Library of
Davidson College

Social Change
and Urban
Politics:
Readings

Social Change and Urban Politics: Readings

Edited by
Daniel N. Gordon
University of Oregon

Prentice-Hall, Inc., *Englewood Cliffs, New Jersey*

© 1973 by Prentice-Hall, Inc.
Englewood Cliffs, N. J.

*All rights reserved. No part of this book may be reproduced
in any form or by any means without permission in writing from the publisher.*

Library of Congress Catalog Card No.: 72–1847

ISBN: C 0–13–815738–3
P 0–13–815712–X

Printed in the United States of America

10 9 8 7 6 5 4 3 2 1

Prentice-Hall International, Inc., *London*
Prentice-Hall of Australia, Pty. Ltd., *Sydney*
Prentice-Hall of Canada, Ltd., *Toronto*
Prentice-Hall of India Private Limited, *New Delhi*
Prentice-Hall of Japan, Inc., *Tokyo*

*Dedicated to Jack Ladinsky,
who first impressed me with the importance
of industrial and technological change in shaping social structure*

Contents

1

Overview, 1

The Bases of Urban Political Change: A Brief History
of Developments and Trends 2
Daniel N. Gordon

2

Changes in Urban Political Structures:
Industrialization, Absentee Ownership, and Changes
in Formal Political Leadership, 19

From Commercial Elite to Political Administrator:
The Recruitment of the Mayors of Chicago 22
Donald S. Bradley and Mayer N. Zald

The Role of Economic Dominants
in Community Power Structure 40
Robert O. Schulze

An Historical Perspective on the Functions of Local Politics 49
Peter H. Rossi and Alice S. Rossi

3

Changes in Urban Political Structures: Industrialization, Absentee Ownership, and Changes in Informal Political Leadership, 61

Absentee-Owned Corporations and Community Power Structure   65
Roland J. Pellegrin and Charles H. Coates

Economic Dominants and Community Power: A Comparative Analysis   74
Donald A. Clelland and William H. Form

Community Influence Systems: Structure and Change   87
Ernest A. T. Barth

4

Changes in Urban Political Structures: Social Classes and Changes in Municipal Government, 97

Jacksonian Democracy and the Working Class   102
Walter Hugins

The Politics of Reform in Municipal Government in the Progressive Era   107
Samuel P. Hays

Class Participation and the Council-Manager Plan   128
Edgar L. Sherbenou

5

Changes in Groups' Participation and Impact on Urban Politics: Nationality Groups and Local Politics, 135

Assimilation in the Political Community   140
Jerome K. Meyers

The Development and Persistence of Ethnic Voting Raymond E. Wolfinger	146
Immigrants and Municipal Voting Turnout: Implications for the Changing Ethnic Impact on Urban Politics Daniel N. Gordon	167

6

Changes in Groups' Participation and Impact on Urban Politics: The Entrance of Blacks into Urban Politics, 187

Negro Politics in the North James Q. Wilson	192
The Making of the Negro Mayors 1967 Jeffrey K. Hadden, Louis H. Masotti, and Victor Thiessen	200
Black Powerlessness in Chicago Harold M. Baron	216
The Political Objectives of Ghetto Violence Harlan Hahn	225

7

Recent Developments in Urban Politics: Professionalization, Bureaucratization, Urban Renewal, and Metropolitan Government, 257

The Bureaucratization of Urban Government Robert R. Alford	263
Community Structure and Innovation: The Case of Urban Renewal Michael Aiken and Robert R. Alford	278
The Political Economy of the Future Robert C. Wood	298

Preface

My belief in the study of urban politics from a historical–social change perspective and the importance of economic change as an independent variable in urban politics has led me to assemble this volume. Too many cross-sectional analyses of urban politics have been made at the expense of truly understanding change and the causation of political phenomena.

My commitment to a social change perspective began with my dissertation research—a panel study of the social correlates of urban governmental and electoral forms. I originally intended my dissertation to be merely a restudy of several cross-sectional analyses on the same topic. However, my results, coupled with my later panel analysis of the ethnic impact on urban government and elections, convinced me that too much information was lost by static approaches to urban phenomena. Because urban areas undergo constant change, these areas should be studied by methods appropriate to analyze those changes. My research led me to review other works dealing with political change, and some of these works are included in this volume.

The readings presented here do not represent a complete survey of urban political change. Space does not permit the inclusion of all relevant studies. Not all areas of urban politics have been adequately studied from a change perspective, and some selections were not available for inclusion in this volume.

I hope that this volume will contribute in a small way to the understanding of urban political change. Moreover, if the works contained herein motivate others to think about and investigate other aspects of urban political change, I will be more than gratified.

As a concluding note I would like to thank Peter and Alice Rossi, Robert Alford, and Harlan Hahn for permitting me to include their previously unpublished works. All of these people made important contributions which have not been widely available until the publication of this volume.

Social Change and Urban Politics: Readings

1
Overview

The Bases of Urban Political Change: A Brief History of Developments and Trends*

DANIEL N. GORDON

Contemporary politics in America's cities are highly diverse. Pyramidal and pluralistic power structures, "reformed" and "unreformed" governments, intense voter activity and voter apathy are a few of the differences which distinguish cities politically. However, available evidence—fragmentary though it is—indicates that prior to industrialization the range of urban politics from city to city was narrower, and politics was often characterized by elite rule. The changing nature of urban politics before and after industrialization is the focus of this paper.

It is impossible to detail all the historical changes in urban politics because of the subject's scope and complexity. Instead I will focus on five major variables which have induced political change—industrialization, the trend toward absentee ownership of major community economic units, changes in urban class composition, changes in urban ethnic composition, and changes in population size—and these variables' effects on the urban political process (governmental forms, formal and informal leadership, mass participation and bureaucratization and professionalization of urban government). These variables have been chosen because they have been the most carefully studied from a change perspective. Diverse sources will be used to sketch a generalized picture of urban political change. Contextual and idiosyncratic factors will be largely ignored here.

Producers of Urban Political Change

Industrialization is the process whereby production is removed from the home or small craft shops and is placed in a factory setting. With the advent of industrialization came rapid technological developments in agriculture, transportation, communication, etc.—developments which spurred the growth of cities (see, e.g., National Resources Committee, 1957; and Davis, 1955 for a discussion of industrialization's effect on city growth) and transformed the political processes within them.

* A paper written for this volume.

The factory system required massive capital outlays to build the centralized production facilities necessitated by the shift from animate (animals and man) to inanimate (steam, etc.) sources of energy. Large-scale financing for industrial development was accomplished through the corporate device—selling shares in a company to obtain necessary working capital. The corporate economy meant that corporations would establish branch plants, offices, warehouses, etc. in many communities. These absentee-owned companies have influenced urban politics in ways described below.

The industrial revolution which transformed America from an agrarian to an urban society also had a profound impact on the class composition, ethnic makeup and size of urban populations.

Initially, industrialization attracted large propertyless masses to fill the labor force demands created by new, urban-based economic enterprises. In *The Economy of Cities* (1969), Jane Jacobs describes how the addition of new work in cities leads to "explosive city growth." A city produces a new product for export. This product often attracts new activity necessary for the production of the new product, i.e., a local supplier (see, e.g., Thompson, 1965). The local production of goods previously imported causes money to be retained within the community for new investment and for local consumption. This newly-retained money works according to the "multiplier principle" to further expand the local economy by the establishment of new indigenous business and by the attraction of further new businesses from outside the community. The continual creation of new work which generates new money for local payrolls and reinvestment, attracts newcomers to the city. Although cities often fail to generate new work and consequently stagnate in their growth, in the past, addition of new work usually attracted a variety of persons to the city.

With developments in transportation (i.e., mass transit, the automobile and the truck) and communication, city dwellers began migrating to the suburbs. Modern metropolitan areas, especially the oldest ones, now often consist of socially heterogeneous central cities surrounded by suburban communities that have their own unique class characteristics. Often these suburbs have higher-status residents than the central city (Schnore, 1963). Suburbs are also economically differentiated—e.g., employing and residential suburbs (Schnore, 1957). The differentiated class composition of metropolitan areas creates differentiated political systems in the component cities. We will see below some of the political effects of class differentiation.

The industrialization of cities and the addition of new work attracted two large migratory streams (in addition to the native white rural-urban migration) to urban America (especially the Northeast and the Midwest). First came immigrants from foreign shores who were both "pulled" to America by greater economic opportunities and "pushed" from their homelands by economic distress, political and religious persecution, etc. The rise and fall of immigration waves during periods of economic growth and recession, respectively, illustrates the importance of economic gains as an attraction for immigrants (Jones, 1960). Blacks also saw the urban North as an economic, social and political haven. During severe labor shortages, e.g., the two World Wars, especially, blacks were attracted to large urban centers—often at the urging of industrial recruiters (see, e.g., Spear, 1967; and Drake and Cayton, 1945). With the passage of time, more and more blacks have left the rural South and have come to the North (Farley, 1968).

Finally, the impetus of industrialization has affected population size and mobility. Large numbers of new cities formed after industrialization (Davis, 1955), and these cities grew in size. The population shifts caused by industrialization and the highly mobile populations necessitated by industrial systems (see, e.g., Litwak, 1960 for a discussion of why industrial societies require mobile populations) meant that some cities grew, some stagnated, and some declined as economic opportunities shifted locations.

Five major variables, then, have produced profound changes in urban politics. Undoubtedly other variables have also affected the urban political scene. For example, economic concentration, the MPO ratio (see, Hawley, 1963 for the definition of this ratio), the percentage unemployed, etc., have been shown to be associated with the shape of community power structure (Aiken, 1970). Also, "structural attachments" are associated with the outcome of political referendums, e.g., fluoridation (Pinard, 1963). The list could go on. However, these other variables have been mainly investigated by cross-sectional techniques, and the static case does not allow us to infer to the dynamic case (Duncan, et al., 1961). To delineate the complex picture of those community social and economic variables that produce political changes will require a great deal more work than has been done to date.

Major Dimensions of Political Change

Several major dimensions of urban politics and government have historically been sensitive to changes in communities' social and economic structure. Governmental forms, recruitment of formal (elected) and informal (influentials not holding formal office) leaders, mass participation, complexity of municipal functions, and the bureaucratization and professionalization of government have all profoundly changed in response to industrialization and other previously mentioned variables.

Governmental form refers to the structure of government—especially the mayor-council, commission, and council-manager forms. The method of electing city councilmen (wards versus at-large) and the form of elections (partisan versus nonpartisan) are also important structural features of city government. Governmental forms are important because they have consequences for communities' patterns of political participation and because they tend to deal differently with cities' functions and problems.

Mayor-council is the one form of American municipal government (excluding the town meeting) which was not "invented" (as were the commission and council-manager forms). Rather, mayor-council's form and functions tended to follow historical trends. This governmental form dates back to before the American Revolution (the office of the mayor being modeled after the mayor in English boroughs [Phillips, 1960:260–61]), when municipal legislatures—city councils, boards of aldermen, etc.—usually selected the mayor (Griffith, 1927:I, 13). This situation did not last very long because of popular democratic movements which occurred in the early nineteenth century. More will be said about this later.

Dissatisfaction with municipal operations led some reformers to look for governmental alternatives to the mayor-council plan. Commission government and later council-manager government were the two major alternatives proposed by reform advocates. Both forms were attempts to centralize power to achieve efficient governmental operation. (See, e.g., MacGregor, 1911; Bradford, 1911; and Hamilton, 1910 for some proponents' views about the merits of commission government. See, e.g., White, 1927; and Childs, 1952 for the alleged merits of council-manager government.) Both forms tend to shift the bases of political power from what they are under mayor-council government. I will discuss this more fully below.

Formal leadership refers to incumbents in elective and appointive municipal offices. Most important are the recruitment patterns of these officeholders because recruitment is an indicator of both the groups which have power and the groups which have an interest and a stake in local government. Recruitment patterns of political leaders have historically been responsive to the previously mentioned dimensions of social and economic change.

Like formal leadership, informal leadership is drawn from a variety of social sectors. Whereas formal leaders occupy legally constituted offices, informal leaders work through various civic groups, *ad hoc* groups, or by themselves to effectuate the passage or rejection of various community policies and projects. Formal leaders generally obtain their influence and power by virtue of holding office, while informal leaders derive their influence from their economic position in the community, their social standing, or their ability to mobilize support.

The converse of leadership patterns is the nature of mass participation—the "followers." Not everyone can or wants actively to influence policy decisions in the urban political arena. Most people are content either to vote, to sign petitions, or to be politically apathetic. The patterns of action—participation or apathy—which urban electorates take is an important component of urban politics because participation patterns influence the overall system.

Finally, two additional important components of urban politics are the number and complexity of urban functions and the bureaucratization and professionalization of city government. The two components are interrelated, of course, since the greater the number and complexity of city tasks, the more likely is urban government to be bureaucratized and professionalized. The number and complexity of city functions refers to how many and how involved are the duties which city governments perform. For example, a simple welfare program might be one where any person with a set minimum income receives a set allowance. A complex welfare program sets various classes of need (unemployment, dependent children, disability, etc.) and formulates various "remedies" which can be applied depending on the category of the recipient and additional situational factors. Bureaucratization and professionalization refer to the method of carrying out municipal functions. If cities employ people who have special skills and training, who are selected on the basis of examination, and who exercise considerable autonomy in their day-to-day activities, those cities' municipal staffs are professionalized (see Alford, 1973). Bureaucratization, consistent with Weber's (1964) model, consists of an administrative structure which is organized into hierarchically arranged specialized units (i.e., units charged with specific tasks) characterized by formal rules, trained and specialized personnel, elaborate record keeping, continuity, etc.

In sum, some major dimensions of urban politics and government are governmental form, formal and informal leadership, mass participation, complexity of municipal functions, and professionalization and bureaucratization. While not all inclusive, these are the dimensions which have received the greatest attention in the literature, especially the literature dealing with change. They affect each other and are affected by the major social and economic shifts in urban communities. The relationships between urban economic, social, and political variables are discussed next.

Economic, Social, and Political Change: Patterns of Interaction

Industrialization has provided the impetus for a major reorientation and recasting of the shape of urban politics. Although the evidence is incomplete, preindustrial American communities were apparently hierarchically ordered social systems capped by elite domination and rule. Politics was not a thing apart from other areas of life, but was intricately intertwined with social institutions. Thernstrom (1964:39) writes about Newburyport, Massachusetts:

Here Newburyport was a community pattern in which every citizen was closely bound to other members of the community by familial, religious, recreational, economic and political ties. The social hierarchy was clear; a series of institutions supported that hierarchy; and the community was so compact that it was difficult to escape the vigilant surveillance of the dominant class.

Even the allegedly democratic town meetings were characterized by deferential voting (Thernstrom, 1964:40–41; and Dahl, 1961:Ch. 2). Open voting in the town meetings was done under the watchful eye of an elite who had social standing in the community and who could apply serious economic sanctions to dissident community members.

The evidence for hierarchical (elite) rule is supported not only by Newburyport (Thernstrom, 1964), but also by New Haven (Dahl, 1961),

Springfield, Massachusetts (Frisch, 1969), "Bay City," Massachusetts (Rossi and Rossi, 1973), "Cibola" (Ypsilanti), Michigan (Schulze, 1958 and 1961), Chicago (Bradley and Zald, 1965), and Nashville (Zald and Anderson, 1968). In the latter four cities, historical investigation has revealed early occupancy of political office by business elites who were replaced by professional politicians. The early business elite of Ypsilanti was also shown to have extensive, interlocking business relations within the community.

Of course, some preindustrial American communities were probably more open and more egalitarian than the elite controlled communities just mentioned. However, it is probably safe to assume that most communities became more politically open after industrialization if for no other reason than the resultant greater complexity of community affairs. No one person or group of persons is likely to want or to be able to control all aspects of community life.

Urban complexity, induced by industrialization, split the interlocking relationship between business and politics into two relatively distinct spheres (although they are certainly not totally separated). In addition, industrialization spurred the rapid growth of cities because large numbers of people were attracted to industrial urban centers by the prospects of economic opportunities. Moreover, transportation and communication technology which developed after industrialization further aided urban development (National Resources Committee, 1957).

Industrialization, then, broke up the elite dominated politics of Federalist America and created a vastly more complex and differentiated urban politics. Industrialization transformed urban politics by several mechanisms—(1) the rise of the working class, (2) the rise of ethnic groups, (3) the increase in importance for business of city functions, (4) the increase in absentee ownership, and (5) population shifts and the creation of metropolitan areas. I will briefly outline the effects on urban politics of these industrialization induced developments.

As mentioned previously, industrialization was a major impetus to the formation of large cities which contain large working-class populations. In fact, even prior to industrialization, some of America's largest cities (i.e., New York) had large working-class populations who agitated for political change. The New York Workingmen's movement is illustrative because it was an early development in urban politics and because it has been extensively studied (Hugins, 1960).

Immediately after the Revolutionary War, property qualifications existed for voting. These qualifications were not to last long because in the early nineteenth century an egalitarian movement which gave the right of suffrage to most adult males spread over this country.[1] Once possessing the vote, Workingmen demanded political reforms so that

---

[1] Some historians (e.g., Schlesinger, 1945) refer to this era in the 1820s as the Age of Jackson or the Era of Jacksonian Democracy because they attribute the spread of this egalitarian ideology to Andrew Jackson and his Democratic Party. Lee Benson (1961), in contrast, agrees that there was an "Age of Egalitarianism," but says that it was not due to Jackson or his party who were politically conservative.

political leadership positions would be open to them. For example, the Workingmen's Party in New York City demanded the election of aldermen from wards because ward election campaigns are cheaper than at-large campaigns and candidates only have to be known in their own local areas. In addition, the Workingmen demanded compensation be paid to political officeholders so that working-class men could afford to take political office if elected. They also wished to discourage people who took nonpaying office simply for the power over patronage appointments inherent in those offices. Also, the Workingmen demanded the direct election of the mayor to put him under electorate control. And, the Workingmen sought to expand the number of elective offices to make government more responsive to the electorate (Hugins, 1960:Chaps. i, ii, and vii).

Class divisions in urban government and politics persisted beyond the Age of Egalitarianism into the era of the governmental reform movement. The rapidly burgeoning ranks of the urban working class created a formidable political force. In the Northeast and Midwest, especially, the urban working classes were often members of ethnic groups, attracted to urban areas by the promise of economic opportunities. Some members of ethnic groups quickly found that their opportunities lay in the political system.

For example, the elite hegemony in Newburyport was broken up by Irish Catholic laborers who joined the Democratic Party (Thernstrom, 1964). New Haven's "Patricians" were replaced by the "Entrepreneurs" who were replaced, in turn, by the "Ex-Plebes"—men who were able to mobilize the working-class ethnic vote (Dahl, 1961). Ethnic politicians also replaced business-class political leaders in Springfield, Massachusetts (Frisch, 1969), "Bay City," Massachusetts (Rossi and Rossi, 1973), and Chicago (Bradley and Zald, 1965).

Several reasons dictated the businessmen's withdrawal from local elective offices. First, as business and government became more complex, it became increasingly difficult for businessmen both to deal adequately with their business affairs and to conduct affairs of government. In effect, both business and government became full-time jobs requiring a distinct set of leaders to run each (Bradley and Zald, 1965; and Zald and Anderson, 1968). Second, businessmen became less able to command a large electoral following as the size of working-class populations increased. In the case of working-class ethnic populations, businessmen had no experience in utilizing ethnic symbols to achieve ethnic support (Dahl, 1961). In addition, some authors contend (e.g., Wilson and Banfield, 1964) that middle and upper-class Protestants and Jews have a different set of values than do working-class ethnics. The latter hold a "private regarding" view of government (i.e., what government can do for the individual) while the former view government in "public regarding" terms (i.e., what is best for the general welfare). Third, businessmen withdrew from political office when the stakes of local government declined. The Rossis (1973) point out that businessmen lost interest in "Bay City's" politics when government shifted its focus from growth and development to maintenance and conservation. Fourth, in one reported instance (Frisch,

1969), the elite lost control of Springfield, Massachusetts' politics when their conception of government's goals no longer prevailed over the entire community. As Springfield grew, diverse groups came to see that government could pursue diverse goals depending upon who was in power. Springfield's business elite was not large enough to hold the reins of government in the face of working-class opposition. Finally, economic dominants withdrew from public office in communities where absentee-owned firms became predominant (see, e.g., Schulze, 1958 and 1961; and Clelland and Form, 1964). Although absentee managers tend to withdraw from public office because their attention is focused on national markets and company operations rather than the community, absentee-owned firms do excercise influence in community affairs through various mechanisms (Mott, 1970).

In many communities businessmen withdrew from politics and remained withdrawn. Especially during the middle and late nineteenth century businessmen were content to go along with the decentralized politics and government of the working class and ethnic groups. Businessmen who needed city permits or franchises often got them by payoffs and bribes, and other businessmen were able to ignore city affairs altogether. However, businessmen could not go on ignoring municipal affairs forever.

As the late nineteenth century gave way to the twentieth, both business and municipal government became more complex and intertwined as business became more dependent on the successful and predictable operation of municipal government. Business needed well-paved roads and streets, good water supplies, effective zoning and building codes, dependable procedures for getting city permits, etc. However, in many cities businessmen were frozen out of government by working-class and lower middle-class politicians. To correct this situation, business-class reformers came up with the commission form and later the council-manager form of government (Hays, 1964; and Weinstein, 1968:Chap. 4).

Commission government was designed to centralize governmental operation by eliminating wards, cutting down on the number of elective offices, making all commission candidates run at large, and giving the commissioners both policy-making (especially appropriations) and administrative powers. However, combining policy-making and administration led to tradeoffs and deals among commissioners. Each commissioner tended to pursue the interests of his own department at the expense of others. Because of the muddling of policy-making and administrative tasks, and because well-trained and competent men were not usually attracted to the poorly paid, part-time commissioner's job, commission government did not work out according to plan, and council-manager government was proposed as an alternative.[2]

Council-manager government separated policy-making (which is formulated by the city council) and administration (which is carried out by a

[2] Council-manager government was first proposed by Richard Childs who assumed that consensus existed in municipal affairs and that differences in governmental performance were due to differences in structure. See John Porter East (1965) for a detailed analysis of Childs' views and a history of manager government.

full-time city manager). Manager government is based on the corporate model with the council analogous to the board of directors and the manager analogous to the president. The city manager ideally should be trained in municipal administration and have the power to appoint (with council ratification) department heads. In addition, advocates of council-manager government favor the abolition of wards and the institution of nonpartisan elections—both measures designed to remove "politics" from government.

For all the idealistic arguments in favor of reform government, this government really represented an attempt to wrest control of local government from the working and middle classes (Hays, 1964). Because business was becoming more dependent on increasingly complex city functions, businessmen wanted a strong voice in the conduct of city affairs. The abolishment of wards was especially important according to Hays (1964: 161–65), because ward councilmen were oriented to the particularistic needs of their own little districts. At-large elections put working-class candidates at a distinct disadvantage since they were generally not known outside their own neighborhoods and they often lacked the funds to finance more expensive at-large campaigns.

The class nature of "reformed" versus "unreformed" government is seen in a variety of ways. Hays (1964) says that in many council-manager referendums the upper-class areas were overwhelmingly for the plan, the working-class neighborhoods were overwhelmingly opposed, and the middle-class areas were evenly divided. Sherbenou (1961) found that when he ordered Chicago's suburbs by median housing values, the wealthiest suburbs were found to have adopted manager government first, some middle-class suburbs adopted the plan later, and no lower-status suburbs (those below the median of median housing value) adopted the plan. Finally, numerous case studies (see, e.g., Stone, et al., 1940a and 1940b) have found that the strongest opposition to the manager plan is located among members of the working class (of both ethnic and nonethnic origin).

Council-manager government, in addition to its ideological and class roots, is an attempt to bureaucratize and professionalize municipal government. However, even where reform governments are not found—i.e., mayor-council cities—government is becoming increasingly professionalized and bureaucratized. Big city mayors are now usually full-time administrators who often make government service a career (see, e.g., Bradley and Zald, 1965; and Zald and Anderson, 1968). As cities become larger and face more complex problems, they must devise new methods to handle new problems—methods usually based on the bureaucratic model with professional staffs (Alford, 1973). And more power has generally been put in the hands of mayors as weak mayor government has given way to strong mayor government and the number of elective offices has been reduced from the numbers found in the nineteenth century.

Regardless of governmental form, then, almost all municipal governments have been involved in the trend toward centralization of power,[3]

---

[3] Even in mayor-council cities there has been a trend away from the use of ward elections for city councilmen. More and more mayor-council cities are adopting at-large

bureaucratization of city agencies and departments, and professionalization of municipal staffs. The complexity of contemporary city functions makes mandatory a rational and planned approach to urban government rather than the informal, often machine dominated arrangements which prevailed in earlier eras.

Currently a racial aspect has been added to the earlier class and ethnic struggles for local political control. In a few cities black politicians have successfully challenged white candidates for the mayoralty. Much like the earlier struggle for leadership positions between business elites and ethnic and nonethnic working-class politicians, blacks struggle with whites for political power. Kenneth Gibson in Newark defeated a white mayor of Italian ancestry. Carl Stokes, in his primary election bid before winning the mayoralty, won nomination from Mayor Ralph Locher, who made a strong appeal to Cleveland's Eastern European working-class groups (Hadden, et al., 1968). And Richard Hatcher defeated Joseph Radigan in machine dominated Gary, Indiana. Unlike earlier class and ethnic struggles for political control, though, blacks have two very serious obstacles in their path to political power. First, the various governmental reforms which were instituted before blacks arrived in Northern cities in great numbers put them (and any minority group) at a severe disadvantage. As I mentioned previously, for example, the abolition of wards decreases the responsiveness of government to minority interests. Second, blacks have had to constitute a larger proportion of the electorate than previously was necessary to capture political office.

Unlike earlier ethnic groups, blacks have also resorted to rioting as a means of calling attention to their needs. Many black rioters and riot observers view their activities as having political ends (Hahn, 1973), although these ends do not include the election of black candidates. Rather, the riots have been attempts to get white politicians to ameliorate problems endemic in ghetto areas. To some extent the riots were successful, but not totally so. Blacks are still frozen out of policy-making positions (see, e.g., Baron, 1968), both public and private, and in many cities many black problems have still not been dealt with by the white political system.

In sum, the recruitment of political leaders and the class and ethnic base of political power has changed several times in American cities—especially in the East and Midwest.[4] However, regardless of the class or ethnic groups in power, machine-style politics has tended to disappear (Banfield and Wilson, 1963) and to be replaced by administratively cen-

---

elections (Gordon, 1968:166 and 171) which act to centralize governmental operations and to do away with particularistic interests.

[4] Many of these class and ethnic struggles for local political control have been avoided in the South and West. Since blacks were excluded from Southern politics and voting for many decades, urban electorates (i.e., people who voted and participated in local politics) tended to be homogeneously Protestant and white. In addition, Southern politics is apparently more likely to be characterized by elite rule, although blacks are now fighting for power in some Southern cities. Western cities, on the other hand, are characterized by relatively recent and rapid growth. Their politics and government, in turn, tend to be nonpartisan and council-manager, respectively, with no major ethnic divisions. (San Francisco and a few other cities are major exceptions.)

tralized, professionalized, and bureaucratized government, whether that government be reformed (i.e., commission or manager) or unreformed (i.e., mayor-council).

Just as the formal (i.e., elected) leadership base in cities has changed, so too has the informal leadership base. However, the reasons for changes in informal leadership appear to be somewhat different from those for elected leaders.

Prominently mentioned as a reason for changes in leadership recruitment is the rise of absentee ownership. As discussed earlier, the financial needs of an industrializing economy created the corporate system and these corporations set up branch facilities across the country. The establishment of a branch facility, especially a large manufacturing plant, often changes the configuration of power in the affected community (Schulze, 1958 and 1961; Clelland and Form, 1964; and French, 1970). Two studies (Schulze, 1958 and 1961; and Clelland and Form, 1964) have shown that absentee managers do not follow in the footsteps of earlier local economic dominants in that they do not seek political office and often do not seek office in voluntary associations (although a somewhat contrary view is put forth by Rossi, 1961). Often the void left by absentee managers is filled by local middle-class businessmen and professionals.

However, the bifurcation of community leadership into economic dominants and middle-class civic leaders is not the only consequence of absentee ownership, and absentee ownership is not the only factor to affect community leadership.

Domination of communities' economies by absentee-owned firms is associated with the presence of factional, coalitional, and amorphous (i.e., diffuse and unstructured) power structures (Walton, 1970; and Aiken, 1970). The introduction of large absentee-owned facilities can have a dramatic effect on communities (e.g., see French, 1970). French (1970) reports that "Cornucopia" went from a monolithic power structure when the community was dominated by a locally-owned sewing machine company to a pluralistic power distribution when a large absentee-owned automobile plant was established in the community.

However, absentee-owned corporations do not totally withdraw from community affairs—rather they operate in more subtle and indirect ways (Pellegrin and Coates, 1956; and Mott, 1970). Pellegrin and Coates write that absentee managers exercise veto power in "Bigtown," but in general a "power vacuum" exists there (i.e., there is no cohesive leadership elite among the community's influentials). Political considerations and the importance of the local market for the absentee corporations probably account for the interest of absentee managers in Bigtown's affairs.[5] Moreover, in Ypsilanti absentee corporations exercise influence in several

[5] In a personal communication, Professor Pellegrin pointed out that "Bigtown" is the state capital of an oil producing state. Because severance taxes, depletion allowances, and oil leases are important to the company, executives participate in the community to maintain good political relations with politically powerful persons in the state. Also, the company owns most of the local service stations which enhances the importance of the local market.

ways (Mott, 1970). Corporations exercise veto power by inaction in community decisions. General Motors, for example, managed to defeat a move to annex their plant into Ypsilanti by simply remaining "neutral." The company's inaction insured defeat of the annexation attempt which is what General Motors wanted. Ecological power is also exercised by absentee-owned companies because they control scarce resources in the community, employ large numbers of people, and supply them with their income. In addition, American society, according to Mott, is still dominated by a set of values compatible with business, and political decisions may be shaped by business-oriented values. Also, informal contractual arrangments are often entered into by a community's political leaders and a corporation as a condition of that corporation moving into the community. Often these arrangements involve a significant restructuring of the community's social structure. Finally, corporations have community relations departments which handle community problems, and some companies (e.g., Ford) encourage their employees to become involved in community affairs—civic associations, elective offices, etc.

Absentee managers, then, apparently have withdrawn from public and voluntary association offices, although even this generalization must be qualified. Rossi (1961) reports that executives of absentee-owned firms in "Mediana" are involved in local civic associations. Also, the metropolitan status of a community appears to influence the rate of absentee manager withdrawal from community offices. In their study of Lansing, Clelland and Form (1964) found that unlike Ypsilanti (Schulze, 1958 and 1961), absentee managers did not withdraw as fast or as completely from voluntary association offices as did the managers in Ypsilanti. Clelland and Form attribute the differences between these cities as stemming from the metropolitan status of each. Ypsilanti is a satellite city of Detroit and the absentee managers only work in Ypsilanti but live in other Detroit suburbs. Lansing, in contrast, is a central city of another metropolitan area and commands, therefore, more loyalty and attention from the absentee managers who reside there.

Not only are absentee managers participating less in community affairs and exerting less direct influence, but power structures in general seem to be changing. When power structures change they tend to become more pluralistic or dispersed (Walton, 1970). Three major reasons for such changes are the increase in absentee-owned corporations (Schulze, 1958 and 1961; Clelland and Form, 1964; Barth, 1961; and French, 1970), population growth (Barth, 1961), and the increasing complexity of community life. (See, e.g., Warren, 1963 for a perspective on the causes and consequences of community complexity, especially relations between communities and outside influences.)

In contrast to urban leadership, not much has been written about changes in urban electorates and their political activity. However, we have seen previously that the influx of large ethnic and nonethnic working-class populations into communities unsettled earlier political arrangements. Men arose who could politically mobilize these urban masses and organize them into a stable and loyal electoral base. Working-class voters will tend to support a political style compatible with unreformed governmental structures and political activities such as using patronage as a reward for political loyalty. Middle and upper-class persons, in contrast, are more amenable to apolitical, reformed (especially nonpartisan, council-manager) government. Middle-class suburbs, for example, are often characterized by voter apathy and lack of interest in political affairs (Greer, 1962:Chap. 5).

Urban political systems and styles tend to persist once established unless the community is disrupted by some great change. The influx of immigrant laborers into Newburyport (Thernstrom, 1964), New Haven (Dahl, 1961), "Bay City" (Rossi and Rossi, 1973), and Springfield (Frisch, 1969) transformed those communities' politics from elite domination to ethnic working-class domination. Similarly, rapid population growth, in general, shifts political systems from the "politics of acquaintance" to the "politics of group mobilization" (Lee, 1960:147). And rapid growth also brings new political problems to communities which unsettle old ways of doing things (Kessel, 1962:617).

On the other hand, evidence for suburban cities (and probably, by implication, other cities) indicates that they tend to maintain their character over long periods of time (Farley, 1964). Since urban social and economic composition determines communities' political style, most cities' political systems will persist over time: to change only if some major social or economic change—e.g., a large new factory, or major population shift—is introduced into the community.

In sum, the major national trends—e.g., industrialization, large-scale migrations, the rise of absentee ownership—have differentially affected urban political systems. For example, cities' governmental forms are differentiated on the basis of class, religious, population, and economic differences (Schnore and Alford, 1963; Alford and Scoble, 1965; Kessel, 1962; and Gordon, 1968), and policy outputs (expenditures and taxation) also differ according to similar criteria (Lineberry and Fowler, 1967). The differential effects of social and economic shifts have produced politically differentiated metropolitan areas—areas which contain "have" and "have not" cities; cities which spend liberally for schools, sanitation, police and fire protection, etc., and those which do not; cities with competitive political systems and those with little political activity, etc. These disparities in political styles, resources, and goals have created both problems of metropolitan coordination and control, and differential abilities to finance municipal operations. In some cases special districts (e.g., sewerage) have been set up to handle metropolitan or area-wide problems. In a very few cases (e.g., Nashville and Davidson County, Tennessee, Indianapolis, Indiana, and Jacksonville and Dade County, Florida) metropolitan governments have been formed to handle these problems. However, the long political histories of many communities have created vested interests against change (Wood, 1961). Community residents usually want to keep their community identity, and legal obstacles have been created to protect the integrity of local political boundaries.

If there is a new national trend building up to reshape urban politics once again, it is the twin problems of municipal finance and lack of regional (especially metropolitan) coordination and control. To date these problems have largely been ignored. However, the current financial crisis in municipal government gives new urgency to the governance of metropolitan areas. Conceivably metropolitan governments will never be adopted on a broad scale, but will be shunned in favor of other solutions, e.g., federal revenue sharing, or more centralized state financing of local services. However, if metropolitan government ever emerges on a large scale, we will witness another major reshaping of urban political systems.

References

AIKEN, MICHAEL. "The Distribution of Community Power: Structural Bases and Social Consequences." In *The Structure of Community Power*, edited by Michael Aiken and Paul E. Mott. New York: Random House, 1970.

ALFORD, ROBERT R. "The Bureaucratization of Urban Government." This volume (1973).

ALFORD, ROBERT R. and HARRY M. SCOBLE. "Political and Socioeconomic Characteristics of American Cities." In *Municipal Yearbook*, edited by Orin F. Nolting and David S. Arnold. Chicago: International City Managers' Association, 1965.

BANFIELD, EDWARD C. and JAMES Q. WILSON. *City Politics*. Cambridge, Mass.: Harvard University Press, 1963.

BARON, MILTON M. "Black Powerlessness in Chicago." *Trans-action* 6 (November 1968): 27–33. Reprinted in this volume.

BARTH, ERNEST A. T. "Community Influence Systems: Structure and Change." *Social Forces* 40 (October 1961): 58–63. Reprinted in this volume.

BENSON, LEE. *The Concept of Jacksonian Democracy*. Princeton, N.J.: Princeton University Press, 1961.

BRADFORD, E. S. *Commission Government in American Cities*. New York: Macmillan, 1911.

BRADLEY, DONALD S. and MAYER N. ZALD. "From Commercial Elite to Political Administrator: The Recruitment of the Mayors of Chicago." *American Journal of Sociology* 71 (September 1965): 153–67. Reprinted in this volume.

CHILDS, RICHARD S. *Civic Victories*. New York: Harper and Brothers, 1952.

CLELLAND, DONALD A. and WILLIAM H. FORM. "Economic Dominants and Community Power: A Comparative Analysis." *American Journal of Sociology* 69 (March 1964): 511–21. Reprinted in this volume.

DAHL, ROBERT A. *Who Governs?* New Haven, Conn.: Yale University Press, 1961.

DAVIS, KINGSLEY. "The Origin and Growth of Urbanization in the World." *American Journal of Sociology* 60 (March 1955): 429–37.

DRAKE, ST. CLAIR and HORACE R. CAYTON. *Black Metropolis*. New York: Harcourt Brace, 1945.

DUNCAN, OTIS D., RAY P. CUZZORT, and BEVERLY DUNCAN. *Statistical Geography*. New York: Free Press, 1961.

EAST, JOHN PORTER. *Council-Manager Government.* Chapel Hill, N.C.: University of North Carolina Press, 1965.

FARLEY, REYNOLDS. "Suburban Persistence." *American Sociological Review* 29 (February 1964): 38–47.

———. "The Urbanization of Negroes in the United States." *Journal of Social History* 1 (Spring 1968): 241–58.

FRENCH, ROBERT MILLS. "Economic Change and Community Power Structure: Transition in Cornucopia." In *Community Power Structure,* edited by Michael Aiken and Paul E. Mott. New York: Random House, 1970.

FRISCH, MICHAEL H. "The Community Elite and the Emergence of Urban Politics: Springfield, Massachusetts, 1840–1880." In *Nineteenth Century Cities,* edited by Stephan Thernstrom and Richard Sennett. New Haven, Conn.: Yale University Press, 1969.

GORDON, DANIEL N. "Immigrants and Urban Governmental Form in American Cities, 1933-60." *American Journal of Sociology* 74 (September 1968): 158–71.

GREER, SCOTT. *Governing the Metropolis.* New York: John Wiley, 1962.

GRIFFITH, ERNEST S. *The Modern Development of City Government in the United Kingdom and the United States,* Vol. 1. London: Oxford University Press, 1927.

HADDEN, JEFFREY K., LOUIS H. MASOTTI, and VICTOR THIESSEN. "The Making of the Negro Mayor 1967." *Trans-action* 5 (January–February 1968): 21–30. Reprinted in this volume.

HAHN, HARLAN. "The Political Objectives of Ghetto Violence." This volume (1973).

HAMILTON, JOHN J. *The Dethronement of the City Boss.* New York: Funk and Wagnalls, 1910.

HAWLEY, AMOS H. "Community Power and Urban Renewal Success." *American Journal of Sociology* 68 (January 1963): 422–31.

HAYS, SAMUEL P. "The Politics of Reform in Municipal Government in the Progressive Era." *Pacific Northwest Quarterly* 60 (October 1964): 157–69. Reprinted in this volume.

HUGINS, WALTER. *Jacksonian Democracy and the Working Class.* Stanford, Calif.: Stanford University Press, 1960.

JACOBS, JANE. *The Economy of Cities.* New York: Random House, 1969.

JONES, MALDWYN ALLEN. *American Immigration.* Chicago: University of Chicago Press, 1960.

KESSEL, JOHN H. "Governmental Structure and Political Environment: A Statistical Note About American Cities." *American Political Science Review* 56 (September 1962): 615–20.

LEE, EUGENE C. *The Politics of Nonpartisanship.* Berkeley and Los Angeles: University of California Press, 1960.

LINEBERRY, ROBERT L. and EDMUND P. FOWLER. "Reformism and Public Policy in American Cities." *American Political Science Review* 61 (September 1967): 701–16.

LITWAK, EUGENE. "Geographic Mobility and Extended Family Cohesion." *American Sociological Review* 25 (June 1960): 385–94.

MACGREGOR, FORD H. *City Government by Commission.* Madison, Wis.: University of Wisconsin Press, 1911.

MOTT, PAUL E. "The Role of the Absentee-Owned Corporation in the Changing Community." In *The Structure of Community Power*. edited by Michael Aiken and Paul E. Mott. New York: Random House, 1970.

National Resources Committee. "The Process of Urbanization: Underlying Forces and Emerging Trends." In *Cities and Society*, edited by Paul K. Hatt and Albert J. Reiss, Jr. New York: Free Press, 1957.

PELLEGRIN, ROLAND J. and CHARLES H. COATES. "Absentee-Owned Corporations and Community Power Structure." *American Journal of Sociology* 61 (March 1956): 413–19. Reprinted in this volume.

PHILLIPS, JEWELL CASS. *Municipal Government and Administration in America*. New York: Macmillan, 1960.

PINARD, MAURICE. "Structural Attachments and Political Support in Urban Politics: The Case of Fluoridation Referendums." *American Journal of Sociology* 68 (March 1963): 513–26.

ROSSI, PETER H. "The Organizational Structure of an American Community." In *Complex Organizations*, edited by Amitai Etzioni. New York: Holt, Rinehart and Winston, 1961.

ROSSI, PETER H. and ALICE S. ROSSI. "Historical Perspectives on the Functions of Local Politics." This volume (1973).

SCHLESINGER, ARTHUR, JR. *The Age of Jackson*. Boston: Little, Brown and Co., 1945.

SCHNORE, LEO F. "The Growth of Metropolitan Suburbs." *American Sociological Review* 22 (April 1957): 165–73.

———. "The Socio-Economic Status of Cities and Suburbs." *American Sociological Review* 28 (February 1963): 76–85.

SCHNORE, LEO F. and ROBERT R. ALFORD. "Forms of Government and Socioeconomic Characteristics of Suburbs." *Administrative Science Quarterly* 8 (June 1963): 1–17.

SCHULZE, ROBERT O. "The Role of Economic Dominants in Community Power Structure." *American Sociological Review* 23 (February 1958): 3–9. Reprinted in this volume.

———. "The Bifurcation of Power in a Satellite City." In *Community Political Systems*, edited by Morris Janowitz. New York: Free Press, 1961.

SHERBENOU, EDGAR L. "Class Participation and the Council-Manager Plan." *Public Administration Review* 21 (Summer 1961): 131–35. Reprinted in this volume.

SPEAR, ALLAN H. *Black Chicago*. Chicago: University of Chicago Press, 1967.

STONE, HAROLD A., DON K. PRICE, and KATHRYN H. STONE. *City Manager Government in Nine Cities*. Chicago: Public Administration Service, 1940a.

———. *City Manager Government in the United States*. Chicago: Public Administration Service, 1940b.

THERNSTROM, STEPHAN. *Poverty and Progress*. Cambridge, Mass.: Harvard University Press, 1964.

THOMPSON, WILBUR R. "Urban Economic Growth and Development in a National System of Cities." In *The Study of Urbanization*, edited by Philip M. Hauser and Leo F. Schnore. New York: John Wiley, 1965.

WALTON, JOHN. "A Systematic Survey of Community Power Research." In *The Structure of Community Power*, edited by Michael Aiken and Paul E. Mott. New York: Random House, 1970.

WARREN, ROLAND. *The Community in America*. Chicago: Rand McNally, 1963.

WEBER, MAX. *The Theory of Social and Economic Organization*. New York: Free Press, 1964.

WEINSTEIN, JAMES. *The Corporate Ideal in the Liberal State: 1900–1918*. Boston: Beacon Press, 1968.

WHITE, LEONARD D. *The City Manager*. Chicago: University of Chicago Press, 1927.

WILSON, JAMES Q. and EDWARD C. BANFIELD. "Public Regardingness as a Value Premise in Voting Behavior." *American Political Science Review* 58 (December 1964): 876–87.

WOOD, ROBERT C. *1400 Governments*. Cambridge, Mass.: Harvard University Press, 1961.

ZALD, MAYER N. and THOMAS A. ANDERSON. "Secular Trends and Historical Contingencies in the Recruitment of Mayors: Nashville as Compared to New Haven and Chicago." *Urban Affairs Quarterly* 3 (June 1968): 53–68.

2

Changes
in Urban
Political Structures

Industrialization,
Absentee Ownership,
and Changes in Formal
Political Leadership

Industrialization and economic change have wrought profound changes in the characteristics of elected urban political leadership. As the three selections in this section indicate, there has been a shift from the political involvement of economic and social notables to their withdrawal and replacement by either professional politicians or middle-class businessmen, depending on the type of community. Five factors—(1) industrialization, (2) the influx of new workers into industrializing communities, (3) the rise of absentee ownership, (4) metropolitanization, and (5) the loss of prestige for urban politics—are apparently responsible for this shift in urban political leadership.

In the first selection Donald Bradley and Mayer Zald discuss the changes in the patterns of recruitment for Chicago's mayors.

During its earliest history, Chicago's mayors were drawn from the ranks of businessmen who sought the part-time office as a prestige symbol. The mayor's office had few duties at the time, but it did serve as a source of publicity for the incumbents who held the office. However, the rise of big industry in Chicago was to put an end to the businessmen mayors. As industry grew in the city, a new group of businessmen came to prominence—men who headed the large manufacturing firms which located in the city. These industrialists were too busy with their business affairs to worry about running for mayor. Moreover, not only was business becoming a full-time job, but so too was the mayor's office. No longer were mayors part-time leaders; they were full-time administrators in their own right.

It is doubtful that businessmen could have continued being elected mayor even if they wanted to run. Their economic successes attracted large numbers of new working-class residents to Chicago—immigrants and others—who gave their support to machine politicians who sought working-class support. Sometimes these machine politicians were party leaders and sometimes they commanded personal organizations of their own. But in either case, they were part of a political machine system. However, these men were yet to give way to political administrators: men who spent their lifetimes coming up the political and governmental ranks. Government had become sufficiently complex to create a class of career politicians and governmental officials.

Industrialization was not the only important determinant of political recruitment. Also important was the rise of absentee ownership and metropolitanization. Both of these factors are seen at work in the second selection, Robert Schulze's "The Role of Economic Dominants in Community Power Structure."

Schulze found a somewhat different picture in "Cibola" (Ypsilanti, Michigan) than did Bradley and Zald. The early mayors of Cibola were drawn largely from the ranks of the economic dominants in the community—"those persons who: (a) occupied the top formal roles in the largest industries and banks in the community; or (b) were members of the boards of directors of two or more of these industries and banks, thus serving formally to interlock the dominant economic units; or (c) were the largest property-owners in the community."

Mayors and other elected leaders in Cibola were drawn from the ranks of the economic dominants until absentee-owned corporations came to dominate the community's economy. With the introduction of these large corporations, the economic dominants (i.e., the managers of these corporations) no longer had a vital interest in the community, but were part of large national enterprises oriented to national rather than local markets. In addition, as Cibola became drawn into the metropolitan orbit of a large nearby metropolis (Detroit), these economic dominants increasingly came to live outside the community. Therefore, Cibola's corporate managers had neither the time nor the interest to seek public office. Economic dominants gave way to local business and professional men: middle-class men whose livelihoods and residences were in the community.

Finally, one additional factor spurring the withdrawal of economic notables from local political office is what Peter and Alice Rossi call "the trivialization of local issues." Interestingly, the initial industrialization of "Bay City" led to the political hegemony of Yankee Republican industrialists. However, population size became stabilized after industrialization in the city ceased, and the composition of the population underwent change. Differential birth rates and out-migration rates produced a population predominantly ethnic in character. Stable population size served to downgrade the importance of local issues from a politics of expansion to a politics of maintenance and conservation. Also, many previously local functions were removed from the community and taken over by state and federal agencies. These trends together downgraded the prestige of local politics and spurred the political withdrawal of the Yankee Republicans.

Although the circumstances differ somewhat in each of the three communities analyzed in this section, industrialization had important consequences in all of them. The economic elite in all three cities withdrew from the local political arena to be replaced by local businessmen or professional politicians. The changing functions of both business and politics and the reordering of bases of political support caused this political shift.

From Commercial Elite to Political Administrator: The Recruitment of the Mayors of Chicago*

DONALD S. BRADLEY AND MAYER N. ZALD

The urbanization and industrialization of American life have had a profound impact on the operations of political institutions and the elements of political power. This political transformation has occurred not only on the national scene but in the structure of local politics as well. There have been changes in the strength and structure of local political, social, and economic elites and in the political coin necessary to win office. While this statement is almost a truism, it is difficult to find valid data which concisely summarize the changes in social structure, politics, and the linkages between them. Indexes of political transformation that reveal underlying changes in community structure and composition are needed.

Our study follows the lead of R. A. Dahl who uses an analysis of the salient features of the life histories of mayors in New Haven, Connecticut, as evidence for shifts in the distribution and differentiation of political resources from 1789 to 1961.[1]

Dahl finds that the social and occupational backgrounds of New Haven mayors fall into three main groupings: (1) "the patricians," well-educated, legally trained men from well-established New Haven families, who dominated the political field from 1784–1842; (2) "the entrepreneurs," heads of the largest and most prominent New Haven industrial and commercial firms who, whether or not they had high social standing, consistently were elected to the office of mayor from 1842–99; and (3) the

---

Reprinted from the *American Journal of Sociology* 71 (1965): 153–67. Copyright 1965 by the University of Chicago. Reprinted by permission of the publisher.

* We are indebted to the Center for Social Organization Studies and its director, Morris Janowitz, for criticism and financial support. A small grant from the Social Science Research Committee, Division of Social Sciences, University of Chicago, helped in the early stages of the study. A critical reading by R. W. Hodge was also of great help.

This paper was based on a more detailed manuscript prepared by Donald Bradley (Working Paper No. 10, Center for Social Organization Studies, University of Chicago, 1963 [Mimeographed]).

[1] Robert A. Dahl, *Who Governs? Democracy and Power in an American City* (New Haven, Conn.: Yale University Press, 1961), pp. 1–81.

"ex-plebes," men from working-class and ethnic backgrounds who capitalized on an arithmetic of ethnic composition and were able to be the major figures in politics from 1899 on. Dahl sees such a man as Richard Lee, mayor since 1953, as possibly the first of "the New Men"; men who build on an ethnic base but also have a wider base of support through advocating such good-government policies as community redevelopment.

To explain these shifts in recruitment Dahl focuses on the relative advantages and disadvantages possessed by the various groupings within the community for gaining important political positions. He does not deal with the motivation to participate in politics. In order to understand the historical shifts in local political elites it is necessary to deal with changes in both the distribution of the resources of political power and the value of political participation for the various social groups, for these are separate aspects of recruitment to political office.

We have used the social characteristics of Chicago mayors as the basis for an analysis of the changes in the political and social structure of Chicago. As compared with New Haven, Chicago has had a more dynamic and restless growth. While New Haven had an established and cohesive elite at the time of its incorporation as a city, the groups that were to make up Chicago's elite migrated there as it grew into a transportation and trading center; where New Haven grew slowly and incorporated a few major ethnic groups, Chicago grew rapidly and assimilated a multitude of diverse immigrant groups. Thus, we were led to expect a rather different pattern of recruitment to the office of mayor. Our central purpose is to present an analysis of the changes in recruitment in Chicago. In order to highlight the differences between the two communities, comparison with New Haven will be reserved for the conclusions.

From a host of biographical sources we gathered information on the social background and political careers of each of the thirty-nine Chicago mayors. By comparing the backgrounds of each of these individuals, we established patterns of common characteristics. The mayors grouped into four periods, which we have labeled according to their most salient characteristics.[2] Changes in the patterned characteristics from one period to another are interpreted in terms of shifts in the social, economic, and ideological conditions of the city. The names and dates of election of the mayors, arranged by the periods to which we have assigned them, are presented in Table 1. In Table 2 we present summaries of the social and occupational backgrounds and of the political background and careers of the mayors of each period.

The Elite of Commercial Expansion: 1837–68

In 1830 Chicago was only a small trading post with a population under 100. As the frontier was pushed further west, Chicago rapidly became a

[2] We recognize that precise dating of periods is risky, but it helps organize reporting of the shifts in recruitment. More important than the dates are the underlying trends.

Table 1. Mayors of Chicago and the years in which they were elected,* by chronological periods

Period	Mayors
Commercial elite (1837–68)	Ogden, 1837; Morris, 1838; Raymond, 1839 and 1842; Lloyd, 1840; F. C. Sherman, 1841, 1862, and 1863; Garrett, 1843 and 1845; A. Sherman, 1844; Chapin, 1846; Curtiss, 1847 and 1850; Woodworth, 1848 and 1849; Gurnee, 1851 and 1852; Gray, 1853; Milliken, 1854; Boone, 1855; Dyer, 1856; Wentworth, 1850 and 1860; Haines, 1858 and 1859, Ramsey, 1861; Rice, 1865 and 1867
Transition mayors (1869–75)	Mason, 1869; Medill, 1871; Colvin, 1873; Hoyne, 1875†
Personalized politics versus party machine (1876–1930)	Heath, 1876‡ and 1877; Harrison I, 1879, 1881, 1883, 1885, and 1893;§ Roche, 1887; Cregier, 1889; Washburne, 1891; Hopkins, 1893; Swift, 1885; Harrison II, 1897, 1899, 1901, 1903, and 1911; Dunne, 1905; Busse, 1907; Thompson, 1915, 1919, and 1927; Dever, 1923
Political administrators (1931–65)	Cermak, 1931; Kelly, 1933,‖ 1935, 1939, and 1943; Kennelly, 1947 and 1951; Daley, 1955, 1959, and 1963.

* Terms were for 1 year 1837–62, two years 1863–1905, four years from 1907 on.
† Hoyne never took office. Colvin refused to yield seat because of change in election procedure.
‡ Special election.
§ Harrison assassinated, Hopkins elected at special election.
‖ Cermak assassinated, Kelly elected at special election.

transportation and trading center. The businessmen who were most prominent in this economic development commanded respect, prestige, and economic resources; they dominated the political scene and, to some extent, other institutional areas of community life. From 1837, the date of Chicago's incorporation, to 1868 the mayor, whether Whig, native American, Democrat, or Republican, was likely to be a leading businessman, highly active in political affairs and active in the affairs of his religious denomination.

Social, Occupational, and Political Characteristics

The speculative fever that characterized the economic development of Chicago at this time led most of the leading citizens to participate in several kinds of economic enterprise at the same time. More than half of this first group of mayors was engaged in between two and four occupations. For instance, a man might be a practicing lawyer, a land speculator, and a forwarding agent.

The first nineteen mayors represent the commercial, transportation, and building interests related to the growing economy. Real-estate speculation and investment were sources of income for at least eight of the first nineteen mayors; eight were associated with the merchandising and trading activities of the city; at least six were active in the development of railroads; three were in banking and building; and four were practicing lawyers. Almost all were extremely prominent in the business world. As Pierce observed, "Indeed, only two of the twenty-seven men running

Table 2.* Summary of social, occupational, and political characteristics, by chronological periods

	Commercial Elite (N = 19)	Transition Mayors (N = 4)	Personalized Politics vs. Party Machine (N = 12)	Political Administrators (N = 4)
Social and occupational background:				
Occupations:				
Multiple occupational practice†	10	....	1	1
Real estate and building	2	....	2	....
Grain and meat processing and packing, and merchandising	5	....	....	....
Wholesale and distribution, Chicago area	....	....	4	1
Law and judiciary	2	1	3	....
Newspaper	....	1	....	....
Career government service	....	....	....	2
Other	....	2	2	....
Education:				
Less than ten years	5‡	....	....	....
High school	3§	1	5	3
College	1	2	1	....
Legal training	4‖	....	5	1
No information	6	1	1	....
Religion:				
Protestant	17	2	6	....
Catholic	....	....	3	3
Other	....	....	....	1
No information	2	2	3	....
Age at arrival in Chicago:				
0–15	1	....	1	3
15–29	10	1	7	1
30 +	8	3	2	....
No information	....	....	2	....
Membership in social elite of modal mayor# (impressionistic rating)	Yes (social elite not highly organized)	Yes	Yes**	No

* The detailed table which this table summarizes has been deposited as Document No. 8387 with the ADI Auxiliary Publications Project, Photoduplication Service, Library of Congress, Washington 25, D.C. A copy may be secured by citing the document number and remitting $1.25 for photoprints or $1.25 for 35-mm. microfilm. Advance payment is required. Make checks or money orders payable to Chief, Photoduplication Service, Library of Congress.

† These men were involved in several lines at once. Almost all speculated in land, two combined this with banking, one was a medical doctor, a contractor, and in banking. Several were also active in railroads.

‡ Includes "very little," "village school," "district school," and "public school."

§ Includes one "superior education for his time."

‖ Two of these four lawyers were "self-educated."

No social registry before 1880.

** Catholics not in social registry.

Table 2.—Continued

	Commercial Elite (N = 19)	Transition Mayors (N = 4)	Personalized Politics vs. Party Machine (N = 12)	Political Administrators (N = 4)
Economic standing of modal mayor at time of first election (impressionistic rating)	Highest	A level below the highest	A level below the highest	Medium—medium high
Political background and experience:				
Party affiliation:				
Democrat	11	....	5	4
Republican	4	2	7	....
Whig	3	....	....	....
Other	1	2	....	....
Mean age at election (years)	36	57	48	54
Mean length of residence before election (years)	13	23	28	49
Political experience prior to election:††				
Alderman	9	....	4	1
Other positions:				
From local system	8	2	9	3
Non-local	2‡‡	....	....	....
No previous position or no information	5	2	3	....
Over-all judgment of prior political experience of modal mayor	High	Low	Moderate	High
Number of mayors serving different lengths in office (including two and more terms):				
1 year	10	§§	....	....
2 years	8	2	6	1
3 years	....	1	1	....
4 years	1	....	2	....
5–7 years	....	....	....	....
8 or more years	....	....	3	3
Later political office (aside from being re-elected mayor):††				
Alderman	4	....	....	....
Other local-based elections	10	....	2	....
No information or no other known position	7	4	10	4
Summary judgment: Amount of office-holding after mayoralty	High	Low	Low	Low

†† A mayor could have been both an alderman and held other positions. Therefore, some mayors have been recorded twice.

‡‡ Two of the first group of mayors had been members of their state legislatures before moving to Chicago.

§§ See Table 1, n. †.

for the office between 1848 and 1869—Isaac L. Milliken, a blacksmith (and self-taught lawyer) and Timothy Wait, a barkeeper—had not attained enviable standing in the business life of the city."[3] Like most of the early migrants to Chicago all but three of these nineteen men came from New York or New England and all were born in the United States.[4]

Although we do not have complete information on the religious and educational background of this group, the available evidence indicates that it was almost entirely Protestant or non-religious. Furthermore, several of this group were instrumental in the organization of their denominations in Chicago. Raymond, Lloyd, Sherman, and Boone were either founders or prominent supporters of their respective congregations. By and large these men did not have extended formal education. Only three—Curtiss, Boone, and Wentworth—can indisputably be said to have had a college education. Although Morris and Milliken were qualified lawyers, their educational backgrounds are in doubt, for a college degree was not one of the requirements for admission to the bar.

The political careers of these mayors reveal extensive political participation. As a group, they had held substantially more offices than the group which immediately follows them. All but five of the commercial elite had anywhere from one year (Lloyd) to twelve years (Wentworth) of experience in some type of public office. After the mayoralty all but two (Ramsey and Rice) went on to serve in other positions.

Although these men were active in politics, none dominated the mayoralty for long periods, as we find happening later in the century. Even though there were no legal restrictions on the number of consecutive terms that one could serve, of the nineteen mayors only four held office for two consecutive terms and none for more than that. On the one hand, long terms in office would not have been consonant with the maintenance of economic and other interests. On the other hand, given the size of the community in its early days, the office of mayor may have had mainly honorific rather than central career importance.

The small size of the community also means that most of these men must have had extensive business dealings with each other and have known one another quite well. This homogeneity of background did not always result in a common approach to the policies of city administration. In fact, Dyer and Chapin were members of the same firm, but they ran on opposite party tickets. Although some differences in viewpoint may have existed, in Chicago, as in other new commercial towns,[5] the views of the commercial elite were stamped on the administration of the city.

The evidence presented above suggests that these first mayors were part of a "multi-institutional" elite; active in political office both before and

---

[3] Bessie L. Pierce, *A History of Chicago* (3 vols.; New York: Alfred A. Knopf, Inc., 1937, 1940, 1957), vol. II, p. 305. This work was an indispensable aid to our study.

[4] *Ibid.*, vol. I, p. 174.

[5] See Richard C. Wade, *The Urban Frontier: Pioneer Life in Early Pittsburgh, Cincinnati, Lexington, Louisville, and St. Louis* ("Phoenix Book" [Chicago: University of Chicago Press, 1964]), esp. chap. iii, pp. 72–101.

after being mayor, heading the largest economic enterprises, and active in school and religious activities, these mayors were the leading figures in the community. They attained their position, not by virtue of family background, but through economic achievement.

Changes in Community Structure

The population of Chicago grew from 4,000 in 1837 to 29,000 in 1850 to 120,000 in 1860. As the town grew, forces developed to displace the original commercial elite from their position of both economic and political dominance. Before discussing those forces we must account for a peculiarity in the recruitment of the early mayors: Of the mayors from 1837 until 1870 all but Rice arrived in Chicago between 1833 and 1837. What accounts for the "entrenchment" of these early arrivals?

A partial explanation is found in the depression of 1837, which ruined many of the businessmen who had made fortunes during the preceding speculative era. The "panic" also served to change the character of the people who continued to come to Chicago; the speculator and the bankrupt merchant left—1838 is one of the few years in Chicago's history that reveals a decline in population—and in their place came the laboring immigrant. Those who stayed and consolidated their positions found themselves in economic ascendancy with the return of prosperity; those who came later found themselves competing against an entrenched and active group of commercial leaders who also were active in politics and dominated the political scene.

Several factors led to the eventual economic and political decline of the commercial elite, however. First, the original business leaders were eclipsed by later arrivals who built large industrial, trading, and meatpacking firms. Second, requirements developed that made the office of mayor less desirable for the businessman. Third, political resources became available to other groups within the community.

The original commercial entrepreneurs of the city had a dominant position during the 1840s, but in the 1850s and 1860s they began to be economically obscured by later arrivals.[6] By the end of the 1860s they had lost their position of economic supremacy. Such firms as Wadsworth, Dyer, and Chapin were obscured by the growth in Chicago of Armour and Company; the Chicago Packing and Provision Company; and Libby, McNeill, and Libby; and others. The new leaders of business did not replace the old commercial elite in politics, however; in part because they did not choose to run for office.

The office of mayor became a less desirable sideline occupation for a businessman as the scope of competing firms was enlarged and more energy and time were required to maintain a commanding position in the business community. Also, to be mayor in an era when the pioneer work of building the physical plant and establishing an order for the growing city was complete was a less valuable financial investment than it had been

[6] Pierce, *History of Chicago*, vol. II, pp. 77–117

in the early days when various city improvements in transportation, sanitation, and waterworks could not but benefit economic interests founded on real-estate and commercial holdings.

At the same time, the growth in the physical size of the city and the expansion of public services made the elected officials responsible for more duties, requiring full-time attention to public office. The increase in municipal expenditures from approximately $45,000 in 1848–49 to over $6,000,000 in 1868 indicates the tremendous growth in municipal complexity. Duties formerly performed by private enterprises were taken over by the administrative authorities of the city.[7] This extension of city services and the increased responsibility of the mayor for the performance of these functions made the office an all-engaging activity.

Furthermore, the proliferation of public services extended governmental responsibility into areas where it conflicted with the interests of some segments of the business community. The business leader in office found it increasingly difficult to resolve his business interests and his public responsibilities, and businessmen found they could buy advantages from the developing ward bosses of the city council. All of these developments—the increased attention demanded by commercial and public activity, the decreasing necessity for active political involvement, and the conflict of interest between the two roles—tended to make the mayoralty less desirable to the leading business notables.

At the same time there was a decline in the political resources of the economic dominants. Specifically, there was a lower popular estimation of the virtues and attainments of the businessman. The commercial elite had dominated the political scene despite rapid changes in the community composition. The city census of 1843 listed almost 30 percent of Chicago's population as foreign-born, and by 1850 this figure had risen to 52 percent. Until 1870, in spite of its numerical superiority and with only minimal residence requirements for voting, the foreign-born population of the city continued to support the Yankee businessman year after year.[8] The only explanation of this support seems to be that they believed they too would be the beneficiaries of the rapidly expanding wealth of the city.[9] The rise of labor consciousness, growing public concern over the extent of graft and spoils in public office, and the growing awareness of a divergence of business and public goals all worked to undercut the ideological legitimation of the commercial elite.

[7] *Ibid.*, p. 344.

[8] With the incorporation of the city in 1837, in addition to an age requirement and a residence requirement of at least six months, there was a requirement that the voter have the status of householder or have paid a city tax of not less than three dollars. The property qualifications were eliminated in 1841 and the naturalization requirements were clarified in 1843, when it was explicitly stated that persons could vote whether naturalized citizens or not. This was not changed until 1871 when naturalization was made a condition of registration (A. A. Lavery [ed.], *Smith-Hurd Illinois Annotated Statutes* [Chicago: Bendette Smith Co., 1944], p. 28).

[9] Ethnic politics began to play some role quite early. The charge was made that "the Irish entirely controlled" a local election of 1840 (Ogden to Edwin Crowell, August 31, 1840, *Ogden Letter Books*, vol. II, p. 494).

Transition Mayors: 1869–75

In 1869, with the election of Rosewell Mason, a change occurred in the social background of the mayors. Supported by radical labor and pledged to the restoration of official morals, Mason no longer typifies the commercial elite. During this short period an interlude occurs between a business-dominated political scene and one controlled by charismatic and party leaders.

This period is characterized by political unorthodoxy, conflict between public moralists and advocates of personal liberty, a high degree of party irregularity, and the formation of successful independent parties. Both the disarray of the regular parties and the need for total unity following the fire of 1871 required men who could build a coalition outside of normal channels. The mayors of this period were generally older men with few local political commitments who had high standing in the community.

The type of individual chosen to serve during this period of transition and political conflict had less commitment to the economic growth of Chicago than did the entrepreneur of the preceding period. It is true that Mason and Colvin represented large transportation concerns, but they were managers rather than owners; all of the nineteen previous mayors had been more or less self-employed. Furthermore, the organizations employing them (Mason was employed by the Illinois Central Railroad and was a well-known civil engineer and Colvin was the resident agent of the United States Express Company) were oriented to a much wider area than just that of Chicago.

That the mayoralty was not the prerogative of the leaders of commerce in this period is also indicated by the election of Joseph Medill (editor and owner of the *Chicago Tribune*) and Thomas Hoyne (lawyer and jurist). Although wealthy, Medill did not hold a position in the commercial, industrial, or financial activities of the city comparable to that of the previous mayors. Wentworth, the figure of the first group of mayors most analogous to Medill, in that he owned a newspaper, was also active in real estate, banking, and railroad development. Medill, on the other hand, was completely committed to managing and editing the *Tribune*. Apparently, Hoyne had no active connection with the business community.

The average age of the transition mayors was older than either the preceding or the following groups of mayors. At the time they became mayor the mean age of the first nineteen mayors was forty-one while that of transition mayors was fifty-seven. Of the first nineteen, only two (Dyer and Rice) exceeded the age of the youngest of the second group (Medill). The transition mayors were older in average age than the subsequent two groups (forty-eight and fifty-four, respectively).

Although these mayors were older than their predecessors they had more limited local political involvements. Hoyne and Medill were active in state and national politics, but neither took the usual route to becoming mayor, that is, via the aldermanic position. Moreover, neither Mason nor Colvin had any prior political experience in the city and at the end of their terms of office they discontinued political participation.

How can we account for the selection of these mayors? The disarray in politics had led to the rise of independent parties such as the reform-minded Citizens' Ticket and the labor and ethnic-based People's Party. The "Union-Fireproof" ticket (headed by Medill) was a response to the fire. For finding a candidate that was acceptable to the diverse parties and elements of the community, who could be more acceptable than highly respected older men who had not become identified with the local political issues?

After the election of 1879 the Republicans were convinced that they could elect one of their own candidates and that a bipartisan coalition was not necessary. Thus, party politics returned to their more usual course, the reform elements of the Citizens' Ticket went over to the Republicans, and many of the ethnic elements of the People's Party returned to the ranks of the Democratic party. The transition period was ended.

Personal Machine Versus Party Machine: 1876–1930

Disunity, self-interest, and apathy characterized the business, labor, and middle-class elements of Chicago during this period. A lack of clear numerical preponderance and a high degree of social mobility prevented a clear victory by any one class or ethnic group. Whereas in other major cities strong machines developed, political factions controlled the various regions and groups of Chicago. The distribution of political resources in the community was such, however, that when the city-wide office of mayor was at stake it took more than these local allegiances to elect a candidate. Because of its "payoff" in patronage and political influence, the office of mayor was the focal point of activity for the politicians of all factions of both parties.

Given these conditions, there seemed to be two chief routes of ascent to the office of mayor during this period: through long and careful service to the party and through charismatic or vote-getting abilities. On the one hand, a potential mayor could extend the range of his influence until he became head of one of the party factions or he could be chosen because he epitomized party loyalty and respectability in reform periods. On the other hand, there were the two Harrisons and Thompson—upper-class notables who came to power because they could at the same time mobilize party support and, through personal qualities, appeal widely to the diverse groups of the community.

Social, Occupational, and Political Characteristics

Even though commerce and industry were growing rapidly, the period from 1880 to 1930 did not see the election of any businessman from the major industrial companies, department stores, or banks which came to dominate the Chicago economy. Legal practice, wholesaling, and real-estate management were the major business connections of the twelve mayors elected during this period. A larger proportion of these than of the previous mayors had legal training (five out of twelve as compared to six out of twenty-three); and, whereas many of the first group of mayors had been involved in shipping and milling grain or were in general merchandising, only one of these mayors was a merchant. Three of the mayors in this period were practicing lawyers and judges; five were involved primarily in the distribution of coal, paint and wood, and machinery; three were wealthy real-estate owners and operators; and one, Cregier, was a mechanical engineer and former city engineer. Both real estate and law permit an easy transition to and from public office; thus running for public office was more feasible for many of these men than for the heads of major companies.

Even the men whose businesses demanded much time differ from those who were mayors in previous eras. In several instances the political activities of these businessmen seem to be more important than their business careers. For instance, Hopkins was active in Democratic politics from his arrival in 1880 organizing several annexation movements. He was one of the organizers and early presidents of the Cook County Democratic Club; chairman of the Democratic County Committee in 1889; delegate to the Democratic National Conventions of 1892, 1900, and 1904; and ofttime chairman of the Democratic State Committee. Although he held office for only a short time, he had much more than a passing interest in politics. The same prolonged involvement is true of Busse and Swift. Not only were the mayors of this period not the leaders of the business community but politics and party work were a major part of their lives. Furthermore, five of them were identified with the large Irish and German populations of the city.

All but three of the mayors between 1880 and 1931 had obtained enough social standing and financial success to be listed in the social directories of their periods. Their educational attainment was considerably greater than that of the previous mayors. Of the twelve mayors between 1880 and 1931 six had received college educations and of the remaining six we know that five graduated from high school. (Of the nineteen mayors of the first period only four had a college education.)

Most of these men had long service in their party, and several were heads of factions. Hopkins, Swift, Busse, and Dunne all worked up to power from unpromising beginnings. Using position in the business world and ethnic communities, each gradually extended the range of his influence over party workers and supporters until each became head of one of the party factions. Once in a position to concoct schemes and negotiate treaties, each was able to parlay his political strength into the mayoralty. The success of these mayors in the party was dependent on political generalship, and their election success was a result of the superior working of their respective party organizations.

Heath, Roche, Cregier, and Dever also spent considerable time in the service of their parties. They differed from the former group, however, in their positions within the parties. None was the head of a party faction; rather each was a party supporter. They were chosen as candidates because of their party loyalty and because of their respectability. They pacified the occasional reform or businessman groups that organized to fight the party bosses.

Although the Yankee businessman and the members of first-generation ethnic groups sought and obtained office, the most successful candidate was the charismatic social leader. During this fifty-five-year period, the two Harrisons and Thompson held the office of mayor for a total of thirty-one years and when not in office were a force to be reckoned with. In a sense the history of the mayoralty of this period is the story of these three individuals. Although quite different in their administration of public office, the Harrisons and Thompson were successful because they could appeal to a wider variety of groups than could their opponents.

Chosen to run initially for minor posts because of their silk-stocking respectability and financial standing, both the senior Harrison and Thompson showed remarkable ability as campaigners. While Harrison, and especially his son, were less raucously flamboyant than Thompson (and were never as involved in scandals), all three had oratorical skills, a sense of showmanship, and an ability to adapt to their audience. Their personal following enabled them to jump to the top of their parties without serving long apprenticeships. Because of their citywide following they were relatively independent of the political fiefs making up the respective party organizations.

Changes in Community Structure

Between 1876 and 1931 Chicago developed into a great central manufacturing center and one of the principal agricultural clearing houses in the country. From virtually complete destruction in the fire of 1871, Chicago became the showplace of the 1893 Columbian Exposition. These radical rearrangements in the economic and physical structure were paralleled by extensive migration to the city and a reordering of its population composition. In the 1890s extensive numbers of Poles, Bohemians, Russians, and Italians arrived, following the Germans, Irish, and Scandinavians. By 1920, 70.6 percent of the population was either foreign-born or of foreign parentage. Finally, in the early 1900s the influx of Negroes increased.[10] The high rate of economic growth, the extent of vertical mobility, and the rapid movement of large numbers of people to and

---

[10] Helen R. Jeter, *Trends of Population in the Region of Chicago* (Chicago: University of Chicago Press, 1927). See also Paul F. Cressy, "The Succession of Cultural Groups in Chicago" (unpublished Ph.D. dissertation, University of Chicago, 1930); Pierce, *History of Chicago*, vol. III, pp. 20–64; Charles E. Merriam, *Chicago: A More Intimate View of Urban Politics* (New York: Macmillan Co., 1949), pp. 134–77.

from the city prevented stable political organizations and traditional groupings.[11]

Of the groupings that arose out of this economic development, the most effectively organized and *potentially* the most influential was the business element. Able to control newspapers, campaign funds, propaganda, and the services of political leaders, they could play—when they cared to act together—an important role in the political game. They seldom, however, chose either to act, or, when they did act, to do so in concert. There was conflict between commerce and industry and railroads and real-estate operators and public utilities. There was also conflict within each of these groups and between them and the public, which felt that its interests had been subordinated to narrow economic goals. Both factors, the lack of group solidarity and the lessening of social legitimation, prevented the business elite of the community from exerting control over the political scene.[12]

The numerically most powerful group, labor, was not notably successful in political participation. Organized in the 1870s and 1880s under the pressures of an expanding labor force, recurring unemployment, rising food prices and falling wages, and the injustices of child labor, the labor movement was beset by strife resulting from the issue of radicalism versus trade unionism. General prosperity between 1887 and 1892 brought quiet to the labor front and a degree of rapprochement within the labor movement. The insecurity of this rapprochement led the leaders who feared the effects of politics upon the unity of their trade-union organizations, to discourage union participation in political contests. Even when this policy was abandoned, as it was in the mayoralty campaign of 1919, lack of solidarity made labor's efforts in politics unsuccessful.

At the same time, the very diversity of ethnic groups prohibited any one group from dominating the scene. The cleavages in the ethnic composition of the community presented natural lines along which political power could be organized. Capitalizing on the neighborhood segregation of their countrymen, and their own ethnic identification, political bosses appeared who were supreme in their own bailiwicks. Chicago politics became more and more controlled by several party organizations able to distribute patronage and to obtain large campaign funds.[13]

The diversity in the community structure did not totally exclude businessmen from political participation; the time had passed, however, when an individual could be elected merely on the basis of his standing within the business community. Thus, Harrison was able to defeat a movement

---

[11] See Merriam, *Intimate View of Urban Politics*, and Lincoln Steffens, *The Autobiography of Lincoln Steffens* (New York: Harcourt, Brace & Co., 1931), pp. 422-29, for a description of the political system at this time.

[12] There is some evidence to suggest that the Republican party was more influenced by the business element of the city than was the Democratic party. Every one of the Republican mayors elected during this period could be found listed in the executive directory of their time, in contrast to the Democratic candidates, only one of whom was listed.

[13] Merriam, *Intimate View of Urban Politics*, pp. 97-98.

in 1881 to nominate in his stead candidates of the highest prestige in the business world, such as Levi Z. Leiter, George L. Dunlap, and Cyrus McCormick, and he defeated the Republican John M. Clark, a leather manufacturer, who had the backing of five hundred leading businessmen.

Although the first-ranking businessmen were not elected, several considerations lead to the conclusion that ethnic identification, while important, was not sufficient to insure election to the office of mayor. Such identification had to be paired with some business success. Roche, Hopkins, Dunne, and Dyer were all only one or two generations removed from Ireland. (Of these four, three were sufficiently wealthy to be listed in the elite directory for the mid-1880s, a precursor to the Social Register.) Busse, an influential leader of the Republican party and quite prosperous, represented the large German population in Chicago. Even when business success was paired with factional strength and ethnic identification, however, the flamboyant appeal of Thompson and the Harrisons could dominate such candidates.

The election of Anton Cermak as mayor in 1931 brought an end to the Thompson era and represented the ascendancy of a party machine that was unparalleled in the history of the city. From a position at the beginning of the depression in which the balance between the two major parties in Chicago was fairly even (seven of the last twelve mayors had been Republicans), the political complexion changed such that by 1936 the Democrats were in complete control of all the governmental agencies within the territorial limits of the city of Chicago. Henceforth, the Democratic party machine was the decisive force in the selection of elected officials. No longer could the competition between the two parties or the divergent factions within them be used as a lever for political success. The route to public office was now limited to ascendancy through the party's ranks.

Political Administrators: 1931–1965

In many other cities the economic crisis and the community disorganization that resulted from the depression led to the introduction of political reforms and the election of rabidly antimachine candidates. In Chicago, however, the effect of the depression was to weld together the political resources of the community into the all-powerful Democratic machine. Thus, at a time when the Tammany Hall machine of New York and the Republican machine of Philadelphia were meeting severe reverses, Chicago was embracing an organization of unparalleled strength.[14] Consequently, that individual able to rise to the top of the organization or chosen by the machine to run for the office was elected to the mayoralty. Under such conditions the mayors of this period had to be, above all else, strongly connected to the local Democratic party structures.

[14] Harold F. Gosnell accounts for the ascendancy of the Chicago machine by referring to an "unfavorable press situation, a lack of leadership, and the character of the party division at the beginning of the depression" (*Machine Politics: Chicago Model* [Chicago: University of Chicago Press, 1937]).

Social, Occupational, and Political Characteristics

The four men who held office between 1931 and 1965 started from rather modest beginnings. They had little formal education—only Daley had college training; the others had a high school diploma or less—and started near the bottom of the occupational hierarchy—Cermak in the coal mines of Illinois, Kelly as an axeman for the Sanitary Department, Kennelly as a laborer in a warehouse, and Daley as a stockyard cowboy.

With the exception of Kennelly, the mayors after 1931 started fairly low in the party organization and served in a variety of elective positions (Cermak spent thirty-three years in elective office) before becoming mayor. Even Kennelly, who has been characterized as an outsider, had a long history of political involvement as a commissioner to the Lincoln Park Board and as a member of the Chicago Park District.

None of these four mayors was among the top leaders in the industrial, commercial, or financial activities of the city (although Cermak's banking and real-estate holdings placed him at the head of his ethnic community of Lawndale). They were not social notables, and none of them appeared in the elite directory of his time.[15] They had demonstrated administrative and managerial abilities, however. For instance, Kelly had been head of a large public-service agency, president of the South Park Board of Commissioners, and heir apparent to the machine; Daley had been the Illinois Revenue Director and Clerk of Cook County. All had shown ability to organize and direct large organizational structures. They were political rather than economic entrepreneurs.

The religious and ethnic identification of most of the Democratic mayors from Hopkins on reflects the domination of the party by Irish Catholics. With the exception of the Harrisons and Cermak, all of the Democratic mayors from 1893 to the present have been first or second-generation Irish Catholics.

Cermak, the only foreign-born Chicago mayor and, besides Busse, the only mayor to fall outside of the old-stock American, English, Scottish, or Irish groups, was able to obtain success as spokesman of the "wet" vote and the other ethnic groups making up the Democratic party. His organization and consolidation of the party, however, enabled the Irish to gain consolidated control after Cermak's death.[16]

A long and intimate participation in the life of Chicago became increasingly important for political success. Each of the ten mayors from Swift to Daley had resided in the city for more than twenty-eight years. Of these, five had been born and raised and a sixth raised in the city. The requisite sensitivity to the issues and social arrangements of the community, the necessity of an extensive network of informal social and busi-

---

[15] This lack of representation of the "silk stocking" element is also reflected in the city council. Of the thirty-four aldermen on the council in 1900, five were listed in the *Chicago Social Directory* for that year. By 1935, of the fifty men who sat on the council, not one was listed. This lack of representation of the "better class" has continued so that in 1965 there is still no alderman to be found in the listed elite of Chicago.

[16] Alex Gottfried, *Boss Cermak of Chicago: A Study of Political Leadership* (Seattle: University of Washington Press, 1962).

ness connections, and the lengthy party apprenticeship made residence in Chicago an imperative for political leadership.

Changes in Community Structure

What led to the rise of the political administrators? We must look at the motives for participating in politics. Judging from the social standing of a number of the aldermen and mayors of the pre-1930 period, political participation was accepted as a legitimate activity for the well-to-do. The activities of the "gray wolves" and the "boodle boys" during the era of the Harrisons, the open protection of a wide-open city during the Thompson period, the breaking of scandal after scandal, and the general circus atmosphere under which the political campaigns were run all led to the destruction of any social prestige that had been attached to office-holding and cast political participation in a negative light.[17] Many social and business leaders refrained from mingling in the rough and tumble of politics. Private welfare and philanthropy offered a much more respectable way of performing one's civic duties.[18] Busily engaged in building up their fortunes, fearful of alienating the populace with an unpopular political stand, and finding it much more profitable to buy the political favors they needed, the business and social elite stood at the sidelines of the political game. Furthermore, movement to the suburbs removed many of them from the political scene.[19]

Even those of the economic and social elite who stayed and wished to participate would have had to do so through the party organization, for the party machine, with its mobilization of the working-class vote, financial resources, and hard core of party workers, could afford to pick its candidate from within the organization.[20] The ward committeemen constituted the core of the party machinery. They controlled the selection of

[17] The following volumes give colorful, if at times overly journalistic, accounts of the history of Chicago's political and social reputation: John Bright, *Hizzoner Big Bill Thompson, an Idyll of Chicago* (New York: J. Cape & H. Smith, 1930); Fletcher Dobyns, *The Underworld of American Politics* (New York: privately printed, 1932); Lloyd Lewis and Henry Smith, *Chicago: The History of Its Reputation* (New York: Harcourt, Brace & Co., 1929); Merriam, *Intimate View of Urban Politics*; William H. Stuart, *The Twenty Incredible Years* (Chicago: M. A. Donahue & Co., 1935).

[18] Much of the motivation dynamics operating in Chicago is similar to that found by Lynd and Merrill in Middletown (Robert S. Lynd and Helen Merrill, *Middletown: A Study in Modern American Culture* [New York: Harcourt, Brace & Co., 1929], p. 421).

[19] William R. Gable, "The Chicago City Council: A Study of Urban Politics and Legislation" (unpublished Ph.D. dissertation, University of Chicago, 1953), p. 10.

[20] It should be noted that, while the socially and economically advantaged moved out of the city and into the suburbs, their places were taken by the migrants from the agrarian areas of the North and South (chiefly southern Negroes and whites), immigrants from Puerto Rico and other Latin American countries, and occasional immigrants from Europe. Thus the often-predicted changing class character of urban politics and the resulting decline in machine dominance has been postponed in Chicago. See Part V of Edward C. Banfield (ed.), *Urban Government: A Reader in Administration and Politics* (New York: Free Press, 1961); especially relevant in this regard are Samuel Lubell, "The New Middle Class" (pp. 301–8) and Frank J. Sorauf, "The Silent Revolution in Patronage" (pp. 308–17).

candidates for public office as well as the operation of the election machinery that elects the candidates. In order to become boss of the party one had to have the backing of the principal ward bosses of the inner city. It is not surprising, therefore, to find the ward bosses giving support to a leader whose identifications were with the inner-city wards.

Once chosen and in office, however, the mayor possessed a great deal of the coin upon which the machine is built—patronage. This resource made the mayor independent of the ward bosses and the ward bosses dependent upon him. This partially accounts for the coincidence of the mayor and the party boss being one and the same. The mayor, however, never gained complete independence—witness Kennelly's defeat when he tried to run without the support of the regular party organization in 1955 —but must always have some measure of support from the ward bosses.[21] Faced with the necessity of centralized leadership, the ward bosses have chosen to follow individuals with working-class backgrounds, intimate knowledge of Chicago and the party organization, Irish Catholic identification,[22] and demonstrated administrative ability. The popular and charismatic qualities that had enabled the Harrisons and Thompson to dominate the political scene during the 1890s and 1920s would in 1950 only hinder their political aspirations. The kind of leader produced by the organization was, above all else, a political executive.

Conclusions

Our conclusions can best be stated by comparison and contrast with those presented by Dahl for New Haven:[23]

1. In New Haven a long and settled history prior to incorporation led to the selection of mayors from among the patrician families—families of long and established social standing; these mayors had had legal training and extensive education. In comparison, Chicago's first mayors were drawn from its commercial leaders, regardless of family background, who were caught up in the growth and speculative investment of the community. This came about partly because Chicago's "old" families were almost non-existent but also because the commercial elite represented the driving force in the new community.

[21] Our analysis draws heavily on Edward C. Banfield's *Political Influence* (New York: Free Press, 1961).

[22] A comment on the success of the Irish: both in the city council and in the party hierarchy, the religious similarity between the Irish and the other nationality groups (the principal ethnic groups in the Democratic party, in descending order of importance, were the Poles, Italians, Bohemians, Lithuanians, Slovaks, and Greeks) and the fact that in a city which has no one single ethnic group in a clear majority, the Irish upset the community balance least, made the Irish Catholics the most logical and acceptable candidates. As one investigator quotes a politician: "A Lithuanian won't vote for a Pole, and a Pole won't vote for a Lithuanian. A German won't vote for either of them, but all three will vote for a 'Turkey' [Irishman]" (Martin Meyerson and E. C. Banfield, "A Machine at Work," in Banfield [ed.], *Political Influence*, p. 136).

[23] Dahl, *Who Governs?* pp. 11–64.

2. After 1842, New Haven's patricians gave way to the leading entrepreneurs, whether recruited from the commercial or from the industrial elite, who were to hold sway until 1900. Chicago's commercial elite were followed in the 1860s and 1870s by the transition mayors, men picked as a compromise because of the disunity and chaos of party alignments. While not unsuccessful in their occupational or social pursuits, they represented neither the commercial elite nor the local politically active.

3. In New Haven, the entrepreneurs were succeeded around 1900 by the ex-plebes, representatives of the city's recent new arrivals. In Chicago, beginning about 1880, two types of men were recruited, social notables with wide popular following and highly politically involved businessmen: men who had status in the business community, but were not from the largest firms or factories; men who had both business, political, and ethnic (Irish or German) connection. While the "ex-plebe" or at least the ethnic, label might fit some of them, ethnic politics seem not to have been as dominant a feature in their election as in that of New Haven's mayors. The diversity of ethnic groups and of the community prohibited giving the simple label of ex-plebe to these men, or to the period, until 1930.

4. Finally, with Cermak, the dominance of the Democratic party machine began. While the new mayors are "ex-plebe," the driving force in community politics becomes the machine, and the style of the mayor becomes that of the political administrator. The machine and city politics had become a full-time career. While a business career parallel to a political one is not impossible in this era, it becomes more and more unlikely.

Dahl suggests that politics and recruitment to the mayoralty may be in a period of transformation in New Haven. Ethnicity is declining as a major criterion of political success; instead Dahl hypothesizes, the "new men" will be those who, by a concern with the fate of the city, expand their political base to the self-interested downtown businessmen and the social-welfare professional. The "new men" expand their support from ethnic organizations by becoming the leaders and initiators of programs of physical and social city renewal.

The parallel with Chicago is difficult to find. As Banfield notes, in a community as diverse as Chicago there is little development of the conditions for consensus supporting a widespread attack on city problems. In such a situation the mayor is more a referee than a combatant in the resolution of the issues facing the city.

There is a parallel of another sort, however. Even though the patronage available to Chicago mayors allows the machine to function with less concession to reform than in other cities, as in other cities there has been a transformation of the posture of its political administrator. Thus, to quote the political slogan of Mayor Richard J. Daley, "Good government is good politics."

With the assimilation of foreign immigrants, the rise of social-security measures, the introduction of civil service, and the transformation of the occupational and educational structure, the only significant source of political support in the traditional patronage-welfare exchange is the Negroes, and even they are becoming increasingly concerned with the ideological dimensions of politics.

Given this transformation of the urban setting, the present mayor of Chicago, like those in Philadelphia, New Haven, and Detroit, must represent the process of collective betterment and not the process of machine greed. A new ethos of "the good of the community" becomes dominant and shapes the administration of the mayor.

The Role of Economic Dominants in Community Power Structure*

ROBERT O. SCHULZE

That persons occupying positions of economic importance are among the key wielders of local influence and control has long been one of the most commonplace assumptions of American sociologists and one of the most consistent findings of research concerned with American communities and community power structures.[1] With very few exceptions, however, most studies relevant to the role of economic dominants in community control structures have focused on current power configurations. Relatively little research attention has yet been devoted to historical shifts in local power structures associated with the metropolitan and bureaucratic drift of American life.[2] Likewise, while most relevant studies have indi-

Reprinted from the *American Sociological Review*, 23 (1958): 3-9. Copyright 1958 by the American Sociological Association. Reprinted by permission of the publisher.

* Expanded version of paper read at the annual meeting of the American Sociological Society, August, 1957. I wish to thank Morris Janowitz and Melvin Reichler, both of the University of Michigan, for their helpful comments on this paper.

[1] In addition to the well-known works of the Lynds, Warner, Hollingshead, Mills, and Hunter, see: Roland J. Pellegrin and Charles H. Coates, "Absentee-Owned Corporations and Community Power Structure," *American Journal of Sociology*, LXI, 5 (1956), pp. 413-19; George Belknap and Ralph Smuckler, "Political Power Relations in a Mid-West City," *Public Opinion Quarterly*, XX, 1 (1956), pp. 73-81; A. Alexander Fanelli, "A Typology of Community Leadership Based on Influence and Interaction Within the Leader Subsystem," *Social Forces*, 34, 4 (1966), pp. 332-38; Robert E. Agger, "Power Attributions in the Local Community," *ibid.*, pp. 322-31; Peter Rossi, "Historical Trends in the Politics of an Industrial Community," paper presented at the 51st annual meeting of the American Sociological Society, September, 1956.

[2] Rossi's study is a notable exception.

cated that a considerable number of persons of significant local influence are men of economic substance, they have not revealed the pattern of community involvement (nor changes in that pattern) of the economically most-powerful considered as a category. Thus, we have heard a good deal about the activities and influence of the "X" family and its equivalents in American communities, but rather less about the "Y" families, and almost nothing at all about the ratio of "Xs" to "Ys" either currently or over time.

This paper reports some findings of an investigation of the power structure of a middle-sized American community—findings concerned primarily with the historical role of the economic dominants in that community's power structure.[3] Although the study has among its numerous limitations those inevitable in any piece of single-community research, it is hoped that it might be theoretically and methodologically suggestive for research in other communities, especially those which—like the subject of this study—have become satellites in a society increasingly dominated by giant metropolitan centers and large national corporations.

The rudimentary theory underlying this research may be briefly summarized. The basic assumption was that as the functional relationship of the community to the larger society changes, so does the nature and form of its control structure, and so, too, does the role of its economic dominants in that structure.

It was hypothesized that in the community *relatively* self-contained and uninvolved in the larger social and economic system, the community with few and scattered commitments beyond its borders, local power would tend to be structured as a pyramid and heavily concentrated at the apex. More specifically, it was surmised that those persons who exercised major control over the community's economic system would tend to be the same persons who exercised preponderant control over its socio-political system, and that this latter control would be reflected, at least in part, by their active leadership and participation in the political and civic life of the community.

With increasing urbanization and as the community passed beyond what Lloyd Warner has called "the period of local capitalism"[4] however, it was suggested that the economic dominants would begin to withdraw their interest and active attention from the local socio-political system. Although the major economic units would have grown in size and potential influence, it was hypothesized that several factors would militate against the effective exercise, the actual "cashing-in" of their power in the community. The most significant of these would be the fact that the local community would have become ever less important to the survival and prosperity of its dominant economic units. As the activities of these units became increasingly directed toward—and by—populations and groups other than the local ones, the relevance of local community

[3] Robert O. Schulze, *Economic Dominance and Public Leadership: A Study of the Structure and Process of Power in an Urban Community*, microfilmed Ph.D. dissertation, University of Michigan, 1956. (University Microfilms, Publication No. 21,359.)

[4] W. Lloyd Warner and J. O. Low, "The Factory in the Community," in William Foote Whyte (ed.), *Industry and Society* (New York: McGraw-Hill, 1946), p. 35.

organizations and the impact of local political influences on the major economic units would accordingly diminish. As this occurred, the local power structure would in effect, bifurcate—with those who exercised primary direction over its socio-political system no longer being essentially the same set of persons who exercised primary control over its economic system.[5]

An effort was made to test this general theory in Cibola, a Midwestern industrial community of some 20,000 inhabitants, located approximately 30 miles from Metro City, one of the nation's largest metropolitan centers. Founded in 1823, Cibola grew rather slowly until World War II. Between 1940 and 1950, however, its population increased over 50 percent, a shift symptomatic of countless other changes to which the community has lately been subject. One of the principal changes has been the gradual absorption of its major industrial plants by large, absentee-owned corporations, a trend sharply accelerated during the World War II period.

In our research, we attempted to reconstruct Cibola's economic dominants from the time of its founding in 1823 until 1955, and to determine the general nature and extent of their overt involvement in the political and civic life of the community.

The economic dominants for the various historical periods were operationally-defined as those persons who: (a) occupied the top formal roles in the largest industries and banks in the community; or (b) were members of the boards of directors of two or more of these industries and banks, thus serving formally to "interlock" the dominant economic units; or (c) were the largest property-owners in the community.[6]

---

[5] It is not suggested that the decline in the economic dominants' leadership and participation in community decision-making processes stems wholly from their diminishing concern with local affairs. With their attenuation of local involvement, it is obvious that effective contact and meaningful communication between economic dominants and diverse elements of the community population are likewise reduced, contributing to what has been referred to as the loss of "multi-class leadership" by the top business groups in American communities. In such a situation, economic dominants—when they occasionally may want to influence community decisions—may find that their local leadership base has so shrunken that their effectiveness is impaired. Somewhat illustrative of this was the case of Cal Lamkin, the general manager of a large industrial plant in the community studied. Long inactive in local political and voluntary associational affairs, Lamkin was eventually prevailed upon to stand for election to the board of directors of the local Chamber of Commerce. To the considerable embarrassment of the Chamber's officials, however, Lamkin failed to muster sufficient votes to win a seat on the board. Cf. Wilbert E. Moore, *Industrial Relations and the Social Order* (New York: The Macmillan Company, 1951), pp. 547–53. Although presented in causal terms somewhat different from those suggested in this paper, the best known and perhaps most sanguine statement of the American business elites' loss of multi-group leadership is contained in Kenneth Galbraith, *American Capitalism and the Concept of Countervailing Power* (Boston: Houghton Mifflin, 1952).

[6] Specific criteria for classification as an economic dominant in each historical period were based on such measures as number of employees (industries), capital worth (banks), and assessed valuation of holdings (property-owners). Various source data were utilized in the determination of these measures, including county tax records, city directories and histories, newspapers, records of individual companies and of the Chamber of Commerce and the State Historical Collections, plus such standard references as *Poor's Register of Directors and Executives* and *Polk's Bank Directory*.

Table 1. Number and percent of economic dominants in public office, 1823–1954 periods

Period	Number of Economic Dominants	Number of Economic Dominants in Public Office	Percent of Economic Dominants in Public Office
1823–1860	12	10	83
1860–1900	21	17	81
1900–1940	43	12	28
1940–1954	31	7	23

Table 2. Changes in number of economic dominants and number of available officies, 1823–1954 periods

Period	Percentage Change in Number of Economic Dominants	Percentage Change in Number of Public Offices in City Government
From 1823–1860 to 1860–1900 periods	plus 7	plus 80
From 1860–1900 to 1900–1940 periods	plus 105	plus 183
From 1900–1940 to 1940–1954 periods	minus 28	minus 30

Insofar as local involvement was reflected by occupancy of formal offices in the political and civic organizations in the community, the research tended clearly to support the basic hypothesis. *The historical drift has been characterized by the withdrawal of the economic dominants from active and overt participation in the public life of Cibola.* Tables 1, 3, and 4 are presented to illustrate this withdrawal.

Table 1 indicates that prior to the turn of the century, fully four-fifths of Cibola's economic dominants held public office in the community, while since 1900, the proportion has declined to approximately one-quarter.[7] Likewise, as shown in Table 3, the proportion of economic dominants who have held the top political office in Cibola has sharply diminished. Not indicated in either of these two tables is the fact that *none* of the most recent type of economic dominant—the managers of the absentee-owned corporations—has held any public office (elective or appointive) in the community.

There was some evidence that in the early decades of this century the arena of active local involvement of Cibola's economic dominants shifted from politics to the important voluntary associations. Even in this area,

---

[7] It might be suggested that the declining proportion of economic dominants in public office was a function of the fact that the number of dominants increased at a greater rate than the number of available offices, and therefore, that the declining proportions are spurious. This was not the case. Changes in the number of economic dominants throughout the four periods were very closely paralleled by proportionately similar changes in the number of available public offices. (See Table 2.)

Table 3. Number and percent of economic dominants in office of village president or mayor, 1823–1954 periods

Period	Number of Dominants in Office of Village President or Mayor	Percent of Dominants in Office of Village President or Mayor	Percent of "Politically-Active" Dominants in Office of Village President or Mayor*
1823–1860	5	42	50
1860–1900	7	33	41
1900–1940	2	5	17
1940–1954	1	3	14

* "Politically-Active": All those economic dominants who had held any public office.

Table 4. Number of economic dominants in offices of the Chamber of Commerce, 1920–1955*

Period	Median Number of Memberships per Year on Board of Directors	Number Serving as President
1920–1927	6	3
1927–1934	3	2
1934–1941	3	0
1941–1948	2	1
1948–1955	1	0

* The Cibola Chamber of Commerce was founded in 1920. From that date until 1953, the number of directors was fifteen; in the latter year, the number was increased to eighteen. Directors serve two-year terms and are eligible for reelection.

however, an appreciable subsequent diminution of active participation has been apparent—perhaps best reflected by the declining number of dominants holding responsible office in the community's most influential association, the local Chamber of Commerce.

It is suggested that the withdrawal of the economic dominants was primarily a consequence of the changing relationship of the community's economic system to that of the larger society. Prior to about 1900, three aspects of Cibola's economic life were especially notable: (a) all of its economic dominants were local residents; (b) all of its dominant economic units were locally-owned; and (c) the majority of its dominants were associated in extensive economic networks *within* the community.

Our research established that in the pre-1900 period, almost 70 percent of the economic dominants had known business or financial ties—as partners, co-officers or co-directors—with other dominants in the community. Thus, throughout most of Cibola's history, its "average" economic dominant was not only a local resident, or merely the head of a single major economic unit; he was also directly and indirectly linked with a considerable number of other major economic units and dominants within the community.

Combined, these factors provided most economic dominants with deep, branching roots in Cibola. The business and financial links, in particular, afforded many of them a basis for shared concern in the local community. The economic networks served to weld together blocs of dominants, giving them frequent and specific occasion for interpersonal contact. By the same token, the very diversity of the "average" dominant's local economic commitments meant that there was always a variety of areas and methods in which local political considerations could impinge upon his pecuniary and related interests. The evidence suggests that these considerations were closely associated with the high incidence of involvement by economic dominants in the socio-political system of the community.

The period since 1900, and more particularly, since 1930, has been marked by the increasing absorption of the local economic system into the larger industrial complex, especially that of Metro City. While several complex social factors were patently involved, the following three seem most closely related to the eventual withdrawal of the economic dominants from active participation in the political-civic life of Cibola: (a) the establishment by a growing number of locally-owned industrial units of direct supplier relationships with a small number of large, non-local manufacturing plants; (b) the subsequent introduction into the local economic system of an increasing number of branch plants of large, absentee-owned corporations; and (c) the concomitant dissolution of the extensive networks of interlocking director and officerships which had formerly served to link significant numbers of local economic dominants within the community.

Consequently, the overt direction of the political and civic life of Cibola has passed almost wholly into the hands of a group of middle-class business and professional men, almost none of whom occupies a position of economic dominance in the community. That this has in fact been the case was suggested in another aspect of our research by the finding that only two of Cibola's seventeen current economic dominants were perceived by the local voluntary association heads to have been among the eighteen most influential leaders in the community.[8] And both of these two, by the way, were heads of relatively small, locally-owned economic units.

Patently, these data reveal changes only in the level of overt and manifest involvement of the economic dominants in the local power structure. It may be suggested, of course, that covertly—"behind-the-scenes"—the economic dominants continue to exercise considerable direction and control of community affairs. However, the findings of another part of our research strongly suggest that things may, in fact, be what they seem.

In an effort to view the community power structure "in action," we endeavored to determine the patterns and processes of local decision-making in a series of recent community episodes (including a successful campaign to change the structure of municipal government from a mayor-aldermen to a city manager form, and an ambitious but unsuccessful

---

[8] The heads of 143 voluntary associations in Cibola were asked a series of five questions intended to elicit their perceptions of the most influential leaders in the community. On the basis of their total "nominations," the eighteen most-frequently cited persons were designated as the "public leaders" of Cibola. See Robert O. Schulze and Leonard U. Blumberg, "The Determination of Local Power Elites," *American Journal of Sociology,* 63, 3 (1957), pp. 290–96.

annexation effort).[9] Our findings in this aspect of the research forced us to conclude that the recent economic dominants—and especially those representing the growing number of large, absentee-owned corporations—appear indeed to have dissociated themselves from active involvement in Cibola's power structure.

These episodes reflected a growing adherence on the part of the absentee-owned corporations in Cibola to a "hands-off" position with regard to local political decision-making. And while it cannot be conclusively documented within the limits of the present paper, this evolving policy is graphically suggested by presenting excerpts from interviews with several executives in the larger economic units.

The general manager of the second largest manufacturing plant in the community, commenting on our findings that but two of the top ten officials in his plant actually resided in Cibola, stated:

> That's a sore spot with me. I've always felt that if I'm going to work in a town, I ought to live there. But there's no consensus on that by a long ways. It's been discussed at the highest levels in our corporation—I know because I've been on the company's community relations committee ever since it was set up. The company has decided that it won't encourage its executives to live in the communities where they work if they don't already or if they don't want to. . . . The company doesn't feel its people—at least its executives—have to live in a town in order to have good community relations. Just about the opposite, as a matter of fact. You're always subject to a hell of a lot of local pressures if you're there. If they know where you are, you're always a target. So maybe it's better not to be in a position to be asked to do something than to have to say, "No."

In discussing the paucity of both formal and informal contacts between corporation officials and local leaders, the assistant general manager of the largest industrial plant in Cibola said:

> No, I've almost never gone downtown for lunch "with the boys." I sometimes get my hair cut in [Cibola], but outside of that I don't show my face any more than I feel I absolutely have to. . . . The people at the Chamber of Commerce seem to fall all over themselves trying to do anything we want—but the point is, we don't really *want* anything there except for the people to have a good opinion of us. But mostly due to this placating attitude of the town's leaders, I'm afraid to say much or be around much.

The corporations were interested, to be sure (as the title of one company's "kit for divisional executives" indicated) in "Making Friends for [U. S. Motors] in the Local Community," but a growing number of them were coming to regard "making friends" and "getting involved" as incon-

---

[9] In these reconstructions, a variety of source materials was utilized, including intensive interviews with the seventeen current economic dominants, the eighteen persons perceived by the 143 local voluntary association heads as the community's most influential leaders, and a selected number of informants. In addition, relevant newspaper files, Chamber of Commerce records and reports, and city council minutes were reviewed.

sonant. The general manager of another large plant summed up his attitude:

> One sure way to give [our firm] a black eye would be for me to get myself into things so deeply in town that no matter what I did, I'd end up alienating a lot of people.

And another:

> You've got to remember that what I do doesn't affect us just here. The guy who represents our company in this area could affect our reputation a lot of other places as well. . . . Why, if I went out and got myself [involved] in local politics, you'd see a new boy in these shoes so damned fast it'd make your head swim.

Meaningful participation in the decision-making processes of a community such as Cibola was mainly regarded by these corporations as entailing risks to their operations and to their positions in the larger social system—risks which could not be offset by any palpable advantages which might accrue to them through playing significant roles in the local power structure. They were clearly cognizant, for example, of the possibility that involvement by their executives in local affairs might induce conflicting loyalties. Likewise, their executives recognized that decisive involvement in critical community decisions posed the threat of alienating significant superiors and publics at the extra-community level, thus endangering their larger occupational and public relations objectives. It seems tenable that it was the very sensitivity of the large corporations to socio-political determinations at the regional and national levels which militated against their involvement in these matters at the level of the local community.

The central finding of the Cibola study—the bifurcation of the community's power structure, stemming from the withdrawal of the economic dominants from active direction of the political and civic life of the community—appears quite generally to corroborate the investigation of Peter Rossi and his associates of the changing patterns of political participation in a middle-sized industrial community in New England.[10] Likewise, our findings seem to be consistent with C. Wright Mills' observations regarding the altered position of large economic units in the power structures of local communities.[11] On the other hand, the Cibola findings do not appear consistent with Hunter's research in Regional City, nor, especially, with that of Pellegrin and Coates in Bigtown.[12]

In addition to the obvious and perhaps significant differences in the sizes of the several communities involved, it will be noted that Hunter and Pellegrin and Coates studied the structures and dynamics of community power in Southern cities, while Rossi's and the present research

[10] Rossi, "Historical Trends."

[11] C. Wright Mills, *The Power Elite* (New York: Oxford University Press, 1956).

[12] Floyd Hunter, *Community Power Structure* (Chapel Hill, N.C.: University of North Carolina Press, 1953); Pellegrin and Coates, "Absentee-Owned Corporations."

concern New England and Midwestern communities, respectively. In correspondence with the writer, Pellegrin has suggested that the disparate findings may be largely the function of regional differences: the historical tradition of paternalism being perhaps stronger in the South than in the North. It has also been suggested that economic dominants may become involved in community power structures independent of the desires of their economic units to guide or influence local decision-making. Thus, for example, to the extent that economic dominants represent the wealthier interests in the community and are a major source of voluntary donations to local charities and similar activities, they may be coopted into decision structures by those actively "in charge" in order to reinforce the latter's control positions and to guarantee a continued source of contributions. Likewise, to the extent that the economic dominants represent the upper prestige levels in a community, they may be drawn into the control structure by the active community leaders in an effort by the latter to legitimize their own prestige positions.

It should be noted, however, that both of the foregoing hypothetical instances cast the economic dominants in the role of rather reluctant participants in local power structures. In such situations, it would be *other* members of the community, not the economic dominants nor the dominant economic units themselves, who would have most stake in the latters' local involvement. And this, in turn, would have, perhaps, significant ramifications for the kinds of roles which the economic dominants played in community power structures and for the degree of interest and local concern with which they acted out these roles.

Whatever the reasons for the apparent differences in the nature and extent of economic dominant involvement in local power structures— and the delineation of these reasons should certainly be one objective of future research—the Cibola study appears to document the absence of any neat, constant, and direct relationship between *power as a potential for determinative action,* and *power as determinative action, itself.* It suggests, likewise, the need to re-examine the role of economic dominance in community power structures in view of the continued drift of American society, on the one hand, toward the concentration of population in suburban and satellite communities, and, on the other, toward the continuing expansion of huge economic bureaucracies.

An Historical Perspective on the Functions of Local Politics*

PETER H. ROSSI and ALICE S. ROSSI

In perhaps a majority of American communities—particularly in our cities—the prestige of local politics is very low. The popular image of the local political figure is often that of the "ward-heeler," a person of obscure accomplishments and doubtful morality whose visible occupation often conceals more lucrative connections. At best, only the very top offices are regarded as legitimate ambitions for men of talent and principle, while our local city councils are considered beneath their aspirations.

The disparagement of local political office is endemic throughout our nation, although this attitude is particularly strong among our higher occupational and educational groups.[1] That this has not always been the case can be seen in the testimony of Bryce[2] or de Toqueville,[3] both of whom remarked on the strength and vitality of local government in the nineteenth century. What happened to transform popular opinion since their day is the subject of this paper.[4] We shall consider the history of a small Massachusetts industrial city as a case in point, tracing the changes in the popular conceptions of local politics as a function of changes in the social structure of the community.

A revision of a paper presented at the 1956 Meeting of the American Sociological Society, Detroit, Michigan. Published for the first time in this volume.

* The research upon which this paper is based was done under a grant from the Kellogg Foundation to the Graduate School of Education of Harvard University. It constitutes part of an intensive analysis of the relationships between community institutions and public education in a Massachusetts city. The preparation of this paper for publication was aided by a grant from the Social Science Research Committee of the University of Chicago, whose assistance is gratefully acknowledged.

[1] National Opinion Research Center, *The People Look at Politics and Politicians*. (Denver: National Opinion Research Center, University of Denver, Report No. 20, March 1944).

[2] James Bryce, *The American Commonwealth* (New York: Macmillan, 1888).

[3] Alexis de Toqueville, *Democracy in America* (New York: Alfred A. Knopf, 1945).

[4] This transformation is also documented in the case of New York by Gabriel Almond, *Plutocracy and Politics in New York City* (unpublished doctoral dissertation, University of Chicago, 1938).

The historical study reported here is part of a larger inquiry into the political life of a small New England city, here given the pseudonym "Bay City."[5] The major attention of the project centered on the contemporary patterns of political and community organization participation. In attempting to account for the present attitudes toward local politics held by various groups in the community—particularly the nostalgia with which the upper-status groups looked to a past Golden Age of local politics—we were drawn inevitably to consider what had been the long-range trends of political participation. Our inquiry brought us back to the earliest days of the city in a search through a fascinating set of historical documents. While these data were tantalizingly incomplete at vital points, it was still possible to reconstruct the gross historical trends and to weave a plausible, although not rigorously sustainable, interpretation of the shifting functions of participation in local politics.

Today Bay City is a typical New England industrial city numbering some 45,000 inhabitants, located just beyond commuting range of Boston. The "Yankee" ethnic stock which founded the settlement in 1760 now comprise less than one-quarter of the population, the remainder being divided among the French Canadians (one-third), Irish (one-fourth), Italians and Finns (one-tenth each), and small numbers of Greeks, Poles, Jews, and Germans. Three out of five residents are Catholics. Bay City's industries include two large, locally-owned paper mills, a pair of nationally-known hardware manufacturers (also locally owned), and a branch factory of a large manufacturer of electrical goods. A number of smaller concerns making both consumer and capital goods also are established there. With the exception of a small insurance company, there are no establishments which hire any significant numbers of white-collar workers. Factories and the business establishments servicing the needs of the city furnish its economic base.

Politically, Bay City reflects the demographic preponderance of the Catholic ethnic groups. On the average, over the past generation, Bay City gave the Democrats about 60% of its votes in national and state elections. In local elections, which operate under non-partisan electoral rules, party lines are often obscured in shifting coalitions and alliances. However, if we count only those mayoralty elections in which Democrats opposed Republicans, whatever disguise may have been employed, we note that each group has been in office about half the time over the past generation.

The prestige of local politics as expressed in the attitudes toward the city government and public office holders is rather low at present. With the exception of the school committee, public office is left to the middle-status groups to occupy. In many segments of the community, the quality of public office holders is considered poor, and few look upon public

---

[5] Because much of the material to be reported in later publications on the contemporary political scene was given to the researchers as confidential communications, we are bound not to reveal the name of the town in formal publications. Unfortunately, therefore, we are unable to cite those historical sources which would identify the city.

office as a proper goal for an ambitious young man. It should be noted that Bay City's government is not in the hands of a corrupt "machine"; the intelligence and ability of the politician is questioned, not his honesty.

In our review of the political history of the city, we shall try to account for the present patterns of regard for and participation in local political office. We shall do this by addressing to the data three major questions:

1. At a given period of time, who are the office holders? From what portion of the community are they recruited? From the answers here we shall infer the status of local politics.
2. What were the major political and ecological problems facing the community at that time? How do the political and ecological exigencies condition the participation in political office of different groups within the community?
3. What functions did political participation fulfill for those who held or contended for political office?

The historical review will be divided into three sections, corresponding to successive phases of development: an Early Phase, from the founding in 1760 to the early part of the 19th Century; a Middle Phase, lasting until World War I; and a Contemporary Phase, containing the present period.

The Early Phase: The Yeoman Republic

In the middle of the 18th Century, the inhabitants of the southwest corner of Moonsville petitioned the Massachusetts General Court to be allowed to set up their own township, because the six- or seven-mile walk to the Moonsville town center over rough terrain for Sunday services was a decided hardship. In 1760 their request was granted, and the twenty-five families residing in the new Bay City organized a town government. Almost the first concern of the town was to obtain a minister and a place of worship, expressing the high place accorded to religion in the value hierarchy. Indeed, religious matters were to be a prime political concern of the town for its first seventy years.

All during this early period—lasting from settlement to around 1830—Bay City was primarily an agricultural community. A few stores, taverns, and a handful of artisans complemented the basically agricultural economy. The farms were small and provided little more than subsistence from the lean New England soil.

The political organization of the town followed the familiar New England pattern. A town meeting, composed of all males with the requisite property qualifications, was the basic legislative body, while between meetings authority rested with six selectmen and a number of minor officials—assessors, fence viewers, tithe collectors, etc. Considering the large number of offices relative to the size of the population in this period, the density of political opportunities was very high.

Throughout this early period, the political elite can scarcely be differentiated from the rest of the citizenry. While one may discern a tendency for storekeepers, artisans, and professionals (doctors and lawyers) to occupy the posts of selectmen and other offices, this may have been due as much to the location of these occupations in the center of the settlement as to their constituting a higher status group. Indeed, many of these are listed in the early records as holding dual occupations—e.g., scythe maker *and* farmer, or tavern keeper *and* farmer.

Many of the political problems encountered by the town during this period had their origins in the larger society. Although the town was not part of the battlefield of the American Revolution, its residents supplied provisions, money, and men. The aftermath of the Revolution was inflation and Shay's rebellion, with which many of the inhabitants had some sympathy, and the town records contain many references to attempts to meet these problems through local legislation.

The major internal political problems had to do with schismatic tendencies within the town. Congregationalism was the established church, supported by tithes collected by town officials. Dissenting Methodists, Baptists, and Universalists submitted petition after petition asking to be relieved from tithes. A running battle between a conservative wing and a liberal wing of the Congregational Church lasted more than a decade, ending with the ouster of the conservative minister who was the focus of contention. Partly corresponding to the religious schisms were a number of geographical cleavages; various sections of the town submitted a number of petitions asking to be allowed to secede to form new townships.

For much of this period, Bay City could hardly be called a unified community. Primary loyalties went to sect and neighborhood, and the sense of community did not extend over the entire thirty square miles of Bay City. Indeed, dissension within the community postponed decisions about the location of the meeting house for almost a decade, with each locality bidding for the meeting house to be built within easy access to itself. It was only with the separation of church and state in Massachusetts in the 1820s that sectional and religious dissensions declined.

The consequence of the separation of church and state in Bay City was a proliferation of religious societies and the beginning of the status ranking of the resulting Protestant churches. With the church separated from the state, the political focus of religious matters declined, not to be noted again until our third, or contemporary, period, when Catholic ethnic group members entered local politics and religion was found as an underlying focus in political contests, particularly school committee elections.

A third type of political problem arose from the physical environment. The rugged terrain comprising the valley of the Bay River which ran through the town made it hard to build and maintain the roads and bridges which bound the various sections together. Early town records contain many references to debates over the locations and costs of these public works.

Reading the old town records, one cannot escape being impressed by the dignity and sophistication with which these politically inexperienced farmers and villagers handled their problems. Town finances were conducted shrewdly; petitions submitted to the town meetings were written with style and clarity. The townsmen's appraisal of the early drafts of the Federal Constitution, before the first ten amendments were added, showed considerable political astuteness. Instructions given to the town's representatives in the General Court showed a good sense of political maneuvers. In short, those who took the most active part in town politics displayed valuable skills in finance, leadership of men in organized enterprises, and in the art of negotiation. Furthermore, they were the town's leading citizens in prestige and perhaps in economic well-being as well.

In tracing the beginnings of industrial development as reflected in the town records of the latter part of this early period, we noted a very interesting pattern. Many of the men who figured so prominently in the political life of Bay City in the 1790s began to appear, in the early 1800s, as the founders of the small precursors to the large industrial enterprises of the post–Civil War period. The major enterprises of the second half of the nineteenth century, and indeed even of today, were started by the farmers and artisans who served prominently over many years as selectmen, assessors, etc.

This pattern indicates that in this early political period the same skills employed in political organization were later to serve in good stead in the development of industrial enterprises. Indeed, it may be that what these men learned from their political experiences about the leadership of men, the conduct of public finances, and the political arts of bargaining and negotiation, was precisely the complex of skills which made the fostering of industrialization possible. At the least, one can assume that for most the holding of political office was their first experience in large-scale organization. At the most, this pattern suggests the interesting possibility that in this early period participation in politics provided an important training experience for the town's future industrialists. It would almost appear as if—our present-day business ideology notwithstanding—men improved their station by applying the methods of government to their private businesses.

Phase II: The Hegemony of Industrialists

In the 1830s Bay City began to lose its agricultural quality. Industrial enterprises grew out of the artisans' shops, and farmers began to turn to manufacture. Outsiders, attracted by the water power resources of the Bay River, came to set up paper mills and textile works. By the end of the Civil War, itself undoubtedly an important stimulus, Bay City was a full-fledged industrial community manufacturing a variety of goods, ranging from textiles and furniture to hardware and heavy machine tools. An important factor in precipitating this spurt of growth was the building of the railroad to Boston, accomplished largely by the initiative of the founder of one of the city's present leading families. The later extension of the railroad beyond Bay City to upper New York State provided excellent transportation. The importance of the railroad can be most dramatically appreciated by contrasting Bay City with the community from which it split in 1760: Moonsville has only recently lost its agricultural character to become one of Bay City's residential suburbs.

It was also during this period of industrialization that Bay City lost its ethnic homogeneity. Irish laborers, brought in to build the railroad, remained to work in the new factories. Wave after wave of new Americans continued to swell the population all during the latter half of the 19th Century.

As industrialization proceeded, the political elite began to be more and more differentiated from the general population. Industrialists, merchants, and lawyers occupied the posts of selectmen and assessors. When the town form of local government was abandoned in the 1870s in favor of a mayor-aldermen-council organization, the transformation of the political elite went even further. Among the first nine mayors of the new city we counted six industrialists, two lawyers, and the owner of a plumbing firm. Among the six aldermen holding office during 1886–87 were two industrialists, three merchants, and an iron moulder. As in the earlier period, many of the local political figures also served as the city's representatives in the state and national legislatures. Local politics was fused with state and national politics.

The political problems of this period no longer concerned religious orthodoxy but were derived from industrialization. The first political issues of the period centered around the new railroad which, when first proposed, met with both ridicule and opposition. An adequate water supply was needed for industry and for the augmented population. A series of public works—initially started as a private enterprise by the same industrialist who undertook to bring the railroad to Bay City—laid out a set of reservoirs which assured adequate water supplies. Roads were built, the school system extended to the high school level, and a public library founded and housed in a building donated by one of the leading paper manufacturers. Law and order prevailed in Bay City, and the community was "free" of labor troubles.

Up to the end of World War I, the prestige of local public office was high. With the Republicans safely in the majority, and the Party safely in the hands of the industrialists, nominations for public office were distributed almost as public recognition of accomplishment in private enterprise. To hold public office was a sign of high status, and the higher the public office within the local government, the greater the meaning of the recognition involved. Political office served as the most visible measure of status in the community.

The sense of community among the industrialists of this period was very strong. Their attention was directed primarily to the local scene and only secondarily to the state and national levels. This is the period when the local historical society was most active, publishing both the early town records and several volumes of proceedings. With great changes underway in the social composition and organization of the community, the industrial elite apparently felt a great need to preserve, intact and in prideful prose, the history of the town and its leading citizens. Industrialists also founded the local private hospital, donated a very impressive library building, and made many other contributions to the city. Whether this sense of community penetrated all the levels of what must have been a highly stratified society we cannot tell, for the Irish immigrants left little in the town records of this period.

Phase III: The Political Ascendancy of the Middle Class

For Bay City, the 19th Century was the time for growth in population and industry. In the present century, expansion came to a halt. Beginning with the Census of 1920, the city reached stability in numbers, and, with minor fluctuations has maintained the 45,000 mark in every subsequent Census. Although new industries have entered the city, they have served primarily as replacements for firms which had either failed or migrated elsewhere. The textile mills, in particular, have been replaced by other industries.

The stability in population size, however, conceals a number of significant changes in population composition. The higher birth rates of the newer ethnic groups, the steady stream of in-migration from French Canada, plus the out-migration of Yankee youth who left to seek the white-collar jobs unavailable locally, have all combined to transform the homogeneous city of the early 19th Century into the culturally heterogeneous one of the present. While these were changes which started in the 19th Century, it was not until the early part of the present period that their implications for local politics became manifest. Politically the new population balance shifted the city out of the Republican and into the Democratic ranks. Since 1928, when the anti-Catholic sentiments of the Republican presidential campaign welded the Catholic French and Italians into a solid political bloc with the Irish, Bay City has not returned a majority for the Republicans in any state or national election. On the local scene, the hegemony of the Yankee industrial elite was successfully challenged in election after election. Only a shift in electoral rules making local elections nonpartisan has saved the local Republicans from being a permanent opposition to local Democratic administrations.

At the same time, the political trends in the nation as a whole changed the character of local politics. The growth of state and national governmental powers and the accompanying increasing regulation of economic activities, shifted attention to the state and national political scenes. Concurrently, the stabilization of population growth resulted in the local political issues becoming narrower in scope. Local problems in Bay City were mainly those of maintenance and replacement, rather than of extension of municipal facilities and services. In many activities which local government once undertook unilaterally—e.g., roadbuilding, care of the poor and aged, support of the schools—the state and national governments provided subsidies, subsidies which were often made contingent on the city's fulfilling certain standards. In short, there has occurred a "trivialization" of local issues as the resolution of the major problems of these decades was effected in either Boston or Washington.

With the disappearance of "bread-and-butter" issues from the local scene and the rise of the political power of the newer ethnic groups, local issues centered more around "style" than economics. *Who* shall control the city government became more important than *what* the city government shall do. More specifically, shall the city be represented by office holders from among the new Americans, or shall the older Yankee stock prevail? Such matters of style reach particular importance in the school board election contests, where the clandestine issues revolve around whether the Catholics or the Protestants will control the school system.

In this post–World War I period, political leadership underwent a corresponding change. Among the nine mayors who held office since 1920, only two could be counted as industrialists, and these came primarily from the managerial rather than the ownership level. Three were small businessmen, including a trucker, a florist, and a truck farmer. A dentist represented the professions, and two mayors were "professional politicians." Even more striking were the ethnic backgrounds of the mayors: Four were from the newer ethnic groups (two Irish, one Italian, and one French Canadian); four come from the old Yankee stock; and one defies classification, having been a recent immigrant from Wales. The defeated mayoralty candidates for this period presented a similar array of occupations and ethnicity. The members of the city council were drawn from slightly lower occupational ranks, with a fair proportion of industrial workers and white-collar employees.

Only the elective school board has had members from the industrial owners categories. Since 1920, the school board has almost always had a member of the city's most prominent industrial family, descendants of the early industrialist who brought the railroad to the city. An element of *noblesse oblige* attends this pattern of participation—a felt obligation to prevent the school system from falling into the hands of the Catholics.

Religious issues thus have again returned to politics, this time reflecting a latent, hidden cleavage in the electorate rather than one which is publicly manifest in the political documents and speeches. In contrast to the earliest period when religious differences were the subject of political debate, in the present phase religion is scarcely mentioned in public utterances, although it is almost the primary basis for political divisions within the community.

In large part, the political struggle between the Catholics and Protestants represents strong value differences. These value differences come out most clearly in school board elections. Bay City's Protestants are fearful of the transformation which would be wrought in the public schools were the Catholics to dominate the school board, and they press hard to elect a majority to this body. Although it is not clear what dire consequences would flow from Catholic domination of the school board, the fear of these changes is quite strong.

In part, the religious differences mask status differences. The Catholic majority comprise the bulk of the industrial workers, with some representatives in the small business and professional occupations. The Protestant minority contributes most of the industrial managers, professionals, and merchants, and has some small representation among the higher ranks of the industrial workers. From the Catholic viewpoint, the major point of difference is one of status, with the Protestant minority occupying positions of control and depriving the Catholics of a proper spot in the status system of Bay City.

Perhaps each group views the basis for the struggle from that perspective which puts its own claims for moral right in the best possible light. Thus, the Protestants view their struggle to maintain control in terms of the superiority and historical fitness of their value position, while the Catholics claim status deprivation and argue from the strength of majority rule. In any event, the depth of the cleavage can be gauged by the way in which it cuts across strong political ideological positions: A small group of Scandinavian descent, with a heavy socialist ideological background but of Protestant (or at least non-Catholic) composition, has aligned itself on the local scene with the conservative Yankee group.

The political solidification of the Catholic majority has meant the election to local public office of individuals whose social status in the community is relatively low. The prestige of public office declined along with the status of incumbents. This loss of status suffered by public office was particularly severe among the industrial, professional, and merchant group, which presently considers local politics to be in the hands of the unsuccessful and incompetent, and an activity that is beneath their consideration. In large part, this derogatory view of politics has permeated the entire community, although among the working classes public office is still viewed as honorific.

Among the town's businessmen and professionals, the evaluation of politics and politicians is decidedly negative. Political activity on the level of running for office is regarded as demeaning, requiring close contact with ethically shady, if not dishonest, compromises and contaminating negotiations. This view covers both the Republican and Democratic parties in Bay City, although the Democratic Party receives the more extreme criticism. It is felt that businessmen and professionals would do best to abstain from political activity except on the national or state levels or as silent partners in the local political party. As a counterpoise to this present situation, the same critics—especially the older generation—point to the "Golden Age," now long past, when businessmen (meaning industrialists) ruled the city with efficiency, intelligence, responsibility, and style.

Indeed, this viewpoint puts the professional Republican politician in the rather anomalous position of serving the interests of a constituency which regards what he is doing as somewhat beneath serious consideration. The city chairman of the Republican Party, a lawyer with many business connections but few social connections with the industrial elite, complained bitterly in our interview with him of the irresponsibility of this position and the resulting necessity for him to rely on the lower occupational ranks for Republican candidates.

The negative appraisal of politics among the middle and upper classes covers, in the more polite language of comparative intelligence and competence, a critique in terms of social class. The origins, manners, and occupational backgrounds of office holders are disparaged, more than the specific acts performed by the office holders. Political skills of compromise, negotiation, and demagogy, necessary in a period of heavy political competition, are not recognized as the special skills of the occupation of public office, but as the consequence of the low social status of the politician. The disparagement of public office and office holders on the local level is in effect a denial of status to achievement along this career line, a line in which the inequality of opportunity now operates more to the benefit of the Catholic majority.

The functions of status allocation and recognition, which were once performed by public office-holding, have been shifted in this period to a relatively new set of institutions, the community service organizations. Beginning around the turn of the century, a number of private organizations came into being which were dedicated to the provision of social services to the community under private financing and control. The local hospital, Red Cross chapter, Community Chest, and Family Welfare Society are examples of the organizations started during the last fifty years which have become the focus of participation in community affairs for the industrial and managerial elite. The numerous offices on the governing boards of these organizations have replaced public office as the channels through which the functions of public recognition and status allocation operate. Since control over the membership of these boards can be maintained by the elite leaders through their heavy donations, being offered the chairmanship of a "drive" or a position on the board of trustees now has the same status meaning that nomination to the board of aldermen did in the nineteenth century. Such positions carry with them an entree into certain social circles, publicity, and recognition of financial worth: In short, it places the individual as a member of the upper status levels of Bay City. While this sort of participation is quite costly to the participant—and those aspiring to raise their social status have to pay more—the tax provisions concerning donations to charity help to remove some of the sting.

The importance of the voluntary associations in defining who is to be admitted to the higher social circles of Bay City can be most dramatically illustrated by the refusal of the board of directors of the Community Chest to elect to membership the owner of one of the largest manufacturing firms, despite his large personal contributions to the Chest. Because this man is Jewish, he is excluded from the Board, although ordinarily persons giving as much as he does are almost automatically elected. In contrast, a recent migrant to Bay City from Tuxedo Park, New York, who occupies a middling managerial position in one of the town's oldest industries, was eagerly accepted as having the proper credentials for participation. It is, perhaps, a consequence of his exclusion that the Jewish manufacturer heavily supports a Jewish community center of considerable size, although there are probably not more than seventy Jewish families in Bay City.

More important than its function of public recognition of high status, the voluntary charitable association and its boards and committees performs the function of providing a rank order within the upper ranks of the community. The boards are ranked in reputation among themselves, and within each board various positions—such as chairman or member of various committees—provide further differentiation. It is perhaps this differentiation which is of most concern to the members of the upper occupational levels, for it is the status differences within this group which are of most immediate social significance to them.

A man's position within the board system is a function in part of his family background and in part of his occupational position. The owners or managers of the largest industrial firms, unless they happen to be Jewish, can count on being offered a key position on one of the middle rank boards or a minor position on the highest boards. If the person is a member of Bay City's old families, his position can be expected to be higher.

Especially for the manager of an absentee-owned firm, the voluntary associations provide the immediate locale for obtaining status and recognition from an occupational position which is defined within an industrial organization typically regional or national in character. Thus, although the local plant manager for a nationwide electrical goods manufacturer has his position defined within the hierarchy of that business firm, the face-to-face rewards accompanying the position have to be defined within Bay City, and the voluntary association system provides the means for this definition.[6] Indeed, many of the plant managers in this and other communities point to recognition accorded to their participation in voluntary associations in small cities as one of the more important rewards available to persons in their occupational positions.

As a consequence of this institutional arrangement, the local community service organizations can count on enlisting the energies and financial support of the wealthiest portions of the community. The direct benefits to the community are considerable. Bay City has a very well equipped and staffed private hospital, and a public library and art collection considerably above average for communities of its size and wealth. Comparable achievements have been made by the other welfare organizations of the city. By tying into the status system of the commu-

---

[6] With an increasing number of such absentee firms, it becomes increasingly difficult for the local political structure to fulfill this function. Political office, based as it is on popular election, is easier to obtain by persons who have lived long in the community and who are consequently widely known. The itinerant plant manager cannot hope to compete for popular acclaim with the homegrown products, and hence public recognition of his position has to be a function of some other institutional arrangement. For a more extensive analysis of the roles of industrial managers in the social life of another community, see Peter H. Rossi, *Industry and Community* (Chicago: National Opinion Research Center, University of Chicago, Report No. 64, October, 1957).

nity, the community organizations have been able to raise considerably the level of living of Bay City.

Our review of Bay City's political history indicates that in each period local politics and political participation have played different roles, conditioned by the social structure of the community and its external ecological exigencies.

In the earliest period, local politics was organized primarily around sectarian and neighborhood differences. Political office served as an opportunity for a rustic yeomanry to acquire or exercise those managerial skills subsequently utilized by the entrepreneurs of the next era.

In the middle period of industrial hegemony, local government was the means by which the local industrialists strengthened their competitive positions *vis-à-vis* other industrial cities. Political office was at its peak of prestige, serving as public recognition of entrepreneurial or professional accomplishment. Political office served as a status allocation mechanism.

In the contemporary period, when the demographic balance shifted against the Republican Party and the leaders of the Catholic ethnic groups were able to win public office, the industrial elite abandoned local politics. At the same time, local politics became trivialized as the power and activities of state and national governments grew. The prestige of local public office underwent a considerable decline, and its former functions of public recognition and status allocation shifted to the private community service organizations.

3

Changes in Urban Political Structures

Industrialization,
Absentee Ownership,
and Changes in Informal
Political Leadership

Many of the same forces which transformed the characteristics of elected political leadership also transformed the characteristics of informal leadership (i.e., leaders who hold no formal municipal office) in American cities. If one could sum up the major overall change in community power with the advent of industrialization, the rise of absentee ownership, and metropolitanization, the major change would be from monolithic power structures to more fragmented power structures. Political and civic life in American communities has become sufficiently complex that no one person or group of persons is likely either to want or to be able to attain power in all areas of community life. Of course, in some cities there are powerful people with a great deal of influence in community affairs. However, the complexity of community affairs, differences of interest, lack of time and resources, all tend to discourage the formation of a monolithic elite with complete hegemony over *all* aspects of community life.

Pellegrin and Coates, in the first selection, find the managers of absentee-owned firms in "Bigtown" to be active in the most influential organizations. Although there is a "power vacuum" in "Bigtown" due to poor coordination and communication among the various influential segments in the community, Pellegrin and Coates claim that no community project can be successfully completed if disapproved by the management of one of the large absentee-owned firms. In addition, a project favored by the management of one of these absentee-owned firms will probably be successfully concluded.

Participation in civic affairs by management personnel is motivated by two considerations. First, company policies can be fostered by sponsoring projects compatible with these policies and by vetoing projects incompatible with them. Second, an executive's successful participation in community organizations increases his visibility and prominence and aids in his career within the company. Success by an executive in his community work is likely to result in his being given greater company responsibilities.

The findings of Pellegrin and Coates are in distinct contrast to the results of Clelland and Form presented in the second selection. Like Robert Schulze, Clelland and Form found that managers of absentee-owned firms were withdrawing from public and civic life in "Wheelsburg," but not to as great an extent as the managers in "Cibola." Clelland and Form attribute this slower withdrawal to the fact that "Wheelsburg" is a central city whereas "Cibola" is a satellite city. Executives are more inclined to participate in the affairs of a central city than a satellite city because central city matters are more relevant to them.

The evidence, then, indicates that absentee managers are not necessarily aloof from the affairs of their communities. In a personal communication to me, Professor Pellegrin said that the greater participation of "Bigtown" executives (especially the executives of a large oil company with a branch facility in "Bigtown") stems from two factors. First, the local area represents a significant market for the oil company's products since the company owns many of the service stations in the "Bigtown" area. Second, "Bigtown" is the state capital of an oil-producing state. Because the oil company is concerned about depletion allowances, oil leases, and severance taxes, the company strives to maintain the image of a good community citizen in order to impress local people who have power in state politics. A large aluminum company located in "Bigtown," in contrast, avoids local involvement because the company has no economic interest in doing otherwise. Professor Pellegrin points out that the explanation for community involvement or lack of it by absentee-owned companies rests on social structural considerations tied up with the companies' economic interests. If economic interests dictate it, companies will participate in community affairs, and vice versa if no economic interests compel local involvement.

In addition, Paul Mott[1] reports that the large absentee-owned firms in "Cibola" do become involved, at least indirectly, in community affairs when they impinge on the companies' interests. For example, an annexation drive failed when a large corporation in the territory to be annexed remained "neutral." In fact, the annexation move could not succeed without the company's concurrence which it would not give. The company's "neutrality" effectively blocked the annexation attempt. Mott also gives other examples of companies' influence in local affairs.

Absentee-owned firms will become involved in local affairs when it is to their economic interest to do so, or if the local area is a focus for company executives. However, the involvement of absentee-owned firms in local affairs may not match the type of involvement shown by local businessmen who have a more all-encompassing interest in their community (since their only market is within the local area).

Finally, the last selection in this section by Ernest A.T. Barth claims that the two most important factors in altering the shape of community power structures are rapid population growth and the community's economic base. These both serve to fragment community power structures. Both types of growth increase the numbers of issues facing communities and also increase the number of influence centers in the community. Therefore, power structures in communities with rapidly growing populations or rapidly growing economic bases develop clique structures or, alternatively, disorganized power structures. Gone from these communities are the monolithic elites.

Economic and population changes influence the shape and dynamics of community power structures. Industrialization, the rise of absentee ownership, and population growth associated with economic growth tend to fragment power and shift the base of community leadership from economic dominants to middle-class business and professional men. The shift in focus of economic dominants from the local community to national markets causes these economically powerful people to withdraw from active and sustained community participation to be replaced by the owners of small local businesses who still have a vital stake in the community.

---

[1] Paul E. Mott, "The Role of the Absentee-Owned Corporation in the Changing Community," in Michael Aiken and Paul E. Mott (eds.), *The Structure of Community Power* (New York: Random House, 1970), pp. 170–79.

Corresponding to the shift to a national economy is the shift of many previously local governmental functions to state and national governments. The declining importance of the local community as a decision-making center also provides impetus for the withdrawal of economically powerful people. No longer do community decisions have the importance to warrant attention by otherwise busy men (although there are exceptions to the withdrawal process).

One final tempering factor with respect to the participation of absentee managers in local affairs appears to be regional differences. The paternalistic traditions of Southern businessmen appear to have permeated the thinking of absentee managers who locate in the South. This paternalism was not observed in Northern cities, and perhaps will decline in the South as its economy develops.

In sum, the participation of economic dominants in community affairs has dramatically changed in some communities whose economies are dominated by absentee-owned industries. The economic dominant who heads a locally-owned company has a broad interest in community affairs because he is part of the community and because all or a significant portion of his market is centered within his community. The absentee manager, in contrast, apparently only concerns himself with local affairs which impinge on his company (and even in many of these cases a specialized community relations department will deal with the matter). In communities where the economic interests of the company are intertwined with community affairs, company executives will participate. That is, community participation is merely a means to an economic end. It is unknown how many communities place a company in such a position. But where such a community and company exist, the executives are probably involved in community affairs.

Absentee-Owned Corporations and Community Power Structure

ROLAND J. PELLEGRIN AND CHARLES H. COATES

The stratification system of a given community attains stability and remains basically unaltered over relatively long periods of time because, as shown in recent studies, the control of community affairs and policies resides in dominant interest groups which feel little incentive to disrupt the existing pattern of superordination and subordination. These groups exercise power[1] which is infinitely out of proportion to their number.

The mechanics of control by minority are clearly revealed in Floyd Hunter's work *Community Power Structure*.[2] Hunter examined the roles in community affairs and policy-making played by various cliques or "crowds" of leaders from the realms of business, finance, and industry. The power of these individuals and groups, he states, is effectively channeled through organizations, committees, and agencies which are concerned with community affairs—plans, projects, and policies.[3] Following his argument, this paper deals with the role played by executives of absentee-owned corporations in organized groups, such as associations, clubs, councils, and committees. Data were gathered between June, 1954, and May, 1955, through intensive interviews with fifty leading executives of the community and other persons who have worked with and observed corporation executives.

Reprinted from the *American Journal of Sociology* 61 (1956): 413–19. Copyright 1956 by the University of Chicago. Reprinted by permission of the publisher.

[1] "Power" is defined herein as the ability to direct and control the activities of others in the pursuit of goals which are established in accordance with a given set of social values.

[2] Floyd Hunter, *Community Power Structure: A Study of Decision-Makers* (Chapel Hill, N.C.: University of North Carolina Press, 1953).

[3] Floyd Hunter, *Host Community and Air Force Base* (Air Force Base Project Technical Rept. No. 8 [Maxwell A.F.B., Ala.: Research Institute, Human Resources, 1952]), p. 5.

The Community Setting

Bigtown, the nucleus of a southern metropolitan area of approximately 200,000 inhabitants, is a fictitious name for a rapidly growing city whose rise to economic prominence in the region and nation has been meteoric. Above all, its growth is a consequence of new industrial plants. The residents of Bigtown derive their livelihoods from a variety of sources, but the most vital elements in the economic structure of the city are a number of absentee-owned corporations which manufacture and process industrial products mainly for non-local consumption. The plants not only employ a large proportion of Bigtown's citizens and set the local wage pattern but make possible the existence of a multitude of smaller industrial and business concerns. The development of community facilities and services is in part dependent upon their financial contributions[4] and their cooperation in programs designed to improve the city. In short, they play a pre-eminent role in the dynamics of Bigtown life.

The Power Structure, Civic Affairs, and the Corporation

American cities apparently vary considerably in the extent to which dominant interest groups are united effectively for coordinated control of community affairs. As Hunter describes the situation in Regional City, groups are drawn together through mutual interests and common values and are held together by strong leadership, which integrates their efforts.[5] The cliques or crowds "go along" with one another's projects in anticipation of future reciprocity.

The leaders of Bigtown, many of whom are of cosmopolitan backgrounds, tend to view this pattern of control as ideal. They dwell at great length upon the power structure of other cities in which they have resided, where an informal "Committee of 50," "Citizens' Council," or like group controls civic affairs with a firm hand. These glowing accounts are typically accompanied by a pessimistic description of the situation in Bigtown. This community, as analyzed by some of its outstanding men, has a number of powerful interest groups but lacks effective liaison among them and leadership to unite them. Under these circumstances, a given "crowd" is unlikely to participate in a proposed project unless it foresees tangible gain.

This situation lends itself neither to effective community planning nor to adequate facilities and services for the citizenry. Many plans and projects are initiated by individuals and groups, but few indeed are carried through to fruition, either because of a lack of cooperation among

---

[4] Corporations not only pay taxes (directly and indirectly) but make outright gifts to community projects and collect contributions from their employees during various fund-raising "drives."

[5] Hunter, *Community Power Structure*, chap. iv.

powerful groups or negative reactions by one or more "crowds." The shortcomings of the city are popularly ascribed, however, not to power conflicts or apathy but to the rapid growth of the city and to the failings of its governmental officials.[6]

In the relative power vacuum which exists in Bigtown, community projects are usually doomed if they lack the approval of the industrial, absentee-owned corporations. There is no single crowd or clique of representatives of them, but their top executives communicate with one another informally and arrive at agreement on matters of policy. The executives of each corporation are then informed of the decision, making it possible for given community projects to be supported or vetoed through united action. Corporation support probably assures the success of a proposed project, while disapproval spells doom for it. Thus absentee-owned corporations are a decisive force in the power structure of Bigtown, since they constitute a balance of power among the competing interest groups of the community. On the other hand, as initiators of projects or policies, the corporations can ordinarily get support from a sufficient number of other enterprises to put across their goals.

Corporate participation in Bigtown's civic affairs has followed an intriguing pattern. While the interests of a corporation extend far beyond the local community and it is primarily concerned with furthering its own goals rather than those of cities in which its branches are located, there has been a tendency for absentee-owned corporations in the South to adopt local customs and practices, including a paternalistic attitude toward both their employees and the community.[7] The corporations of Bigtown have exhibited considerable interest in civic affairs, justifying their participation publicly in terms of "making this a better place for all of us to live." In past decades, of course, additional motivation for becoming community-conscious has been found in the corporation's concern for favorable taxation rates and good labor relations and for securing needed local facilities and services for its expanding enterprises. Thus a need for a favorable public conception of the corporation has been felt for a considerable period.

Recent changes in the region and nation, however, have also promoted the corporate concern with public sentiment. The threat posed by the gains of organized labor in the South has greatly stimulated the desire

---

[6] The typical interviewee in this study described local governmental officials as relatively powerless figures who do not have the backing of influential groups but secured their positions through the support of working-class voters. Indeed, these officials were more often than not targets of ridicule for those who evaluated their positions in the power structure. Note the differences in roles between these officials and those of Regional City, where governmental figures are subservient to the dominant interest groups (see *ibid.*, p. 102). The relative lack of integration of Bigtown's interest groups makes it possible for governmental officials to sponsor civic projects which are sometimes successful, in spite of opposition from one or another of the "crowds." Interest groups find it difficult to express publicly opposition to projects which attract widespread public support. To do so would be "bad public relations," perhaps unprofitable in the long run.

[7] Cf. Harriet L. Herring, "The Outside Employer in the Southern Industrial Pattern," *Social Forces*, 18 (1939): 115–26.

to develop and maintain a favorable public image as a weapon for use in labor–management controversy. There exists in Bigtown, as elsewhere in the nation, an almost incredible preoccupation with "public relations" —i.e., a constant and vociferous campaign designed to apprise the populace of the magnanimity and generosity of the corporations. Local media of communication constantly provide tangible evidence of corporate altruism in the form of statements concerning substantial financial contributions to civic projects and the heavy burdens of civic duties carried by top executives.

David Riesman has called attention to the emerging pattern of "conspicuous production" or "conspicuous corporate consumption," by means of which a corporation seeks prestige and plaudits for providing new employee benefits and services, luxurious buildings, machinery designed with aesthetic values in mind, and the like—much of which can hardly be justified economically.[8] In the same way, the corporations are contributing money and time to community projects as a favored means of creating and reinforcing a favorable public image of the corporation.

It must be strongly emphasized, however, that this active participation in civic affairs is motivated primarily by a desire to present the corporation to the citizenry in as favorable a light as possible and to maintain zealous guard over the corporation's interest and prerogatives. Not only does the corporation dictate the terms, but it decides what *social values* are to be implemented by its choice of projects and the policies followed by its agents. This is indeed participation with a purpose, the purpose being a double one: to further corporate interests and to exercise control over civic affairs in order to preserve the values of a conservative, business-oriented ideology. This is clearly revealed by an analysis of the role of the corporation executive in civic affairs.

The Executive's Civic Participation

Extent and Types of Participation

The executives of Bigtown's absentee-owned corporations are discriminating in their choice of civic associations. The modal number of affiliations with local organizations per person is but two, as contrasted with a modal number of four organizational memberships for executives in all other types of industrial, business, and financial enterprises.[9] Citing

---

[8] "New Standards for Old: From Conspicuous Consumption to Conspicuous Production," in his *Individualism Reconsidered and Other Essays* (New York: Free Press, 1954), pp. 228–29.

[9] In contrast, executives in absentee-owned corporations had twice as many memberships in state and national organizations as did the other executives (modal numbers, 2 and 1, respectively). These comparisons of local and non-local affiliations of the two groups may indicate the relative lack of dependence of the former upon the community for a livelihood, prestige, etc. The personal futures of the former group are much less tied in with the fortunes of Bigtown than are those of the latter.

the number of memberships, however, is likely to give a misleading impression of the influence of corporation executives civic affairs. When the types of organizations to which they belong are analyzed, it is discovered that in 60 percent of the cases they belong to *both* of the two most powerful organizations in the community.[10] These two are policy- and decision-making bodies that play a vital role in charting the course of Bigtown's plans and projects.

Conversely, the executives of the absentee-owned corporations are heavily underrepresented in the less powerful organizations of the community. The restriction of their memberships primarily to the "elite" organizations not only shows a personal lack of interest in the lesser ones but means that the numerous youth, welfare, "uplift," fraternal, and other agencies are dependent upon others for support, direction, and sponsorship. A few of the top corporation executives participate in the work of these groups, primarily as members of boards of directors. They are especially likely to be found in organizations charged with the responsibility of disbursing large sums of money, since they are interested in the uses to which the money will be put. In general, however, the least influential organizations of Bigtown are forced to content themselves with membership from middle management and junior executive levels.[11]

The Assignment of Civic and Committee Memberships

Typically, the absentee-owned corporation in Bigtown has a list of executives eligible for membership in power-wielding civic organizations and for service on various "citizens' " committees and commissions created to plan for and supervise important special community projects. Community leaders generally expect the corporation to provide civic leadership commensurate with its size and influence; similarly, the corporation anticipates adequate representation in groups which chart the course of community affairs.

[10] In 90 percent of the cases, membership was held in at least one of these two top organizations. Executives from other types of enterprises were also well represented in the two organizations—42 percent belonged to both, and 77 percent to one or the other. Being from many enterprises, these persons outnumber the executives from absentee-owned corporations in these two organizations. It should be noted, however, that, because of the size and influence of the large absentee-owned corporations, each is allotted more memberships in these organizations than are given to smaller enterprises. Since there is agreement within the absentee-owned corporation as to policies and procedures to be followed by its executives and since the interests of these corporations are generally not conflicting, their executives constitute an effective minority in dealing with the executives from other enterprises, which frequently represent conflicting interests.

[11] To his superiors, "excellent service" in these civic groups identifies the junior executive as responsible and clear-thinking. The young executive, in turn, may regard his civic duties as a means of demonstrating an ability to serve his employers in a higher capacity.

The assignment of junior executives to civic projects is discussed in Aileen D. Ross, "The Social Control of Philanthropy," *American Journal of Sociology*, 58 (1953): 451–60. This article provides keen insight into corporate participation in civic "drives" or "canvasses."

Almost without exception, the men chosen to represent the corporation are high-level executives with lengthy service. They have demonstrated time and again that they are familiar with corporation policies and that they can be relied upon to do a good job of representing the company and its interests. They will express opinions on any subject which indicate that they cherish the "proper" social values.

Executives are expected to belong to civic organizations and serve on committees as part of their jobs. The process by which an individual receives a committee assignment was described by an interviewee as follows:

> Let's suppose that Mr. X, a community leader or government official, is lining up men to serve on an important new committee or commission. He will contact the top executive in a corporation, Mr. Y, and explain the situation to him. Mr. X will then ask Mr. Y to provide him with a certain number of men. Sometimes the two disagree concerning the number to be assigned. Mr. Y will demand more representation if he evaluates the matter as important to the corporation's interests or if it involves basic community policy. If he feels the matter relatively unimportant, he will try to cut down the number of men he has to assign. If Mr. X especially wants a specific executive, say Mr. Z, to serve on his committee, he might ask Mr. Y for him. Mr. Y may agree to this choice, or he may not. In any case, his decisions are the final ones. He can always justify denying the request by stating that Mr. Z is too busy.
>
> Sometimes, if Mr. Z is widely known to have clearance for such activities from his superiors, Mr. X will contact him directly. In such a case, Mr. Z would O.K. the matter "upstairs" before committing himself.

If an executive is not on the "approved list," he is unlikely either to be given permission to serve or to absent himself from his job during working hours, even if he should volunteer. Interviewees emphasized that only if there were a great deal of "public pressure," would a man not on the list obtain clearance to serve.[12] Another interviewee, who is in a position to be well acquainted with the practices of his own corporation, put the matter this way:

> Only a man who is naïve would accept invitations to participate in important community affairs without the blessings of Mr. A, the top executive in our company. For a man to ignore the usual procedures for getting clearance, he'd either have to be unconcerned about his career or else be a complete ass. In fact, in my company, *executives at any level have to clear all their organizational memberships with top management.*

POLICY AND TACTICS

As an agent of his corporation, the executive is cautious in his public pronouncements. His superiors expect him to keep in mind company

---

[12] This "public pressure," the authors concluded, consists of demands for an individual's services after he had demonstrated at a lower level that he is either an unusually competent "idea man" or a workhorse.

policies and interests, and he knows that he should emphasize at opportune moments a firm conviction that what is good for the corporation is good for the community. These expectations are not difficult to adhere to when he participates in organized groups, such as associations and clubs. The individual is informed ahead of time what the position of his company will be, and no decisions on his part are required. He merely has to proceed in accordance with predetermined policies and tactics.

It is through an examination of the executive's role in committees and councils created for specific projects that we gain insight into the extent to which his behavior is conditioned by the expectations of his superiors. Prior to the first meeting of a given committee or other similar group, the executive usually receives a briefing from his superiors on the company's position in the matter involved. In committee meetings he listens carefully for sentiments expressed by others and then reports the proceedings to his company. Thus his superiors are kept informed of what transpires, and he receives instructions as the project proceeds. If a committee unexpectedly seeks a vote on an issue which is not on the prepared agenda, the executive may plead for a recess in order to telephone for instructions. If the word must come from the national head office, he may seek a longer delay by suggesting "Let's sleep on it!"

In civic matters, as remarked, the corporation seeks not only to protect and foster its own interests but to promote a conservative, business-oriented ideology. The general procedure is for Bigtown's executives to state their opinions in such a manner as to imply that anyone holding different ones is stupid, uninformed, or possbly subversive. The implication is that all "right-thinkers" must believe as the executives do. Thus a dissenter would be forced into a defense not only of his social values but of his intelligence and his patriotism.

Executives are constantly on guard lest fellow committee members divert funds to new projects suggestive of the "welfare state." Advocates of such measures are speedily labeled "controversial" and, if they persist, are referred to as "cranks" or "subversives"—a term once used only for political traitors. Deviants of this nature are, in the long run, however, weeded out; they are not able to obtain appointments to other committees. An old-timer, involved in such measures scores of times during the previous thirty years, observed:

We freeze out these New Dealers and other Reds. When we appoint people to important committee posts, we look at their record. If an individual has gone all out on some crazy idea, his goose is cooked. If I am chairman of a group that is making appointments, I go stone deaf whenever someone suggests the name of one of these radicals. My hearing improves when a good, reliable person is mentioned as a possibility.

Said another informant:

It frequently happens in the course of a meeting that someone will call attention to the heavy burden of civic responsibilities that is being carried by a small proportion of the population. Someone will say, "My God, it's a shame that just a few of us have to do all the work. Why, this community is just full of talented people who could help a lot, if only they wouldn't shirk their civic duties."

At this point heads will nod vigorous assent, and comments along the same lines will be made by several persons. Then someone else will say, "Yes, all of this is true, but we have to select people we can depend on." Everybody agrees emphatically with this too, so the idea of enlarging the circle of policy-makers is dropped.

Thus a bow is made in the direction of what might be termed more democratic participation of the citizenry in policy-making. As Hunter has pointed out in the case of Regional City, however, community projects can be carried out successfully only if the small group of policy-makers can marshal the cooperation of large numbers of lower-level workers who will perform the labor required to transform the policies and decisions into reality.[13] When Bigtown's leaders speak of the desirability of increasing participation in community affairs, they are referring to their wish for more followers, not leaders.

The Individual's Motivation for Civic Participation

C. Wright Mills and Melville J. Ulmer have pointed out that the executive depends for his career advancement upon his superiors rather than upon local individuals or institutions, and hence he is much more concerned with the affairs of the corporation than he is with those of the community.[14] This correctly implies that his civic participation tends to be a by-product of his job and his desire for career advancement. In the modern corporation the executive role requires a considerable capacity for organizing and manipulating ideas, men, and materials. A demonstration of ability in civic matters may well lead a man's superiors to exploit his talents in the administration of the corporation's internal affairs. Moreover, in his work with influential people in civic organizations and committees, the individual acquires experience and contacts which contribute to his personal development. Hence the executive may, through his outside activities, gain promotion for himself within his own organization.

Top executives of Bigtown are afforded many opportunities for gaining publicity for themselves and their corporations. Not only are these men granted clearance for civic participation by their superiors, but they are invited to join many civic organizations. It is even possible for an executive to migrate to Bigtown from outside the South and in a short time become known as an outstanding civic leader.

The junior executive, through his participation in the lower levels of civic organizations of less prestige and power, can likewise build a reputa-

---

[13] Hunter, *Community Power Structure*, p. 65.

[14] *Small Business and Civic Welfare: Report of the Smaller War Plants Corporation to the Special Committee to Study Problems of American Small Business* (Senate Doc. No. 135 [79th Cong., 2d sess.]) (Washington: Government Printing Office, 1946), p. 26.

tion in a hurry. This attention-getting activity is especially important for young men employed in corporations in which the individual tends to be just one of a large and "anonymous" mass of junior executives.

Thus the desire for advancement in his career motivates a man to play a part in civic affairs. It would be a mistake, however, to assume that executives are active in community affairs solely to promote their own careers or the interests of the corporation. Not only are there many reasons why men become concerned with the affairs of the community, but a given individual may have several reasons for his activities. Some executives, for example, seem quite concerned with the "sorry state" of community services in Bigtown and cherish an altruistic hope of contributing toward improvement.

It should be added that another motive for civic participation is emerging from the peculiar role which the corporation executive plays in modern society. As contrasted with the earlier elite of the capitalistic world, the business owner, the modern executive is not an entrepreneur. He manages his corporation, but he does not own it. He is usually not wealthy and cannot indulge in flagrant conspicuous consumption. Subject to control by his own superiors, he is not free and independent. This situation led several interviewees, both corporation and non-corporation men, to speculate on civic participation as a means of compensating for the executive's lack of real power. One of Bigtown's entrepreneurs, quite conscious of his own powerful position, made the following remarks:

> I've been observing these corporation executives in action for about thirty years. Two things about them have really impressed me. One is their frustrated desire to be free and independent—that is, to be able to make independent decisions and exercise personal power. The other thing is the lengths to which they will go to conceal from their subordinates and the public at large their subservience to their masters up above, either locally or in the corporation's national headquarters.
>
> The fact is that these fellows nurse a tremendous desire to be big-shot capitalists. But they are not, and they know it. Some of them try to hide this fact by holding a tight rein on their subordinates, using this means to demonstrate their power. Others try to further the impression that they are big shots by being hyperactive in community affairs.

Thus, lacking many of the satisfactions and powers of the entrepreneur, the corporation executive seeks means of displaying authority and independence which he knows to be functions of his position rather than his personal prerogatives. He may conceal his frustrations by playing to the hilt the role of entrepreneur, so long as his own superiors do not see fit to curtail his activities and restrict his powers.

This research report has focused upon the influence of absentee-owned corporations and their executives in the civic affairs of a single community; hence the extent to which the phenomena described and analyzed are typical of American cities must be determined by further comparative research. Future investigations may identify circumstances making for variation in the patterns of informal control in various types of urban environment.

It should be observed that this analysis of Bigtown's power structure has centered attention solely upon one interest group—the absentee-owned corporations. A broader investigation would examine the structures and functions of the multitude of other competing-cooperating factions which actively seek to influence policy-making in civic affairs.

Attention has also been concentrated in this study upon the role of executives in civic matters deemed important to those in control of the corporation and which are potentially controversial—i.e., matters involving decisions to be made in terms of goals and values. Happily, perhaps, not all community affairs are decided in an arena in which the combatants are hostile and competing interest groups. Some matters are resolved through quick consensus, since all agree on the desirability of certain goals.

Economic Dominants and Community Power: A Comparative Analysis*

DONALD A. CLELLAND and WILLIAM H. FORM

Introduction

Three avenues to the study of American community power structure have received widest attention during the last decade. The earliest approach studied a single set of community influentials who allegedly made the major community decisions.[1] Adherents of this method have generally concluded that business leaders are the "ruling elite" or at least *primi inter pares* in the community power structure. The second method discerned the power structure by examining how specific persons and groups

---

Reprinted from the *American Journal of Sociology*, 69 (1964): 511–21. Copyright 1964 by the University of Chicago. Reprinted by permission of the publisher.

* We are grateful to Professor James B. McKee for a critical reading of the manuscript.

[1] The tradition of Robert S. Lynd and Helen Merrill Lynd, *Middletown in Transition* (New York: Harcourt, Brace & Co., 1937); C. Wright Mills, *The Power Elite* (New York: Oxford University Press, 1956); Floyd Hunter, *Community Power Structure* (Chapel Hill, N.C.: University of North Carolina Press, 1953); and many others.

behaved in specific community issues and decisions.[2] Those using this technique have generally found a pluralistic system of decision-making. The third avenue has investigated the forces changing the character of persons holding positions of potential power.[3] Irrespective of approach, an ideological question has been persistent—whether the community is governed informally by an economic elite or whether the dominant pattern is political pluralism, a situation where decision-makers represent groups with differing interests.

One instructive way of posing this controversy is to ask what types of relationships characterize the stratification orders in American communities in the past and in the present.[4] More specifically, the sociological question is: To what extent has private economic power been translated directly into community or public power? Although R. O. Schulze did not formally place his research within the Weberian framework, operationally he did study the question we have posed by tracing historically the place of economically powerful figures in the public life of Cibola.[5] The study reported here attempts to replicate his investigation in a different type of community, which we shall call "Wheelsburg."

Schulze's findings upheld his hypothesis that as a city grows from an isolated, self-contained entity to an urbanized community "increasingly involved and interrelated in the large social complex," its sociopolitical power structure changes from a monolithic one dominated by persons possessing great economic power to a bifurcated structure comprising "two crucial and relatively discrete power sets, the economic dominants and the public leaders."[6] Economic dominants were defined as "those persons who occupy the top formal statuses in the major economic units within the community area,"[7] and public leaders (or top influentials) as

---

[2] E.g., Robert A. Dahl, "Equality and Power in American Society," in *Power and Democracy in America*, William V. D'Antonio and Howard J. Ehrlich (eds.) (Notre Dame, Ind.: University of Notre Dame Press, 1961); Nelson W. Polsby, "The Sociology of Community Power: A Reassessment," *Social Forces*, XXXVII (1959), pp. 232–36; Linton C. Freeman *et al.*, "Local Community Leadership," *Syracuse College Paper No. 15* (Syracuse, N.Y.: Syracuse University, 1960); Edward C. Banfield, *Political Influence* (New York: Free Press of Glencoe, 1961); and many others.

[3] Robert A. Dahl, *Who Governs?* (New Haven, Conn.: Yale University Press, 1961); Constance Green, *Holyoke, Massachusetts* (New Haven, Conn.: Yale University Press, 1939); Thorstein Veblen, *Absentee Ownership* (New York: Viking Press, 1939); and the works of R. O. Schulze cited in n. 5.

[4] In the framework of Max Weber as explicated in "Class, Status and Power," in *From Max Weber: Essays in Sociology*, Hans H. Gerth and C. Wright Mills (trans. and eds.) (New York: Oxford University Press, 1946).

[5] Robert O. Schulze, "Economic Dominance and Public Leadership: A Study of the Structure and Process of Power in an Urban Community" (microfilmed Ph.D. dissertation, University of Michigan, 1956); "The Role of Economic Dominants in Community Power Structure," *American Sociological Review*, XXIII (1958): 3–9; "The Bifurcation of Power in a Satellite City," in *Community Political Systems*, Morris Janowitz, ed. (New York: Free Press, 1961), pp. 19–80.

[6] Schulze, "The Bifurcation of Power," pp. 21–22.

[7] *Ibid.*, p. 21. For Schulze's operational criteria for determining economic dominants and public leaders see *ibid.*, Appendixes A and B, pp. 73–75. Essentially the same criteria

those who, in the opinion of community "knowledgeables," exercise major influence and leadership in community affairs.[8]

Schulze tentatively explained the dissociation of economic dominants from local political-civic affairs by the following three trends:

(*a*) the establishment by a growing number of locally-owned industrial units of direct supplier relationships with a small number of large, non-local manufacturing plants; (*b*) the subsequent introduction into the local economic system of an increasing number of branch plants of large, absentee-owned corporations; and (*c*) the concomitant dissolution of the extensive networks of interlocking directorates and officerships which had formerly served to link significant numbers of local economic dominants within the community.[9]

These trends have also occurred in Wheelsburg, but to a more limited degree. The greatest variation between Cibola and Wheelsburg is in the first factor, because in Wheelsburg many local supply plants were established to serve the local automobile firms.

Comparison of the Communities

The two communities differ significantly in a number of ways. For most of its history Cibola was a small independent town. It is now a satellite city of approximately 20,000 inhabitants located just beyond the Standard Metropolitan Area of a large midwest industrial center containing more than 3,000,000 people. The five largest of its eight major industrial plants were absentee-controlled. Cibola is an extreme example of a city that "has felt the full impact of the metropolitan drift of American life."[10] A period of rapid expansion began during World War II with the establishment just outside the city's boundaries of a gigantic war-

---

were utilized to identify the dominant economic units (and consequently economic dominants themselves) in the two cities. Number of employees, capital worth, and assessed valuation were used as measures. However, since Wheelsburg is a much larger city than Cibola, the minimum figures for cutoff points were necessarily larger. In Cibola the only dominant economic units were manufacturing plants, banks, and savings and loan companies. In Wheelsburg a wider variety of economic units was included in the dominant group, e.g., department stores, utilities, and insurance companies. In addition to the heads of the major economic units, all who were on the board of directors of two or more of the major economic units were also identified as economic dominants.

[8] As suggested by Hunter, *Community Power Structure*. The "knowledgeables" who were interviewed in the two studies differed somewhat. Schulze's knowledgeables were the heads of local voluntary associations. This research relied on the nominations of fourteen high-ranking officials from seven institutional sectors of the community (mass communication, business, union, welfare, education, government, religion). David A. Booth and Charles A. Adrian compared the results of the method used by Schulze with the simpler method we employed, and found almost identical results (see their "Simplifying the Discovery of Elites," *American Behavioral Scientist*, 5 [1961]: 14–16).

[9] Schulze, "The Role of Economic Dominants," p. 6.

[10] Schulze, "The Bifurcation of Power," p. 24.

production plant which employed over 40,000 workers at its peak. After the war the economic instability of absentee-owned companies occupying this plant caused wide and rapid fluctuations in the local labor force. Consequently, during the 1940s the community experienced rapid fluctuation and high turnover in population. At the time of Schulze's study employment at the main plant had leveled off at 9,500 as it became tied securely to the motor vehicle industry.

Wheelsburg is located about 60 miles west of Cibola. It is an independent city of over 100,000 dominating a metropolitan area with a population of approximately 180,000. Like Cibola, its economy is based primarily on motor vehicle production. In fact, the same motor vehicle company is the largest single employer in both communities. In Wheelsburg the company employs nearly 15,000 workers. However, significant sections of Wheelsburg's labor force are employed in state government and in a nearby state university. Wheelsburg's period of most rapid industrial and population growth occurred earlier than Cibola's, between 1900 and 1920. This growth largely reflected the success of locally owned automobile and supplier plants. Since 1920 Wheelsburg's growth has been moderate and steady even with the large invasion of absentee-owned companies. Such companies came earlier to Wheelsburg, but entered and grew more gradually than in Cibola.

Currently, thirteen of the twenty non-financial dominant economic units are absentee-controlled.[11] Unlike Cibola, (a) Wheelsburg's major firms have been fairly stable operations, (b) the vast majority of its labor force has always been employed within the city limits, (c) very few of its economic dominants have lived beyond the city's contiguous suburbs, and (d) the city is removed from the influence of a large competing metropolis. Wheelsburg, then, is a much more stable and "normal" type of community setting in which to test Schulze's hypothesis.

Following Schulze's method closely, we tested his main hypothesis by (1) reconstructing the formal participation patterns of economic dominants over the past century in the political and civic activities of the community; (2) ascertaining the representation of current economic dominants among public leaders, that is, in the "reputational" power structure; and (3) analyzing the role of current economic dominants in specific community issues and programs.

Economic Dominants as Political and Civic Leaders

In Wheelsburg, as in Cibola, the proportion of economic dominants who occupied high local governmental offices declined dramatically over the century. Data in Tables 1 and 2 reveal that in both communities prior to

[11] An absentee-controlled company is defined as one having a majority of its board of directors living outside of the local community. In both Cibola and Wheelsburg, slightly less than 5 percent of the dominant economic units were absentee-controlled—five of eleven units in Cibola and thirteen of twenty-seven units in Wheelsburg. In both cities, all of the financial units (three and seven, respectively) were locally owned.

Table 1. Economic dominants serving in public office in Wheelsburg and Cibola

Period	No. of Economic Dominants	Percent In Public Office	In Elective Office	On Governing Body	In Highest Public Office
1823–60:					
Wheelsburg	*	......	......	......	......
Cibola	12	83	83	75	50
1860–1900:					
Wheelsburg	44	73	64	57	30
Cibola	21	81	67	57	33
1900–1940:					
Wheelsburg	80	25	11	4	0
Cibola	43	26	16	12	5
1940–59:					
Wheelsburg	71	14	0	0	0
Cibola	31	23	13	10	3

*Wheelsburg was not incorporated until 1859.
Source: Cibola data, see Schulze, "The Bifurcation of Power," pp. 37–38.

Table 2. Offices held by politically active economic dominants in Wheelsburg and Cibola*

Period	No. of Politically Active Economic Dominants	Percent In Elective Office	On Governing Body	In Highest Public Office
1823–1860:				
Wheelsburg	......	......	......	......
Cibola	10	100	90	60
1860–1900:				
Wheelsburg	32	88	78	41
Cibola	17	88	71	41
1900–1940:				
Wheelsburg	20	45	15	0
Cibola	12	64	45	18
1940–1959:				
Wheelsburg	10	0	0	0
Cibola	7	57	43	14

* "Politically active" refers to economic dominants holding any appointive or elective office.
Source: Cibola data, see Schulze, "The Bifurcation of Power," pp. 37–38.

1900 the economic dominants were highly represented in local government. The comparable percentages in each table are virtually identical. Although the twentieth century ushered in a sharp decline in the proportion of economic dominants holding public office in both communities, this decline was sharper in Wheelsburg than in Cibola. Moreover, in both cities, but especially in Wheelsburg, the offices held by economic dominants have been increasingly appointive rather than elective. Indeed, no economic dominant has served as mayor since 1899, or as councilman since 1932.

Table 3. Economic dominants as board members of Chamber of Commerce

	Median No. of Memberships per Year on Board of Directors*		No. Serving as President	
Period	Wheelsburg	Cibola	Wheelsburg	Cibola
1901–6	8	......	3	......
1906–13	9	......	4	......
1913–20	9	......	4	......
1920–27	10	6	3	3
1927–34	9	3	2	2
1934–41	9	3	2	0
1941–48	4	2	0	1
1948–55	3	1	3	0
1955–59	5	......	0	......

* The number of directors varied from 15 to 18 in Cibola and from 15 to 21 in Wheelsburg.

Source: Cibola data, Schulze, "The Bifurcation of Power," p. 49. Since the Cibola Chamber was founded in 1920, there are no data for earlier periods.

The trend of these developments in Wheelsburg may be seen more clearly by examining the data in terms of twenty-year periods. A precipitous decline in public officeholding by economic dominants occurred in the 1900–1920 period, with relatively little change thereafter. However, there has been a continuing change in the type of office held. In each succeeding twenty-year period, fewer of the economic dominants who held office were elected. Increasingly, they have come to hold advisory and honorary positions in local government. Since it is probably fair to assume that the power potential of appointive offices is less than that of elective offices, the shift of economic dominants from the latter may be taken as evidence of continuing loss of formal political power.

Schulze suggests that after 1900 the arena of local involvement of the economic dominants shifted from politics to voluntary associations. The Wheelsburg data confirm his observation. Thus data in Table 3 show that at the beginning the economic dominants were highly represented among the members and officers of the Chamber of Commerce, and that their representation declined at a later era. Apparently the Wheelsburg economic dominants were even more powerful in the Chamber than their Cibola counterparts, for one of their number was president during nineteen of the first twenty years of the organization's existence. During the past two decades their representation in the Chamber has declined, but not so sharply as in Cibola. An historical analysis of the proportion of officerships held by Wheelsburg economic dominants in other civic organizations (major service clubs, community chest, and the board of trustees of the leading local hospital) reveals patterns of withdrawal similar to that evident in Table 3. While it is difficult to estimate the power potential of these officerships, current public leaders or top influentials regard the Chamber of Commerce as the single most influential organization in the city. Yet, as indicated above, direct control of this organization by economic dominants has probably declined over the years.

In both Wheelsburg and Cibola economic dominants reduced their incumbency in public offices at the turn of the century. A similar withdrawal from civic leadership positions began about 1940.[12] A comparative analysis of the economic development of the two communities corroborates some of Schulze's explanations and contradicts others. The evidence fails to support Schulze's position that the growth of absentee ownership and the dissolution of local business ties (interlocking directorates) among the economic dominants account for their withdrawal from public office. In both communities these phenomena occurred *after* the withdrawal; in Cibola, the first absentee-controlled plant was established in 1932, and in Wheelsburg as late as 1940 two-thirds of the major economic units were locally owned. Moreover, 80 percent of the Wheelsburg economic dominants maintained local business ties with other economic dominants as late as 1940. A third factor which Schulze associated with withdrawal, namely, the growth of direct supplier relationships to non-local industries by locally owned plants, must also be discarded, for in Wheelsburg no such growth took place and yet the pattern of withdrawal was similar to that of Cibola. Moreover, in Wheelsburg this withdrawal does not seem to have been forced by the growing political power of ethnic groups as was the case in many American cities.[13] There has never been a large ethnic proletariat in Wheelsburg, nor have local politics ever been heavily based on ethnic lines or class conflict.

What factors, then, are associated with the sharp decline in political participation by economic dominants (i.e., the bifurcation of political and economic power structure) since the turn of the century? At the broadest level of explanation, the increased involvement of the community and its economic units in state and nationwide social economic systems was, no doubt, an important factor. More specifically, in Wheelsburg, the end of the period in which political and economic power tended to coincide was marked by the rise of a new breed of economic elite, namely, managers and owners of the new automobile and supply plants. Younger, wealthier, operating larger businesses, more directly involved in the day-to-day operation of their businesses, introducing a wide variety of new products, these men did not participate in local politics probably largely because they lacked the time and because they probably found that business was much more exciting. A growing separation of wealth and social honor may have been a second factor, but the new economic elite was partly based on old local wealth and the

[12] Withdrawal" is probably an apt phrase, because no evidence is available to suggest that there was community pressure on the economic dominants to reduce their community involvement. However, individual economic dominants were constantly changing. Their withdrawal consisted not so much in dropping civic leadership positions as in the failure of new economic dominants to seek such positions.

[13] E.g., in New Haven, from the late nineteenth century until recently, local politics were controlled primarily by "ex-plebes," individuals on the rise from the ethnic proletariat, who gained office through "the skills of ethnic politics." From 1843 to 1898, New Haven politics were dominated by the leading entrepreneurs. It may be significant that the period of dominance by economic dominants is almost identical in New Haven, Wheelsburg, and Cibola (see Dahl, *Who Governs?* chap. iii and iv).

majority were entrepreneurs rather than simply managers of companies financed by non-local capital. However, in the absence of ethnic and class cleavage in the community, it is doubtful that the new economic dominants, many of whom were classed Horatio Alger success models, lacked the popularity needed for election. They probably did not choose to run.

On the other hand, later withdrawal from civic leadership positions seems to be associated with the introduction of absentee-owned plants and the related decrease in common local business ties (interlocking directorates) among the economic dominants. The importance of the latter factor is underscored in Wheelsburg where economic dominants not only have more local economic linkages but also comprise a larger proportion of the local civic leaders.[14]

The so-called pattern of withdrawal needs to be interpreted within a broad context of the local participation. In Wheelsburg, the historical pattern has been for the economic dominants to become officers of new organizations as they emerged in the community, then to retain membership, and later to withdraw from active participation. Thus when the Chamber of Commerce was created, dominants were its earliest officers; when the service clubs arose they again became officers; when the Community Chest arrived they became its sponsors and officers; and they sponsored the largest hospital and dominated its board. This pattern of domination and later "withdrawal" is subject to various interpretations. We are inclined to believe that it demonstrates two related phenomena: (a) assumption of officerships in new organizations validated not only their importance to the community but the power and status of the original officers, namely, the economic dominants, and (b) the policies, direction, and administration of the new organizations were set and institutionalized by the original officers. After this initial period the organizations needed only informal and non-official guidance from the dominants and not their active officeholding. In other words, a change in officers did not necessarily mean a change in policy or loss of power and control by dominants.[15]

Community Influence of Economic Dominants

In order to assess the community influence of current economic dominants in Wheelsburg, two procedures were used. First, their reputational influence was investigated by assessing their representation in the list of public leaders (community influentials as determined by the method out-

[14] Sixty-five percent of the economic dominants in the 1940–59 period were associated as officers, partners, or directors in at least one other business with other economic dominants.

[15] Lest the concentration on "withdrawal" be overwhelming, it should be noted that almost half the economic dominants in the 1940–59 period held civic leadership positions in Wheelsburg and that their participation in the Chamber of Commerce was increasing.

lined in n. 8). Second, their "actual" influence was probed by examining their role in a number of community issues or projects.

In 1958–59, thirty-nine individuals were found to be economic dominants, and coincidentally, thirty-nine people were designated as public leaders. The names of twelve persons (31 percent) appeared on both lists. This overlap is considerably higher than that found in Cibola where only two of seventeen economic dominants were among the community's eighteen public leaders. Moreover, eight of the top fifteen public leaders in Wheelsburg, including the top four, as rated by the public leaders themselves, were economic dominants. Although major absentee-owned corporations were "underrepresented" among the economic dominants who were also public leaders, "U.S. Motors" (the absentee-owned industrial giant in the community) was represented by three executives (two of whom were not defined as economic dominants). From these observations we cannot conclude that two discrete power sets are found in Wheelsburg.

In order to substantiate the basic dissimilarities between the economic dominants and public leaders in Cibola, Schulze examined their patterns of political and civic participation. He found that the economic dominants had held only about half as many governmental offices as the public leaders. The same was true in Wheelsburg, although both groups were less active. Somewhat surprisingly, economic dominants were as well represented as the public leaders in the five most influential associations. Table 4 reveals a similar situation of high participation by both economic dominants and public leaders in Wheelsburg's most influential associations. However, the Cibola situation of wide differences between public leaders and economic dominants in the number of officerships held in these associations was not in evidence. Table 5 reveals that a higher proportion of economic dominants in Wheelsburg (from both locally and absentee-owned companies) have in the past held office in the five most influential organizations. Differences are small between the two communities in the proportions currently holding such offices. In short, both Tables 4 and 5 document no deep bifurcation in associational participation between Wheelsburg's economic dominants and public leaders. The relatively high rate of participation by absentee-owned corporation executives is especially notable.[16]

One of the reasons for the failure of economic dominants to participate in the civic life of Cibola was that they regarded the city mainly as the locus of their work life and not their community life.[17] Moreover, their private economic interests were primarily non-local. This may not be

---

[16] Although managers of the largest absentee-owned corporation did not dominate the local scene as extensively as in the case of Bigtown, they did have representatives on most of the local bodies to coordinate knowledge of what was going on in the city. For data on Bigtown see Roland J. Pellegrin and Charles H. Coates, "Absentee-owned Corporations and Community Power Structure," *American Journal of Sociology*, 59 (1956): 413–19.

[17] A large proportion lived in other communities in the metropolitan area and may have participated in the associational life of these other communities.

Table 4. Membership of current public leaders and economic dominants in the most influential associations*

	Percent Belonging to Association			
	Public Leaders	Economic Dominants		
Association		Local	Absentee	Total
Chamber of Commerce:				
Wheelsburg	87	96	100	97
Cibola	78	100	87	94
Rotary:				
Wheelsburg	49	38	40	38
Cibola	50	70	14	47
Kiwanis:				
Wheelsburg	18	13	7	10
Cibola	44	30	0	18
Lions:				
Wheelsburg	5	8	0	5
Cibola	11	0	0	0

* In Cibola the five most influential associations were determined by polling the voluntary association heads, public leaders, and economic dominants. The four associations listed above and the Junior Chamber of Commerce were named by all of the groupings questioned. These organizations were also designated by Wheelsburg public leaders as highly influential. Since few public leaders or economic dominants were young enough to be eligible for membership in the Junior Chamber of Commerce in either city, and none were members, this association was omitted from the table.
Source for Cibola data: Schulze, "The Bifurcation of Power," p. 47.

Table 5. Officerships of public leaders and economic dominants in five most influential community associations

	Public Leaders		Economic Dominants					
			Local		Absentee		Total	
	Wheelsburg	Cibola	Wheelsburg	Cibola	Wheelsburg	Cibola	Wheelsburg	Cibola
Percent having served as president of at least one of the five associations	31	61	25	20	20	0	23	12
No. of presidencies occupied in the five associations	17	14	8	2	3	0	11	2
Percent *currently* serving as officer or board member in at least one of the five associations*	18	44	4	10	27	30	13	18
No. of officerships or board memberships *currently* held in the five associations	7	12	1	1	4	2	5	3

* "Currently" refers to the year of research: 1954 for Cibola, 1958–59 for Wheelsburg.
Source: Cibola data, Schulze, "The Bifurcation of Power," p. 48.

Table 6. Number of known local economic ties among public leaders and economic dominants

	Public Leaders	Economic Dominants	
		Local Firm	Absentee Firm
Public leaders:			
Wheelsburg	23	31	8
Cibola	4	3	2
Local-firm dominants:			
Wheelsburg:	......	47	11
Cibola	......	15	0
Absentee-firm dominants:*			
Wheelsburg	......	......	2
Cibola	......	......	2

* In neither Wheelsburg nor Cibola were there any economic ties between absentee-firm dominants from *different* corporations. In the case of two absentee firms in Wheelsburg, a second person in addition to the general manager was defined as an economic dominant because he held a directorship in a local bank as well as an officership in the absentee-owned firm.

Source: Cibola data supplied by Robert O. Schulze in an unpublished manuscript.

surprising since the city's largest economic units were absentee-owned and oriented toward a national market. However, Table 6 indicates that a much more extensive network of economic ties exists in Wheelsburg than in Cibola.[18] Despite a high degree of absentee ownership in Wheelsburg, a fairly extensive network of economic ties unites the interests of the economic dominants and the public leaders. These ties may explain the higher rate of civic participation by its economic dominants and their closer social integration to public leaders.

As a final demonstration of the bifurcation of Cibola economic dominants and public leaders, Schulze analyzed the decision-making process on two important community issues. The economic dominants refused to become involved in resolving either of them, leaving the public leaders autonomous but perhaps without a solid power basis for community action.

In Wheelsburg, an analysis of eleven community issues[19] revealed

---

[18] "Economic ties" are instances in which a pair of individuals serves as officers or directors of the same firm. Each pair is counted as one economic tie. For example, if four public leaders serve on the board of directors of a bank, there are six economic ties (pairs).

[19] These issues were selected and recapitulated by the public leaders in interviews. They included hospital expansion drive, downtown development, establishment of a metropolitan planning agency, improvement of airport terminal facilities, establishment of a tricounty planning agency, annexation of a school district to the city, widening of a city street, ban on Sunday shopping, proposed shift of location of city hall, proposed sale of bonds by the city to finance construction of parking facilities, and proposed annexation of a suburban shopping center. Our inspection of newspapers and other documents reveals that these indeed represent nearly the full range of community issues during the last five or six years. One or two others might be added by other local interests such as organized labor (see William H. Form and Warren L. Sauer, "Community and Labor Influentials: A Comparative Study of Participation and Imagery," *Industrial and Labor Relations Review*, 18 [1963]: 8–19).

that eight of the economic dominants who were also public leaders were among those mentioned as influential in initiating and resolving these issues. Economic dominants, including some representing absentee-owned corporations, either initiated or co-initiated programs of action for six of the eight issues in which they were involved. Although this evidence suggests that economic dominants have not withdrawn from community decision-making and that they are not just ceremonial leaders, apparently they do not form a monolithic power elite. Different individuals became involved in different issues, doing so in the process of playing their own "games."[20]

Not all of the broad community issues in which economic dominants were involved were controversial. Some of them may more properly be called "projects." The major issues in Cibola seemed to involve a higher degree of conflict in the political arena. Perhaps this conflict reflected the inertia of partisan party politics which existed in the community as late as 1947. In addition, both of the major issues in Cibola—adoption of a new city charter and annexation—were the direct results of rapid urbanization and industrialization, processes which had occurred at a more gradual rate in Wheelsburg. There, political life seemed less marked by conflict, for local government not only was nonpartisan but it traditionally and customarily responded to the needs of business.[21] It is highly probable that the lack of political conflict and the tendency for community decision-making to be channeled to the private rather than public sphere are interdependent. In Wheelsburg there was little evidence of basic differences in values among the economic dominants, the public leaders, and the elected officials. If representation of conflicting interests or values is chosen as the indicator of pluralism in the power structure, Wheelsburg (and most American communities) will be judged less pluralistic than if a weaker test of pluralism, such as the participation of separate individuals in different issues, is used.[22]

Thus, the social climate of the decision-making roles of the economic dominants in the two cities is not identical. Whether Wheelsburg dominants would become involved in highly conflictful issues should they arise is not known. Certainly they hesitated to publicize their involvement in controversial issues.[23] One large firm, for example, refused to become overtly involved in an annexation issue despite the fact that its

---

[20] Norton E. Long, "The Urban Community as an Ecology of Games," *American Journal of Sociology*, 64 (1958): 251–61.

[21] Form and Sauer, "Community and Labor Influentials."

[22] For a fuller discussion of this problem see Marshall N. Goldstein, "Absentee Ownership and Monolithic Power Structures: Two Questions for Community Studies," in *Current Trends in Comparative Community Studies*, Bert E. Swanson (ed.) (Kansas City, Mo.: Community Studies, Inc., 1962), pp. 49–59.

[23] The same attitudes were revealed in interviews conducted by Rossi in Mediana. This does not mean that economic dominants had withdrawn from local influence systems because, as Rossi points out, "this is the age of community projects" (Peter H. Rossi, "The Organizational Structure of an American Community," in *Complex Organizations*, Amitai Etzioni [ed.] [New York: Holt, Rinehart & Winston, 1961], p. 301).

economic interests were involved. However, it made its position known. What covert influence this might have had cannot be accurately appraised. Yet, since executives of the absentee-owned corporations were less likely to become involved in community decision-making than economic dominants from locally owned enterprises, possibly Wheelsburg's pattern of influence is evolving toward the type found in Cibola. On the other hand, both economic dominants and public leaders work hard to solve issues without conflict, and controversial issues probably arise less often in gradually expanding cities such as Wheelsburg than in cities which have grown very rapidly and have experienced extreme economic fluctuations, such as Cibola. Further research is required to determine the power roles of economic dominants in cities differing in size, social composition, economic composition, and economic history.

Conclusions

Comparative analysis of the roles of economic dominants in power structures of a satellite and an independent city reveals that in both communities the formal political and economic power structures which were once melded have tended to become bifurcated over time. This process seems to have paralleled the integration of local economic units into national markets and the process of governmental centralization. The economic dominants, once highly active leaders in civic associations, have tended to reduce their participation in this area, especially in the satellite community. This withdrawal coincided roughly with the rapid extension of absentee ownership in both cities. Currently, the nearly complete bifurcation of economic dominants and public leaders (top influentials) found in the satellite city was not as evident in the independent city, where an extensive network of economic ties bound the two groups together. Moreover, unlike the economic dominants in the satellite city, those in the independent city have not abandoned their decision-making role in community issues.

While the evidence cited in this research is not conclusive, it points to variable patterns of relations between economic dominants and public leaders in different types of communities. Apparently the absence of local party politics, a history of local industries becoming absentee-owned rather than the introduction of branch plants from outside the community, the institutionalization of local political controls, and the absence of ethnic, class, or other cleavages which contribute to partisan politics reduce the withdrawal rate of economic dominants from participation in community associations and local power arrangements. The time is ripe for many rapid comparative studies of a wide range of communities to determine more precisely the factors responsible for the bifurcation or persistence of ties between economic dominants, civic leaders, and community influentials.

Community Influence Systems: Structure and Change

ERNEST A. T. BARTH

Although there have been numerous studies of community power and influence systems reported in the literature over the past several years, few of these have been specifically designed to make use of the comparative method. As a result, no systematic attention has been devoted to identifying the determinants of the shape of influence systems, and little attention has been devoted to the dynamics of change in the shape of such systems. The research reported in this paper was carried out during the summer of 1952 by two research teams under the sponsorship of the Institute for Research in Social Science of the University of North Carolina at Chapel Hill. The principal focus of that study was the investigation of the relational system involving Air Force Bases and their host communities. During the course of the study data were obtained by means of intensive personal interviews with key officers stationed at each base and similar interviews with key leaders in the host community. The study was formulated explicitly within the framework of a comparative design and within Blackwell's theoretical framework for research in community organization.[1] Hunter's nominational technique was used to identify community influentials.[2] Six communities are compared on the basis of the "shape" of their influence systems. Two community variables, the rate of growth of the total population and the nature of the economic base of the community, are related to the structure and patterns of change in the influence system.

The literature on community power structure provides several hypotheses concerning the "determinants of the shape" of the influence system. In their article on the role of absentee-owned corporations in a community influence system, Pellegrin and Coates note that: "American cities

---

Reprinted from *Social Forces*, 40 (1961): 58–63. Copyright 1961 by the University of North Carolina Press. Reprinted by permission of the publisher.

[1] Gordon W. Blackwell, "A Theoretical Framework for Research in Community Organization," *Social Forces*, 33, No. 1.

[2] Floyd Hunter, *Community Power Structure: A Study of Decision Makers* (Chapel Hill, N.C.: The University of North Carolina Press, 1954).

apparently vary considerably in the extent to which dominant interest groups are united effectively for coordinated control of community affairs."[3] They appear to view this variation as related to the patterns of leadership exhibited by the executives of absentee-owned corporations in the local community. Clapp and Padgett relate the dynamics of expansion of the population of Tijhuana to the structure of influence in that city.[4] They suggest that under conditions of rapid expansion of population the dominance of the influence structure by a single clique is modified and a "flattening" of the structure occurs. Barth and Abu-Laban report that Negro leaders in Pacific City do not appear to wield power (although they are influential).[5] The relatively small Negro population and its rapid rate of growth appear to be linked with this lack of power in that subcommunity.

These studies suggest three hypotheses concerning the shape of the influence system:

1. The rate of growth of the population base of a community is related to the shape of the community influence system. Other things being equal, the more rapid the rate of growth, the more diffuse will be the distribution of community influence.
2. Absentee-owned businesses or businesses headed by persons not living in the community are found in communities with flat, or disorganized influence patterns. In such communities those who control the means of power do not participate in community affairs.
3. The rapid expansion of the economic base of a community (especially where the community population is small prior to this expansion) is related to the development of clique structures in the influence system.

The six communities for which data will be discussed are classed into three general types according to the "shape" of their influence systems. The main dimension along which shape is being measured is "the degree of integration," or the degree of schism, characteristic of leadership in that community. Miller in his comparative study of "community power structure" in three cities utilized this dimension.[6]

Type I—Pyramidal

The first type of influence system could be classified as having a "pyramidal" shape. A small and well-integrated "clique" of influentials, often

[3] Roland Pellegrin and Charles Coates, "Absentee-Owned Corporations and Community Power Structure," *American Journal of Sociology*, 61 (1956).

[4] Orrin E. Klapp and Vincent Padgett, "Power Structure and Decision-making in a Mexican Border City," *American Journal of Sociology*, 65 (1960).

[5] Ernest A. T. Barth and Baha Abu-Laban, "Power Structure and the Negro Subcommunity," *American Sociological Review*, 24 (1959).

[6] Delbert C. Miller, "Decision-Making Cliques in Community Power Structure: A Comparative Study of an English and an American City," *American Journal of Sociology*, 64 (1958).

Community Influence Systems: Structure and Change 89

dominated by a single leader, exercises a dominant position over the decision-making processes of the community. Two communities of this type were studied: Sanford, Louisiana and Amory, Texas. (All communities have been given fictitious names.)

Incorporated in 1839, Sanford experienced rapid growth in the thirty year period prior to 1950. This growth was stimulated primarily by the discovery of gas and oil reserves in the area. In 1950 the total population of the community was 127,206 representing an increase of 29.5 percent over 1940. Influence in Sanford was clearly structured. One man was repeatedly mentioned by respondents as the "most powerful man in the city." He was the president of the Consolidated Gas Corporation. One respondent, himself classified as a member of the power structure, told the interviewer: "Now the biggest man in Sanford is B. C. O'Swan, but I don't think that you could even get in to talk to him. He's pretty hard to get to. He's the most powerful man in Sanford. As he goes, so goes the city." In describing the power structure of the community the field worker had the following to report:

> At the top of the power structure is a wealthy, powerful group of business executives. The man identified as being the most influential was the president of the Consolidated Gas Corporation. He is said to be difficult to reach but very "civic-minded." The impression was gained that he operates behind the scenes, letting the executives of his corporation attend to details but passing judgment himself on civic matters. He is a very active Catholic layman and made a contribution of $100,000 toward a fund for a new Catholic hospital for the city.
>
> Almost as powerful as O'Swan, and more active in community affairs, is a wealthy oil man, Colonel C. W. Wilde. He is a widower and is said to be more active in community affairs than most of the economically powerful men because of this. He is a past president of the Chamber of Commerce. He too, made a sizeable contribution to to the drive for the Catholic hospital.
>
> A third member of the top level group is H. A. Ceaser, president of the State Gas Company. His younger brother is a four star general in the Air Force. He has been chairman of the Community Chest Drive in previous years.
>
> A politically but not economically powerful figure is Congressman Lee. He is a major figure in the House Military Affairs Committee. Apparently he has the support and approval of the top men in the power structure. The Mayor and "working members" of the chamber of commerce, while not members of the top-level, wealthy group, also have their support.

Thus, the field reports indicate that at the top of the influence structure of Sanford is a small well-integrated and closely knit group of businessmen who combine their efforts to direct the community decision-making process.

A second community in this class was Amory, Texas. Founded in 1887, Amory's greatest growth has taken place since 1920. It is the center of a tri-state cattle, wheat and oil area, and its economy was built on these three commodities. The total population of the city increased 43.6 percent between 1940 and 1950 when it reached a figure of 74,246.

Amory had many wealthy citizens whose fortunes had been made in wheat, oil, and cattle. The dominant figure in the power structure, L. R.

Olds, had both oil and wheat interests. During World War II he was placed in charge of the rehabilitation of refineries in Russia and adjoining countries by the United States Government. He had been on intimate terms with such figures as Eisenhower, Harriman, and Marshall Vorishilov. It was said of him that he owned half of the Panhandle. It was further said that what he did not own, Jack Woods, an oil man, and Pat Bird, a cattleman, did own. While these were not the only very wealthy men in the Panhandle, they appeared to be the dominant ones, particularly in an economic way. Olds and Bird were active in state and national politics, and Olds was formerly the mayor of Amory.

The incumbent mayor of the city was not as powerful as these men, but he was wealthy enough to be on intimate terms with them. He was by no means a figurehead.

L. R. Olds and a few of his fellow industrialists, Mayor Lean and Ted Faller, were in on every important decision that affected the city. They were powerful enough to have access to Washington through two Texas legislators and a congressman from their district. The process by which the community secured the reactivation of Arnold Air Force Base illustrates the power of these leaders and the manner in which they operated. The field worker reported it in the following way:

The land on which Arnold Air Force Base is located has never been owned by the United States Government. During World War II it was owned by the city, and at the end of the war the lease was terminated on a revocable basis, and the land reverted to the city. The buildings on the base were declared surplus by the government and most of them were removed, although the hangars remained standing.

When the Korean crisis arose in June of 1950, the leaders of Amory went into action quickly. Two successive wheat crop failures had hit the economy of the Panhandle hard blows and the leaders saw in the reactivation of the base a means of bolstering the economy.

Immediately some of the community leaders, including such men as Olds and Bob Giles, General Manager of the Southwest Public Service Company and the President of the Chamber of Commerce, got together and decided on the reactivation of the base. Ted Faller was in Washington at the time, and Mayor Lean went to join him. The day after the Korean outbreak these men went to the Pentagon and got in touch with an Air Force officer who had formerly commanded Arnold Air Force Base. After several months of work, they received word from their two Texas Senators and their Congressman that if the city would make certain commitments to the Air Force, there was reasonable assurance that the base would be reactivated.

The mayor and the chamber of commerce then called a meeting of the leaders of all the organizations and agencies in Amory who would be affected by the reactivation of the base and got certain commitments from them in writing.

Again, as was the case in Sanford, the field reports indicate that a small and integrated clique of leaders headed the informal influence structure of Amory. When issues of significance for the total community developed, it was these men and their associates who made the decisions and wielded the influence necessary to see that they were carried out.

Type II—Clique-based Truncated Pyramid

In this type of community the number of active members in the top reaches of power is greater than in Type I. As many as twenty to twenty-five people may operate at roughly equal levels of power. Often two or more "influential cliques" operate semi-autonomously within the influence system. Such a pattern of organization is associated with a rapid rate of population growth and a diversification of the industrial base of the community. The following dynamics seem to underly this type of structure. Efforts to expand the economic base of the community (often engaged in by an "old influential crowd") are successful. New businesses enter the community creating a rapid expansion of population, and in turn creating new positions of industrial and business leadership. Frequently the individuals filling these positions have been "imported" from other communities and are relatively unfamiliar with the local culture and traditions. The old leadership group finds itself unable to handle the problems of urban expansion (i.e., the need for sewers, increased water supply, new streets, housing, schools, etc.), and so a leadership gap appears. Men filling the new managerial positions in the new industries are "forced to step in" and participate in top levels of the influence system. As community decisions are often related to the interests of their company, they are, if for no other reason than self interest, forced to participate in decision-making activities. This is the type of dynamic exemplified in Clapp and Padgett's Mexican border city. Two communities surveyed in this study, Algona, Georgia and Gretna, South Carolina, fall into this category.

Algona, Georgia was a rapidly growing community of approximately 31,000 located in southeast Georgia. Its rate of population increase in the decade 1940 to 1950 was 62 percent. The community functions as a trade center for a large portion of southeast Georgia. In 1949 the retail sales for the community totaled $42,000,000. Community leaders were actively engaged in attempts to secure further business locations in the area. Theirs was a philosophy of optimism and business expansion.

The survey team was unable to locate any single individual or clique of individuals who were considered by their fellow community residents as "most influential." To the extent that influence was structured in the community, it appeared to be diffuse, rather than centrally located. Several community leaders reported that it took a group of 20 or more men in coordinated activity to make decisions for the community. There was some indication of a two-clique structure emerging in the community with an "old guard" group of conservative interests opposed to some extent by a "new clique." The "new clique" included the officers of two "new businesses" in the community as well as some of the "younger men" in town.

Gretna, South Carolina was a booming textile community with a population of about 58,160 in 1950. This 1950 population represented a 67 percent increase over the total for 1940. Surrounded by a large metropolitan area, Gretna had an atmosphere of growth similar to that in Algona.

The picture of the Gretna influence structure as developed by the field research team is not clear. Apparently there were at least two influntial cliques operating as rivals in the community. It appears that Gretna's rate of growth was a factor in dispersing the structure of influence in the community. One of the respondents, a professional sociologist living and teaching in Gretna, reported that "the leadership in town was no longer centered in the hands of two or three people." "There were," she believed, "several constellations of powerful people in town rivaling with one another." None of them had steady control over the situation. She attributed this to the rapid growth of the community which, she said, had necessitated the delegation of power and had not permitted any one individual or group to keep control of all of the multiplying activities in the town.

She reported that the Rotary Club was one of the groups which was fairly representative of a large number of leaders. The various textile groups were rival power centers. Other respondents substantiated these judgments about the community influence system. Among the more powerful leaders in town were the President of the Rotary Club, a corporation president (textiles), a local banker, and another local businessman.

Type III—Influence System
(Disorganized, No Identifiable Structure)

Although it seems paradoxical to discuss a disorganized structure, in this case the term is used in lieu of a better one. Communities characterized by this type of influence system exhibit no clear-cut leadership system at least at the informal, nongovernmental level. The two communities discussed below manifested this pattern. Each was also characterized by a relatively stagnant population (rates of population increase from 1940 to 1950 were 18 percent and 00 percent respectively), and a high level of absentee ownership of local businesses. In both cases these communities were located near major metropolitan centers. In one case the business executives who might normally have been looked to for leadership in the influence system lived in a residential community 30 miles removed from the community, and they consistently refused to participate in its activities.

Milton, Michigan was a small east central Michigan community with a population of approximately 17,000 in 1950. This represented an increase of approximately 18 percent over that of 1940. Well within the orbit of Detroit, this town was considered a suburb of the larger metropolitan community.

Historically, Milton had been a recreational and health center offering mineral baths and warm springs. Prior to the First World War the community had been regarded as one of the major centers for this type of service in the entire nation. The hotels were lavishly equipped and attracted many of the wealthiest people in the nation. Due to rising competition from other areas and a general decline in public belief in the medical values of these treatments, the industry waned. At the time of the survey, the community appeared to be in a transitional phase of development. Some of the older families whose fortunes had been made and lost in the bath industry were still active in community affairs. However, their influence had been threatened by an influx of small industries and the expanding control of Detroit.

The survey team was not able to discover a well-defined structure of power in the community. Community leaders who were interviewed on this question generally responded that there was no power structure nor was any individual a dominant power figure. Decisions involving action by the whole community were handled mainly through two channels. These included the board of commerce, which represented most of the business interests of the community, and the city government. One of the native residents of the community explained the power situation in this way:

> The power in this town used to be in the hands of the hotel people. Since the depression these businesses have been losing ground rapidly although the old families still have some power in town. There are no really big factories in town so no one has "taken over" for this reason. Usually, a fairly large number of the business men are involved in making decisions in Milton.

One of the men who was reported to be "very influential" in town reported that:

> There is no concentrated local leadership in town. It is widespread. It takes the whole town to get anything done usually. This is partly due to the fact that there is no industry here.

The community of Norwood, New York, is located on the upper Hudson River about 50 miles from New York. It is one of a cluster of small cities in that area. Industry in the community is dominated by out-of-town owners and managers. In 1950 the total population of the community stood at 31,956. This represented a .02 percent increase over the 1940 figure.

Power in Norwood appeared to have been diffusely organized if any power were exercised at all. The field researcher reported evidence pointing to the conclusion that on many issues facing the community, no effective decisions were ever made. Among the residents of the community there appeared to be a general unwillingness to "identify" with the community. When asked to indicate their "home town," they would frequently say, "I come from the 'New York area'." For several years the town had failed to meet its Community Chest goals in spite of the fact that each year they were lowered.

This lack of leadership in the community probably stems from the lack of a resident owner and a resident managerial class. Some of the businesses are controlled by owners working out of New York and a large proportion of the local managerial stratum lived in a residential suburb several miles from the town. It was reported that this latter group evidenced little interest in local community problems and almost never participated in local affairs.

The executive director of the local Red Cross unit, a long time resident of the town, gave the following account of the organization of influence in the community:

> Old families control the social situation in Norwood but not the political situation. The Jews control the economic situation, but most of them do not live in town. No one group controls the political situation. Both the Protestants and the Catholics contest for control.

The secretary of the chamber of commerce gave the following picture of the community:

> There's no one big industry here in town. Correspondingly, there's no small group of men who control things in town. The control is rather diffuse.

Even the chamber of commerce was divided into small "pressure" groups. This agency's executives agreed that it was very difficult to get any concerted action on a project due to the factional organization of the town. Three men were identified as potential future leaders in the community. They included Samuel Street, the president of the Community Chest for the past few years; Colonel Donald Monroe III, the head of the National Guard in town; and a local businessman.

In concluding his field report the observer noted that "undoubtedly the official representatives of the Norwood government, the mayor and the city manager, wielded some influence." In fact, it is probable that these positions were vested with more power than would ordinarily be the case in a similar community situation where a well-defined power structure existed.

In this case then, the combination of a lack of growth, both in population and in the economic base, plus the absence of the community's "natural leaders" provided a setting in which many community decisions were not made. The community was stagnant, its population lacked *esprit de corps*, and community integration was low.

Summary and Conclusions

On the basis of the evidence from the six cases presented in this study, two conclusions can be drawn. First, community influence systems vary in their shape from those which are highly integrated and peaked to those with virtually no structure of influence. Second, the dynamics of population growth and expansion and the structure of the economic base of the community are two major determinants of the shape of the influence system.

A rapid rate of urban growth is associated with a rapid increase in the number of issues facing community leaders and also with the complexity of these issues. At the same time, the expansion produces new positions of influence and new sources of power. These processes are associated with the development of power cliques and with a reduction of the integration of the influence system. In certain types of disorganized communities no identifiable structure of influence exists. This perhaps is associated with the dominance exerted over the community by a metropolitan regional center.

In view of the profitability of this type of comparative research, it is suggested that future research on the nature of social influence within the community setting be designed within a comparative framework. Additional dimensions, such as the size and composition of the population, the nature of the political structure, the historical background of the community, and the nature of its class system could be systematically investigated for a better understanding of their relation to the structure of the influence system.

4

Changes in Urban Political Structures

Social Classes and Changes in Municipal Government

Industrialization produced a shift in the American occupational structure from an agricultural to an industrial base. The mechanization of agriculture and the creation of new occupational opportunities in our urban centers produced a vast migration from rural to urban areas and from foreign countries to urban America. The settled class hierarchy of Colonial and Federalist America was replaced by an urban class hierarchy laden with propertyless members of the working class.

The emergence of a large urban working class had profound effects on the organization and operation of urban government. The class struggle for local political control was to produce two essentially different conceptions of government in the late nineteenth and early twentieth centuries. In this section we will examine the impact of class participation and class conflict on local governmental structure. Whereas in previous sections we have seen the impact of structure on participation, here we will examine the impact of participation on structure.

The history of municipal government is replete with instances of class struggle for local control. Local government in pre-revolutionary America was controlled by officials named by royally appointed governors and legislatures. This system of appointment continued even after the Revolutionary War—appointment power usually being transferred to the newly formed state legislatures. However, appointed local government was not to last.

The era of Jacksonian Democracy ushered in sweeping changes in the form of local government and the method of selecting municipal officials. The number of elective offices in cities was greatly expanded, wards were instituted, compensation for elected officials was begun, etc. All these changes were designed to increase the responsiveness of local government to the people and to facilitate access to public office by working-class citizens.

The first selection by Walter Hugins outlines one such movement for governmental change—the Workingmen's movement in New York. This movement was directed toward more than governmental change; however, it is the effort to change the structure of New York City's government which concerns us here.

We saw in the first section of this volume that prior to industrialization, mayors in at least three cities (and undoubtedly more) were drawn from the economically powerful segments of the community. The hegemony of the elite over local politics stemmed from many sources which need not concern us here. However, when universal male suffrage was instituted in this country, it provided the basis for sweeping governmental changes to assure the representation of the working classes in government.

New York, according to Hugins, had a government which the working classes felt was unresponsive to their needs. To the Workingmen, government represented a mechanism to destroy the social and political barriers which blocked social betterment for the working classes. In 1829, the Workingmen's Party was formed with the expressed intent of working for the election to office of "the industrious classes." To accomplish this end, several reforms were necessary.

Two of the major reforms pursued by the Workingmen were salaries for public office holders and the establishment of small election districts.

Workingmen could not run for nonremunerative offices since they had no independent means of support. In addition, the Workingmen claimed that unsalaried or low salaried offices attracted men who wanted elected office to exploit the power inherent in patronage appointments or for financial gain to be made by unethical practices. Small election districts were also necessary reforms, the Workingmen contended, in order to insure the representation of all interests in government. Moreover, election campaigns from small districts are cheaper and easier to conduct.

The democratization of local government proceeded to the point where, in many cities, there were a multitude of elected offices with fragmented powers and responsibilities. It is contended by some writers that these decentralized governmental structures were incapable of responding to the growing urban problems found in expanding cities. Often, therefore, a political boss arose who could informally centralize power through the auspices of a political machine. The boss was able to get things done, although at the price of graft and corruption in government.

In the early twentieth century, some men began to propose new types of governmental forms to meet the needs of urban America. The governmental reform movement crusaded for municipal government based on a business model, first with the commission plan and then with the council-manager plan. To these reformers local government was not political, but was a business to be run efficiently so that the "stockholders" (i.e., the citizenry) received the most value for their tax dollars. They viewed the electorate as desirous of efficiency. In other words, the reform movement viewed local government as government by consensus and that consensus was to obtain efficiency. No admission was made by the reformers that all people do not share the same governmental priorities, and that governments resolve conflicting demands through the political process.

Reformers were usually recruited from the ranks of businessmen or professionals (and sometimes the clergy), whereas opponents to reform often were members of the working classes, especially union leaders. The working classes were an opponent of reform in part because it was usually couched in business terms and they distrusted the business community. In addition, there were reasons for working-class opposition which ran deeper than the ideological terms used to promote governmental reform. Some of these reasons are stated in the selection by Samuel P. Hays.

In the second selection Hays contends that studying the ideology of the municipal reform movement is not enough because it can often mask the real reasons behind events. In addition, he says that historians who have studied reform by use of collective biographies are being misled by their results. Most of these studies conclude that the reform movement was a middle-class effort. However, Hays maintains that this tells us very little since most people classify themselves as middle class even though they come from a wide variety of class levels.

Hays begins his presentation of results by saying that reformers were not middle class (or lower class) at all, but were upper-class businessmen. In study after study it has been found that reform movements were spearheaded by chambers of commerce. In one study it was reported that the vote for commission governments was overwhelmingly negative in the working-class districts, overwhelmingly positive in the upper-class districts, and more evenly divided in the middle-class areas. In addition, Hays writes that reformers intended, by their own admission, to install businessmen in their reform governments. Reform government was equated with business-like government by the reformers.

As the economic development of the United States progressed, the interests of businessmen expanded from their own little areas of residence or business to encompass an entire city. Often these businessmen would move to the periphery of a city, but their businesses and their cultural institutions (libraries, concert halls, etc.) remained in the central city. Although it was in the businessmen's interests to control city-wide affairs, city government was quite decentralized. Ward systems especially meant that lower and middle-class interests were represented in city government at the expense of the upper-classes. In order to seize control of municipal government, the business-class reformers worked to substitute more centralized government for the decentralized government of the lower and middle classes. The governmental interests of the lower and middle classes were, according to Hays, diametrically opposed to upper-class interests.

The most crucial reform for the establishment of upper-class political hegemony was the switch from ward to at-large election of councilmen. The elimination of wards effectively eliminated the lower classes from representation in local government. In fact, Hays writes that in some cities, the change from wards to at-large elections was the only reform sought by reform elements.

Although reform was an attempt to change the class base of political control, upper-class interests were not without influence in city government before reform. Often business interests, e.g., utility companies and traction companies, established influence with municipal officials via corrupt practices. However, these corrupt methods were unreliable sources of influence and were abandoned for efforts at reform.

Hays also brings up the question of the "extension of popular democracy" in the reform movement. Many reform charters were presented to cities with the initiative, referendum, and recall incorporated as features of the charter. However, reformers were not consistent in their advocacy of these features, but only favored them when it was in their interests. And, the number of signatures required to call an initiative, referendum, or recall election were often so large that these democratic options were all but inoperable.

The upper-class bias toward reform and the working-class opposition to it is also seen in Edgar Sherbenou's paper, "Class Participation and the Council-Manager Plan." Sherbenou studied suburban cities around Chicago, Illinois. These cities all share a common dependency upon Chicago, but they vary widely in their class composition. Using median housing value as a measure of class composition, Sherbenou studied adoption patterns of council-manager government.

He found that when he arranged the suburban cities in descending order of median housing value, the frequency of council-manager government decreased as he went from the communities with the highest housing values to those with the lowest. In fact, below the median level of median housing value, manager government ceases to appear. Also, the year of adoption of this type of government varies with median housing value. The communities which adopted council-manager government earliest were also those with the highest median housing values. Later adoptions were made by communities down the list. Finally, per capita municipal expenditures, municipal debt, and property taxes differed between the manager and nonmanager cities. Manager cities tended to have higher per capita expenditures, lower municipal debts, and higher per capita property taxes.

Although Sherbenou does not directly address himself to the differing political interests of working and upper-class citizens, his data have definite implications which support the previous works in this section. The wealthiest communities presumably are also the communities with the most homogeneously upper-class populations and these communities would have the least opposition to reform government. As one goes from wealthy communities to less wealthy ones, the latter probably have socially heterogeneous populations. These communities would adopt manager government later than the wealthier communities because of greater resistance to the plan. The least wealthy communities, those most homogeneously working or lower middle class, do not adopt manager government at all because their populations are almost uniformly opposed to the plan. Of course, this explanation is speculative since Sherbenou's aggregate data are not directly applicable to this explanation. However, they are consistent with such an explanation, especially in the light of the other selections included in this section.

In sum, then, class divisions have historically been important in determining the shape of municipal government. Changes in government are related to class composition and the economic structure of communities. (Of course, class structure is a reflection of a community's economic structure.) The lower end of the class spectrum has traditionally favored more grass-roots oriented local government whereas the upper-class elements have favored more centralized government: government which is amenable to their control and which fosters their interests.

Jacksonian Democracy and the Working Class

WALTER HUGINS

The election of Andrew Jackson in 1828 has been viewed as a result of "the rising of the masses"; certainly the scenes at his inauguration seemed, in the eyes of the old order, to demonstrate that King Mob had been enthroned.[1] In New York, the most populous city in the Republic, citizens for the first time voted directly for Presidential electors, and Jackson's triumph was overwhelming. Yet this was not wholly attributable to "the common man," for the Jackson ticket received widespread support in all but the formerly Federalist lower wards.[2] Although both were doubtless symptoms of the same ferment, the rise of the Workingmen's Party during the first year of Jackson's administration was totally unrelated to the political changes in Washington. Neither was it a conscious imitation of the similar political organization which had been active the previous year in Philadelphia.[3] The New York movement, although its origins are somewhat obscure, was largely the result of local factors, economic and social as well as political.

The initial impetus was economic, a protest against unemployment and a defense of the ten-hour day, but social and political grievances soon came to the fore. Increasingly conscious of their subordinate status in society, "mechanics and workingmen" listened avidly to the lectures of Frances Wright and Robert Dale Owen at the newly opened Hall of Science, and pored over their editorials and articles in the *Free Enquirer*, recently transferred to New York from the defunct New Harmony com-

Reprinted from *Jacksonian Democracy and the Working Class: A Study of the New York Workingmen's Movement, 1829–1837* by Walter Hugins with the permission of the publishers, Stanford University Press. © 1960 by the Board of Trustees of the Leland Stanford Junior University.

[1] See Claude G. Bowers, *Party Battles of the Jackson Period* (Boston and New York, 1922), chap. 2.

[2] Fox, *Decline of Aristocracy*, pp. 347–50; Jackson's statewide majority was about 25,000 less than that of Governor Van Buren. See also *American*, November 10, 13, 1828.

[3] For the history of the Philadelphia Workingmen's Party cf. Commons, *History of Labour*, I, 184–216; and Arky, "The Mechanics' Union of Trade Associations," pp. 142–76. It is difficult, if not impossible, to assess the influence of this movement, though it seems inconceivable that New Yorkers could have been ignorant of its existence.

munity.⁴ Not all shared their anticlericalism, but their attacks on banks and other "aristocratical tendencies," and their emphasis on mass education as a solution to social ills, found receptive ears. To this social unrest was joined a deep-seated animosity to caucus politics, as exemplified particularly by the entrenched Tammany machine. Not only were the recently enfranchised restive under its control, but many former adherents of the discredited Adams-Clay party were in search of a new political alignment as their only hope for the future. In many instances disenchantment with apparent obstacles in the way of the popular will was reinforced by specific complaints against the ruling party; significant among these were the lack of mechanics' lien law and the failure to reform the auction system.⁵ All these elements played a part in the rise, and ultimate decline, of the Workingmen's Party.

During the winter of 1828–29 New York City suffered from business stagnation. Unemployment, combined with unusually severe weather, produced widespread destitution, as evidenced by numerous meetings held in February and March to encourage the leading citizens of the metropolis to practice "benevolence" as a palliative for pauperism.⁶ When spring came, some employers attempted to revive the eleven-hour day, even though ten hours had long been established as the norm in most trades. On April 23, 1829, a meeting of "mechanics and others" was called to resist this demand, and the Workingmen's Party was born.⁷ This meeting was sparsely attended, so after some discussion it was adjourned until April 28, when a second and much larger meeting was held. At this time a resolution was passed announcing that all concerned would refuse to work for any employer asking more than "ten hours, well and faithfully employed." A Committee of Fifty was then appointed to collect a relief fund, but little use was made of the money as the employers quickly retreated from their stand. The Committee was also instructed to prepare a report for later presentation on "the causes of the present condition of the poor."⁸ According to George Henry Evans, one of the leaders and first historian of the movement, "great care was taken to have no 'Boss' on the committee . . . [so] a large majority . . . were journeymen."⁹

---

⁴ Miss Wright delivered a series of lectures in New York before Owen's arrival; *Free Enquirer* (New Harmony, Ind.), February 11, 1829. The first issue of the paper published in New York was that of March 4, 1829; both Owen and Miss Wright were listed as editors.

⁵ An anti-auction ticket was nominated in 1828 in opposition to the Democratic Congressional candidates.

⁶ *Morning Herald*, February 26 to March 4, 1829; *American*, March 3, 20, 1829.

⁷ [George H. Evans], "History of the Origin and Progress of the Working Man's Party in New York," *Radical* (Granville, N.J.), January 1842; Evans does not so state, but it is probable that the building trades were most concerned by this demand. A brief notice of the meeting appeared in *Commercial Advertiser*, April 25, 1829.

⁸ Brief proceedings of the meeting were published in *Free Enquirer*, April 29, 1829, and *Morning Herald*, May 1, 1829. See also *Farmers', Merchants', and Working Men's Advocate* (Albany, N.Y.), June 30, 1930.

⁹ *Radical*, January 1842; this assertion cannot be proved, as no list of the Committee members has been found.

The Workingmen's Party, which had arisen out of economic and social grievances and opposition to Tammany management, found itself drifting reluctantly into the Democratic orbit. Its initial success had not only wrung concessions from the enemy—causing some desertions at the hour of triumph—but induced National Republican adventurers to infiltrate its ranks in an effort to capture and utilize the enthusiasm generated by the new party. Personal animosites intensified doctrinal differences until party objectives were nearly subordinated to factional striving for advantage. But, although this movement of "the producing classes" was sundered by ambition and dogmatism, the basic aspirations of the Workingmen remained. Optimistic even in the face of disaster, "A Mechanic" wrote Evans after the election, urging his fellows never to despair of "the progressive improvement of the human mind," which would in time bring the triumph of their cause.[10]

The workingman, incessantly urging that reform proceed further and faster, represented the radical fringe in New York City politics during the evolution of Jacksonian Democracy. Yet is is obvious that this movement must not be epitomized as the anticapitalist striving of a submerged proletariat, nor can it be satisfactorily explained by the epithet "middle class." The source and nature of this radicalism . . . is more complex, and can be further elucidated only with reference to the party platform. Varied and often visionary as were the Workingmen's demands throughout this period, they represented for the most part real grievances and offered concrete solutions. An analysis of this program, showing its relationship to the composition of the movement, provides a key to its socioeconomic orientation.

State and local politics, being more immediate, received their greatest attention and called forth their loudest cries for reform. The Workingmen's advocacy of direct election of the Mayor received support from other groups in 1831, the movement achieving success two years later.[11] Following New York's first experience with the new law in the bitter and violent election of 1834, Evans admitted that "something is necessary to prevent the delay, immorality, and confusion attendant on the present mode of voting in this city." The solution of the Whigs in the newly elected Common Council was compulsory registration of voters, but the Workingmen joined Tammany in denouncing this device as an unconstitutional curtailment of the right of suffrage. Evans objected that not only would it "cause a loss of time, which loss would be more burdensome to the poor than the rich, and would consequently deprive many poor men of their votes," but it would also be ineffective in eliminating illegal voting. "A man *disposed* to vote illegally," he argued, "would stand much

---

[10] Letter published in *Working Man's Advocate*, November 13, 1830.

[11] *Evening Journal*, March 31, 1830; *Working Man's Advocate*, April 3, 1830; *Farmer's, Mechanics', and Working Men's Advocate*, March 12, 1831.

less chance of detection, when registering his name, with few eyes upon him, than when liable to be cross questioned, surrounded by persons interested in detecting him, at the polls." Six years later, when the Whigs revived the registration plan, former Workingmen took a leading part in Tammany meetings called to denounce this "odious and unconstitutional law" for the "disfranchisement of hundreds of our most useful citizens."[12]

Although often finding allies in Tammany Hall in their attacks on the "aristocracy," the Workingmen more frequently denounced "the misrule of the dominant party in this state, and especially in this city." They especially cited the "general ticket" system of nominations as the principal means by which the "dominant corrupt party" maintained its power, and regarded the party convention as no more democratic than the caucus which it had supplanted. Demanding the establishment of election districts smaller than the senatorial district or the county, the Workingmen emphasized that this had worked well in the election of the Common Council; the nomination and election of Aldermen and Assistants by wards allowed *"all interests to be represented"* and resulted in a governing body seldom dominated by one party. In support of this proposal, Evans attacked the existing system for "the facility which it affords for combinations and parties to take the power of nominating candidates out of the hands of the people, and to confer it upon 'committees' and 'conventions' for their own special advantage." Furthermore, he declared, the nomination of candidates is left to "idlers, office holders, and office seekers; for the industrious citizen cannot afford to be absent from his business for a week to attend conventions."[13]

One of the principal reasons given in 1829 for organizing the Workingmen's Party was to elect representatives of "the industrious classes" to office. Yet it was apparent that this was impracticable in the case of offices, like the Common Council, for which no compensation was given. This situation led the Workingmen to advocate that Aldermen and Assistants be paid for their services, pointing out that under the system of gratuitous service "none but large property holders can be elected, . . . for poor men cannot afford to spread their time without receiving an equivalent for their labor." This reform, Evans believed, would also tend to decrease extravagance and corruption. Others, such as the *American*, an anti-Tammany paper, remarked on the "eager competition for places to which no compensation is attached," concluding: "Such places do afford, either by the patronage which results from them, or the opportunities of private jobs, abundant equivalents for the demands upon the time and ordinary

---

[12] *Working Man's Advocate*, April 19, 1834; see also *ibid.*, April 12, November 29, 1834; *Man*, February 20, 1834. The brunt of the Whig attack was directed against naturalized citizens, most of whom voted for the Democrats. For the 1840 agitation on this question see *Democratic-Republican New Era*, February 29, March 19, 20, 25, 1840.

[13] *Sentinel and Working Man's Advocate*, June 23, 1830; *Working Man's Advocate*, August 21, September 18, November 6, 1830. Evans' statement was in *ibid.*, October 29, 1831; see also *ibid.*, March 21, 1835. Congressional districts were first established for the election of 1842; *Plebeian*, November 5, 1842.

avocations of those who occupy them.[14] But Evans disagreed with those who suggested increasing salaries in order to improve the quality of elected officials, declaring that "if *salaries* were not too high, office seekers would be less numerous." Such salaries, he asserted,

> should neither be so high as to make them an inducement for those engaged in useful occupations to *seek* for office, nor so low as not to compensate officials for their time as well as the majority of useful occupations compensate those who follow them. And one *qualification* for public officers of every description should be that they had been brought up to a *useful occupation*, to which they might at any time return if the will of the people should require it.[15]

It was realized, however, that because of strict party control of nominations "the working people" generally choose for legislators men who "have not a single feeling in common with their constituents." To some extent, according to Evans, this could be ascribed to an inordinate respect for formal education, and he reminded his readers that "men who maintain our cause are entitled to our unqualified support at the polls, even though they should not be so well read, as those who *never work*." The Workingmen expressed a special animosity toward lawyers, from whose ranks both major parties drew a high proportion of their candidates. Although a few men of this profession were enlisted in the movement, attorneys were generally denounced as lackeys of the aristocracy and "unceasing promoter[s] of strife" who were "educated, . . . if not in habits of idleness, at least in the habit of looking with contempt . . . upon all sorts of manual labor." As "A Working Man" argued: "The lawyers want office, power, patronage, sinecures, pensions. . . . To obtain distinction and emoluments of this sort, they very naturally unite with men of wealth, and give them banks, monopolies, etc., and with priests and other literary men, to endow colleges and universities for the benefit of a class of men separate and distinct from the working men."[16]

. . . The Workingmen represented an amalgam of skilled mechanics and small businessmen struggling to improve their lot by removing or mitigating social, economic, and political disabilities. While the agitation for enactment of a lien law, like their attack on specific monopolies, was directly related to the interests and aspirations of a particular occupational element in the movement, . . . other issues . . . had a more general appeal. The emphasis upon free public education, abolition of imprisonment for debt, and legal and electoral reform was part of the humanitarian impulse of the times, expressed in equally uncompromis-

---

[14] *Courier and Enquirer*, October 23, 1829; *Farmers', Mechanics', and Working Men's Advocate*, September 1, 1830; *Working Man's Advocate*, June 16, 1832, February 9, 1833; *American*, April 13, 1831.

[15] *Working Man's Advocate*, December 31, 1831; see also *Man*, May 16, 1834.

[16] *Working Man's Advocate*, June 23, 1832; *Sentinel*, October 8, 1832; *Man*, June 28, 1834. For the letter from "A Working Man" see *Working Man's Advocate*, June 23, 1832; cf. other denunciations of lawyers in *Evening Journal*, March 31, 1830; *Sentinel and Working Man's Advocate*, June 23, 1830; Byrdsall, *History*, pp. 73–74.

ing terms by "aristocratic" reformers intellectually descended from the Enlightenment. But for the Workingmen these demands were both based on principle and rooted in experience. Few of them had been able to acquire more than a rudimentary education, and all had been subject to the nuisance of a militia muster; furthermore, though refusing to be cautious or conservative about the future, most of them were intimately acquainted with the dangers of debt. Probably most important was their experience with the legal and political machinery of the Republic, their disillusionment leading them to view it as a denial of justice and democracy. The Workingmen reflected the hopes and fears, as well as the discouragement, of the first generation of enfranchised commoners. Yet they endeavored to exercise this power, not only to gain an effective voice in their own government, but to use political means to break down the barriers standing in the way of their social and economic betterment. That they largely succeeded in these reformist objectives, and in a relatively short time, demonstrates the broad base of the movement and indicates the respect that the evidence of this power engendered in the major political parties.

The Politics of Reform in Municipal Government in the Progressive Era

SAMUEL P. HAYS

In order to achieve a more complete understanding of social change in the Progressive Era, historians must now undertake a deeper analysis of the practices of economic, political, and social groups. Political ideology alone is no longer satisfactory evidence to describe social patterns because generalizations based upon it, which tend to divide political groups into the moral and the immoral, the rational and the irrational, the efficient and the inefficient, do not square with political practice. Behind this contemporary rhetoric concerning the nature of reform lay patterns of political behavior which were at variance with it. Since an extensive gap

Reprinted from the *Pacific Northwest Quarterly* 55 (1964): 157–69. Copyright 1964 by the University of Washington. Reprinted by permission of the author and the publisher.

separated ideology and practice, we can no longer take the former as an accurate description of the latter, but must reconstruct social behavior from other types of evidence.

Reform in urban government provides one of the most striking examples of this problem of analysis. The demand for change in municipal affairs, whether in terms of over-all reform, such as the commission and city-manager plans, or of more piecemeal modifications, such as the development of the city-wide school boards, deeply involved reform ideology. Reformers loudly proclaimed a new structure of municipal government as more moral, more rational, and more efficient and, because it was so, self-evidently more desirable. But precisely because of this emphasis, there seemed to be no need to analyze the political forces behind change. Because the goals of reform were good, its causes were obvious; rather than being the product of particular people and particular ideas in particular situations, they were deeply imbedded in the universal impulses and truths of "progress." Consequently, historians have rarely tried to determine precisely who the municipal reformers were or what they did, but instead have relied on reform ideology as an accurate description of reform practice.

The reform ideology which became the basis of historical analysis is well known. It appears in classic form in Lincoln Steffens' *Shame of the Cities*. The urban political struggle of the Progressive Era, so the argument goes, involved a conflict between public impulses for "good government" against a corrupt alliance of "machine politicians" and "special interests."

During the rapid urbanization of the late 19th century, the latter had been free to aggrandize themselves, especially through franchise grants, at the expense of the public. Their power lay primarily in their ability to manipulate the political process, by bribery and corruption, for their own ends. Against such arrangements there gradually arose a public protest, a demand by the public for honest government, for officials who would act for the public rather than for themselves. To accomplish their goals, reformers sought basic modifications in the political system, both in the structure of government and in the manner of selecting public officials. These changes, successful in city after city, enabled the "public interest" to triumph.[1]

Recently, George Mowry, Alfred Chandler, Jr., and Richard Hofstadter have modified this analysis by emphasizing the fact that the impulse for reform did not come from the working class.[2] This might have been suspected from the rather strained efforts of National Municipal League

---

[1] See, for example, Clifford W. Patton, *Battle for Municipal Reform* (Washington, D.C., 1940), and Frank Mann Stewart, *A Half-Century of Municipal Reform* (Berkeley, 1950).

[2] George E. Mowry, *The California Progressives* (Berkeley and Los Angeles, 1951), pp. 86–104; Richard Hofstadter, *The Age of Reform* (New York, 1955), pp. 131–260; Alfred D. Chandler, Jr., "The Origins of Progressive Leadership," in Elting Morrison *et al.*, (eds.), *Letters of Theodore Roosevelt* (Cambridge, 1951–54), VIII, Appendix III, pp. 1462–64.

writers in the "Era of Reform" to go out of their way to demonstrate working-class support for commission and city-manager governments.[3] We now know that they clutched at straws, and often erroneously, in order to prove to themselves as well as to the public that municipal reform was a mass movement.

The Mowry-Chandler-Hofstadter writings have further modified older views by asserting that reform in general and municipal reform in particular sprang from a distinctively middle-class movement. This has now become the prevailing view. Its popularity is surprising not only because it is based upon faulty logic and extremely limited evidence, but also because it, too, emphasizes the analysis of ideology rather than practice and fails to contribute much to the understanding of who distinctively were involved in reform and why.

Ostensibly, the "middle-class" theory of reform is based upon a new type of behavioral evidence, the collective biography, in studies by Mowry of California Progressive party leaders, by Chandler of a nationwide group of that party's leading figures, and by Hofstadter of four professions—ministers, lawyers teachers, editors. These studies demonstrate the middle-class nature of reform, but they fail to determine if reformers were distinctively middle class, specifically if they differed from their opponents. One study of 300 political leaders in the state of Iowa, for example, discovered that Progressive party, Old Guard, and Cummins Republicans were all substantially alike, the Progressives differing only in that they were slightly younger than the others and had less political experience.[4] If its opponents were also middle class, then one cannot describe Progressive reform as a phenomenon, the special nature of which can be explained in terms of middle-class characteristics. One cannot explain the distinctive behavior of people in terms of characteristics which are not distinctive to them.

Hofstadter's evidence concerning professional men fails in yet another way to determine the peculiar characteristics of reformers. For he describes ministers, lawyers, teachers, and editors without determining who within these professions became reformers and who did not. Two analytical distinctions might be made. Ministers involved in municipal reform, it appears, came not from all segments of religion, but peculiarly from upper-class churches. They enjoyed the highest prestige and salaries in the religious community and had no reason to feel a loss of "status," as Hofstadter argues. Their role in reform arose from the class character of their religious organizations rather than from the mere fact of their occupation as ministers.[5] Professional men involved in reform (many of

[3] Harry A. Toulmin, *The City Manager* (New York, 1915), pp. 156–68; Clinton R. Woodruff, *City Government by Commission* (New York, 1911), pp. 243–53.

[4] Eli Daniel Potts, "A Comparative Study of the Leadership of Republican Factions in Iowa, 1904–1914." M.A. thesis (State University of Iowa, 1956). Another satisfactory comparative analysis is contained in William T. Kerr, Jr., "The Progressives of Washington, 1910–12," *PNQ* 55 (1964): pp. 16–27.

[5] Based upon a study of eleven ministers involved in municipal reform in Pittsburgh, who represented exclusively the upper-class Presbyterian and Episcopal churches.

whom—engineers, architects, and doctors—Hofstadter did not examine at all) seem to have come especially from the more advanced segments of their professions, from those who sought to apply their specialized knowledge to a wider range of public affairs.[6] Their role in reform is related not to their attempt to defend earlier patterns of culture, but to the working out of the inner dynamics of professionalization in modern society.

The weakness of the "middle-class" theory of reform stems from the fact that it rests primarily upon ideological evidence, not on a thorough-going description of political practice. Although the studies of Mowry, Chandler, and Hofstadter ostensibly derive from behavioral evidence, they actually derive largely from the extensive expressions of middle-ground ideological position, of the reformers' own descriptions of their contemporary society, and of their expressed fears of both the lower and the upper classes, of the fright of being ground between the millstones of labor and capital.[7]

Such evidence, though it accurately portrays what people thought, does not accurately describe what they did. The great majority of Americans look upon themselves as "middle class" and subscribe to a middle-ground ideology, even though in practice they belong to a great variety of distinct social classes. Such ideologies are not rationalizations of deliberate attempts to deceive. They are natural phenomena of human behavior. But the historian should be especially sensitive to their role so that he will not take evidence of political ideology as an accurate representation of political practice.

In the following account I will summarize evidence in both secondary and primary works concerning the political practices in which municipal reformers were involved. Such an analysis logically can be broken down into three parts, each one corresponding to a step in the traditional argument. First, what was the source of reform? Did it lie in the general public rather than in particular groups? Was it middle class, working class, or perhaps of other composition? Second, what was the reform target of attack? Were reformers primarily interested in ousting the corrupt individual, the political or business leader who made private arrangements at the expense of the public, or were they interested in something else? Third, what political innovations did reformers bring about? Did they seek to expand popular participation in the governmental process?

There is now sufficient evidence to determine the validity of these specific elements of the more general argument. Some of it has been available for several decades; some has appeared more recently; some is presented here for the first time. All of it adds up to the conclusion that reform in municipal government involved a political development far different from what we have assumed in the past.

Available evidence indicates that the source of support for reform in municipal government did not come from the lower or middle classes, but

---

[6] Based upon a study of professional men involved in municipal reform in Pittsburgh, comprising eighty-three doctors, twelve architects, twenty-five educators, and thirteen engineers.

[7] See especially Mowry, *The California Progressives*.

from the upper class. The leading business groups in each city and professional men closely allied with them initiated and dominated municipal movements. Leonard White, in his study of the city manager published in 1927, wrote:

The opposition to bad government usually comes to a head in the local chamber of commerce. Business men finally acquire the conviction that the growth of their city is being seriously impaired by the failures of city officials to perform their duties efficiently. Looking about for a remedy, they are captivated by the resemblance of the city-manager plan to their corporate form of business organization.[8]

In the 1930s White directed a number of studies of the origin of city-manager government. The resulting reports invariably begin with such statements as, "the Chamber of Commerce spearheaded the movement," or commission government in this city was a "businessmen's government."[9] Of thirty-two cases of city-manager government in Oklahoma examined by Jewell C. Phillips, twenty-nine were initiated either by chambers of commerce or by community committees dominated by businessmen.[10] More recently James Weinstein has presented almost irrefutable evidence that the business community, represented largely by chambers of commerce, was the overwhelming force behind both commission and city-manager movements.[11]

Dominant elements of the business community played a prominent role in another crucial aspect of municipal reform: the Municipal Research Bureau movement.[12] Especially in the larger cities, where they had less success in shaping the structure of government, reformers established centers to conduct research in municipal affairs as a springboard for influence.

The first such organization, the Bureau of Municipal Research of New York City, was founded in 1906; it was financed largely through the efforts of Andrew Carnegie and John D. Rockefeller. An investment banker provided the crucial support in Philadelphia, where a Bureau was founded in 1908. A group of wealthy Chicagoans in 1910 established the Bureau of Public Efficiency, a research agency. John H. Patterson of the National Cash Register Company, the leading figure in Dayton municipal reform,

---

[8] Leonard White, *The City Manager* (Chicago, 1927), pp. ix–x.

[9] Harold A. Stone et al., *City Manager Government in Nine Cities* (Chicago, 1940); Frederick C. Mosher et al., *City Manager Government in Seven Cities* (Chicago, 1940); Harold A. Stone et al., *City Manager Government in the United States* (Chicago, 1940). Cities covered by these studies include: Austin, Texas; Charlotte, North Carolina; Dallas, Texas; Dayton, Ohio; Fredericksburg, Virginia; Jackson, Michigan; Janesville, Wisconsin; Kingsport, Tennessee; Lynchburg, Virginia; Rochester, New York; San Diego, California.

[10] Jewell Cass Phillips, *Operation of the Council-Manager Plan of Government in Oklahoma Cities* (Philadelphia, 1935), pp. 31–39.

[11] James Weinstein, "Organized Business and the City Commission and Manager Movements," *Journal of Southern History* XXVIII (1962): 166–82.

[12] Norman N. Gill, *Municipal Research Bureaus* (Washington, 1944).

financed the Dayton Bureau, founded in 1912. And George Eastman was the driving force behind both the Bureau of Municipal Research and city-manager government in Rochester. In smaller cities data about city government was collected by interested individuals in a more informal way or by chambers of commerce, but in larger cities the task required special support, and prominent businessmen supplied it.

The character of municipal reform is demonstrated more precisely by a brief examination of the movements in Des Moines and Pittsburgh. The Des Moines Commercial Club inaugurated and carefully controlled the drive for the commission form of government.[13] In January, 1906 the Club held a so-called "mass meeting" of business and professional men to secure an enabling act from the state legislature. P. C. Kenyon, president of the Club, selected a Committee of 300, composed principally of business and professional men, to draw up a specific proposal. After the legislature approved their plan, the same committee managed the campaign which persuaded the electorate to accept the commission form of government by a narrow margin in June, 1907.

In this election the lower-income wards of the city opposed the change, the upper-income wards supported it strongly, and the middle-income wards were more evenly divided. In order to control the new government, the Committee of 300, now expanded to 530, sought to determine the nomination and election of the five new commissioners, and to this end they selected an avowedly businessman's slate. Their plans backfired when the voters swept into office a slate of anticommission candidates who now controlled the new commission government.

Proponents of the commission form of government in Des Moines spoke frequently in the name of the "people." But their more explicit statements emphasized their intent that the new plan be a "business system" of government, run by businessmen. The slate of candidates for commissioner endorsed by advocates of the plan was known as the "businessman's ticket." J. W. Hill, president of the committees of 300 and 530, bluntly declared: "The professional politician must be ousted and in his place capable businessmen chosen to conduct the affairs of the city." I. M. Earle, general counsel of the Bankers Life Association and a prominent figure in the movement, put the point more precisely: "When the plan was adopted it was the intention to get businessmen to run it."

Although reformers used the ideology of popular government, they in no sense meant that all segments of society should be involved equally in municipal decision-making. They meant that their concept of the city's welfare would be best achieved if the business community controlled city government. As one businessman told a labor audience, the businessman's slate represented labor "better than you do yourself."

The composition of the municipal reform movement in Pittsburgh dem-

---

[13] This account of the movement for commission government in Des Moines is derived from items in the Des Moines *Register* during the years from 1905 through 1908.

onstrates its upper-class and professional as well as its business sources.[14] Here the two principal reform organizations were the Civic Club and the Voters' League. The 745 members of these two organizations came primarily from the upper class. Sixty-five percent appeared in upper-class directories which contained the names of only 2 percent of the city's families. Furthermore, many who were not listed in these directories lived in upper-class areas. These reformers, it should be stressed, comprised not an old but a new upper class. Few came from earlier industrial and mercantile families. Most of them had risen to social position from wealth created after 1870 in the iron, steel, electrical equipment, and other industries, and they lived in the newer rather than the older fashionable areas.

Almost half (48 percent) of the reformers were professional men: doctors, lawyers, ministers, directors of libraries and museums, engineers, architects, private and public school teachers, and college professors. Some of these belonged to the upper class as well, especially the lawyers, ministers, and private school teachers. But for the most part their interest in reform stemmed from the inherent dynamics of their professions rather than from their class connections. They came from the more advanced segments of their organizations, from those in the forefront of the acquisition and application of knowledge. They were not the older professional men, seeking to preserve the past against change; they were in the vanguard of professional life, actively seeking to apply expertise more widely to public affairs.

Pittsburgh reformers included a large segment of businessmen; 52 percent were bankers and corporation officials or their wives. Among them were the presidents of fourteen large banks and officials of Westinghouse, Pittsburgh Plate Glass, U.S. Steel and its component parts (such as Carnegie Steel, American Bridge, and National Tube), Jones and Laughlin, lesser steel companies (such as Crucible, Pittsburgh, Superior, Lockhart, and H. K. Porter), the H. J. Heinz Company, and the Pittsburgh Coal Company, as well as officials of the Pennsylvania Railroad and the Pittsburgh and Lake Erie. These men were not small businessmen; they directed the most powerful banking and industrial organizations of the city. They represented not the old business community, but industries which had developed and grown primarily within the past fifty years and which had come to dominate the city's economic life.

These business, professional, and upper-class groups who dominated municipal reform movements were all involved in the rationalization and systematization of modern life; they wished a form of government which would be more consistent with the objectives inherent in those developments. The most important single feature of their perspective was the rapid expansion of the geographical scope of affairs which they wished to

[14] Biographical data constitutes the main source of evidence for this study of Pittsburgh reform leaders. It was found in city directories, social registers, directories of corporate directors, biographical compilations, reports of boards of education, settlement houses, welfare organizations, and similar types of material. Especially valuable was the clipping file maintained at the Carnegie Library of Pittsburgh.

influence and manipulate, a scope which was no longer limited and narrow, no longer within the confines of pedestrian communities, but was now broad and city-wide, covering the whole range of activities of the metropolitan area.

The migration of the upper class from central to outlying areas created a geographical distance between its residential communities and its economic institutions. To protect the latter required involvement both in local ward affairs and in the larger city government as well. Moreover, upper-class cultural institutions, such as museums, libraries, and symphony orchestras, required an active interest in the larger municipal context from which these institutions drew much of their clientele.

Professional groups, broadening the scope of affairs which they sought to study, measure, or manipulate, also sought to influence the public health, the educational system, or the physical arrangements of the entire city. Their concerns were limitless, not bounded by geography, but as expansive as the professional imagination. Finally, the new industrial community greatly broadened its perspective in governmental affairs because of its new recognition of the way in which factors throughout the city affected business growth. The increasing size and scope of industry, the greater stake in more varied and geographically dispersed facets of city life, the effect of floods on many business concerns, the need to promote traffic flows to and from work for both blue-collar and managerial employees—all contributed to this larger interest. The geographically larger private perspectives of upper-class, professional, and business groups gave rise to a geographically larger public perspective.

These reformers were dissatisfied with existing systems of municipal government. They did not oppose corruption per se—although there was plenty of that. They objected to the structure of government which enabled local and particularistic interests to dominate. Prior to the reforms of the Progressive Era, city government consisted primarily of confederations of local wards, each of which was represented on the city's legislative body. Each ward frequently had its own elementary schools and ward-elected school boards which administered them.

These particularistic interests were the focus of a decentralized political life. City councilmen were local leaders. They spoke for their local areas, the economic interests of their inhabitants, their residential concerns, their educational, recreational, and religious interests—i.e., for those aspects of community life which mattered most of those they represented. They rolled logs in the city council to provide streets, sewers, and other public works for their local areas. They defended the community's cultural practices, its distinctive languages or national customs, its liberal attitude toward liquor, and its saloons and dance halls which served as centers of community life. One observer described this process of representation in Seattle:

The residents of the hill-tops and the suburbs may not fully appreciate the faithfulness of certain downtown ward councilmen to the interests of their constituents. . . . The people of a state would rise in arms against a senator or representative in Congress who deliberately misrepresented their wishes and imperiled their interests, though he might plead a higher regard for national good. Yet people in other parts of the city seem to forget that under the old system the ward elected councilmen with the idea of procuring service of special benefit to that ward.[15]

In short, pre-reform officials spoke for their constituencies, inevitably their own wards which had elected them, rather than for other sections or groups of the city.

The ward system of government especially gave representation in city affairs to lower- and middle-class groups. Most elected ward officials were from these groups, and they, in turn, constituted the major opposition to reforms in municipal government. In Pittsburgh, for example, immediately prior to the changes in both the city council and the school board in 1911 in which city-wide representation replaced ward representation, only 24 percent of the 387 members of those bodies represented the same managerial, professional, and banker occupations which dominated the membership of the Civic Club and the Voters' League. The great majority (67 percent) were small businessmen—grocers, saloonkeepers, livery-stable proprietors, owners of small hotels, druggists—white-collar workers such as clerks and bookkeepers, and skilled and unskilled workmen.[16]

This decentralized system of urban growth and the institutions which arose from it reformers now opposed. Social, professional, and economic life had developed not only in the local wards in a small community context, but also on a larger scale had become highly integrated and organized, giving rise to a superstructure of social organization which lay far above that of ward life and which was sharply divorced from it in both personal contacts and perspective.

By the late 19th century, those involved in these larger institutions found that the decentralized system of political life limited their larger objectives. The movement for reform in municipal government, therefore, constituted an attempt by upper-class, advanced professional, and large business groups to take formal political power from the previously dominant lower- and middle-class elements so that they might advance their own conceptions of desirable public policy. These two groups came from entirely different urban worlds, and the political system fashioned by one was no longer acceptable to the other.

Lower- and middle-class groups not only dominated the pre-reform governments, but vigorously opposed reform. It is significant that none of the occupational groups among them, for example, small businessmen or white-collar workers, skilled or unskilled artisans, had important representation in reform organizations thus far examined. The case studies of city-manager government undertaken in the 1930s under the direction of Leonard White detailed in city after city the particular opposition of labor. In their analysis of Jackson, Michigan, the authors of these studies wrote:

[15] *Town Crier* (Seattle), Feb. 18, 1911, p. 13.
[16] Information derived from same sources as cited in n. 14.

The *Square Deal*, oldest Labor paper in the state, has been consistently against manager government, perhaps largely because labor has felt that with a decentralized government elected on a ward basis it was more likely to have some voice and to receive its share of privileges.[17]

In Janesville, Wisconsin, the small shopkeepers and workingmen on the west and south sides, heavily Catholic and often Irish, opposed the commission plan in 1911 and in 1912 and the city-manager plan when adopted in 1923.[18] "In Dallas there is hardly a trace of class consciousness in the Marxian sense," one investigator declared, "yet in city elections the division has been to a great extent along class lines."[19] The commission and city-manager elections were no exceptions. To these authors it seemed a logical reaction, rather than an embarrassing fact that had to be swept away, that workingmen should have opposed municipal reform.[20]

In Des Moines working-class representatives, who in previous years might have been council members, were conspicuously absent from the "businessman's slate." Workingmen acceptable to reformers could not be found. A workingman's slate of candidates, therefore, appeared to challenge the reform slate. Organized labor, and especially the mineworkers, took the lead; one of their number, Wesley Ash, a deputy sheriff and union member, made "an astonishing run" in the primary, coming in second among a field of more than twenty candidates.[21] In fact, the strength of anticommission candidates in the primary so alarmed reformers that they frantically sought to appease labor.

The day before the final election they modified their platform to pledge both an eight-hour day and an "American standard of wages." They attempted to persuade the voters that their slate consisted of men who represented labor because they had "begun at the bottom of the ladder and made a good climb toward success by their own unaided efforts."[22] But their tactics failed. In the election on March 30, 1908, voters swept into office the entire "opposition" slate. The business and professional community had succeeded in changing the form of government, but not in securing its control. A cartoon in the leading reform newspaper illustrated their disappointment; John Q. Public sat dejectedly and muttered, "Aw, What's the Use?"

The most visible opposition to reform and the most readily available target of reform attack was the so-called "machine," for through the "machine" many different ward communities as well as lower- and middle-income groups joined effectively to influence the central city government. Their private occupational and social life did not naturally involve these groups in larger city-wide activities in the same way as the

---

[17] Stone *et al.*, *Nine Cities*, p. 212.

[18] *Ibid.*, pp. 3–13.

[19] *Ibid.*, p. 329.

[20] Stone *et al.*, *City Manager Government*, 26, 237–41, for analysis of opposition to city-manager government.

[21] Des Moines *Register and Leader*, March 17, 1908.

[22] *Ibid.*, March 30, March 28, 1908.

upper class was involved; hence they lacked access to privately organized economic and social power on which they could construct political power. The "machine" filled this organizational gap.

Yet it should never be forgotten that the social and economic institutions in the wards themselves provided the "machine's" sustaining support and gave it larger significance. When reformers attacked the "machine" as the most visible institutional element of the ward system, they attacked the entire ward form of political organization and the political power of lower- and middle-income groups which lay behind it.

Performers often gave the impression that they opposed merely the corrupt politician and his "machine." But in a more fundamental way they looked upon the deficiencies of pre-reform political leaders in terms not of their personal shortcomings, but of the limitations inherent in their occupational, institutional, and class positions. In 1911 the Voters' League of Pittsburgh wrote in its pamphlet analyzing the qualifications of candidates that "a man's occupation ought to give a strong indication of his qualifications for membership on a school board."[23] Certain occupations inherently disqualified a man from serving:

Employment as ordinary laborer and in the lowest class of mill work would naturally lead to the conclusion that such men did not have sufficient education or business training to act as school directors. . . . Objection might also be made to small shopkeepers, clerks, workmen at many trades, who by lack of educational advantages and business training, could not, no matter how honest, be expected to administer properly the affairs of an educational system, requiring special knowledge, and where millions are spent each year.

These, of course, were precisely the groups which did dominate Pittsburgh government prior to reform. The League deplored the fact that school boards contained only a small number of "men prominent throughout the city in business life . . . in professional occupations . . . holding positions as managers, secretaries, auditors, superintendents and foremen" and exhorted these classes to participate more actively as candidates for office.

Reformers, therefore, wished not simply to replace bad men with good; they proposed to change the occupational and class origins of decision-makers. Toward this end they sought innovations in the formal machinery of government which would concentrate political power by sharply centralizing the processes of decision-making rather than distribute it through more popular participation in public affairs. According to the liberal view of the Progressive Era, the major political innovations of reform involved the equalization of political power through the primary, the direct election of public officials, and the initiative, referendum, and recall. These measures played a large role in the political ideology of the time and were frequently incorporated into new municipal charters. But they provided at best only an occasional and often incidental process of

[23] Voters' Civic League of Allegheny County, "Bulletin of the Voters' Civic League of Allegheny County Concerning the Public School System of Pittsburgh," Feb. 14, 1911, pp. 2–3.

decision-making. Far more important in continuous, sustained, day-to-day processes of government were those innovations which centralized decision-making in the hands of fewer and fewer people.

The systematization of municipal government took place on both the executive and the legislative levels. The strong-mayor and city-manager types become the most widely used examples of the former. In the first decade of the 20th century, the commission plan had considerable appeal, but its distribution of administrative responsibility among five people gave rise to a demand for a form with more centralized executive power; consequently, the city-manager or the commission-manager variant often replaced it.[24]

A far more pervasive and significant change, however, lay in the centralization of the system of representation, the shift from ward to city-wide election of councils and school boards. Governing bodies so selected, reformers argued, would give less attention to local and particularistic matters and more to affairs of city-wide scope. This shift, an invariable feature of both commission and city-manager plans, was often adopted by itself. In Pittsburgh, for example, the new charter of 1911 provided as the major innovation that a council of twenty-seven, each member elected from a separate ward, be replaced by a council of nine, each elected by the city as a whole.

Cities displayed wide variations in this innovation. Some regrouped wards into larger units but kept the principle of areas of representation smaller than the entire city. Some combined a majority of councilmen elected by wards with additional ones selected at large. All such innovations, however, constituted steps toward the centralization of the system of representation.

Liberal historians have not appreciated the extent to which municipal reform in the Progressive Era involved a debate over the system of representation. The ward form of representation was universally condemned on the grounds that it gave too much influence to the separate units and not enough attention to the larger problems of the city. Harry A. Toulmin, whose book, *The City Manager*, was published by the National Municipal League, stated the case:

The spirit of sectionalism had dominated the political life of every city. Ward pitted against ward, alderman against alderman, and legislation only effected by "long-rolling" extravagant measures into operation, mulcting the city, but gratifying the greed of constituents, has too long stung the conscience of decent citizenship. This constant treaty-making of factionalism has been no less than a curse. The city manager plan proposes the commendable thing of abolishing wards. The plan is not unique in this for it has been common to many forms of commission government. . . .[25]

---

[24] In the decade 1911 to 1920, 45 percent of the municipal charters adopted in eleven home rule states involved the commission form and 35 percent the city-manager form; in the following decade the figures stood at 6 percent and 71 percent respectively. The adoption of city-manager charters reached a peak in the years 1918 through 1923 and declined sharply after 1933. See Leonard D. White, "The Future of Public Administration," *Public Management* XV (1933): 12.

[25] Toulmin, *The City Manager*, p. 42.

Such a system should be supplanted, the argument usually went, with city-wide representation in which elected officials could consider the city "as a unit." "The new officers are elected," wrote Toulmin, "each to represent all the people. Their duties are so defined that they must administer the corporate business in its entirety, not as a hodge-podge of associated localities."

Behind the debate over the method of representation, however, lay a debate over who should be represented, over whose views of public policy should prevail. Many reform leaders often explicitly, if not implicitly, expressed fear that lower- and middle-income groups had too much influence in decision-making. One Galveston leader, for example, complained about the movement for initiative, referendum, and recall:

> We have in our city a very large number of negroes employed on the docks; we also have a very large number of unskilled white laborers; this city also has more barrooms, according to its population, than any other city in Texas. Under these circumstances it would be extremely difficult to maintain a satisfactory city government where all ordinances must be submitted back to the voters of the city for their ratification and approval.[26]

At the National Municipal League convention of 1907, Rear Admiral F. E. Chadwick (USN Ret.), a leader in the Newport, Rhode Island, movement for municipal reform, spoke to this question even more directly:

> Our present system has excluded in large degree the representation of those who have the city's well-being most at heart. It has brought, in municipalities . . . a government established by the least educated, the least interested class of citizens.
>
> It stands to reason that a man paying $5,000 taxes in a town is more interested in the well-being and development of his town than the man who pays no taxes. . . . It equally stands to reason that the man of the $5,000 tax should be assured a representation in the committee which lays the tax and spends the money which he contributes. . . . Shall we be truly democratic and give the property owner a fair show or shall we develop a tyranny of ignorance which shall crush him?[27]

Municipal reformers thus debated frequently the question of who should be represented as well as the question of what method of representation should be employed.

That these two questions were intimately connected was revealed in other reform proposals for representation, proposals which were rarely taken seriously. One suggestion was that a class system of representation be substituted for ward representation. For example, in 1908 one of the prominent candidates for commissioner in Des Moines proposed that the city council be composed of representatives of five classes: educational and ministerial organizations, manufacturers and jobbers, public utility cor-

---

[26] Woodruff, *City Government*, p. 315. The Galveston commission plan did not contain provisions for the initiative, referendum, or recall, and Galveston commercial groups which had fathered the commission plan opposed movements to include them. In 1911 Governor Colquitt of Texas vetoed a charter bill for Texarkana because it contained such provisions; he maintained that they were "undemocratic" and unnecessary to the success of commission government. *Ibid.*, pp. 314–15.

[27] *Ibid.*, pp. 207–8.

porations, retail merchants including liquor men, and the Des Moines Trades and Labor Assembly. Such a system would have greatly reduced the influence in the council of both middle- and lower-class groups. The proposal revealed the basic problem confronting business and professional leaders: how to reduce the influence in government of the majority of voters among middle- and lower-income groups.[28]

A growing imbalance between population and representation sharpened the desire of reformers to change from ward to city-wide elections. Despite shifts in population within most cities, neither ward district lines nor the apportionment of city council and school board sets changed frequently. Consequently, older areas of the city, with wards that were small in geographical size and held declining populations (usually lower and middle class in composition), continued to be overrepresented, and newer upper-class areas, where population was growing, became increasingly underrepresented. This intensified the reformers' conviction that the structure of government must be changed to give them the voice they needed to make their views on public policy prevail.[29]

It is not insignificant that in some cities (by no means a majority) municipal reform came about outside of the urban electoral process. The original commission government in Galveston was appointed rather than elected. "The failure of previous attempts to secure an efficient city government through the local electorate made the businsss man of Galveston willing to put the conduct of the city's affairs in the hands of a commission dominated by state-appointed officials."[30] Only in 1903 did the courts force Galveston to elect the members of the commission, an innovation which one writer described as "an abandonment of the commission idea," and which led to the decline of the influence of the business community in the commission government.[31]

In 1911 Pittsburgh voters were not permitted to approve either the new city charter or the new school board plan, both of which provided for city-wide representation; they were a result of state legislative enactment. The governor appointed the first members of the new city council, but thereafter they were elected. The judges of the court of common pleas, however, and not the voters, selected members of the new school board.

The composition of the new city council and new school board in Pittsburgh, both of which were inaugurated in 1911, revealed the degree to which the shift from ward to city-wide representation produced a change in group representation.[32] Members of the upper class, the advanced professional men, and the larger business groups dominated both. Of the fifteen members of the Pittsburgh Board of Education appointed in 1911 and the nine members of the new city council, none were small business-

---

[28] Des Moines *Register and Leader*, Jan. 15, 1908.

[29] Voters' Civic League of Allegheny County, "Report on the Voters' League in the Redistricting of the Wards of the City of Pittsburgh" (Pittsburgh, n.d.).

[30] Horace E. Deming, "The Government of American Cities," in Woodruff, *City Government*, p. 167.

[31] *Ibid.*, p. 168.

[32] Information derived from same sources as cited in n. 14.

men or white-collar workers. Each body contained only one person who could remotely be classified as a blue-collar worker; each of these men filled a position specifically but unofficially designed as reserved for a "representative of labor," and each was an official of the Amalgamated Association of Iron, Steel, and Tin Workers. Six of the nine members of the new city council were prominent businessmen, and all six were listed in upper-class directories. Two others were doctors closely associated with the upper class in both professional and social life. The fifteen members of the Board of Education included ten businessmen with city-wide interests, one doctor associated with the upper class, and three women previously active in upper-class public welfare.

Lower- and middle-class elements felt that the new city governments did not represent them.[33] The studies carried out under the direction of Leonard White contain numerous expressions of the way in which the change in the structure of government produced not only a change in the geographical scope of representation, but also in the groups represented. "It is not the policies of the manager or the council they oppose," one researcher declared, "as much as the lack of representation for their economic level and social groups."[34] And another wrote:

There had been nothing unapproachable about the old ward aldermen. Every voter had a neighbor on the common council who was interested in serving him. The new councilmen, however, made an unfavorable impression on the less well-to-do voters. . . . Election at large made a change that, however desirable in other ways, left the voters in the poorer wards with a feeling that they had been deprived of their share of political importance.[35]

The success of the drive for centralization of administration and representation varied with the size of the city. In the smaller cities, business, professional, and elite groups could easily exercise a dominant influence. Their close ties readily enabled them to shape informal political power which they could transform into formal political power. After the mid-1890s the widespread organization of chambers of commerce provided a base for political action to reform municipal government, resulting in a host of small-city commission and city-manager innovations. In the larger, more heterogeneous cities, whose subcommunities were more dispersed, such community-wide action was extremely difficult. Few commission or city-manager proposals materialized here. Mayors became stronger, and steps were taken toward centralization of representation, but the ward system or some modified version usually persisted. Reformers in large cities often had to rest content with their Municipal Research Bureaus through which they could exert political influence from outside the municipal government.

[33] W. R. Hopkins, city manager of Cleveland, indicated the degree to which the new type of government was more responsive to the business community: "It is undoubtedly easier for a city manager to insist upon acting in accordance with the business interests of the city than it is for a mayor to do the same thing." Quoted in White, *The City Manager*, p. 13.

[34] Stone *et al.*, *Nine Cities*, p. 20.

[35] *Ibid.*, p. 225.

A central element in the analysis of municipal reform in the Progressive Era is governmental corruption. Should it be understood in moral or political terms? Was it a product of evil men or of particular sociopolitical circumstances? Reform historians have adopted the former view. Selfish and evil men arose to take advantage of a political arrangement whereby unsystematic government offered many opportunities for personal gain at public expense. The system thrived until the "better elements," "men of intelligence and civic responsibility," or "right-thinking people" ousted the culprits and fashioned a political force which produced decisions in the "public interest." In this scheme of things, corruption in public affairs grew out of individual personal failings and a deficient governmental structure which could not hold those predispositions in check, rather than from the peculiar nature of social forces. The contestants involved were morally defined: evil men who must be driven from power, and good men who must be activated politically to secure control of municipal affairs.

Public corruption, however, involves political even more than moral considerations. It arises more out of the particular distribution of political power than of personal morality. For corruption is a device to exercise control and influence outside the legal channels of decision-making when those channels are not readily responsive. Most generally, corruption stems from an inconsistency between control of the instruments of formal governmental power and the exercise of informal influence in the community. If powerful groups are denied access to formal power in legitimate ways, they seek access through procedures which the community considers illegitimate. Corrupt government, therefore, does not reflect the genius of evil men, but rather the lack of acceptable means for those who exercise power in the private community to wield the same influence in governmental affairs. It can be understood in the Progressive Era not simply by the preponderance of evil men over good, but by the peculiar nature of the distribution of political power.

The political corruption of the "Era of Reform" arose from the inaccessibility of municipal government to those who were rising in power and influence. Municipal government in the United States developed in the 19th century within a context of universal manhood suffrage which decentralized political control. Because all men, whatever their economic, social, or cultural conditions, could vote, leaders who reflected a wide variety of community interests and who represented the views of people of every circumstance arose to guide and direct municipal affairs. Since the majority of urban voters were workingmen or immigrants, the views of those groups carried great and often decisive weight in governmental affairs. Thus, as Herbert Gutman has shown, during strikes in the 1870s city officials were usually friendly to workingmen and refused to use police power to protect strikebreakers.[36]

---

[36] Herbert Gutman, "An Iron Workers' Strike in the Ohio Valley, 1873–74," *Ohio Historical Quarterly*, LXVIII (1959): 353–70; "Trouble on the Railroads, 1873–1874: Prelude to the 1877 Crisis," *Labor History*, II (1961): 215–36.

Ward representation on city councils was an integral part of grass-roots influence, for it enabled diverse urban communities, invariably identified with particular geographical areas of the city, to express their views more clearly through councilmen peculiarly receptive to their concerns. There was a direct, reciprocal flow of power between wards and the center of city affairs in which voters felt a relatively close connection with public matters and city leaders gave special attention to their needs.

Within this political system the community's business leaders grew in influence and power as industrialism advanced, only to find that their economic position did not readily admit them to the formal machinery of government. Thus, during strikes, they had to rely on either their own private police, Pinkertons, or the state militia to enforce their use of strikebreakers. They frequently found that city officials did not accept their views of what was best for the city and what direction municipal policies should take. They had developed a common outlook, closely related to their economic activities, that the city's economic expansion should become the prime concern of municipal government, and yet they found that this view had to compete with even more influential views of public policy. They found that political tendencies which arose from universal manhood suffrage and ward representation were not always friendly to their political conceptions and goals and had produced a political system over which they had little control, despite the fact that their economic ventures were the core of the city's prosperity and the hope for future urban growth.

Under such circumstances, businessmen sought other methods of influencing municipal affairs. They did not restrict themselves to the channels of popular election and representation, but frequently applied direct influence—if not verbal persuasion, then bribery and corruption. Thereby arose the graft which Lincoln Steffens recounted in his *Shame of the Cities*. Utilities were only the largest of those business groups and individuals who requested special favors, and the franchises they sought were only the most sensational of the prizes which included such items as favorable tax assessments and rates, the vacating of streets wanted for factory expansion, or permission to operate amid antiliquor and other laws regulating personal behavior. The relationships between business and formal government became a maze of accommodations, a set of political arrangements which grew up because effective power had few legitimate means of accomplishing its ends.

Steffens and subsequent liberal historians, however, misread the significance of these arrangements, emphasizing their personal rather than their more fundamental institutional elements. To them corruption involved personal arrangements between powerful business leaders and powerful "machine" politicians. Just as they did not fully appreciate the significance of the search for political influence by the rising business community as a whole, so they did not see fully the role of the "ward politician." They stressed the argument that the political leader manipulated voters to his own personal ends, that he used constituents rather than reflected their views.

A different approach is now taking root, namely, that the urban political organization was an integral part of community life, expressing its needs and its goals. As Oscar Handlin has said, for example, the "machine" not only fulfilled specific wants, but provided one of the few avenues to success and public recognition available to the immigrant.[37] The political leader's arrangements with businessmen, therefore, were not simply personal agreements between conniving individuals; they were far-reaching accommodations between powerful sets of institutions in industrial America.

These accommodations, however, proved to be burdensome and unsatisfactory to the business community and to the upper third of socio-economic groups in general. They were expensive; they were wasteful; they were uncertain. Toward the end of the 19th century, therefore, business and professional men sought more direct control over municipal government in order to exercise political influence more effectively. They realized their goals in the early 20th century in the new commission and city-manager forms of government and in the shift from ward to city-wide representation.

These innovations did not always accomplish the objectives that the business community desired because other forces could and often did adjust to the change in governmental structure and reestablish their influence. But businessmen hoped that reform would enable them to increase their political power, and most frequently it did. In most cases the innovations which were introduced between 1901, when Galveston adopted a commission from of government, and the Great Depression, and especially the city-manager form which reached a height of popularity in the mid-1920s, served as vehicles whereby business and professional leaders moved directly into the inner circles of government, brought into one political system their own power and the formal machinery of government, and dominated municipal affairs for two decades.

Municipal reform in the early 20th century involves a paradox: the ideology of an extension of political control and the practice of its concentration. While reformers maintained that their movement rested on a wave of popular demands, called their gatherings of business and professional leaders "mass meetings," described their reforms as "part of a world-wide trend toward popular government," and proclaimed an ideology of a popular upheaval against a selfish few, they were in practice shaping the structure of municipal government so that political power would no longer be broadly distributed, but would in fact be more centralized in the hands of a relatively small segment of the population. The paradox became even sharper when new city charters included provisions for the initiative, referendum, and recall. How does the historian cope with this paradox? Does it represent deliberate deception or simply political strategy? Or does it reflect a phenomenon which should be understood rather than explained away?

The expansion of popular involvement in decision-making was fre-

[37] Oscar Handlin, *The Uprooted* (Boston, 1951), pp. 209–17.

quently a political tactic, not a political system to be established permanently, but a device to secure immediate political victory. The prohibitionist advocacy of the referendum, one of the most extensive sources of support for such a measure, came from the belief that the referendum would provide the opportunity to outlaw liquor more rapidly. The Anti-Saloon League, therefore, urged local option. But the League was not consistent. Towns which were wet, when faced with a county-wide local-option decision to outlaw liquor, demanded town or township local option to reinstate it. The League objected to this as not the proper application of the referendum idea.

Again, "Progressive" reformers often espoused the direct primary when fighting for nominations for their candidates within the party, but once in control they often became cool to it because it might result in their own defeat. By the same token, many municipal reformers attached the initiative, referendum, and recall to municipal charters often as a device to appease voters who opposed the centralization of representation and executive authority. But, by requiring a high percentage of voters to sign petitions—often 25 to 30 percent—these innovations could be and were rendered relatively harmless.

More fundamentally, however, the distinction between ideology and practice in municipal reform arose from the different roles which each played. The ideology of democratization of decision-making was negative rather than positive; it served as an instrument of attack against the existing political system rather than as a guide to alternative action. Those who wished to destroy the "machine" and to eliminate party competition in local government widely utilized the theory that these political instruments thwarted public impulses, and thereby shaped the tone of their attack.

But there is little evidence that the ideology represented a faith in a purely democratic system of decision-making or that reformers actually wished, in practice, to substitute direct democracy as a continuing system of sustained decision-making in place of the old. It was used to destroy the political institutions of the lower and middle classes and the political power which those institutions gave rise to, rather than to provide a clear-cut guide for alternative action.[38]

The guide to alternative action lay in the model of the business enterprise. In describing new conditions which they wished to create, reformers drew on the analogy of the "efficient business enterprise," criticizing current practices with the argument that "no business could conduct its affairs that way and remain in business," and calling upon business practices as the guides to improvement. As one student remarked:

[38] Clinton Rodgers Woodruff of the National Municipal League even argued that the initiative, referendum, and recall were rarely used. "Their value lies in their existence rather than in their use." Woodruff, *City Government*, p. 314. It seems apparent that the most widely used of these devices, the referendum, was popularized by legislative bodies when they could not agree or did not want to take responsibility for a decision and sought to pass that responsibility to the general public, rather than because of a faith in the wisdom of popular will.

The folklore of the business elite came by gradual transition to be the symbols of governmental reformers. Efficiency, system, orderliness, budgets, economy, saving, were all injected into the efforts of reformers who sought to remodel municipal government in terms of the great impersonality of corporate enterprise.[39]

Clinton Rodgers Woodruff of the National Municipal League explained that the commission form was "a simple, direct, businesslike way of administering the business affairs of the city . . . an application to city administration of that type of business organization which has been so common and so successful in the field of commerce and industry."[40] The centralization of decision-making which developed in the business corporation was now applied in municipal reform.

The model of the efficient business enterprise, then, rather than the New England town meeting, provided the positive inspiration for the municipal reformer. In giving concrete shape to this model in the strong-mayor, commission, and city-manager plans, reformers engaged in the elaboration of the processes of rationalization and systematization inherent in modern science and technology. For in many areas of society, industrialization brought a gradual shift upward in the location of decision-making and the geographical extension of the scope of the area affected by decisions.

Experts in business, in government, and in the professions measured, studied, analyzed, and manipulated ever wider realms of human life, and devices which they used to control such affairs constituted the most fundamental and far-reaching innovations in decision-making in modern America, whether in formal government or in the informal exercise of power in private life. Reformers in the Progressive Era played a major role in shaping this new system. While they expressed an ideology of restoring a previous order, they in fact helped to bring forth a system drastically new.[41]

The drama of reform lay in the competition for supremacy between two systems of decision-making. One system, based upon ward representation and growing out of the practices and ideas of representative government, involved wide latitude for the expression of grass-roots impulses and their involvement in the political process. The other grew out of the rationalization of life which came with science and technology, in which decisions arose from expert analysis and flowed from fewer and smaller centers outward to the rest of society. Those who espoused the former looked with fear upon the loss of influence which the latter involved, and those who espoused the latter looked only with disdain upon the wastefulness and inefficiency of the former.

[39] J. B. Shannon, "County Consolidation," *Annals of the American Academy of Political and Social Science* 207 (1940): 168.

[40] Woodruff, *City Government*, pp. 29–30.

[41] Several recent studies emphasize various aspects of this movement. See, for example, Loren Baritz, *Servants of Power* (Middletown, 1960); Raymond E. Callahan, *Education and the Cult of Efficiency* (Chicago, 1962); Samuel P. Hays, *Conservation and the Gospel of Efficiency* (Cambridge, 1959); Dwight Waldo, *The Administrative State* (New York, 1948), pp. 3–61.

The Progressive Era witnessed rapid strides toward a more centralized system and a relative decline for a more decentralized system. This development constituted an accommodation of forces outside the business community to the political trends within business and professional life rather than vice versa. It involved a tendency for the decision-making processes inherent in science and technology to prevail over those inherent in representative government.

Reformers in the Progressive Era and liberal historians since then misread the nature of the movement to change municipal government because they concentrated upon dramatic and sensational episodes and ignored the analysis of more fundamental political structure, of the persistent relationships of influence and power which grew out of the community's social, ideological, economic, and cultural activities. The reconstruction of these patterns of human relationships and of the changes in them is the historian's most crucial task, for they constitute the central context of historical development. History consists not of erratic and spasmodic fluctuations, of a series of random thoughts and actions, but of patterns of activity and changes in which people hold thoughts and actions in common and in which there are close connections between sequences of events. These contexts give rise to a structure of human relationships which pervade all areas of life; for the political historian the most important of these is the structure of the distribution of power and influence.

The structure of political relationships, however, cannot be adequately understood if we concentrate on evidence concerning ideology rather than practice. For it is becoming increasingly clear that ideological evidence is no safe guide to the understanding of practice, that what people thought and said about their society is not necessarily an accurate representation of what they did. The current task of the historian of the Progressive Era is to quit taking the reformers' own description of political practice at its face value and to utilize a wide variety of new types of evidence to reconstruct political practice in its own terms. This is not to argue that ideology is either important or unimportant. It is merely to state that ideological evidence is not appropriate to the discovery of the nature of political practice.

Only by maintaining this clear distinction can the historian successfully investigate the structure of political life in the Progressive Era. And only then can he begin to cope with the most fundamental problem of all: the relationship between political ideology and political practice. For each of these facets of political life must be understood in its own terms, through its own historical record. Each involves a distinct set of historical phenomena. The relationship between them for the Progressive Era is not now clear; it has not been investigated. But it cannot be explored until the conceptual distinction is made clear and evidence tapped which is pertinent to each. Because the nature of political practice has so long been distorted by the use of ideological evidence, the most pressing task is for its investigation through new types of evidence appropriate to it. The reconstruction of the movement for municipal reform can constitute a major step forward toward that goal.

Class Participation and the Council-Manager Plan

EDGAR L. SHERBENOU

While the council-manager form of municipal government continues to develop and expand, the argument concerning its nature and value continues unabated. Much of the formal discussion turns about the policy role of the manager, and the participation of councilmen and citizens in the initiation and determination of policy. There is little formal discussion of the relationship of the council-manager form of government to the class system of either the particular community or the nation. The absence of such formal discussion is consistent with historic reluctance to give overt recognition to social class as a fact or as an issue. However, council-manager adoption and abandonment campaigns and elections often turn, at least covertly, about social class as an issue, and about the relationship of the council-manager plan to the class issue.

Election at large and nonpartisan election are ordinarily part óf the council-manager approach, and it is in terms of these devices that the lower status person is most often able to objectify his apprehension that the council-manager form means government by and for the upper classes. It is ordinarily claimed, for example, that election at large produces a higher quality councilman. The most obvious dynamic of election at large is that the candidates who are known and respected by the whole city will be of upper middle or upper class position. Without the aid of partisan organization the lower status person will be at a severe disadvantage indeed. The term "quality" has several meanings in this country.

The Manager and Social Class

It is possible to imagine that the council-manager form could be combined with ward elections or even with partisan elections. Such conces-

Reprinted from the *Public Administration Review*, 21 (1961): 131–35. Copyright 1961 by the American Society for Public Administration. Reprinted by permission of the publisher.

sions, however, might not calm all the fears or nullify all the resistance of the plan's opponents. It is entirely probable that the systematic rationalization of administrative structure is bewildering and offensive to many persons, and perhaps especially to those who have been least effective in securing their social, economic, and political goals. To many persons such terms as "efficiency" and "management" are associated with insensitivity to human values. The adoption of the plan is usually associated with a drive to get "politics" out of city administration. This often means that the privatization of municipal offices is to be systematically reduced, and that purely personal fiefs are to be eradicated in the interest of the community. The interests of the upper status persons are protected by civilization's laws and customs while a sentiment of ownership in a municipal job may be the extent of the lower status person's attempt to protect his interests politically. Thus the rationalization of administrative organization may seem to injure only the poor and benefit only the wealthy.

In considering the relationship of the council-manager plan to social class it is important to remember that the plan does not create a class structure. The change from an aldermanic or commission form to a council-manager form is certainly important and significant, but as a revolution it is strictly minor. Class systems are much too deeply imbedded in the beliefs and practices of the society to be greatly modified by a relatively small change in local governmental structure. Thus if there is any causal relationship between the class system and the council-manager plan, the latter is the dependent variable.

Study Suburban Chicago Cities

The suburban cities which surround the central city in a great metropolitan area offer a special opportunity to investigate certain phases of the relationship between classes and the council-manager plan. These suburban cities are more specialized in function than cities with comparatively greater independence. Several of the suburban cities have an entirely residential function, but some have commercial and industrial development of their own. However, all the suburban cities exist in a basically dependent relationship to the great metropolitan complex. In other words, each suburban city represents a very limited part of the total system and depends upon the other cities in the metropolitan area to perform the other functions essential to a complete social, economic, or political system. The specialization of the suburb may serve to isolate variables so that we are able to compare them with other variables.

The research to be reported here is a study of the suburban cities which surround the City of Chicago. During the first phase of the study the seventy-four suburban cities nearest to Chicago in Cook, Lake, and DuPage counties which had more than 2,500 people were arranged in the order of their median dwelling unit values as reported by the Housing Census of 1950. At a later stage in the study the forty-nine suburban cities with more than 5,000 population in 1950 were divided into two groups. The council-manager cities were placed in one group and the non-manager cities in a second group. This division made it possible to compare some of the over-all aspects of the expenditure, debt, and tax patterns in manager suburbs with the patterns in the non-manager suburban cities. It should be noted that the group of seventy-four cities and the group of forty-nine cities overlap. The forty-nine cities are merely the larger cities among the seventy-four cities.

Housing Values as a Private Measure of Class

The objective of arranging the seventy-four cities in the order of their median dwelling unit values is to compare their forms of government with a measure of socio-economic class. Precise measurement of class position may require combination of residence with other variables. W. Lloyd Warner and his associates developed measures of ethnicity, education, amount of income, source of income, dwelling area, house type, and occupation as parts of their measurement of social class.[1] However, the purposes of this project require only a general measure of the socio-economic position of each suburb, and housing values reveal the social positions of the neighborhoods in this general way.

The Chicago suburbs in Illinois describe an arc which begins on the lake shore north of the central city and continues around the city to the Indiana line on the South Side. When the seventy-four suburban cities are arranged from top to bottom according to their median dwelling unit values, the resultant pattern generally resembles the geographic pattern. With only a few exceptions the cities with very high residential values appear to the north of the central city near the lake in the area commonly known as the "North Shore." As one moves away from the lake and around to the west of the central city, the median values drop noticeably to distinctly middle class levels. River Forest on the West Side has one of the highest medians, but the other cities in the western area are definitely below the top residential values. With one or two exceptions the South Side is an area of lower median residential values.

When the seventy-four suburban cities are ranked from top to bottom according to their median housing values, a definite coincidence of high housing values and the council-manager form of municipal government becomes apparent. Council-manager governments are found in all but two of the top twenty cities. As the median value of the housing drops, a few more non-manager cities appear. About halfway down the list, manager and non-manager cities are in about the same proportion, but as we move past the middle of the scale of medians the manager cities cease to appear entirely. Oak Lawn, number forty-three on the list, is the last council-manager city. Above Oak Lawn there are twenty-nine

---

[1] W. Lloyd Warner, Marcia Meeker, and Kenneth Eells, *Social Class in America* (P. Smith, 1957).

Class Participation and the Council-Manager Plan 131

manager cities and fourteen non-manager cities, while below Oak Lawn there are thirty-one non-manager cities and not a single manager city. The pattern is very striking. When we consider the generally close relationship between residential values and social class, the definite coincidence of the council-manager form with middle and upper class patterns is unmistakable.

Manager Adoption Pattern

The order in which the manager cities adopted the council-manager form suggests a further hypothesis. As measured by the median housing values of 1950, the council-manager plan was adopted by the top suburbs on the North Shore in 1914 and 1915. Riverside, on the West Side, but tenth in median housing value, chose the manager plan in 1925. Two more adoptions were made on the North Side in 1930 and 1931. Brookfield and Western Springs, neighbors to Riverside, adopted the plan in 1947 and 1948. From these beginnings several adoptions were made after more favorable legislation was passed by the legislature in 1951. The first interpretation suggested by this pattern is that once the council-manager plan is adopted by a city, it is more likely to be adopted by other cities in the same area. But more interesting yet, from the viewpoint of this paper, is the possibility that the plan spreads downward from the upper class suburbs into the middle class suburbs. The evidence is far from conclusive even for the Chicago area, but other suburban areas might be checked for the presence of such a relationship.

The second phase of the study involved a modification in method. The smaller cities were set aside, and only the forty-nine relatively larger suburban cities which had populations of 5,000 or more in 1950 were used. The forty-nine cities included twenty-four council-manager cities and twenty-five non-manager cities. The manager cities and non-manager cities were then compared by computing means of several variables for each group. For example, between 1950 and 1960 the manager cities averaged 89.9 percent population growth as compared to 76.7 percent in the non-manager cities.[2]

Table 1. Comparison of housing values for selected suburban Chicago manager and non-manager cities over 5,000 population in 1950

	Twenty-four Manager Cities	Twenty-five Non-Manager Cities
Average of the median dwelling unit values	$16,972	$12,513
Median of the median dwelling unit values	$17,809	$12,114

[2] Computed from field reports of the 1960 census.

Comparison of the housing values supplied by the Housing Census of 1950 for the manager and non-manager cities offers vivid evidence of the relatively affluent position of the residents of the manager cities. This comparison is set forth in Table 1. The Census Bureau lists high medians merely at $20,000 plus. Thus an average (arithmetic mean) of the medians expresses only a part of the total difference between the housing values of the two groups. Eight of the forty-nine cities were listed as having median dwelling unit values of more than $20 thousand. Seven of these eight employ the council-manager form of government.

Public Measures of Social Class

Expenditure for housing is primarily a private matter. Since we Americans customarily satisfy our private wants before we seek public approaches to the common good, no measure of public affluence offers the same degree of contrast between the manager and non-manager cities as does the comparison of their mean housing values. However, comparison on the basis of arithmetic means of three important variables in public finance is offered in Table 2. Table 3 supplies the ranges of the same variables for the manager cities and for the non-manager cities. In Table 2 it is made clear that on the average the manager cities had a higher expenditure per capita, a lower net municipal debt per capita, and higher property taxes per capita.

A few of the council-manager cities have lower expenditure and tax patterns than the majority of the non-manager cities in the sample. These cities demonstrate that the council-manager form may be used primarily for frugal purposes. However, the general pattern is definitely

Table 2.[a] Comparison of per capita average total expenditures, net municipal debt, and average municipal property tax for selected suburban Chicago manager and non-manager cities over 5,000 population in 1957

	Twenty-four Manager Cities	Twenty-five Non-Manager Cities
Average total expenditure per capita[b]	$68.42	$54.24
Average net municipal debt[c] per capita	$26.43	$34.81
Average municipal property tax per capita	$18.84	$13.99

[a] The 1957 Census of Governments is the primary source.

[b] The Census Bureau conducted several special censuses of cities in the area in 1957. Population figures for other cities were obtained by interpolation from the 1950 census and the field count reports of the 1960 census. Estimates supplied by the Chicago Association of Commerce and Industry were used as supplementary evidence in a few cases.

[c] The debt figure was obtained for each city by subtracting total cash and security holdings from total debt outstanding.

Table 3.[a] Comparison of the range of per capita total expenditures, municipal debt, and property tax for selected suburban Chicago manager and non-manager cities over 5,000 population in 1957

	Twenty-four Manager Cities	Twenty-five Non-Manager Cities
Range of total expenditure per capita	$ 21.75 to $167.57	$ 28.52 to $ 82.02
Range of municipal debt per capita	$113.63 debt to $115.38 surplus	$159.05 debt to $ 56.17 surplus
Range of property tax per capita	$ 7.02 to $ 70.48	$ 7.63 to $ 32.72

[a] Sources are the same as those for Table 2.

toward higher expenditures, higher property taxes, and a more conservative policy toward the incurrence of debt. The major variable in this pattern is undoubtedly the greater wealth of many of the suburban cities which have chosen the council-manager plan. Recalling the strikingly higher level of the housing in many of the manager cities, we infer that they have more money. Having more money, they spend more. Proponents of the plan argue that council-management tends to develop a public confidence in the efficiency and responsibility of municipal government. Greater public confidence leads naturally to demands for an expanded program of municipal services and an increased willingness to spend by way of the municipality. Such evidence as the present study affords tends to support this argument.

Significance of Occupational Expense

The relative willingness of the middle and upper classes to try the council-manager government may be at least partly explained by their occupational experiences. Many members of these groups are executives in corporations or other business groups. Other middle and upper class persons may practice a profession or otherwise have acquaintance with professional approaches to organization. It is natural that such people find it relatively easy to visualize a professional approach to municipal administration. It should be noticed also that any particular middle or upper class suburb is more likely to exist in geographical proximity to suburbs currently using the council-manager plan. Vicarious acquaintance with the plan is thus more likely to be obtained from the neighboring cities. In many ways the upper and upper middle class groups have relatively ready access to an accurate impression of the council-manager plan. We might infer that they choose it because they know it and like it.

The counterpart of these logics is that those further down the scale lack experience in executive or professional positions and thus do not have a ready-made basis for sympathetic vision of professional public management. Also, the further down the status scale, the less likely that neighboring cities will use the council-manager form. Thus, a clear impression of the plan is geographically less available. . . .

5

Changes in Groups' Participation and Impact on Urban Politics

Nationality Groups and Local Politics

The industrialization of America gave impetus to the formation of large urban centers where new manufacturing and service facilities were located. As mentioned previously, these large centers of economic activity necessitated infusions of new residents to fulfill the needs of an expanding job market. Many of these new residents came from rural America where agricultural advancements shrank the need for agricultural labor. Also, many additional newcomers were recruited from foreign shores. It is the politics and political activity of these immigrants which are the focus of this section.

Although some of the earliest immigrants settled in rural America, the vast majority of all immigrants became urban dwellers. Several reasons dictated this predominantly urban settlement. First, free or inexpensive rural land rapidly ran out with the heavy demand of westward settlers. Since large proportions of the foreign immigration to America came after the era of abundant land, there were not sufficient opportunities for immigrants to acquire farms. Second, many of the immigrants to these shores—the Irish, the Italians, Eastern European Jews, Poles, etc.—arrived here with little or no money in their pockets. They tended to settle in the cities where they landed, or at least fairly close to them. Third, the major economic opportunities for the immigrants lay in the new urban-based industries. The importance of economic opportunities as attractions for immigrants is demonstrated by the nature of immigration cycles to this country. The great immigration waves to this country came in periods of economic prosperity, and the inflow was reduced to a trickle during periods of economic depression or recession.

The preponderance of the new arrivals to America's shores were poor. Aside from the economic attractions of America which served as "pull" mechanisms, the severe economic hardships which they suffered in their own countries served to "push" the immigrants from their homelands. The Irish potato famine, the backward peasant societies of southern Italy and Sicily, etc., were examples of societies which could not support their residents.

One of the earliest immigrant groups to arrive in America in large numbers was the Irish. They scored early political successes as they seized control of local politics in many northeastern and midwestern cities. The early successes of the Irish placed later-arriving immigrant groups at a severe political disadvantage in their quest for political power. One city where the Irish scored early political gains was New Haven, Connecticut, where later-arriving Italians found difficulty in breaking into the political process.

The slow political assimilation of New Haven's Italians is discussed by Jerome Meyers in the first selection. The Italians comprise the largest ethnic group in New Haven, yet they are not represented in political positions in accordance with their numbers. To examine the representation of Italians in local governmental positions—elective, appointive (i.e., boards and commissions), and salaried (i.e., city jobs such as laborers, policemen, firemen, teachers)—Meyers used a "quota fulfillment index." This index consists of the percentage of Italians in a particular class of jobs divided by the percentage of Italians in New Haven's population. An index value of 100 means that Italians are represented in proportions equivalent to their rank in the general population, whereas an index less than 100 means they are underrepresented, an index value over 100 that they are overrepresented.

Through the use of the "quota fulfillment index" Meyers found several patterns in the representation of Italians in city positions. First, Italians obtained elective office first and have always had their greatest proportional representation in these offices. It is true, though, as Meyers points out, that among elective offices, Italians have tended to gain their greatest representation in minor offices rather than major ones such as the mayor's office. Second, Italians have not attained nearly as great representation as appointed board or commission members or as city employees as they have as elected officials. Third, the Italians entered the political system at the bottom and have always had the greatest representation at the bottom. Finally, Italians are steadily advancing in representation at all levels.

Meyers attributes his findings to the utility of positions for gaining Italian electoral support. The "balanced ticket" is most necessary for gaining this Italian support because elective offices are the most visible to the electorate. (Wolfinger, in the next selection, goes into the role of political nominations as a mechanism for attracting ethnic support.) Therefore, Italians are most likely to get nominated for elective offices. Second, since boards and commission memberships are the next most visible sign of ethnic attainments, Italians have also been given recognition by appointment to these boards and commissions—although not in proportionately the same numbers as nominations to elective offices. Third, and finally, since there are large numbers of city jobs to be filled, Meyers says that it is possible to appoint large numbers of Italians, but in proportions not nearly equal to their numbers in the population. That is, Italians are appointed in large enough numbers to be visible to the electorate, yet they do not have to be appointed in numbers proportional to their representation in the general population. The appointment of Italians, then, has been partially in response to the need for their electoral support.

The use of ethnic candidates to attract ethnic voters is gone into further by Raymond Wolfinger in the next selection. He says that it is commonly thought that as ethnics win their way into the middle class they abandon their ethnic loyalties and vote like old-stock native Americans. Not so, says Wolfinger. The attainment of middle-class status facilitates the entrance of ethnics into the race for elective office. And the presence of a "fellow ethnic's name" on the ticket (Wolfinger focuses especially on the head of the ticket—the mayor's office) is a strong inducement to the ethnic voter.

Therefore, he contends that ethnic voting will get stronger with second and third generation ethnics rather than decline as assimilation theorists might assume. To prove his point, Wolfinger shows that Italians' loyalty in local elections shifted from the Democrats to the Republicans when an Italian was nominated as the Republican mayoral candidate. The Italian identification with the local Republican Party has persisted regardless of the ethnicity of the mayoral candidate. To explain these findings, Wolfinger formulates his "mobilization theory of ethnic voting."

> The strength of ethnic voting depends on both the intensity of ethnic identification and the level of ethnic relevance in the election. The most powerful and visible sign of ethnic political relevance is a fellow ethnic's name at the head of the ticket, evident to everyone who enters the voting booth. Middle-class status is a virtual prerequisite for candidacy for major office. . . . Therefore, ethnic voting will be greatest when the ethnic group has produced a middle class, i.e., in the second and third generations. . . .

The selections concerned with representation in various municipal offices and the mobilization of ethnic voting deal basically with methods used to obtain ethnic political support. However, none of these approaches to ethnic politics looks at the impact which ethnic groups have on the operation of the political system itself. Using ethnic group members—either through patronage positions or political nominations —to attract broad ethnic-group electoral support indicates a high degree of competitiveness in cities with large ethnic populations. That is, ethnic groups tend to be associated with a competitive style of politics. Because competitive elections are known to produce greater voter turnout than noncompetitive elections (such as those represented by nonpartisan suburban communities), cities with large ethnic populations should be associated with higher levels of voter turnout than cities with small ethnic populations.

I tested this hypothesis (for the period 1940–60) in the third selection presented here. The data indicate that the relationship is not quite as simple as initially stated. The presence of large ethnic populations does produce higher levels of voting turnout in nonpartisan cities for three elections (1940, 1950, and 1960), but not after 1940 in partisan cities. Although the aggregate data used in this selection are not sufficient to discern the reasons for this difference, case studies provide some possible reasons.

In a nonpartisan city election in Newark, New Jersey, and a partisan state election contest in the same city, ethnicity was found relevant in the former election but not in the latter. The author of this study (see my article for a complete citation of this study by Pomper) concludes that where party loyalties are absent, voters look to ethnic characteristics as an aid in making their choice. In the partisan contest, however, both parties are careful to balance their tickets so that ethnic considerations are cancelled out and partisan considerations take their place. It is possible that these ethnic accommodations in partisan cities are fairly recent, hence the disappearance of an ethnic effect on turnout after 1940 in the partisan cities. Perhaps ethnic competition has been built into partisan systems where there are large numbers of ethnic voters.

In conclusion, ethnic groups came to urban America seeking the economic opportunities to be found here. While most of these opportunities lay in America's growing industrial system, some opportunities were also found in municipal politics. Patronage appointments, election to public office, recognition and status, were all inducements to ethnic groups to become involved in local politics. Although the nature of ethnic participation in the political system has changed over the years, this participation has remained at fairly high levels. And, in the aggregate, the ethnic influence on governmental structures and municipal voting is still observed in cities with large ethnic populations. Although assimilation can be expected eventually to take its toll on ethnic politics, the demise of this type of politics is a long way off in cities with long histories of ethnic political involvement.

Assimilation in the Political Community

JEROME K. MEYERS

Since the cessation of large-scale European immigration to the United States a quarter century ago, much of the former interest in the study of assimilation has lessened. With the first generation of recent immigrants dying off and the third reaching maturity, it is often assumed that ethnic groups will soon be absorbed into American society.[1] It is true that most of them can no longer be differentiated by such external characteristics as dress and language. It is also true that their members have adopted many practices of American culture. Actually, they have little in common with their original culture and on visits abroad appear as Americans. Nevertheless, they have not been completely absorbed into the society. Every large northeastern city, for example, has its ethnic settlements, members of ethnic groups remain overrepresented in the lower-paid jobs, and their in-marriage rates continue high.[2] Furthermore, discrimination against them still exists, and terms like *dago, wop, kike,* and *hunky* are in common usage.

To determine the rate at which ethnic groups are incorporated into American society in an urban community, we studied the assimilation of Italians in New Haven. In this paper we shall specifically examine their assimilation into the community's political system.[3] Because of the belief in democracy and political equality in the United States, the participa-

---

Reprinted from *Sociology and Social Research*, 35 (1951): 175–82. Copyright 1951 by the University of Southern California. Reprinted by permission of the publisher.

[1] See W. Lloyd Warner and Leo Srole, *The Social Systems of American Ethnic Groups* (New Haven: Yale University Press, 1945), p. 295, for such a view.

[2] See the following for examples of such evidence: Leonard Covello, "Italian Americans," in F. J. Brown and J. S. Roucek (eds.), *Our Racial and National Minorities* (New York: Prentice-Hall Inc., 1937), pp. 373–74; Samuel Koenig, "Ethnic Groups in Connecticut Industry," *Social Forces*, 20 (1941): 96–105; Elin L. Anderson, *We Americans* (Cambridge: Harvard University Press, 1938); Jerome K. Myers, "The Differential Time Factor in Assimilation," unpublished doctoral dissertation, Yale University, 1949; Milton L. Barron, *People Who Intermarry* (Syracuse: University Press, 1947).

[3] The author has also studied assimilation in the residential, occupational, and educational systems, as well as intermarriage. See Myers, "Differential Time Factor."

tion of ethnic groups in local government is a valuable index of assimilation.

New Haven is a predominantly industrial city with a 1940 population of 160,605, of which slightly over three-fifths was of foreign stock. The Italians were the largest of the immigrant groups, with the first and second generations comprising 27 percent of the population. The first year in which a sizable number of Italians resided in the community was 1890, when they totaled 2,330, or 3 percent of the population. We shall trace their participation in the New Haven political system from 1890 to 1940.

The political system with its two-party structure is both a channel and a measure of assimilation. When they first settled in New Haven Italians did not possess the franchise but were encouraged to become citizens and acquire voting rights. Certain members among them were selected by political parties to run for office. Politicians thus used them as a means to attract Italian votes. Other opportunities for membership and advancement in the party organization also came to them. Party activity resulted not alone in political appointment but in interest and responsibility beyond their own group in the New Haven community as well, thus serving them as a channel of mobility.

Political participation also indicates the rate of assimilation. When the Italians first entered New Haven none held political office. Thereafter, however menial were their first positions, securement of them meant they were getting a foothold in politics. Since the political system is a hierarchy, with the positions in it having different degrees of prestige, participation in it serves as a measure of assimilation.

But the number of Italians in political positions is of little value in measuring assimilation unless their distribution in the total population is also known. Therefore, we utilized a "quota fulfillment index" to measure incorporation in numerical terms. This index represents the ratio between the percentage of officeholders who are Italian and the percentage of Italians in the New Haven population.[4] An index of 100 indicates that there are as many Italians holding office as would be expected on a population basis. An index less than 100 signifies that the group is underrepresented on a proportional population basis, while one over 100 means overrepresentation.

Positions in the New Haven political system may be divided into three main groups for purposes of discussion: (1) elective offices (e.g., mayor, alderman, sheriff); (2) appointive board and commission positions (e.g., member of the Board of Education, the Board of Health, and the Civil Service Commission); and (3) municipal employee positions (e.g., fireman, clerk, and school teacher).

[4] Data on Italians and total population in political positions were secured from New Haven city yearbooks, New Haven manuals of city government, and municipal records such as lists of departmental employees and pay roll records. Italian nationality was determined by name. Although errors are bound to occur in utilizing names as an index of ethnic origin, it is the only means of identification we have in such a study. Evidence in this and other studies in New Haven indicates that Italian names are easily identified and that name changing is not common among the group.

Italians in Elective Offices

Of the 104 elected officials in New Haven in 1890, one, a justice of the peace, was of Italian origin. Since then the number of Italian officials has increased steadily until in 1940 26 of New Haven's 112 elected officeholders were of Italian descent. This increase is indicated by the following quota fulfillment indices:

Table 1. Italian quota fulfillment indices in elective offices: 1890–1940

1890	33	1920	57
1900	50	1930	67
1910	45	1940	87

While it appears that Italians are approaching a distribution similar to that of the total population in elective positions, it is apparent that not all such positions are of equal status value. The mayoralty obviously possesses more prestige than the office of selectman or justice of the peace. Therefore, we grouped the elective positions according to status value to see how Italians have been distributed in them. The evaluations were made after discussions with public officeholders, such as the registrar of vital statistics and town clerk; municipal employees, such as clerks, janitors, and policemen; and various citizens. In addition, the author's knowledge of the situation gained through actual field work and library research was utilized.

The top status elective positions, called major elective offices for our purposes, include the following: mayor, city clerk, treasurer, collector of taxes, sheriff, town clerk, registrar of vital statistics, registrars of voters, and aldermen.[5] Then come the minor elective offices of selectmen, constables, grand jurors, and justices of the peace.

The Italian quota fulfillment indices in terms of these major and minor offices are shown in Table 2.

Table 2. Italian quota fulfillment indices: major and minor offices, 1890–1940

	Major	Minor		Major	Minor
1890	0	49	1920	47	61
1900	0	77	1930	46	80
1910	20	56	1940	72	97

An examination of these indices indicates that Italians secured minor elective positions several decades before major ones and have always had greater representation in them. Although the Italians approached their

---

[5] The office of mayor has more prestige than any other elective position, but it is grouped with the major offices instead of being considered a class by itself.

expected distribution (on a population basis) in minor offices in 1940, they had only about 70 percent of such a distribution in major positions. Nevertheless, the Italians have advanced steadily over the years into major as well as minor offices and are being incorporated into the political system.

Italians in Appointive Board and Commission Positions

Elective officials comprise only a portion of the personnel responsible for the management of municipal affairs in New Haven. Much top level work is done by boards and commissions appointed by the mayor. Examples are the Board of Education, Board of Finance, Board of Parks, Civil Service Commission, and City Plan Commission. Membership on any of them carries high prestige in the political system. These positions are nonpaid and usually are held by prominent businessmen, professional persons, and civic-minded individuals. Were such appointments remunerative, these persons would consider their time too valuable to serve in them for the financial rewards involved. Being nonpaid, however, the positions are considered above "ordinary politics," and important people consider it their civic duty to serve in them. The only elective position that has comparable high status value is that of mayor.

The distribution of Italians in such positions in terms of the quota fulfillment index is as follows:

Table 3. Italian quota fulfillment indices in board and commission positions: 1890–1940

1890	0	1920	24
1900	0	1930	13
1910	0	1940	34

It is important to note that there were no Italians on any board or commission until 1920 and that their numbers in these high status positions have always been far below those elected to office. They have been, quite apparently, underrepresented in top status positions in the political system.

Italians as Municipal Employees

It is also instructive to examine the proportion of Italians employed by the city in jobs necessary to keep an urban community operating. In these are found the rank and file of the persons who carry out the duties and functions of local government. These positions, as is true of others in the political system, can be arranged according to status value. In the top status group (Group 1) are department heads and city executives, including such key administrative personnel as the health officer, superintendent of education, and corporation counsel. In Group 2 are school teachers and such other professional and executive personnel as assistant city engineer, probation officer, and assistant librarian. Group 3 is comprised of clerical workers, firemen, and policemen. In the lowest status group (Group 4) are janitors, custodians, and laborers.

The Italian representation in these positions in terms of the quota fulfillment index is as follows:

Table 4. Italian quota fulfillment indices in municipal employee positions: 1890–1940

Group	1890	1900	1910	1920	1930	1940
1	0	0	0	0	0	33
2	0	0	3	9	14	22
3	0	0	2	6	16	21
4	0	0	0	15	47	56

Several facts stand out in the employment of Italians by the city. First is their late entrance into municipal employee positions. Second is their considerable underrepresentation in such jobs. With the exception of laboring and janitorial positions, less than half as many Italians were employed by the city, even in 1940, as would be expected on a population basis. Third, only in 1940 were Italians represented in the highest status positions of department head and key personnel. Finally, despite their underrepresentation, there have been steady increases in the quota fulfillment indices of the Italians at all levels.

Thus far three patterns are discernible in the incorporation of Italians into the New Haven political system. First, Italians obtained elective positions before any other kind and have always had their greatest proportional representation in them. The group is not nearly as well represented, however, in high status board and commission positions. Neither is it well represented among municipal employees. In fact, except for janitorial and laboring jobs, the proportion of Italians employed by the city has usually been even less than the percentage appointed to boards and commissions.

The second pattern to be noted is that Italians entered the political system at the bottom and have always had a much greater proportional representation in minor positions than in high status ones. Even in elective positions the group is underrepresented in the major offices. Third, despite their great underrepresentation the Italians are advancing in the political system.

Perhaps the main reason for the first pattern is the amount of "vote appeal" attached to the different positions. The "balanced ticket" on which nominees are distributed among nationality groups has been used to appeal to the ethnic vote. Therefore, it is not surprising to find the greatest proportional representation of Italians in elective positions. Their nomination for elective office is a most direct appeal to the Italian vote. Board and commission positions probably have the next greatest amount of "vote appeal." Appointments to them are a strong appeal to the Italian vote and a means of rewarding prominent Italians for party activity. The group's proportional representation is low in city employee positions. Since these jobs are the most numerous, a relatively large number of Italians can be employed in them without their proportional representation being very high.[6] Apparently, just enough Italians are employed to appeal to the group's vote. The conclusion to be drawn is that Italians are being incorporated into the political system at a rapid rate only in positions which have a direct connection with the winning of votes. In other positions discrimination remains very great.

Italian Distribution in Total Political Positions

Since there are few elective offices compared with the total number of positions in the political system, the high proportional representation of Italians in them because of "vote appeal" tends to give a distorted picture of the group's assimilation to the political system. A more accurate picture can be obtained by considering the distribution of Italians in all positions. Whether elective or appointive, the many positions in the political system have varying degrees of status value attached to them, and they fall into a hierarchy of four main levels. We shall label the top status group Level I and arrange the others in descending status value. The positions included in each of these are as follows:

Level I: mayor, department heads and key executives, board and commission positions
Level II: aldermen, city clerk, treasurer, collector of taxes, sheriff, town clerk, registrar of vital statistics, registrars of voters, other executive and professional personnel, teachers
Level III: clerical workers, justices of the peace, selectmen, grand jurors, constables, policemen, firemen
Level IV: janitors, custodians, laborers

The distribution of Italians at these various levels in terms of the quota fulfillment index is as follows:

Table 5. Italian quota fulfillment indices according to political level: 1890–1940

Level	1890	1900	1910	1920	1930	1940
I	0	0	0	21	12	33
II	0	0	3	10	15	24
III	12	14	9	13	21	28
IV	0	0	0	15	47	56

[6] For example, in 1940 there were 112 elected officials, 190 members of boards and commissions, and 1,989 municipal employees in New Haven.

The summary, in numerical terms, of the incorporation of Italians into the New Haven political system in Table 5 makes clear that at no level have they come near approaching an expected distribution on a population basis. In fact, only once (Level IV, 1940) have there been even half as many Italians in political positions as would be expected. Only in elective offices, particularly minor ones, have they approached their expected proportional quota. In other positions they are underrepresented, especially in those of top status.

In conclusion, the early or quick assimilation of New Haven Italians in the political system does not seem very probable. Nevertheless, the Italians have been steadily becoming more active politically. Upon their settlement in New Haven over half a century ago, they were unrepresented in the political system. Since then they have not only advanced into it but have climbed upward, even though at a slow rate, until today they are found at all levels. All indications are that political assimilation is inevitable, although it is at least several generations away.

The Development and Persistence of Ethnic Voting*

RAYMOND E. WOLFINGER

Mass immigration ended fifty years ago, but national origins continue to be a salient dimension in many people's perceptions of themselves and of others.[1] Where this salience is widespread, ethnicity plays a major

Reprinted from the *American Political Science Review* 59 (1965): 896–908. Copyright 1965 by the American Political Science Association. Reprinted by permission of the publisher.

* This article is part of a paper delivered at the 1964 annual meeting of the American Association for Public Opinion Research, Excelsior Springs, Missouri. I am indebted to Martha Derthick, Heinz Eulau, Joan Heifetz, and my wife, Barbara Kaye Wolfinger, for help in formulating my argument, and to more friends than I can mention for many helpful comments on an earlier draft of the paper.

[1] For a recent statement of this theme see Nathan Glazer and Daniel Patrick Moynihan, *Beyond the Melting Pot* (Cambridge, MIT Press and Harvard University Press, 1963). "Ethnic consciousness" or "ethnic salience" exists when: (1) many people think of themselves, and are regarded by others, as members of a particular nationality group; and (2) such classification is salient. The two aspects of ethnic consciousness reinforce each other.

role in politics.[2] Ethnicity is often an important independent variable in voting behavior. "Ethnic voting," as I shall call it, has two manifestations. (1) Members of an ethnic group show an affinity for one party or the other which cannot be explained solely as a result of other demographic characteristics. Voters of Irish descent, to take a familiar example, are more likely than other voters of similar economic status to be Democrats. (2) Members of an ethnic group will cross party lines to vote for—or against—a candidate belonging to a particular ethnic group.[3]

This article deals with the development and persistence of ethnic voting. The customary theory holds that ethnic voting is strongest during an ethnic group's earliest residence in this country and subsequently declines from this peak as the group's members make their way out of the working class.[4] This might be called an "assimilation theory." It sees a direct relationship between the proportion of a nationality group in the working class and that group's political homogeneity. As more and more of the group join the middle class, its political unity is progressively eroded. Along with middle-class status, these group members are said to acquire different political interests and to identify more with the majority society and less with their nationality group: in short, they become assimilated. Presumably the end of the process is reached when group members are as occupationally differentiated as the whole population. At this point they are politically indistinguishable from the general population, or from a control group with similar non-ethnic characteristics, and ethnicity is no longer a factor in their voting behavior.[5]

This is a plausible argument, but it is not consistent with voting pat-

---

[2] Conflict among ethnic groups is a central topic in descriptions of politics in the Northeast; see, for example, Duane Lockard, *New England State Politics* (Princeton, Princeton University Press, 1959). For treatments of ethnicity in personnel appointments see Theodore J. Lowi, *At the Pleasure of the Mayor* (New York, 1964); and Daniel Patrick Moynihan and James Q. Wilson, "Patronage in New York State, 1955–1959," *American Political Science Review*, 58 (1964): 296–301. For a discussion of the social and political consequences of ethnic politics see Raymond E. Wolfinger, "Some Consequences of Ethnic Politics," in Harmon Zeigler and Kent Jennings (eds.), *The Electoral Process* (Englewood Cliffs, N. J., 1966).

[3] A good deal of data to support these propositions will be found in this article. For additional evidence see Angus Campbell, Gerald Gurin and Warren E. Miller, *The Voter Decides* (Evanston, 1954), pp. 77–79; Edward C. Banfield and James Q. Wilson, *City Politics* (Cambridge, Harvard University Press, 1963), pp. 230–31; and Lucy S. Davidowicz and Leon J. Goldstein, *Politics in a Pluralist Democracy* (New York, Institute of Human Relations Press, 1963). Ethnicity is only one variable in voting behavior. This article concerns secular trends in its importance. Many short-term influences on voting decisions that also affect its importance are not discussed here; this omission should not be interpreted as an implicit assertion that these short-range factors are not relevant.

[4] I will use the terms "ethnic group" and "nationality group" interchangeably to refer to individuals whose national origins set them apart from the predominantly Protestant old American society.

[5] The assimilation theory is most clearly and explicitly stated in Robert A. Dahl, *Who Governs?* (New Haven, Yale University Press, 1961), pp. 34–36.

terns in New Haven, Connecticut.[6] People of Italian descent there comprise about one-third of the city's population. Although the Italians are the poorest segment of the white population, they are also one of the strongest Republican voting blocs. If the assimilation theory held in New Haven, this Italian Republicanism would have been strongest some generations ago when Italians first settled there in numbers, and would have declined with the passage of time. But the overwhelming support that New Haven Italians give to the Republican party is a development of the past 25 years. It began when the first New Haven Italian candidate for a major city office won the Republican mayoralty nomination. Since then Italians have been the mainstay of Republican voting strength in New Haven, even in elections with no Italian candidates.

These events may not be as anomalous as they seem. They can be explained by a theory that may also be pertinent to many other places. I will discuss this alternate theory after a detailed description of the development of ethnic voting in New Haven. Finally, I will consider available evidence on the persistence of ethnic voting.

The Conditions of Ethnic Politics

The history of nationality group relations in New Haven is from all accounts typical of many industrial cities in the Northeastern states. In the course of the 19th and early 20th centuries the descendants of New Haven's original Anglo-Saxon Protestant settlers were outnumbered by waves of immigrants from Ireland and later from Southern and Eastern Europe. By 1910, according to the census data, two-thirds of the population were first- or second-generation Americans; in 1960 some 42 percent of the population were in these categories. More detailed information on the ethnic composition of the population comes from a sample survey of 525 registered voters conducted in the summer of 1959.[7] White Protestants comprised less than 20 percent of this sample; 31 percent of the respondents were born in Italy or were in the second or third generation of Italian immigrants. Eleven percent were of similarly recent Irish origin,[8] 9 percent were Negroes; and 15 percent were Jews.

Beginning with the first mass Irish immigration the old settlers met the non-Protestant newcomers with hostility, economic exploitation, and religious discrimination. The immigrants were usually penniless and could get only the least desirable jobs. The affronts of everyday life enhanced their ethnic consciousness; so did the obvious gap in well-being between them and the old settlers.

[6] Data on New Haven are from an intensive study of that city's politics conducted primarily by Dahl, William H. Flanigan, Nelson W. Polsby, and Raymond E. Wolfinger. It is reported in Dahl, *Who Governs?* and in Polsby, *Community Power and Political Theory* (New Haven, Yale University Press, 1963), chap. 4; and Wolfinger, *The Politics of Progress* (New Haven, Yale University Press, forthcoming).

[7] The sample was randomly chosen from voting lists. Sampling procedures are described in greater detail in Dahl, *Who Governs?* pp. 338-39. The survey was directed by William H. Flanigan.

[8] This figure undoubtedly underrepresents the number of Irish in New Haven, since 83% of all Irish immigrants came to the United States before 1900; see U. S. Bureau of the Census, *Statistical Abstract of the United States: 1955* (Washington, 1955), p. 95.

In addition to Yankee hostility, other forces tended to maintain ethnic solidarity. For European peasants trying to live in an American city, a familiar language, religion and culture were comforting when so much else was different. Members of any given nationality group usually settled in the same neighborhoods, lived together and married among their kind and not with Yankees or other immigrants, formed nationality associations, and worshipped in national churches.

Needless to say, the ethnics often responded to the Yankees with a hatred that has not yet vanished, while many Yankees continue to look down on the ethnics. Members of each of the major ethnic groups still regard the others with varying amounts of good will, of jealousy and suspicion. As the years have passed, the immigrants and their descendants have moved, in varying numbers, into the middle class. This economic mobility did not result in equivalent geographical dispersion, in part because some of the new prosperity came from neighborhood enterprises such as groceries and mortuaries, in part because of the continuing comforts of ethnic proximity.

One consequence of this history is a persistent emphasis on ethnic differences, which continue to be a major organizing principle in the city's social structure. There are, for example, no less than six Junior Leagues in New Haven, including one each for the not very numerous local young ladies of Swedish and Danish extraction. There are also Jewish organizations with similar functions but different names.[9] The major Catholic ethnic groups have their own national churches.

Ethnic consciousness is an important and pronounced regional characteristic. It is difficult to suggest an objective measure for comparing ethnic salience, much less to find data on this subject, but on the basis of impressionistic evidence it appears that concern with national origins is much greater in the Northeast than in some other parts of the country. The reasons for this regional difference are not immediately apparent. The numerical prevalence of ethnics does not account for it, for the major cities of the West Coast have sizable ethnic populations.[10] San

[9] August B. Hollingshead and Frederick C. Redlich, *Social Class and Mental Illness* (New York, 1958), pp. 64–65. These authors report that ethnic identification divides New Haven's social structure "horizontally" just as economic distinctions organize it "vertically."

[10] This table, taken from Banfield and Wilson, *City Politics*, p. 39, shows the proportion of first- and second-generation Americans in cities with more than 500,000 population in 1960:

Rank	City	%	Rank	City	%
1	New York	48.6	12	Philadelphia	29.1
2	Boston	45.5	13	San Antonio	24.0
3	San Francisco	43.5	14	San Diego	21.5
4	Chicago	35.9	15	Baltimore	14.8
5	Buffalo	35.4	16	St. Louis	14.1
6	Los Angeles	32.6	17	Washington	12.6
7	Detroit	32.2	18	Cincinnati	12.0
8	Seattle	31.4	19	Houston	9.7
9	Cleveland	30.9	20	New Orleans	8.6
10	Pittsburgh	30.3	21	Dallas	6.9
11	Milwaukee	30.0			

Francisco has about the same proportion of first- and second-generation Americans as New Haven (43 as against 42 percent) but there is no comparison between the two cities with respect to ethnic salience.[11]

This regional difference may be due to the fact that in the Northeast the non-British immigrants came to settled communities with relatively stable class structures and systems of status ascription. Only menial jobs were open to them. The distribution of economic rewards and opportunities reinforced the unambiguous class system. On the other hand, immigrants came to the West at the same time as the Yankees, or on their heels. "The Forty-Niners came from all parts of the world, and foreign accents were as common in the mining camps as American ones."[12] The two groups shared the same pioneering experiences[13] and lived in communities with wildly fluctuating economies and unsettled social systems. Economic advantage was not so closely associated with ethnicity, and class distinctions were not so rigid.

The immigrants in New England were equal to the older settlers in only one relevant respect: they could vote. Little in their previous experience suggested that their opinions had much to do with government, and so their votes had no abstract value to them. But these votes mattered to American politicians, who solicited them with advice, favors, petty gifts, and jobs.

Two typical loci of immigrant politicization were the bosses of casual labor gangs on public works, who owed their positions to their ability to deliver their gangs' votes and their vote-delivering ability to their command of jobs; and the leaders of nationality associations, usually men who were the first to achieve some economic success.[14] Such relationships set the pattern for ethnic politics. Each nationality group in a city had leaders who bargained with politicians, trading their followers' vote for money, favors and jobs.[15] For their part the politicians found it convenient and efficient to classify the electorate by ethnicity and to dispense rewards on this basis.

There are some regional differences in the national origins of these ethnic populations; the Western cities tend to have more Scandinavians, for example. On the other hand, San Francisco, for one, has sizable Irish and Italian groups.

[11] For similar observations about regional differences see Glazer and Moynihan, *Beyond the Melting Pot*, pp. 10, 250. They mention an alternate explanation: residents of western cities moved there after living in the East, hence they are less conscious of their European origins.

This point about regional differences applies only to concern about national origins among whites and does not deal with racial prejudice.

[12] Louis Berg, "Peddlers in Eldorado," *Commentary* (July 1965), p. 64.

[13] This shared experience is thought to be the reason for the inclusion of Jews in San Francisco high society: "the early Jews in the West could boast that they were pioneers among pioneers" (*ibid.*, p. 65).

[14] For a description of these social patterns see Oscar Handlin, *The Uprooted* (Boston, 1952), chaps. 7, 8.

[15] An excellent description of ethnic politics that expresses the style and flavor of these negotiations may be found in William F. Whyte, *Street Corner Society*, enlarged edition (Chicago, University of Chicago Press, 1955).

The tangible political rewards were limited. Not everyone could be given a job or a Christmas basket. Nor did everyone want such things; or need to get a son out of jail, or a relative into the United States, or a pushcart license from City Hall. But when one Italian was appointed to a public position his success was enjoyed vicariously by other Italians; it was "recognition" of the worth of the Italians. Ethnic solidarity let politicians economize on the indulgences they bestowed. It was unnecessary to do a favor for every individual to win his vote. Rewards given to the few were appreciated by the many. Money or jobs given to a few leaders earned political returns in two ways: (1) through the votes that the recipient could deliver directly; and (2) through appreciation of the "recognition" he had earned. Public office was much the most effective such reward, for it was most visible and hence conveyed most glory.[16]

Certain of New Haven's other political characteristics were (and are) conducive to ethnic politics. In particular, the city's wards were small enough to be ethnically homogeneous. Politicians need schemes for classifying voters and they tend to look for such taxonomies in election returns. In New Haven the ward is the politicians' unit of electoral analysis, which facilitates explaining the outcome of elections on the basis of ethnic preferences.[17] Since results were understood in ethnic terms, strategies were developed in the same terms. Politicians appealed to the electorate on the basis of ethnic rather than class differences. Moreover, many local political issues concerned the allocation of governmental services and facilities among different neighborhoods, and so contests for these rewards could also be interpreted as competition among ethnic groups.

For many years the urban immigrants were mostly Irish and the "outside" politicians were Yankees. In addition to minor rewards for many people, politics offered a few immigrants a path to real wealth and power, a path that was all the more important because prejudice and lack of education drastically narrowed the chances of a lucrative career in legitimate business or the professions. By the time later waves of immigrants arrived, the Irish had a attained considerable political influence, largely in the Democratic party. Where this happened they replaced or joined the "outside" politicians with whom the leaders of newer ethnic groups bargained.

Ethnic Politics in New Haven

The first Irishman was elected to the New Haven Board of Aldermen in 1857. Henceforth Irishmen and other ethnics held municipal office in

[16] Lowi suggests that, unlike success in other fields, political eminence has a strong impact on ethnic perspectives: "Success in economic fields is highly individualized; ... there is relatively little group symbolization of success. In contrast, political success, particularly in the big cities, is symbolized very highly in group terms" (*Pleasure of the Mayor*, p. 46).

[17] The present Mayor of New Haven was one of the first politicians to make use of professional sample surveys of the electorate. Data from the surveys he commissions are analyzed by ethnic group, rather than income, occupation, or education.

increasing numbers. Democratic mayoralty candidates continued for a while to be Yankee businessmen, demographically indistinguishable from their Republican opponents. The election of 1899 marked the end of Yankee dominance in local politics. Cornelius Driscoll, born in County Cork, was elected mayor on the Democratic ticket. As the Irish subsequently strengthened their hold on the party, some Yankee Democrats defected to the Republicans.

The Irish were not reluctant to take the spoils of victory. In the early 1930s first- and second-generation Irishmen comprised 13 percent of a sample of 1600 family heads in New Haven, but they accounted for 49 percent of all governmental jobs. The Italians suffered most of all from Irish chauvinism: there were *no* government employees among the 27 percent of the sample who were Italian.[18] These survey data exaggerate the Italians' exclusion from political rewards, but not by very much. In 1930 the proportion of Italians in low-paying municipal jobs was only a quarter of the proportion of Italians in the total population, and the ratio for better city jobs was much lower. By 1940 the Italians had attained half their "quota" of the poorer positions, and only about a fifth in white collar posts.[19] Subsequently their representation in both appointive and elective positions has increased enormously.[20]

The explanation of the New Haven Italians' Republicanism may then be thought to lie here: shut out of the Democratic party, they had no place to go but to the Republicans. This argument has two crippling

---

[18] John W. McConnell, *The Evolution of Social Class* (Washington, American Council on Public Affairs, 1942), p. 214. The data are from the Sample Family Survey conducted by the Yale Institute of Human Relations in 1931–33.

[19] Jerome K. Myers, "Assimilation in the Political Community," *Sociology and Social Research* 35 (1951): 175–82. Myers estimated the number of Italians in various categories of municipal jobs from the names in city directories and manuals. The Republicans lost control of City Hall in 1932 to John W. Murphy, a Democrat of the old school. Murphy, who stayed in office until 1946, usually carried the Italian wards, but by somewhat smaller margins than he received in other working-class neighborhoods.

As these findings suggest, there are impediments to a rational strategy of ethnic politics. (1) Party leaders may refrain from cultivating ethnic groups out of prejudice. In much of the East Coast the exclusiveness of Yankee Republican politicians aided the Democrats' proselytizing of immigrants. (2) Party leaders may be reluctant to share political spoils with "outsiders." This seems to have been true of many Irish Democrats. Until a very few years ago, one Democratic ward organization in a New Haven Irish neighborhood would not let Italians participate in any form of campaign activity. (3) There may be principled objections to making appointments on the basis of ethnicity rather than other forms of merit. For examples of this attitude see James Q. Wilson, *The Amateur Democrat* (Chicago, University of Chicago Press, 1962), pp. 283–88. It is quite possible, however, that such scruples are forgotten when the men who hold them actually attain power. Moynihan and Wilson describe the appointment policy followed by the young, liberal, intellectual staff of the newly elected New York Governor Averell Harriman: "...great efforts were extended to 'recognize' certain groups and careful records were kept of the racial and religious identity of the appointees" ("Patronage in N.Y. State," p. 296).

[20] See Myers, "Assimilation in Political Community"; and Dahl, *Who Governs?* pp. 43–44. In the 1950s, during a period of Democratic success, Italians held slightly more than their share of municipal elective offices.

Table 1. Party identification of Italians and Irish in the Northeast, 1952, 1956, and 1958

Party Identification	Irish	Italian
	(%)	(%)
Democratic	51	57
Independent	18	13
Republican	32	30
	101a	101
N	152	143

a Does not sum to 100 because of rounding.

Source: Inter-University Consortium for Political Research. I am indebted to Ralph Bisco and Richard T. Lane of the Consortium staff for their assistance.

limitations. (1) The Italians became more Republican during the period when they finally came closer to getting their "fair share" of municipal jobs. (2) Irish control of the local Democratic party is common in Northeastern industrial cities, but the level of Italian Republicanism found in New Haven is not. Allegations about the Republican inclinations of Italians abound in scholarly and journalistic literature, but concrete and systematic evidence for this general proposition is hard to find. Some Italians will split their ballots to vote for an Italian Republican, but the same is true for an Italian Democratic candidate. The best present source of data on this subject is the series of national election studies conducted over the past dozen years by the Survey Research Center of the University of Michigan. I have compared the party identification of the Italian and Irish respondents in the 1952, 1956 and 1958 studies who lived in the New England and Middle Atlantic states. As Table 1 shows, the Italians are a little more inclined than the Irish to consider themselves Democrats.[21]

Since the level of Italian Republicanism found in New Haven is not common in the Northeast, local history is more likely to provide an explanation than are more widespread political events. Two such local causes can be identified. The first was the determined courting of the Italian vote by Louis and Isaac Ullman, the leaders of the New Haven Republican party in the first part of the 20th century. The Ullman brothers realized that the large and hitherto passive Italian population was an untapped source of potential Republicans. They set out to capture the Italians, using the familar techniques of ethnic politics. They helped them take out citizenship papers, registered them as voters, found them jobs, used their considerable political influence to smooth over ad-

[21] For other data casting doubt on the notion of Italian Republicanism see Lockard, *New England State Politics*, pp. 210, 305–19; Samuel Lubell, *The Future of American Politics* (Garden City, N. Y., 1956), pp. 225–26; Davidowicz and Goldstein, *Politics in Pluralist Democracy*, pp. 11–12, 30–32; Bernard R. Berelson et al., *Voting* (Chicago, University of Chicago Press, 1954), p. 62; and J. Joseph Huthmacher, *Massachusetts People and Politics 1919–1932* (Cambridge, Harvard University Press, 1959), pp. 173, 179–84, 252, 260–61.

ministrative and legal difficulties, subsidized Italian-American fraternal and political clubs, and so on.

It is not too much to say that the Ullman brothers' foresight and political skill kept the Republican party competitive in New Haven. Although the Italians were the poorest part of the population, they were, in the thirty years after 1910, less favorable to Democratic candidates than any other immigrant group, except perhaps the Jews.[22] In the 10th Ward, with the city's heaviest concentration of Italians, the Democratic share of the presidential and mayoralty vote fluctuated around 50 percent. In fact, the 10th voted much like the city as a whole, a remarkable similarity in view of its residents' modest economic position.[23] The other wards in which Italians predominated were also less wholeheartedly Democratic than one would expect from their low income levels. It seems likely that this situation was due largely to the extent and intensity of the Ullmans' proselytizing.

Critical Elections

The Ullman brothers' efforts gave the Republicans a certain advantage with Italian voters. Yet for some thirty years the result was no more than a stand-off; the Italians split their votes more or less evenly between the two parties until the end of the 1930s. Since then they have been very strongly Republican. The big shift in Italian voting habits came when William C. Celentano, a self-made mortician and son of a fruit peddler, won the Republican nomination for mayor in 1939. Celentano was the first New Haven Italian to win either party's nomination for a major city office. He cut 10,000 votes from the enormous majority that the incumbent Democrat, John W. Murphy, had won two years earlier, and came close to winning the election. The Second World War kept Celentano from getting the nomination again until 1945, for the city's Republican leaders did not think it prudent to nominate an Italian while Italy was fighting against the United States. But in that year he defeated Murphy by 6,000 votes.

Celentano's candidacy brought thousands of Italians into the Republican party, as the voting history of the heavily Italian 10th Ward illustrates. In 1937 Murphy received 52 percent of the Tenth's vote. Two years later, running against Celentano for the first time, he got 22 percent and fared almost as badly in other Italian neighborhoods.[24] Matters

---

[22] Jews in New Haven, like those elsewhere, tended to vote Republican until the New Deal; see, e.g., Glazer and Moynihan, *Beyond the Melting Pot*, pp. 168–69.

[23] Except for the 1928 election, when the 10th was 18% ahead of the city in its support of Al Smith, and the 1932 and 1936 elections, when Roosevelt ran about 10% ahead of the city-wide vote there. In other mayoralty and presidential elections prior to 1939, differences were generally minor; see Dahl, *Who Governs?* pp. 48–50.

[24] President Roosevelt's 1940 "stab-in-the-back" speech and World War II are supposed to have cost him some Italian votes in 1940 and 1944. Whatever the extent of this loss, it seems to have been recouped in the 1948 election; see Lubell, *Future of American Politics*, 225–26. For differing assessments of the impact of Roosevelt's speech, see Whyte, *Street Corner Society*, pp. 230–31; and V. O. Key, *Public Opinion and American Democracy* (New York, 1961), pp. 271–72.

Table 2. Deviations from New Haven city-wide Democratic vote by selected wards with concentrations of various ethnic groups—mayoralty elections, 1949–61

Year and ethnicity of Republican mayoralty candidate[a]	City-wide Democratic vote[b]	10th & 11th Wards (Italian)[c]	16th & 17th Wards (Irish)[d]	19th Ward (Negro)[e]
	(%)	(%)	(%)	(%)
1949—Italian	46.6	−21.9	8.5	7.9
1951—Italian	49.9	−24.3	8.0	4.3
1953—Italian	51.9	−27.3	9.0	8.3
1955—Italian	65.3	−21.3	8.1	13.4
1957—Yankee	64.8	−14.4	11.5	14.2
1959—Italian	61.8	−20.2	11.0	16.3
1961—Yankee	53.5	−10.7	15.9	24.3
1950 median family income	$3301	$2660	$3174	$2117
		$2318	$3280	

[a] In all these elections the Democratic candidate was Richard C. Lee.

[b] Percentages are of the total vote cast for mayor.

[c] In 1960 population shifts caused by an urban renewal project began to change the composition of the 10th and 11th Wards. By 1963 a substantial fraction of the old residents had been replaced by newcomers, most of whom were neither Italians nor Republicans.

[d] Since about 1958 these wards have had an influx of Negroes.

[e] Negroes comprised 72% of the 19th Ward in 1950. Increasing Democratic majorities there may be due *in part* to continued growth of the ward's Negro population.

Sources: Voting returns for 1949–57 are from official sources; for 1959–61, from newspapers. Choice of wards was based on a combination of Census data and political lore. (Census tracts do not coincide with wards. The 1950 Census data were matched with wards, but this was an expensive process and was not repeated for the 1960 Census.) One of the three wards with the highest proportion of Italian-born residents, the 12th, has a dissident Democratic organization and was excluded for this reason. Since the first sizable numbers of Irish came to New Haven 120 years ago, Census data on the birthplace of present ward residents are an unreliable index of Irish predominance. I have followed the advice of New Haven politicians in choosing the 16th and 17th as the most Irish wards.

improved somewhat for the Democrats during the war, but Celentano's second candidacy produced an even greater Republican swing; in 1945 Murphy won only 17 percent of the 10th Ward's vote.

In 1947 the Democrats tried to match Celentano's appeal by giving the mayoralty nomination to an obscure Italian dentist. Thereby they recouped most of their losses in Italian neighborhoods—their share of the 10th Ward vote rose from 17 to 42 percent and was about this high in the other Italian wards—but lost heavily elsewhere in the city. Furthermore, a Socialist candidate won a sixth of the total vote and made his best showing in middle-class neighborhoods. Since this was several times greater than any third-party vote in a generation, anti-Italian sentiment may have motivated many of these Socialist votes.[25] The 1947 election

---

[25] The success of the Socialist party in nearby Bridgeport was due to different causes. Capitalizing on public revulsion at corrupt "double machine" collusion between the two major parties, the Socialist leader, Jasper McKevy, won the mayoralty there in 1933 and stayed in office for 24 years.

was the only one in the city's history in which both major party candidates were Italians.

In every mayoralty election since 1947 the Democratic candidate has been Richard C. Lee, a Catholic of mixed English, Scottish, and Irish descent who, for obvious reasons, emphasizes his Irish side. Lee unseated Celentano in 1953 after two unsuccessful attempts. Celentano did not run for mayor again, preferring to bide his time until Lee left the scene. Since then Lee has defeated a series of Republican candidates, usually by sizable margins.

Although Celentano has not run for office for more than ten years, his impact on the political allegiance of New Haven's Italians appears to have been enduring. In a well known article some years ago the late V. O. Key suggested "the existence of a category of elections . . . in which the decisive results of the voting reveal a sharp alteration of the pre-existing cleavage within the electorate. Moreover, . . . the realignment made manifest in the voting in such elections seems to persist for several succeeding elections."[26] Key called such contests "critical elections." As the following data show, Celentano's several mayoralty campaigns were critical elections with respect to the voting behavior of at least the Italians in New Haven.

Since 1947 the Italian wards have been the most Republican ones in the city. Table 2 shows the city-wide Democratic percentage of the vote in mayoralty elections from 1949 through 1961 and the deviations from this percentage of wards with the heaviest concentrations of Italians, Irish, and Negroes, respectively. As the table indicates, even a Yankee Republican will make his best showing in the Italian wards. In fact, the Tenth is the only ward that Lee has never carried. Since the Italian wards are among the poorest in town, their marked Republican inclinations can be attributed to ethnic voting.

Italian support for Republican candidates has been so lopsided that the customary relationship between Democratic voting and foreign birth is reversed in New Haven. The ward-by-ward correlation coefficient (Pearson's r) between percentage of foreign-born residents and percentage of the vote for Democratic mayoralty candidates has been *negative* for most elections since 1937.[27]

While Italian Republicanism is a product of local politics, it is also expressed in state and national elections. The ethnic voting that resulted from Italian solidarity in New Haven is now manifested in elections where "recognition" of Italians is not an issue. As Table 3 shows, the 10th Ward (for example) has been considerably more Republican than the city as a whole in elections where neither candidate was Irish or Italian. For instance, ex-Governor Ribicoff barely carried the Tenth in 1958, while in the Irish 17th Ward, where the median family income was more than $600 higher, he won by a three-to-one ratio.

---

[26] V. O. Key, Jr., "A Theory of Critical Elections," *Journal of Politics* 7 (1955): 4.

[27] Except for the 1941 and 1943 elections, when Celentano was not a candidate, and 1947, when both candidates were Italians.

Table 3. Democratic vote for state and national candidates in New Haven and in selected wards

Year and Election	City-wide Vote	10th Ward (Italian)	17th Ward (Irish)
1956 Presidential	45%	34%	51%
1958 Gubernatorial[a]	69	52	75
1962 Senatorial[b]	65	52	75

[a] The candidates were the incumbent Democrat, Abraham A. Ribicoff, and Fred Zeller.
[b] The candidates were Ribicoff and Horace Seely-Brown.
Source: Official voting returns.

Table 4. Percentage in working class occupations and percentage Democrats of a sample of New Haven voters, by ethnic groups, 1959

Number in Sample		Manual Workers Percent	Rank	Democratic Percent	Rank
47	Negroes	76	1	57	2
157	Italian Catholics	61	2	37	5
53	European Catholics	58	3	48	4
56	European Protestants	35	4	16	6
34	American Protestants[a]	27	5	9	7
53	Irish Catholics	20	6	64	1
74	European Jews	15	7	52	3

[a] "American" here means parents and grandparents born in the U. S.
Source: The table is based on 474 persons (of an original sample of 525 voters) who could be identified by religion and by place of birth of themselves, parents, or grandparents. The percentages Democratic are those who identified themselves as Democrats in response to the question: "Generally speaking, do you usually think of yourself as a Republican, a Democrat, or what?"

Most Italians not only vote for Republican candidates, but consider themselves Republicans. Their party identification was changed and fixed by Celentano's several campaigns. Table 4 shows the percentages of blue-collar workers and of Democrats in various ethnic groups. Little more than a third of the Italians are Democrats, although they are second only to Negroes in proportion of manual workers.

These tables show why New Haven politicians customarily explain the outcome of elections in terms of nationality groups rather than social classes: the most important lines of division in the electorate are ethnic rather than economic. In fact, ethnic cleavages wash out the usual relationships between socio-economic status and partisan preference. When New Haven wards are correlated by median income and Republican vote in the 1959 mayoralty election, the coefficient is −.02.[28] Similarly, there is no relationship between the proportion of manual workers in an ethnic group and the percentage of the group's members who consider themselves Democrats, as Table 4 shows. The salience of ethnicity explains the apparent anomaly that the Republican party's stronghold is in the poor-

[28] The 1st Ward was excluded because most of its residents are Yale students.

est parts of town, while the Democrats draw their strongest support from middle-class Jews and Irishmen, as well as low-income Negroes.[29] Since the two best examples of ethnic voting are the Republican inclinations of working-class Italians and the Democratic affiliation of middle-class Irishmen, the political correlates of ethnicity do not merely represent underlying economic differences.

Plainly, the assimilation theory does not fit the development of Italian bloc voting in New Haven. The New Haven case can be explained by a different view of ethnic voting that I will call a "mobilization theory." I will introduce it by reexamining in greater detail the assumptions of the assimilation theory.

The Mobilization of Ethnic Political Resources

The assimilation theory is based on the assumption that the strength of ethnic voting depends on the intensity of the individual's identification with his ethnic group.[30] The theory supposes that this identification is never stronger than in the early years of residence in this country[31] and declines thereafter as the immigrants gain some measure of well being. There is another prerequisite to ethnic voting that the assimilation theory overlooks: no matter how salient an individual's ethnic identification may be, it will not influence his voting behavior unless he sees a connection between this identity and the choice he makes on election day.[32] How does the Irishman know which candidate (if any) is friendlier to the Irish? The implications of this problem are worth further exploration.

Established politicians appealed to immigrants with tangible rewards and recognition. While one party may have been more vigorous in its efforts, both parties usually made some attempt to win their votes. These

[29] Dahl has an interesting table comparing the Negro 19th Ward to the Italian 11th. The two wards have similarly low occupational, income and educational levels, yet the 19th is overwhelmingly Democratic and the 11th is very Republican. This is the reverse of their partisan affinities in 1930 (Dahl, *Who Governs?*, p. 57).

[30] Cf. Berelson et al., *Voting*, pp. 67–72; and Angus Campbell et al., *The American Voter* (New York, 1960), chap. 12.

[31] This may be a dubious assumption, although it is not crucial to my argument. There are indications that the previous identification of many immigrants was not with the old nation, but the old village or old province. In this view, it was not until the immigrants saw that Americans classified them by nationality that they themselves developed some sense of belonging to a nationality group.

One could also argue that, whatever the locale of his previous identity, the immigrant's first impulse was to forget this old identity and become an American, but that he was forced back into ethnic consciousness by old-settler prejudice. Recurring nativist phenomena like Know-Nothingism, the Ku Klux Klan, Prohibition, and the end of mass immigration probably increased many ethnics' self-consciousness. See, *e.g.*, Richard Hofstadter, *The Age of Reform* (New York, 1955), p. 297.

[32] Cf. the discussion of "political proximity" in Campbell et al.: "Groups as perceived objects may be located according to their proximity to the world of politics... at the individual level: as *perception of proximity between the group and the world of politics becomes clearer, the susceptibility of the individual member to group influence in political affairs increases*" (*American Voter*, p. 311; emphasis in original).

campaign efforts posed a twofold communication problem of pervasiveness and persuasion: how could the party get its message to every ethnic voter, and how could it make the message credible? Only some ethnics would get a job or favor, and only some would know of the recognition given by one party or the other; or, confusingly, by both. How did the ethnic know which party was friendlier to his people?

Precinct workers who talk directly to the individual voter are the most effective means of electioneering.[33] There are no systematic data on precinct workers' activity at the peak of the immigrant era. Contemporary accounts indicate that, in at least some cities, few prospective voters could escape the attention of the political organizations.[34] At present the level of precinct work is much lower. In northern cities with over 100,000 population less than 20 percent of the adults reported contact with a party worker in a single presidential election.[35] In New Haven, where both parties have very strong and active campaign organizations, 40 percent of the registered voters have *never* been reached by a precinct worker.[36]

Let us assume that precinct organizations were able to contact almost every potential voter fifty years ago. What if both parties sent workers around? What if both parties had won—or bought—the support of some ethnic leaders?[37] No matter how fervently the ethnic might identify with his group, the appropriate political expression of this identification might not be clear to him.

First-generation ethnic groups seldom had many political resources aside from their votes. Many of their members were illiterate; except for the Irish, many could not speak English. At this stage it was easiest for the parties to compete for ethnic votes, for the enticements least in demand by party activists were most suitable for the immigrants. As time passed children went to school, men prospered, and the ethnic group produced representatives with the organizational and communications skills necessary for political leadership. There were greater demands on both parties for recognition and the men making the demands were more skilled at pressing their claims. Such demands raised the level of bidding between the parties, for now the ethnics were asking for rewards that were both scarcer and more highly prized by the people already established in the party organizations. The ethnics' ambitions were resisted

---

[33] Cf. Handlin, "The immigrant might sometimes read an article on such a matter in his newspaper but was less likely to be persuaded by any intrinsic ideas on the subject than by the character of the persuader" (*Uprooted*, p. 211). Such persuaders included, in addition to overt party workers, priests and the types of immigrant leaders discussed earlier.

[34] See, e.g., Robert A. Woods, *Americans in Process* (Boston, 1903), pp. 155–56.

[35] Source: data from the 1956 SRC study reported in Fred I. Greenstein, "The Changing Pattern of Urban Party Politics," *The Annals* 353 (1964): 8–9.

[36] Raymond E. Wolfinger, "The Influence of Precinct Work on Voting Behavior," *Public Opinion Quarterly* 27 (1963): 387–98.

[37] Whyte's discussion of bribery indicates that cash can have a powerful, if temporary, distracting effect on ethnic loyalties.

by those who would be displaced. Because of this resistance and the time it took to develop political skills, a generation or more went by before members of the new nationality group found their way into positions of any visibility and influence.[38]

Sooner or later some ethnics will occupy party positions. One party will nominate an ethnic for a minor office. Such positions are unimportant, and if the bid seems to pull votes the other party will soon match the offer.[39] Most ethnic voters still have the problem of figuring out the "right" ticket to vote for, since it is still not evident which party is friendlier. The ethnic group may be given some unity if it has an unquestioned leader who can deliver its vote to the party with which he has made a deal, but this does not appear to have been a common phenomenon. Customarily, ethnic groups were fragmented, with several leaders each telling his constituents about his exclusive inside track to the political bigwigs.[40]

The day will come when an ethnic will win a party nomination for a major elective office.[41] When this happens the problems of pervasiveness and persuasion will be solved for many of his fellow ethnics. They will all see his name on the ballot, and many will take this as proof that the party that nominated him is the right party for them because it has given the most recognition to their group. The bigotry that often accompanies a "first" candidacy is likely to enhance the political relevance of ethnicity for the members of the candidate's group.

It seems plausible that an ethnic group will get such a major nomination when adversity forces one party or the other to appeal to new sources of support. This seems to have been the case with Celentano's nomination. In the late 1930s the New Haven Republicans were in dire straits.

[38] Cf. Lowi, "The representation of a new minority in places of power occurs long after it has reached considerable size in the population and electorate" (*Pleasure of the Mayor*, p. 39). Elmer E. Cornwell, Jr. reports that in Providence, Rhode Island, "Members of a new group are not likely to appear as ward committeemen at all until some three decades after their first arrival in substantial numbers"; see his "Party Absorption of Ethnic Groups: The Case of Providence, Rhode Island," *Social Forces* 38 (1960): 208.

See also Lubell: "The key to the political progress of any minority element in this country would seem to lie in just this success in developing its own middle class" (*Future of American Politics*, p. 79). Lubell does not discuss specifically the importance of candidacy for major office, which is the key point in any group's mobilization.

[39] Huthmacher has an interesting description of this competitive bidding process in Massachusetts (*Mass. People and Politics*, pp. 119–26). His discussion makes clear the dangers of such strategies because of the jealousies aroused when newer groups are recognized.

[40] Prior to Celentano's nomination the Italian community in New Haven was reported to be fragmented; see McConnell, *Evolution of Social Class*, pp. 159–60.

[41] For present purposes "major office" may be loosely but serviceably defined as any public elective office which is the central prize in a political system: mayor, governor, perhaps U. S. senator, and, of course, the presidency. Candidacy for minor office does not seem to produce so much ethnic impact, at least where candidates for such positions appear on the ballot below more important ones. This is particularly true in states like Connecticut where one can vote for an entire party slate with one choice. Such arrangements discourage split-ticket voting; see Campbell et al., *American Voter*, pp. 275–76.

Some of the state party's leading figures had been implicated in the spectacular "Waterbury scandals." In 1937 the local party had suffered its most crushing loss in any mayoralty election in a century. Coming on the heels of Roosevelt's overwhelming re-election victory, Murphy's 1937 landslide must have suggested the need for a new campaign strategy to the city's Republicans; they had little more to lose. It was in this desperate situation that a member of New Haven's most numerous voting bloc was first nominated for mayor.

Celentano was chosen for the 1939 nomination by leaders of the Republican organization. In 1941 and 1943 the party had come close to beating Murphy with non-Italian candidates and by the summer of 1945 the city administration had suffered such a decline in popularity that Republican leaders were confident of winning the election that fall. They did not then want to give the nomination to Celentano, preferring a non-Italian who would be more dependent on their support. Celentano had to wage a hard fight in ward primaries to win the nomination.

The Democrats had nominated Driscoll, their first Irish mayoralty candidate, under similar circumstances a half century earlier. The great controversy over free coinage of silver had split the party and given the 1897 mayoralty election to the Republicans. The defection of Gold Democrats may well have driven the Democratic leaders of that day to adopt a strategy of maximizing their party's appeal to the Irish.[42]

The mobilization theory of ethnic voting states that: *The strength of ethnic voting depends on both the intensity of ethnic identification and the level of ethnic relevance in the election. The most powerful and visible sign of ethnic political relevance is a fellow-ethnic's name at the head of the ticket, evident to everyone who enters the voting booth. Middle-class status is a virtual prerequisite for candidacy for major office; an ethnic group's development of sufficient political skill and influence to secure such a nomination also requires the development of a middle class. Therefore ethnic voting will be greatest when the ethnic group has produced a middle class, i.e., in the second and third generations, not in the first. Furthermore, the shifts in party identification resulting from this first major candidacy will persist beyond the election in which they occurred.*

This is not to say that the growth of a middle class past the point of mobilization will necessarily produce increasing ethnic voting. Nor does the theory state that the resulting alignment is impervious to other political and social developments, or that more than one such shift cannot take place. But it does say that, in a given political arena and for a given nationality group, the development of voting solidarity is a product of leadership; that such leadership requires a middle class; and that such

---

[42] Lowi, who has analyzed top-level mayoral appointments in New York City from 1898 to 1958, reports similar findings: "It has been the role of the minority party in New York to provide a channel of mobility for new ethnic groups.... The dominant Democratic organizations of the twentieth century have made efforts to attract the immigrants, but the minority Republicans made greater use of top patronage for these purposes" (*Pleasure of the Mayor*, pp. 37–39).

alignments are more durable than the political candidacies that produce them.

The mobilization theory seems to be more useful than the assimilation theory in explaining ethnic voting at the national level. Most members of ethnic groups in big cities are, by and large, strongly Democratic. It is often forgotten that this is a rather recent development. In the early part of the 20th century, when the foreign population of many big cities was predominantly first and second generation, these cities were carried by Republican presidential candidates as often as not. In 1920, shortly after the ending of unrestricted immigration, the Republicans carried most cities with big immigrant populations. Harding swept New York, Cleveland, Boston, Chicago, Philadelphia, Pittsburgh, and Detroit by an aggregate plurality of 1,330,000 votes. The Republicans did almost as well in 1924. But in 1928 the aggregate Democratic margin in these seven cities was 307,000, and since then they have gone Democratic in every election, usually by substantial margins.[43]

Smith's candidacy seems to have been particularly important in its impact on partisan alignments in Southern New England. Connecticut, Massachusetts, and Rhode Island, with the highest ethnic populations in the country, were also, until 1928, stoutly Republican in state and national elections. Since then they have been in the Democratic column as often as not. Key's article on critical elections demonstrates this point more precisely. Cities which underwent a sharp and durable pro-Democratic change in 1928 had large Catholic, foreign-born populations; cities which reacted in the opposite way were largely Protestant and native-born. In short, the ethnic population of Southern New England has become more Democratic as the duration of its residence in this country has increased.

The Persistence of Ethnic Voting

I have argued that the importance of ethnicity in voting decisions does not steadily diminish from an initial peak, but instead increases during at least the first two generations. What next? While the assimilation theory may be inadequate for the first development of ethnic voting, what about succeeding generations? Does the importance of ethnicity diminish rapidly with more general acculturation and occupational differentiation?[44] Or does it persist as a major independent variable, although perhaps declining somewhat in importance? It is commonly thought that the first alternative is more correct. I shall argue here for the second proposition and suggest some factors that seem to be associated with the persistence of ethnic voting.

Useful trend data on this subject are scarce. Data on Catholic voting patterns are suggestive since Catholicism is analogous to ethnicity as a

---

[43] Samuel J. Eldersveld, "The Influence of Metropolitan Party Pluralities in Presidential Elections Since 1920: A Study of Twelve Cities," *American Political Science Review*, 43 (1949): 1196.

[44] For a statement of this point of view see Dahl, *Who Governs?*, pp. 34–36, 59–62.

variable in voting behavior. Catholics, too, tend to be more Democratic than Protestants, and this difference persists when income, occupation, or education is controlled—it is not simply an artifact of Protestants' higher status.[45]

The passage of time by itself does not reduce ethnic salience: witness Quebec. Nationality groups seem to vary in their rates of assimilation. Few Irishmen have ancestors who came to the United States after the turn of the century, yet from all indications there are many places where Irish self-consciousness is still very strong—notably in New York City, for instance. But the Germans, who immigrated there in considerable numbers at about the same time as the Irish, no longer seem to be a self-conscious nationality group.[46] Catholic preference for the Democratic party does not seem to be a result of the disproportionately heavy representation of Catholics among more recent arrivals to this country. When generation of American residence is controlled, Catholic–Protestant differences do not disappear nor even diminish significantly.[47]

The passage of time is thought to be associated with weakening ethnic consciousness not just through attenuation of immigrant memories, but because members of any given ethnic group will get better jobs and, after two or three generations, be represented among all occupational levels, more or less in proportion to their numbers.[48] Occupational mobility is believed to reduce the importance of ethnicity in voting decisions for two reasons: (1) it will produce economic interests inconsistent with ethnic voting; and (2) the mobile individuals will come into contact with a broader, socially heterogeneous environment that will dilute ethnic salience.[49]

The extent to which social mobility alters the political expression of ethnic feelings undoubtedly varies with a number of other circumstances. The voting behavior of the New Haven Irish seems to have been relatively impervious to their changed social status. Although they are almost

[45] Berelson et al., *Voting*, pp. 61–71; Campbell, Gurin and Miller, *Voter Decides*, p. 71; Campbell et al., *American Voter*, chap. 12; and Scott Greer, "Catholic Voters and the Democratic Party," *Public Opinion Quarterly* 25 (1961): 611–25. Berelson's study found that Catholicism was a stronger independent variable than socio-economic status in voting behavior. Like ethnicity, its importance is subject to much short-term variation. For example, Catholicism was much more important in the 1960 presidential election than in 1956; see Philip E. Converse et al., "Stability and Change in 1960; a Reinstating Election," *American Political Science Review*, 55 (1961): 269–80.

[46] On the "disappearance" of the Germans see Glazer and Moynihan, *Beyond the Melting Pot*, p. 311; and Moynihan and Wilson, "Patronage in N. Y. State," pp. 299–300.

[47] Greer, "Catholic Voters," p. 621; and Campbell, Gurin and Miller, *Voter Decides*, p. 79. The latter study found that the partisan difference between Catholics and Protestants was as great in the fourth generation as in the first.

[48] All ethnic groups are not, of course, equally represented in various occupations; see, e.g., Glazer and Moynihan, *Beyond the Melting Pot*, pp. 317–24.

[49] This assumes that the direction of ethnic influences will favor the Democratic party. When ethnic pressures are pro-Republican, as in the case of New Haven Italians, the problem of predicting the political consequences of social mobility becomes more complicated.

all in the middle class, their support of the Democratic party is so pronounced that it could not have declined very much as they went from manual labor to white collar jobs. Even when mobility does produce changes in political perspectives, these changes do not obliterate all hitherto existing predispositions. Social change begins from a "base point" of previous habits. Occupational mobility will change the politics of many of the immigrants' children, but it will do the same for old Americans. The net political difference between the two groups may be as great in the middle class as in the working class. This proposition is supported by the Elmira study, which found that differences between Catholics and Protestants in their support of the Republican presidential candidate were actually greater in the middle and upper than in the lower class.[50] If anything, social mobility had heightened the importance of religion as an independent variable.

Upward-mobile members of the middle class have political characteristics intermediate between those typical of their old and their new status positions. While more Republican than their parents, they are considerably more likely to be Democrats than are status-stable members of their class.[51] The voting behavior studies have established that as many as four-fifths of all voters identify with the same party as their parents.[52] This is not just a reflection of similar life conditions; the authors of *Voting* report that most of their respondents whose vote was "inconsistent" with their social class were following parental political preferences.[53]

The data in Table 2 indicate that ethnic voting has not declined in New Haven in the postwar period. Deviation from the city-wide vote by Italian and Irish wards was as great in 1959 as in the 1940s. The smaller Italian deviation in 1961 may be a sign of declining ethnic salience, but it may also reflect Italian coolness to a Yankee Republican candidate, or the first wave of population changes resulting from the Wooster Square Renewal Project. At least in New Haven, all the social changes of the 1940s and 1950s do not seem to have reduced the political importance of national origins.

One contemporary trend that may be relevant to ethnic voting has not been mentioned. Most of the data in this paper describe only those

---

[50] Berelson, et al., *Voting*, p. 65.

[51] James A. Barber, Jr., "Social Mobility and Political Behavior," unpublished dissertation, Stanford University, 1965. See also Berelson et al., *Voting*, p. 91.

[52] *Ibid.*, p. 89; Campbell et al., *American Voter*, p. 147.

[53] Berelson et al., *Voting*, p. 90. For discussion of the varying strength and characteristics of the relationships between social class and voting behavior, see Campbell et al., *American Voter*, chap. 13; and Heinz Eulau, *Class and Party in the Eisenhower Years* (New York, 1962). As these books make clear, associations between class and party are mediated by a number of other personal and historical variables. One such is the difference between social class as measured by objective indicators like income, and subjective class, i.e., what the individual considers his class position to be. When middle-class people identify with the working class their political attitudes and behavior tend to resemble those of members of the working class. Possibly middle-class ethnics are more likely to consider themselves working class than are middle-class Yankees. This suggests one mechanism that would modify the political impact of social mobility.

ethnics who have chosen to remain in the old core cities. Their neighborhoods tend to be ethnically homogeneous but economically diverse, with working-class and middle-class families intermingled. It is plausible that those ethnics who have decided to stay in such neighborhoods despite their financial ability to move to the suburbs have stronger ethnic identifications, whether as a consequence or as a cause of continued proximity. What about the ethnics who have moved to the suburbs? They should be less ethnically conscious. Suburbs tend to be economically homogeneous and ethnically diverse; in these respects they are the reverse of the old city neighborhoods. It seems likely that these new suburbanites break off the interpersonal and institutional relationships that sustain and transmit ethnic consciousness. Since group solidarity is maintained by personal contact,[54] it is probable that geographical dispersion will dilute ethnic salience. At the same time, however, it will help to maintain the solidarity of the urban survivors by draining off those with the weakest ethnic identifications.[55]

There are not many data relevant to these speculations. *The American Voter*'s discussion of suburbanization is tentative and inconclusive, while an earlier analysis of some of the same data produced findings consistent with the line of argument in the preceding paragraph.[56] The most useful evidence comes from Scott Greer's study of Catholic voting behavior in and around St. Louis. He found that, with education and generation of American residence controlled, suburban Catholics were more likely than urban Catholics to defect to the Republicans.[57]

Several political circumstances are also associated with the strength of ethnic voting. In general, it appears that ethnicity will be more important in the absence of other plain cues to guide voters' decisions. It is likely to play a greater role in nonpartisan elections, where voters cannot rely on the party label.[58] But, while party identification may impede the free play of ethnic salience, it also stabilizes and prolongs ethnic voting by providing a vehicle for continuing perception of ethnic relevance. Celentano's candidacy won Italian support not only for him, but also for the Repub-

---

[54] This proposition is stated in Berelson, et al., *Voting*, p. 74; and is supported by data in their chap. 6.

Ethnic groups may differ in their willingness to move from old urban habitats. Glazer and Moynihan report that Italians in New York, unlike some other groups, seem to remain, generation after generation, in the same areas where they first settled. The areas of Italian concentration in 1920 and 1960 are substantially the same except where land clearance has displaced people (*Beyond the Melting Pot*, pp. 186–87).

[55] Immigration continues to provide a diminished but by no means negligible fresh supply of ethnics. Most of the 2,500,000 people who entered the United States as immigrants from 1950 to 1959 probably settled in neighborhoods inhabited by earlier arrivals from their respective countries.

[56] Campbell et al., *American Voter*, pp. 457–60; Fred I. Greenstein and Raymond E. Wolfinger, "The Suburbs and Shifting Party Loyalties," *Public Opinion Quarterly* 22 (1958): 473–82.

[57] Greer, "Catholic Voters," p. 621. Even in the suburbs, however, Catholicism is a potent independent variable in voting behavior.

[58] Cf. James Q. Wilson, *Negro Politics* (New York, 1960), p. 43.

lican party in subsequent elections because his association with the party led Italians to think that it gave them more recognition. Ethnic voting also seems to be less important when some great issue dominates political perspectives, as the Depression did in the 1930s.[59] This may explain the unusually pro-Democratic voting of New Haven Italians in the 1932 and 1936 presidential elections.

The major proposition of this section is that ethnicity is still an important factor in voting behavior and is not eliminated by changes in the economic characteristics of the individuals affected. This is not to say that perspectives formed in the first generations of American residence will persist forever. Ethnic consciousness is fading; it is already faint in some parts of the country and for some ethnic groups. Continuing increases in education, geographical dispersion, intermarriage and intergroup contacts are all likely to reduce ethnic consciousness.

Even when ethnic salience has faded, however, its political effects will remain. One of the most remarkable tendencies in political behavior is the persistence of partisan affiliations for generations after the reasons for their formation have become irrelevant to contemporary society. Key and Munger's article on county voting patterns in Indiana is one of the best-known demonstrations of this proposition. Some Indiana counties were consistently Democratic while others, apparently identical in demographic characteristics, were consistently Republican. The roots of these variations seemed to be the origins of the counties' first settlers—New England or the South: "If one plots on the map of Indiana clusters of underground railroad stations and points at which Union authorities had difficulties in drafting troops, he separates, on the whole, Republican and Democratic counties."[60] Key and Munger conclude that for many voters elections are merely "a reaffirmation of past decisions." It seems plausible that this will be the legacy of ethnic politics: when national origins are forgotten, the political allegiances formed in the old days of ethnic salience will be reflected in the partisan choices of totally assimilated descendants of the old immigrants.

[59] See Dahl, *Who Governs?*, pp. 49–51.

[60] V. O. Key, Jr., and Frank Munger, "Social Determinism and Electoral Decision: the Case of Indiana," in Eugene Burdick and Arthur J. Brodbeck (eds.), *American Voting Behavior* (Glencoe, Ill., 1959), pp. 281–99, and p. 457 n. Similar findings for Ohio are reported in V. O. Key, Jr., "Partisanship and County Office: The Case of Ohio," *American Political Science Review* 47 (1953): 529–31; and Thomas A. Flinn, "The Outline of Ohio Politics," *Western Political Quarterly* 13 (1960): 702–21.

Immigrants and Municipal Voting Turnout: Implications for the Changing Ethnic Impact on Urban Politics*

DANIEL N. GORDON

The ethnic impact on American urban politics has allegedly been widespread, enduring, and significant. And, according to Parenti, ethnic-group presence is still a relevant factor in city politics.[1] However, Parenti drew this particular inference from recent evidence gathered in New Haven, Connecticut. As suggestive as his discussion is, it lacks both a large sample base and historical data. This study will attempt to overcome both shortcomings by examining the relationship between the size of immigrant populations and municipal electoral turnout for the period 1934 to 1960.

Immigrant Populations and Voting Turnout as Measures of Ethnic Political Impact

This study uses the percentage of foreign-born persons as the indicator of nationality groups' presence (the independent variable). Immigrant

---

Reprinted from the *American Sociological Review* 35 (1970): 665–81. Copyright 1970 by the American Sociological Association. Reprinted by permission of the publisher.

* Collection of the voting turnout data reported here was financed by a grant from the Dartmouth College Faculty Research Committee. The collection of the governmental and Census data reported here was financed by a dissertation fellowship from the Russell Sage Foundation Program in Sociology and Law, University of Wisconsin. I would like to thank George W. Bohrnstedt for his advice on the analysis of panel data. I would also like to thank Michael Parenti and Raymond E. Wolfinger for their comments on an earlier draft of this paper. The assistance of these men in no way absolves the author of responsibility for the contents of this paper.

[1] See Michael Parenti, "Ethnic Politics and the Persistence of Ethnic Identification," *American Political Science Review* 61 (1967): 717–26.

The terms "ethnic," "ethnic group," and "nationality group" are used here to designate all groups which differ from the majority old American stocks in their national origins. The terms "foreign born," "immigrants," and "immigrant groups" refer only to actual immigrants from foreign shores. Not included in any of these terms are black Americans who are not covered here because their urban political participation differs from white nationality groups in too many respects to discuss here. Primarily, though, this study is historical in its approach and covers a period (1934–60) in which black Americans had less political power in cities than they do currently. Finally, in Northern cities which form the major part of the analysis presented here, nonwhites have tended to settle in cities which do not have large immigrant populations.

groups in American cities—be they the Irish of Boston, New Haven, New York, or Chicago;[2] the Italians of New Haven;[3] the Germans and Polish in Milwaukee,[4] etc.—have traditionally influenced the pattern of municipal politics. In short, municipal politics cut across national origin lines, and involve many immigrant groups.[5]

In addition, the percentage of foreign born correlates highly (Pearsonian $r = .87$) with the percentage of second-generation Americans in cities.[6] Therefore, the size of foreign-born populations is also a strong indicator of the size of second-generation populations and, presumably, third and subsequent generations. (Unfortunately, the Census does not supply data on the numbers of third and subsequent generations.)

The percentage of adults voting in municipal elections for the period 1934 to 1960 is used as the indicator of voting activity (the dependent variable).[7] I assume that turnout in local elections increases as the stakes and competitiveness of electoral contests increase. People vote in local elections if they conceive of voting as relevant to themselves. As the stakes of elections increase, more people will feel affected by the electoral outcome and will participate as voters. For example, the hard-fought black–white mayoralty contests in Cleveland, Gary, and Los Angeles caused

---

[2] Edward M. Levine, *The Irish and the Irish Politicians* (South Bend: University of Notre Dame Press, 1966); Raymond E. Wolfinger, "The Development and Persistence of Ethnic Voting," *American Political Science Review* 59 (1965): 896–908; Nathan Glazer and Daniel P. Moynihan, *Beyond the Melting Pot* (Cambridge: M.I.T. Press, 1963).

[3] Wolfinger, "Development and Persistence of Ethnic Voting."

[4] Leon D. Epstein, *Politics in Wisconsin* (Madison: University of Wisconsin Press, 1958).

[5] Of course, probably not all nationality groups have been involved in urban politics. However, involvement has been sufficiently widespread to consider these groups as an entity. Also see Robert E. Lane, *Political Life* (New York: Free Press, 1959), chap. 17.

[6] Jeffrey K. Hadden and Edgar F. Borgatta, *American Cities: Their Social Characteristics* (Chicago: Rand McNally, 1965), p. 128.

[7] One might argue for the use of the percentage of registered persons voting since the issue of restrictive registration requirements would be bypassed: all registered persons are presumably eligible to vote. However, historical registration data are less available than turnout data. Nevertheless, the question of restrictive registration laws should not invalidate the results for two reasons. First, a control for region (South vs. North) is used to correct for the most prevalent source of disfranchisement, i.e., Southern blacks. Second, in 1960 the correlations between the size of immigrant populations and the percentage of adults voting and the size of immigrant populations and the percentage of registered persons voting differ in magnitude but not in sign. See Ruth B. Dixon, "Predicting Voter Turnout in City Elections," unpublished M. A. thesis, University of California, Berkeley (1966).

Voting data were gathered primarily from postcard questionnaires sent to reference librarians, city clerks, and election officials. For the municipal elections closest to 1934, 1940, 1950, and 1960 the postcards asked for the number of persons registered, the number of persons voting, and whether the elections were concurrent with a state or national contest. In some cases, missing turnout data for 1934 were obtained from the *Municipal Yearbook*: 1935, and missing data for 1960 were obtained from the Lee electoral turnout data. These data were purchased from the Survey Research Center, University of California, Berkeley. They were collected by Eugene C. Lee and analyzed in his article "City Elections: A Statistical Profile," in Orin F. Nolting and David S. Arnold, eds., *Municipal Yearbook* (Chicago: Internat. City Managers' Assoc., 1963).

very high turnout in those cities. In fact, the 1969 Bradley–Yorty election in Los Angeles had a turnout of 80 percent: 15 percent higher than any previous mayoralty election.[8] In contrast, the nonpartisan noncompetitive politics of suburbia are characterized by voter apathy.[9]

Case studies indicate that cities with large ethnic populations often have highly competitive political systems organized around ethnic cleavages. Freeman's study of "Bay City," Massachusetts,[10] uncovered a political split between Yankee Protestants and Catholic ethnics which was reflected in voting preferences at the polls. Wolfinger's study of New Haven also revealed competitive politics with partisan loyalties partially based on ethnic considerations.[11] Also, New York City politics shifted over the years from a social class basis to an ethnic basis as politicians realized that the "ethnic short-hand" is politically less risky than controversial class politics.[12] In addition, Lane mentions several instances of ethnic conflict.[13] And the history of the American municipal reform movement has often included native American upper-class persons' attempts to wrest local political control from nationality groups.[14] Finally, Banfield and Wilson write that the size of a "particular ethnic group in a city seems to affect turnout. This is often called the 'bandwagon effect.' "[15] Since ethnically-oriented municipal politics are often competitive, the presence of large immigrant populations in cities should be associated with high municipal voting turnout.

Turnout and Other Related Factors

Previous studies have shown that various governmental, regional, and demographic factors are also associated with voting turnout. I employ these variables (1) to guard against spurious correlations between the size of immigrant populations and turnout, and (2) as indicators of *structural potentialities* in urban political systems.

Governmental Factors

Mayor-council (versus commission and council-manager) government, partisan (versus nonpartisan) elections, and concurrency of elections (ver-

[8] Steven V. Roberts, "Yorty Fashions Victory Largely Out of Fear," *The New York Times*, 1 June 1969, Section 4, p. 1.

[9] Scott Greer, *Governing the Metropolis* (New York: John Wiley, 1962), chap. 5.

[10] J. Leiper Freeman, "Local Party Systems: Theoretical Considerations and a Case Analysis," *American Journal of Sociology* 64 (1958): 282–89.

[11] Wolfinger, "Development and Persistence of Ethnic Voting."

[12] Glazer and Moynihan, *Beyond the Melting Pot*.

[13] Lane, *Political Life*.

[14] Daniel N. Gordon, "Immigrants and Urban Governmental Form in American Cities, 1933–60," *American Journal of Sociology* 74 (1968): 158–71.

[15] Edward C. Banfield and James Q. Wilson, *City Politics* (Cambridge: Harvard University Press, 1965).

sus nonconcurrency) with a state or national contest are all associated with high electoral turnout.[16]

Registration laws, especially provisions regarding literacy tests and the closing dates for registration have an impact on registration and subsequent voting turnout.[17] I have no data on registration laws since these data are difficult to collect for the present and nearly impossible to collect for the past. However, difficulties in registration should affect all potential voters equally, with the exception of literacy tests. Foreign-born persons with non-English mother tongues might have difficulty passing such tests. However, Kelley, et al.[18] found that the association between the provisions for literacy tests and the percentage of adults registered became statistically insignificant when they removed Southern cities (which have few members of nationality groups) from their sample.[19]

Regional Factors

Because literacy tests and other registration requirements have historically been used to disfranchise black people in the South, a regional control (South versus North) is necessary.[20] Also related to region in general is the question of historical factors within regions as determinants of political outcomes. Wolfinger and Field argue for the importance of region because their controls for region attenuated the association between ethnicity and various governmental variables.[21] However, this attenuation

---

[16] Lee, "City Elections: A Statistical Profile."

[17] Stanley Kelley, Jr., Richard E. Ayres, and William G. Bowen, "Registration and Voting: Putting First Things First," *American Political Science Review* 71 (1967): 359–79.

[18] *Ibid.*, p. 367.

[19] The above discussion implicitly assumes that registration laws are not uniformly easier in cities with large immigrant populations. Since some states did pass literacy tests in attempts to disfranchise immigrants, and since I will be using a series of controls in my analysis (especially region), this assumption is probably not unreasonable.

[20] The Southern states are Alabama, Arkansas, Florida, Georgia, Louisiana, Mississippi, North Carolina, South Carolina, Tennessee, Texas, and Virginia. These are the states which V. O. Key, Jr. [*Southern Politics* (New York: Vintage Books, 1949)] described as restricting black suffrage. Since all of the elections analyzed here came before the Federal Voting Rights Act, separation of Southern from Northern states is necessary.

The remaining regional divisions are as follows:

The Eastern states are Maine, New Hampshire, Massachusetts, Connecticut, Rhode Island, New York, New Jersey, Pennsylvania, Maryland, and Delaware. No Vermont cities were in the original 306 city sample. Washington, D.C. was excluded because it does not have home rule.

The Midwestern and West Border states are Ohio, Indiana, Illinois, Michigan, Wisconsin, Minnesota, Iowa, Kansas, Oklahoma, Missouri, West Virginia, Kentucky, and Nebraska.

The Western states are South Dakota, Montana, Idaho, Utah, Colorado, Arizona, California, Oregon, and Washington. No North Dakota, Wyoming, New Mexico, Nevada, Alaska, or Hawaii cities were in the original 306 city sample.

[21] Raymond E. Wolfinger and John Osgood Field, "Political Ethos and the Structure of City Government," *American Political Science Review* 56 (1966): 306–26.

does not agree with my earlier results.[22] Since there has been some controversy over regional effects, this factor will also be used as a control variable.

Demographic Factors

Population growth is inversely related to turnout and urban class structure is also negatively related to turnout.[23] Cities with large lower-class populations have higher municipal turnout rates than cities with smaller lower-class populations.

I define urban class composition as the percentage of blue-collar males residing in the city. Alford and Lee used educational measures instead of occupation.[24] However, Hadden and Borgatta demonstrate that urban educational and occupational composition are highly interrelated.[25] Hence, educational and occupational indicators are, in effect, interchangeable.

Finally, the proportion of population change is also related to turnout.[26] High population growth tends to be associated with low turnout and vice versa.

In sum, governmental, regional, and demographic factors may affect turnout, and are accounted for in this analysis of municipal voting turnout.

Sample Characteristics and Methodology

The initial sample for this study was the 306 American cities which had 30,000 or more population in 1930. Complete voting data were obtained for 198 (65 percent) of these 306 cities.

The initial set of 306 cities are those covered in the first report of governmental data published by the International City Managers' Association in 1934. My desire to obtain governmental data for the earliest possible year dictated the selection of this group of cities. In relation to all cities of 25,000 or more population in 1960, the principal bias of the 306 cities is the underrepresentation of rapidly growing cities. This bias is corrected by using population change as a control variable. (A detailed comparison of the 306 cities with all 25,000+ cities is found in my 1968 article.)

The 198 cities for which complete voting data were obtained appear to be highly representative of the original 306 city sample. There is a

---

[22] Gordon, "Immigrants and Urban Governmental Form."

[23] Dixon, "Predicting Voter Turnout," p. 70.

[24] Robert R. Alford and Eugene C. Lee, "Voting Turnout in American Cities," *American Political Science Review* 62 (1968): 796–813.

[25] Hadden and Borgatta, *American Cities*.

[26] Dixon, "Predicting Voter Turnout," and Alford and Lee, "Voting Turnout."

maximum difference between the original (N = 306) and the final (N = 198) sample of two percentage points in the distribution of governmental forms for all four years (1934, 1940, 1950, and 1960). Similarly, the distributions of ward councils, partisan elections, and regions (1934–60) show only small percentage point differences between the 306 city and 198 city samples: the largest difference is 7 percent. And the correlations between the completeness of voting data (1934–60) and the percentage of foreign born, the percentage of blue-collar workers, and the proportion of population change for three decades (1930–40, 1940–50, and 1950–60)[27] show only slight tendencies for cities with complete voting data to have larger foreign-born populations and smaller blue-collar populations.

The data are analyzed by a technique described by Bohrnstedt.[28] The percentage of immigrants at time 1 is correlated with the percentage of adults voting at time 2 while holding constant the percentage of adults at time 1. A complete description of this technique can be found in Bohrnstedt or the original version of this paper (pp. 668–70).

Results: Immigrant Populations and Turnout

The percentage of foreign-born persons has an impact on turnout (Table 1). However, this relationship is not uniform over time. The highest partial correlations between the percentage of foreign born and turnout occur for the elections of 1940 (partial $r = .40$) and 1950 (partial $r = .37$).

In addition, Table 1 shows the partial correlations between turnout and several control variables to be used below.

Eastern cities tend to have high turnouts. Midwestern and Western location of cities does not consistently contribute to low turnouts over time (although Midwestern and Western location is one determinant of low turnouts for one of the three elections).

Region as a determinant of turnout might be a reflection of different city types within regions. (More will be said about this shortly.) For example, Eastern cities tend to have large foreign-born populations and few rapidly growing cities. In contrast, Southern cities are more likely to be rapidly growing and to have small foreign-born populations. Yet historical factors within regions, especially the South, also play a part. Southern cities are generally characterized by lower turnout than any other region. This lower turnout is apparently traceable, in part, to the disfranchisement of black people. The partial correlation between the size of the nonwhite population and turnout for the elections of 1940 and 1950 is negative. When Southern cities are removed from the sample, the partial correlations between the percentage of nonwhite and turnout

---

[27] These correlations were obtained by the use of "dummy" variables. A city with complete voting data was scored as 1 and a city with missing data was scored as 0.

[28] George W. Bohrnstedt, "Observations on the Measurement of Change," in *Sociological Methodology*, Edgar F. Borgatta and George W. Bohrnstedt, eds. (San Francisco: Jossey-Bass, 1969), pp. 113–36.

Table 1. Partial correlations of selected city characteristics at time 1 with the percentage of adults voting[a] at time 2 by the percentage of adults voting at time 1 (N = 198).

City Characteristics	Partial Correlations with Turnout in Year[b]		
	1940	1950	1960
Percentage of foreign born[c]	.40**	.37**	.16**
Proportion population change	−.25**	−.24**	−.23**
Percentage of blue collar[d]	.20**	.17**	.16**
Governmental variables:[e]			
Mayor-council vs. other	.10	.26**	.10
Wards vs. at-large	.05	.22**	.09
Partisan vs. nonpartisan	.09	.11	.19**
Concurrent vs. nonconcurrent	.19**	−.06	.35**
Region:[f]			
East vs. other	.31**	.45**	.25**
Midwest vs. other	−.02	−.23**	.08
West vs. other	−.09	−.08	−.23**
South vs. other	−.33**	−.20**	−.18**

* Significant at the .05 level.
** Significant at the .01 level.

[a] The percentage of adults voting is the total number of voters divided by the number of city residents 21 years or older. Data sources for the number 21 or older are U. S. Bureau of the Census, *Population*, Vol. III, *Reports by States* (Washington, D. C.: U. S. Government Printing Office, 1932), Table 15; U. S. Bureau of the Census, *Population*, Vol. II, *Characteristics of the Population* (Washington, D. C.: U. S. Government Printing Office, 1943), Tables 32 and 34; U. S. Bureau of the Census, *Census of Population: 1950, Characteristics of the Population* (Washington, D. C.: U. S. Government Printing Office, 1952), Table 33; and U. S. Bureau of the Census, *Census of Population: 1960*, Vol. I *Characteristics of the Population* (Washington, D. C.: U. S. Government Printing Office, 1963), Table 20.

[b] The year in the table head is the year of the election for which turnout is being correlated with the selected city characteristics of the previous decade. Turnout in the previous decade is always partialed out.

[c] The percentage of foreign born is the number of foreign born divided by the total city population. Data sources for the number of foreign born are U. S. Bureau of the Census, *Population*, Vol. III, *Reports by States*, Table 15; U. S. Bureau of the Census, *Population*, Vol. II, *Characteristics of the Population*, Tables 31 and 34; U. S. Bureau of the Census, *Census of Population: 1950, Characteristics of the Population*, Table 35; and U. S. Bureau of the Census, *Census of Population: 1960*, Vol. I *Characteristics of the Population*, Table 34. These sources were also used to obtain population sizes from which the proportion of population change was computed by dividing the population size at time 1 by the population size at time 2.

[d] The percentage of blue collar is the total employed male labor force divided into the number of males employed in blue-collar occupations. Occupational data sources are U. S. Bureau of the Census, *Population*, Vol. IV, *Occupations by States* (Washington, D. C.: U. S. Government Printing Office, 1932), Tables 4 and 5; U. S. Bureau of the Census, *Population*, Vol. II, *Characteristics of the Population*, Table 33 and U. S. Bureau of the Census, *Population*, Vol. III, *The Labor Force* (Washington, D. C.: U. S. Government Printing Office, 1943), Table 11; U. S. Bureau of the Census, *Census of Population: 1950, Characteristics of the Population*, Table 35; and U. S. Bureau of the Census, *Census of Population: 1960*, Vol. I, *Characteristics of the Population*, Table 74.

[e] Mayor-council government was scored as 1 and commission and council-manager governments were scored as 0. Wards, partisan elections, and concurrent elections were also scored as 1 while their opposites were scored 0. Partisan elections are those where party labels appear on the ballot, whereas nonpartisan elections have no party labels. Ward elected city councils have some or all of their councilmen elected from wards, whereas all councilmen are elected at large on at-large

Table 1.—Continued

councils. Governmental data sources are Clarence E. Ridley and Orin F. Nolting (eds.), *Municipal Yearbook* (Chicago: International City Managers' Association, 1934), Table 1; Ridley and Nolting (eds.), *Municipal Yearbook* (Chicago: International City Managers' Association, 1941), Table 2; Ridley and Nolting (eds.), *Municipal Yearbook* (Chicago: International City Managers' Association, 1951), Table 3; and Orin F. Nolting and David S. Arnold (eds.), *Municipal Yearbook* (Chicago: International City Managers' Association, 1961), Table 5.

f States within regions are listed in n. 20.

remains only for the election of 1950 (partial r = −.20). The partial correlations for the elections of 1940 and 1960 are virtually nil (partial r = .01 and .05, respectively). Moreover, there is some evidence that the turnout figures reported for some Southern cities were mixtures of primary turnout in some years and general election turnout in others. Therefore, because of the special problems posed by Southern cities, these cities should be separated from Northern cities for the analysis of immigrant populations and turnout. But since there are only 28 Southern cities in the 198 city sample, there are too few cases to carry out parallel analyses between North and South. Only Northern cities will be analyzed in the remainder of this paper.

Finally, with the exception of the percentage of blue collar, the remaining variables are generally related to turnout as predicted, although these relationships do not always hold from decade to decade. The percentage of blue collar, contrary to expectation, has a positive impact on turnout. This result is consistent with the results presented by Alford and Lee to the effect that education is negatively related to turnout.[29] Since the correlations between city populations' occupational and educational characteristics are high,[30] there is a great deal of overlap between these measures.[31]

In Northern cities, large immigrant populations tend to raise turnout in a variety of city types (see Table 2). In general, the impact of ethnicity on turnout is seen only for the elections of 1940 and 1950. Except for cities with at-large councils, nonpartisan elections, nonconcurrent elections, and Midwestern location, the size of immigrant populations has no effect on turnout in the 1960 elections. Of all the control variables, region appears to be the most powerful factor in attenuating some of the relationships between the size of immigrant populations and turnout over time. Also, the temporal pattern of the partial correlations between the percentage of foreign born and the percentage of adults voting is not similar to the pattern seen in other types of cities. Previously, I mentioned that there is disagreement as to the meaning of region as a variable. Wol-

[29] Alford and Lee, "Voting Turnout."

[30] Hadden and Borgatta, *American Cities*, pp. 138, 140, 142. Hadden and Borgatta used the percentage of white collar as their measure of class composition. This measure is merely the reverse of the percentage of blue collar used here. The percentage of white collar in 1960, according to Hadden and Borgatta's data, correlates .80 with median school years completed, −.51 with the percentage who have completed less than five years of school, and .81 with the percentage of college graduates.

[31] Alford and Lee, "Voting Turnout," pp. 811–12.

Immigrants and Municipal Voting Turnout 175

Table 2. Partial correlations with and without control variables between the percentage of foreign born at time 1 and the percentage of adults voting at time 2 by the percentage of adults voting at time 1 in Northern cities.

Control Variable	Partial Correlations with Turnout in Year[a]		
	1940	1950	1960
None	.33** (170) [b]	.32** (170)	.15* (170)
Governmental variables:			
Mayor-council govt.	.34** (96)	.35** (88)	.13 (84)
Commission govt.	.26* (41)	.30* (38)	.21 (31)
Council-manager govt.	.39** (33)	.22 (44)	.15 (55)
Ward council	.34** (82)	.40** (78)	.08 (80)
At-large council	.32** (88)	.23 (92)	.19** (90)
Partisan election	.32** (61)	.14 (60)	.12 (58)
Nonpartisan election	.34** (109)	.47** (110)	.25** (112)
Concurrent election	.54** (35)	.27 (34)	.06 (34)
Nonconcurrent election	.25** (135)	.35** (136)	.16* (136)
Percentage of blue collar:[c]			
Low (61 or less)	.26** (76)	.31** (70)	.14 (93)
Medium (62–67)	.23* (58)	.36** (62)	.07 (49)
High (68 or more)	.30* (36)	.26 (38)	.00 (28)
Proportion population change:[d]			
Decrease (.9999 or less)	.24* (59)	.39 (19)	.04 (70)
Stable–small increase (1.0000–1.1002)	.16 (85)	.24* (80)	.15 (38)
Large increase (1.1003+)	.50** (26)	.28** (71)	.16 (62)
Region:			
East	.04 (75)	.22* (75)	—.12 (75)
Midwest	.39** (65)	—.01 (65)	.28** (65)
West	.29 (30)	.17 (30)	.09 (30)

* Significant at the .05 level.
** Significant at the .01 level.

a The year in the table head is the year of the election for which turnout is being correlated with the percentage of foreign born of the previous decade. Turnout in the previous decade is always partialed out. Some examples of this method are: foreign born in 1930 with turnout in 1940 by turnout in 1934, foreign born in 1950 with turnout in 1960 by turnout in 1950. The year in which the control variables were measured is the year of the election, e.g., the form of government in 1940 for the partial correlation between turnout in 1940 with the percentage of foreign born in 1930 by turnout in 1934.

b The numbers in parentheses are the number of cities in each category. This is also true for all the subsequent tables presented.

c The categories were derived as follows: First, the lowest and highest boundaries possibly occurring in any of the four years (1934, 1940, 1950, and 1960) were determined. These became the lowest and highest boundaries, respectively. Then, the percentages of blue collar were divided into three equal categories of ascending magnitude at each of the four time periods. The boundaries between the first and second categories (low and medium) and the second and third (medium and high) were determined at each time period. The final boundaries were obtained by averaging the values of the two middle boundaries obtained at each time period.

d The categories were derived as follows: First, all declining cities were considered as one category. Second, the boundary between the second and third categories (stable–small increase and large increase, respectively) was obtained by averaging the median boundaries of all stable and growing cities for all three growth decades.

finger and Field assigned major importance to region as a determinant of local political structures. The importance of region, they argued, was probably due to "regional historical experiences related to the influx of immigrants and the responses to their needs reflected in municipal political systems."[32] In effect, Wolfinger and Field are arguing that ethnicity was at least historically important in local politics. And, recent case studies (including one of Wolfinger's[33]) indicate that ethnicity may still have some importance in local politics.

However, Lineberry and Fowler claim that "to 'control' for 'region' is to control not only for history, but for demography as well . . . , since regions are differentiated on precisely the kinds of demographic variables" which are related to turnout.[34] In other words, to control for region is, in part, to control for ethnicity and other factors which affect turnout. This contention is borne out by Table 3 which shows a strong tendency for large immigrant populations to live in Eastern cities. In contrast, there is an almost equally strong tendency for foreign-born persons *not* to live in Midwestern cities. The size of immigrant populations in Western cities tends to be intermediate between Eastern and Midwestern cities.

In addition, cities within regions are characterized by other demographic and governmental characteristics which are related to turnout. For example, Eastern cities tend to have large blue-collar populations, decreasing or slowly growing populations, partisan elections, ward councils, and mayor-council government, whereas Western cities (and to a lesser extent Midwestern cities) tend to have the opposite characteristics. Of course, the East, Midwest, and West have undergone different historical experiences. Whether regional historical experiences are responsible for turnout levels in cities, or whether the characteristics of cities themselves are responsible, is impossible to ascertain definitively. However, I lean toward the "redundancy" explanation rather than the "historical" one because of the results when partisan and nonpartisan cities within regions are separated.

Partisan and nonpartisan cities were seen (Table 2) to have different temporal patterns with respect to the ethnic impact on turnout. When Eastern cities are separated into partisan and nonpartisan, large immigrant populations affect turnout in the Eastern *nonpartisan* cities (partial correlations are .28, .36, and .21 for the elections of 1940, 1950, and 1960, respectively), whereas the size of immigrant populations has no effect on turnout in Eastern *partisan* cities. The partial correlations in Eastern partisan cities are −.04, .10, and −.12 for the elections of 1940, 1950, and 1960, respectively. Also partial correlations for the 1940 and 1960 elections in *nonpartisan* Midwestern cities are similar to the partials for *all* Midwestern cities. The partial correlation for Midwestern nonpartisan cities in 1950 is .16 compared to a partial correlation of −.01 in all Midwestern

[32] Wolfinger and Field, "Political Ethos and Structure of City Government."

[33] Wolfinger, "Development and Persistence of Ethnic Voting."

[34] Robert L. Lineberry and Edmund P. Fowler, "Reformism and Public Policy in Cities," *American Political Science Review* 61 (1967): 701–16.

Table 3. Intercorrelations of region with selected city characteristics for all Northern cities (N = 170).

	Region		
City Characteristic	East vs. other[a]	Midwest vs. other	West vs. other
% foreign born, 1930	.58**	−.43**	−.20**
1940	.57**	−.48**	−.13
1950	.58**	−.51**	−.11
1960	.57**	−.51**	−.10
% blue collar, 1930	.32**	−.08	−.32**
1940	.41**	−.15*	−.35**
1950	.59**	−.35**	−.33**
1960	.55**	−.21**	−.44**
Pop. change, 1930–40	−.33**	.04	.39**
1940–50	−.35**	−.06	.53**
1950–60	−.29**	.00	.37**
Form of govt., 1934[b]	.19*	−.01	−.24**
1940	.16*	.03	−.25**
1950	.09	.06	−.20**
1960	.16*	.00	−.21**
Council election, 1934	.17*	.02	−.26**
1940	.19*	−.01	−.23**
1950	.13	.00	−.18*
1960	.16*	−.01	−.19*
Elections, 1934	.35**	−.19*	−.21**
1940	.35**	−.13	−.28**
1950	.31**	−.10	−.28**
1960	.34**	−.13	−.27**

* Significant at the .05 level.
** Significant at the .01 level.

[a] East was scored 1 and the other regions were scored 0. The same technique was used for Midwest vs. other and West vs. other.

[b] Mayor-council government was scored as 1 and commission and manager government were scored as 0. The same technique was used for council elections (ward councils scored 1 and at-large councils scored 0) and elections (partisan elections scored 1 and nonpartisan elections scored 0).

cities. (There were not enough Midwestern partisan cities to analyze separately.)

In sum, although historical factors within regions may affect turnout, these factors are probably not solely responsible for the attenuations observed in the partial correlations between ethnicity and turnout. It is likely that these attenuations by region are largely due to the clustering of different city types within regions.

Another perspective can be added to the above findings by analyzing the effect of foreign-born populations on turnout in cities which have not changed their governmental structures for the period covered in this study. In this way we can see the effects over time of a constant governmental influence.

Table 4. Partial correlations between the percentage of foreign born at time 1 and the percentage of adults voting at time 2 by the percentage of adults voting at time 1 in Northern cities with stable governmental structures.[a]

City Type	Partial Correlations with Turnout in Year[b]		
	1940	1950	1960
Stable mayor-council (N = 76)	.40**	.33**	.11
Stable commission (N = 26)	.24	.15	.19
Stable council-manager (N = 30)	.41**	−.20	.09
Stable ward council (N = 65)	.34**	.34**	.04
Stable at-large council (N = 73)	.34**	.22**	.15
Stable partisan election (N = 47)	.29*	.10	.22
Stable nonpartisan election (N = 98)	.33**	.51**	.24**
Stable concurrent election (N = 24)	.32	.14	.28
Stable nonconcurrent election (N = 120)	.28**	.44**	.16*

* Significant at the .05 level.
** Significant at the .01 level.

[a] "Stable" means that the cities had the particular governmental structure designated for the entire period of this study, 1934–60.

[b] The year in the table head is the year of the election for which turnout is being correlated with the percentage of foreign born of the previous decade. Turnout in the previous decade is always partialed out. For some examples of this method, see n. a in Table 2.

The results presented in Table 4 are similar to those seen in Table 2. In general, the effect of ethnicity on turnout decreases between the elections of 1950 and 1960. The most striking result is the comparison between partisan and nonpartisan cities. In nonpartisan cities, ethnicity raises turnout in all three election years, while in partisan cities this impact is seen only for the 1940 elections. A similar result was seen in Table 2. Of the three "unreformed" governmental structures considered here (mayor-council government, ward city council, and partisan election), immigrant populations in *partisan* cities evidenced the lowest impact on turnout and for only one election—1940 (Tables 2 and 4). Of the four "reformed" governmental structures (commission and council-manager government, at-large city council, and nonpartisan election), ethnic populations in *nonpartisan* cities had an impact on turnout in all three election years.

To analyze further the effects of partisan and nonpartisan elections on the relationships between ethnicity and turnout, mayor-council, ward, and partisan cities are compared with mayor-council, ward, and nonpartisan cities. (See Table 5.) The *nonpartisan* mayor-council and ward cities show a tendency to high turnout for the elections of 1940–60 when large immigrant populations are present. In *partisan* mayor-council and ward cities, large immigrant populations effect turnout in the 1940 elections only.

One possible explanation for these results in partisan cities is that party considerations are more all-encompassing than ethnic considerations. The all-encompassing nature of partisan considerations was demonstrated by Pomper whose study will be discussed below.

Table 5. Partial correlations between the percentage of foreign born at time 1 and the percentage of adults voting at time 2 by the percentage of adults voting at time 1 in Northern mayor-council, ward, partisan and nonpartisan cities.[a]

City Type	Partial Correlations with Turnout in Year[b]		
	1940	1950	1960
Mayor-council, ward—partisan	.43** (38)	.21 (37)	.11 (35)
Mayor-council, ward—nonpartisan	.30* (39)	.61** (34)	.34* (32)

* Significant at the .05 level.
** Significant at the .01 level.

[a] There were not sufficient cases to compare any other combinations of three governmental structures.

[b] The year in the table head is the year of the election for which turnout is being correlated with the percentage of foreign born of the previous decade. Turnout in the previous decade is always partialed out. Examples of this method are found in n. a of Table 2.

As a check on the earlier results and to give the reader some idea as to the actual differences foreign-born populations make on turnout, partial regressions of the percentage of foreign-born at time 1 on the percentage of adults voting at time 2 by the percentage of adults voting at time 1 in different types of Northern cities are presented in Table 6.

The temporal pattern of the partial regression coefficients is similar to the earlier partial correlation results presented in Table 2. The partial regression coefficients generally decline in magnitude between the elections of 1950 and 1960.

Substantively, the results indicate that with some exceptions an increase in the percentage of immigrants will generally not raise the level of turnout in 1960. Again, a significant exception is nonpartisan cities. In contrast, an increase in the size of immigrant populations raises turnout in partisan cities in the 1940 elections only.

Finally, the question of changes in levels of voting turnout as concomitants of changes in the size of immigrant populations remains to be answered. Table 7 presents the correlations between the residual change scores of the percentage of foreign born and the percentage of adults voting in different types of Northern cities. Most of the correlations are nearly zero in value. Of the few correlations which are larger in magnitude, none are statistically significant. It appears, therefore, that there is no relationship between concurrent changes in the size of immigrant populations and the size of turnout.[35]

[35] Another method of looking at change is by the use of turnover tables for voting turnout at times 1 and 2 which are stratified for the percentage of foreign born at times 1 and 2 and for any other control variables of interest. The major drawback of this technique is that cases are used up very quickly. However, as a check on the results obtained in Table 7, I generated turnover tables and calculated net turnover for all strata with 20 cases or more. (Many tables had less than 10 cases.) The results with turnover tables are the same as those obtained in Table 7. That is, in different types of cities (e.g., mayor-council, ward, low blue collar), there is no significant pattern of change in turnout levels between decades regardless of stability or change in the percentage of immigrants.

Table 6. Partial regressions of the percentage of foreign born at time 1 on the percentage of adults voting at time 2 by the percentage of adults voting at time 1 within different types of Northern cities.[a]

Partial Regressions with Election in Year

Type of City	1940 N	1940 a	1940 b	1940 s	1950 N	1950 a	1950 b	1950 s	1960 N	1960 a	1960 b	1960 s
All	170	7.69	.49**	.11	170	12.81	.57**	.13	170	14.29	.38**	.20
Mayor-council	96	10.09	.45**	.13	88	17.49	.66**	.19	84	22.56	.26	.23
Commission	41	13.74	.40	.24	38	14.05	.31*	.16	31	21.34	.64	.55
Council-mgr.	33	3.31	.96*	.41	44	11.55	.48	.33	55	5.30	.48	.42
Ward council	82	6.97	.50**	.16	78	10.49	.77**	.20	80	19.79	.20	.27
At-large council	88	7.42	.51**	.16	92	14.89	.36**	.16	90	11.71	.51*	.28
Partisan	61	22.81	.47**	.18	60	33.03	.25	.24	58	12.78	.25	.28
Nonpartisan	109	4.65	.50**	.14	110	7.32	.77**	.14	112	17.44	.72**	.26
Concurrent	35	6.53	.96	.27	34	23.34	.58	.38	34	25.11	.14	.41
Nonconcurrent	135	8.21	.35**	.12	136	10.22	.58**	.13	136	14.39	.37*	.20
Eastern	75	15.50	.07	.19	75	24.28	.39*	.21	75	28.53	−.27	.27
Midwestern	65	10.43	.64**	.19	65	20.72	−.02	.23	65	15.96	.77**	.33
Western	30	5.16	.72	.45	30	10.31	.39	.44	30	28.17	.35	.71
Low blue collar	76	3.61	.45**	.20	70	6.84	.54**	.20	93	12.07	.44	.33
Med. blue collar	58	16.09	.35	.20	62	15.73	.64**	.21	49	11.84	.17	.35
High blue collar	36	13.14	.40	.22	38	28.77	.49	.31	28	41.90	.00	.37
Pop. decrease	59	9.04	.38*	.20	19	27.52	.46	.27	70	18.23	.09	.30
Stable-small increase	85	14.69	.22	.15	80	19.71	.46*	.22	38	28.41	.44	.49
Large increase	26	8.00	.85**	.31	71	9.31	.49**	.20	62	5.13	.39	.33

* Significant at the .05 level.
** Significant at the .01 level.

[a] The regression analysis is based on the equation $Y = a_{12.3} + b_{1.23}X$, where Y is the percentage of adults voting, a is the intercept constant, b is the slope of the regression line, and X is the percentage of foreign born. Also reported in the table is N which is the number of cases on which the regression is based and s which is the standard error of the regression coefficient. The value of F (not reported) which is used to determine whether the regression coefficient is statistically significant is determined by the ratio $(b/s)^2$.

Immigrants and Municipal Voting Turnout

Table 7. Pearsonian product moment correlations in different types of Northern cities between the residual change scores of the percentage of foreign born and the percentage of adults voting.

City Type	\multicolumn{3}{c}{Period for Which the Residual Change Scores are Computed}		
	1934–40	1940–50	1950–60
All Northern	.04 (170)	.08 (170)	.02 (170)
Governmental variables:			
Mayor-council govt.	−.03 (96)	−.02 (88)	.09 (84)
Commission govt.	.16 (41)	.31 (38)	−.01 (31)
Council-manager govt.	.12 (33)	.11 (44)	.02 (55)
Ward council	−.05 (82)	.02 (78)	.19 (80)
At-large council	.11 (88)	.14 (92)	−.11 (90)
Partisan election	.14 (61)	.04 (60)	.13 (58)
Nonpartisan election	−.06 (109)	.08 (110)	−.10 (112)
Concurrent election	.01 (35)	.12 (34)	−.03 (34)
Nonconcurrent election	.05 (135)	.07 (136)	−.01 (136)
Percentage of blue collar:			
Low (61 or less)	.06 (76)	−.02 (70)	.07 (93)
Medium (62–67)	.07 (58)	.26 (62)	.13 (49)
High (68 or more)	.15 (36)	−.06 (38)	−.20 (28)
Proportion population change:			
Decrease (.9999 or less)	.02 (59)	−.36 (19)	.13 (70)
Stable–small increase (1.0000–1.1002)	.06 (85)	.12 (80)	.03 (38)
Large increase (1.10033+)	.06 (26)	.08 (71)	−.09 (62)
Region:			
East	.09 (75)	.02 (75)	.01 (75)
Midwest	−.05 (65)	.13 (65)	−.16 (65)
West	.21 (30)	−.14 (30)	.12 (30)

Apparently, changes in the size of immigrant populations are not associated with immediate changes in electoral outcomes. This should not be surprising since electoral systems have a great deal of continuity built into them. Hence, changes in the size of immigrant populations (as well as changes in any other factors which affect urban political systems) would not be reflected as changes in the political system until after some (albeit unknown) time lapse. This time lag, of course, is the assumption built into the partial correlation technique employed in the foregoing analysis.

In addition to the continuity built into electoral systems, changes in the size of immigrant populations do not necessarily provide information on the size of second, third, and subsequent generation ethnic populations. Presumably, cities which have large immigrant populations will also have large second and subsequent generation ethnic populations. Therefore, even though immigrant populations are shrinking in size, the size of ethnic populations in general may be increasing. If sufficient data were available, changes in the total size of ethnic populations might be accompanied by changes in the level of turnout.

Immigrants and Turnout: Discussion of the Results

Large-scale immigration to America ended in the 1920s.[36] The effective curtailment of immigration is evidenced by (1) a decline in the number of immigrants since 1930, (2) an increase in their median age,[37] and (3) a decline in their proportions in *all* the cities used in this study. However, the cities analyzed here generally maintained their ranks with respect to the size of their immigrant populations.[38] Finally, Hadden and Borgatta report that in 1960 the percentage of foreign born correlates .87 with the percentage of native born of foreign or mixed parentage.[39]

In addition, immigrants and their children have shown significant occupational advancement over time—1910–50.[40] Immigrants have shown more rapid occupational advancement than native whites to the point where the immigrants' occupational distribution is nearly similar to natives. And the occupational distribution through the years of the second generation conforms quite closely to the distribution of the white labor force as a whole.

In light of the above data, the following conclusions seem likely:

First, a portion of the immigrants living in my sample of cities in 1930 live in the same cities in 1960. Of course, some immigrants moved away since 1930 and some (probably a major share since the median age of immigrants increases with each succeeding decade) died of old age. Second, the immigrants who died or moved away were not essentially replaced since the immigrant populations declined in all cities. Third, the high correlation between the percentage of immigrants and the children of immigrants indicates that they probably tend to remain in their parents' home city. Finally, immigrants have advanced occupationally to the point where they are nearly similar to the native white labor force. And immigrants' children are occupationally similar to the native old American stocks. Therefore, with the passage of time, immigrants and their children have lost their close ties to the Old World and have increasingly become Americans of foreign descent. If declining numbers and occupational mobility indicate a dilution of ethnic ties, the ethnic impact on urban politics should, *a priori*, be on the decline. With respect to voting turnout, this appears to be the case in partisan but not in nonpartisan cities.

[36] Maldwyn Allen Jones, *American Immigration* (Chicago: University of Chicago Press, 1960).

[37] E. P. Hutchinson, *Immigrants and their Children, 1850–1950* (New York: John Wiley, 1956), Chap. 1, pp. 14–18.

[38] The percentage of foreign born in 1930 correlates .96, .95, and .89 with the percentage of foreign-born persons in 1940, 1950, and 1960, respectively, which demonstrates the relative stability of cities' ranks with respect to the size of their immigrant populations.

[39] Hadden and Borgatta, *American Cities*, p. 128.

[40] Hutchinson, *Immigrants and their Children*, pp. 215–16.

Among all the control variables used above, the distinction between partisan and nonpartisan cities appears to be crucial. Large immigrant populations have no effect on turnout in partisan cities after the 1940 elections. The ethnic impact on turnout persists for all three elections (1940, 1950, and 1960) in nonpartisan cities. Also, when two other governmental variables were held constant (mayor-council government and ward elections, Table 5), the differences between partisan and nonpartisan cities with respect to the ethnic effect on turnout remained. Finally, all other types of cities—e.g., mayor-council, high blue collar, population decrease, Eastern—are mixtures of partisan and nonpartisan cities. Therefore, the pattern of partial correlations should be intermediate, in a temporal sense, between those observed in partisan and nonpartisan cities. In the case of Eastern cities, for example, we saw that nonpartisan Eastern cities had a temporal pattern of partial correlations similar to nonpartisan cities generally. Eastern partisan cities evidenced negligible partial correlations for all these elections. *All* Eastern cities had still a third pattern of partials—no relationship between ethnicity and turnout for 1940 elections, a statistically significant partial for 1950 elections, and no relationship again in 1960.

A possible explanation for the differences between partisan and nonpartisan cities is found in Pomper's 1966 study.[41]

Pomper studied two elections—a nonpartisan municipal election held in 1962 and a partisan state assembly contest held in 1961—in Newark, New Jersey. Rank order correlations were computed by ranking precincts within wards with respect to their total vote percentages given to pairs of candidates. If there was a high correlation in a ward between the votes given to candidates of the same ethnic background, ethnicity was assumed to be a factor in voting. For example, if the rank order correlation between two Italian candidates was highly positive, Pomper concluded that the candidates' nationality was relevant to the voters. He found by this technique that nationality was generally relevant in the nonpartisan municipal election, but not in the partisan state assembly contest.

Pomper concluded that party loyalties were generally stronger than nationality loyalties. However, he points out that *both* political parties had ethnically balanced slates of candidates. Obviously, ethnicity was a factor recognized by both parties. Yet, in the actual election, voters apparently did not split their tickets in an effort to vote for candidates of similar ethnic background. However, in nonpartisan municipal elections like Newark's, there are generally no party loyalties to override ethnic loyalties. Hence, these loyalties are substituted for party loyalties in nonpartisan cities.

These results probably illustrate why the presence of large immigrant populations has no effect on turnout after the 1940 elections in partisan cities, whereas in nonpartisan cities, ethnicity continues to affect turnout.

[41] Gerald Pomper, "Ethnic Group Voting in Nonpartisan Municipal Elections," *Public Opinion Quarterly* 30 (1966): 79–97.

More people vote in partisan than nonpartisan elections. In part, the mere presence of two competing parties, with their advertising campaigns, their organized political campaign events, their images which are held by voters, and their organized get-out-the-vote campaigns, acts to raise turnout levels. In many cities with large ethnic populations, members of ethnic groups become active in partisan politics. In effect, ethnicity becomes built into the competitive framework of party activity. Such is the case in cities like New York, New Haven, and Newark.[42] Perhaps if turnout data were available from the turn of the century, we would see a pattern of a decreasing impact of ethnicity on turnout in partisan cities. This might indicate that as ethnic groups struggled to gain access to the political system in different cities, there was a high degree of competitiveness reflected by high turnout levels. Once ethnic groups were successful in their struggle, then interethnic conflict subsided, and partisan cities with large ethnic populations resembled other partisan cities in their pattern of turnout. In effect, ethnicity becomes built into the partisan framework and therefore persists for long periods of time. As a case in point, New York City is illustrative of ethnic interests being built into the political system.

Electoral politics in New York are organized on an ethnic basis by politicians who try to accommodate diverse ethnic interests. One method of accommodating these interests is by the use of the "balanced ticket," i.e., a slate of candidates which represents the major ethnic groups in the city. For example, the mayoralty slate (for the offices of mayor, city council president, and comptroller) usually includes an Italian, an Irish, and a Jewish candidate. (John Lindsay, of course, is an exception to this rule because he is an Anglo-Saxon Protestant. However, his running mates have been Italian and Jewish.) And, the Manhattan Borough President's office is reserved for a black man.

In sum, New York's parties try to nominate candidates attractive to the city's diverse ethnic interests. Parties "build in" these ethnic interests by insuring that there is a representative ethnic makeup among their candidates, party functionaries, and patronage appointments. In other words, the building in of ethnic interests does not generally consist of promises to economically benefit particular ethnic groups (although appeals to the black populations in cities may be an exception to this). Rather, the building in of ethnic interests consists of making sure that people with desired ethnic backgrounds are represented in the city's political structure, and that this representation is made known to the relevant ethnic segments of the electorate.

Of course, partial correlations revealed that partisan cities with small ethnic populations do not have lower turnouts after 1940 than partisan cities with large immigrant populations. Political parties in cities with small ethnic populations are probably organized around bases other than

---

[42] Glazer and Moynihan, *Beyond the Melting Pot*, pp. 301–10; Robert A. Dahl, *Who Governs?* (New Haven: Yale University Press, 1961), Chap. 4; Pomper, "Ethnic Group Voting."

ethnic loyalties. Such bases of organization could be around social class or other relevant urban factors.

The fact that ethnic interests can be built into the party structure in cities with large ethnic populations, and that other factors can be built into the party structure in cities with small ethnic populations, perhaps can explain why the presence of large ethnic populations did not raise turnout levels in partisan cities after 1940. During the early part of this century, ethnic competition for a place in the political system could have created more voter interest in partisan cities with large ethnic populations than in partisan cities with small ethnic populations. As diverse ethnic groups work out accommodations with each other (accommodations such as those reflected in New York's "balanced ticket"), political competition between ethnic groups subsides and becomes no more than the competition found in partisan cities with small ethnic populations. Currently, then, regardless of what issues or interests (e.g., class or ethnic) are encompassed in the party structures, parties in partisan cities do manage to make elections sufficiently relevant to insure relatively high turnout levels.

Nonpartisan cities, on the oter hand, do not have party structures with which to build in ethnic competition. Therefore, this competition persists from election to election in nonpartisan cities with large ethnic populations, and these nonpartisan cities are characterized by high rates of turnout. However, Tables 2, 4, and 5 show that the partial correlations between the percentage of foreign born and turnout increased between the 1940 and 1950 elections and decreased between the 1950 and 1960 elections. If the latter decrease portends a decline in the ethnic impact on turnout in nonpartisan cities, it is probably attributable to the facts that ethnic populations are becoming more similar to the native population as a whole, and there are no political parties to keep ethnic differences alive.

The persistence of ethnic factors in urban elections has interesting implications for the melting pot view of assimilation.

The melting pot view held that with the passage of time, immigrants and their descendants would be absorbed into American society and become indistinguishable from the American population as a whole. Reacting to this overly simplistic view of assimilation, later writers on the subject contended that ethnic groups are now culturally assimilated (acculturated) but not structurally assimilated.[43] That is, members of ethnic groups in America act like other Americans while at the same time preserving many separate ethnic institutions (the church, social and recreational clubs, the family, etc.). Gordon went on to contend that political institutions (among others) were characterized by the fact that they cut across entire populations and were not uniquely ethnic institutions.

Glazer and Moynihan and Parenti carried Gordon one step further and said that political systems do have unique ethnic characteristics and can

[43] Milton M. Gordon, *Assimilation in American Life* (New York: Oxford University Press, 1964).

serve to foster and maintain ethnic loyalties.[44] (They drew this inference from partisan electoral systems.) That is, political systems become more than a dependent variable but also act as an independent variable to foster and maintain the relevancy of ethnicity in urban populations. My data, although not directly testing this idea, are not inconsistent with it.

Although the points made in this discussion are merely suggestive and not concrete conclusions, the data show that large ethnic populations in nonpartisan cities persist as an influence on the political process. Although the data indicate no ethnic impact on turnout in partisan cities after 1940, evidence from previously cited case studies indicates that ethnicity is still relevant in partisan cities. (Data different from those used here are needed to arrive at any concrete generalizations about the current state of ethnic politics in partisan cities.) This persistence of ethnicity in politics exists despite the fact that new immigrants have not been significantly supplementing the numbers of already present ethnic groups, and that ethnic groups are generally upwardly mobile. How long ethnicity will influence urban elections is impossible to tell. However, the ethnic impact on politics will probably persist for some time to come in cities with large ethnic populations and long histories of ethnic political activity.

[44] Glazer and Moynihan, *Beyond the Melting Pot*; and Parenti, "Ethnic Politics."

6

Changes in Groups' Participation and Impact on Urban Politics

The Entrance of Blacks into Urban Politics

Many of the same economic forces—declining job opportunities at home and increasing opportunities in the large cities—which attracted immigrants to the urban North also attracted black Americans from the rural South. The mechanization of southern agriculture and the partial replacement of cotton farming by tree farming and other crops not requiring large amounts of hand labor drastically curtailed the number of agricultural opportunities for blacks in the South. Concurrent with the decline of southern agricultural job opportunities was the growth of industrial jobs in the urban North. Especially during the First and Second World Wars when severe labor shortages arose, northern cities held out the promise of jobs.

There are other than economic factors which spurred the black migration from North to South. The denial of civil rights—equal justice, voting, etc.—to blacks and the economic, physical, and social harrassment visited upon them lessened the desirability of the South as a place of residence; whereas the greater freedom held out by the North served as an attraction.

Of course, many of the attractions of the urban North were merely illusory. Crammed into ghettos, black people found themselves at the bottom of the social heap, just as had the immigrants who preceded them. And just as the immigrants found local politics to be one avenue of social advancement, blacks, too, entered the urban political process—although their entrance was much slower and met more resistance than did the entrance of earlier immigrant groups. And blacks must often battle the entrenched political powers (who are often European ethnic groups) for a part in the political process.

James Q. Wilson begins the first selection by pointing out that black politics is shaped by white politics. That is, the form and nature of black participation in urban politics will follow the form and nature of white participation. For example, Chicago's black population formed a black machine organization along lines similar to the white machine. Blacks in Detroit, to take another example, were aided in their entrance into city politics by powerful CIO unions.

There is a time lag between the attainment of large numbers in an urban population and the acquisition of political power by blacks. Wilson points out that the political situation of blacks is similar to other ethnic groups struggling for power against entrenched political interests who are trying to maintain their position. For example, in many communities Irish political leaders resisted the political advances of Italians, Poles, and others. This time lag in acquiring power, however, is not uniform from city to city.

Wilson writes that sheer numbers and the nature of the political system are insufficient to explain the differential access of blacks to the political process. He sees three other variables—the rate of in-migration, the density of the black area, and the size of the basic political unit—as important to the political success or failure of blacks.

Chicago witnessed the earliest black successes in local politics. These successes, according to Wilson, were due to a heavy black concentration in one or a few black areas and the basing of Chicago's political system on wards drawn to conform to racial, nationality, or religious lines.

Ward positions were the first political offices captured by blacks. New York's blacks attained political power later than they did in Chicago, even though the black population was larger than Chicago's. New York, in contrast to Chicago, has larger political units which were often gerrymandered to split the black vote among several districts. As a consequence its black population had to reach much larger proportions than Chicago's in order to insure black political representation. And even now, Wilson argues, New York politics still balance diverse ethnic interests so that blacks achieve only certain allotted positions with the remainder going to other ethnic groups.

Detroit and Los Angeles were the last cities to see black representation in the political process—Los Angeles being the slowest of all. Both cities have nonpartisan systems with at-large elections for city offices. At-large elections put blacks at a serious political disadvantage because they must secure city-wide support rather than backing only from black residential areas. Black Detroiters have been more successful in politics than their Los Angeles counterparts, though, largely because of Detroit's powerfully organized labor bloc. Since the 1930s, organized labor has been taking blacks into its associations and has been promoting, in city and state politics, those black interests which are not incompatible with the interests of their white membership.

Although sheer numbers are not sufficient to insure the black entrance into positions of political power, the second selection demonstrates that numbers are crucial to get black mayors elected. Jeffrey Hadden, Louis Masotti, and Victor Thiessen review the 1967 mayoral elections in Cleveland and Gary which pitted black candidates against white candidates.

Cleveland's black electorate is only 34 percent of the city's population, while Gary's is slightly less than a majority of the electorate. Therefore, both cities required overwhelming black support and some white votes for the black candidates to claim victory. And this is exactly what happened in both cities. In Cleveland, Stokes managed both to bring out about 80 percent of the eligible black voters, who gave him about 95 percent of their votes, and to capture about 15 percent of the white votes. With the large black vote and some white support, he easily won the primary election. In the general election, Stokes still held on to massive black support and he was also able to increase his white support to approximately 20 percent of the white vote. Gary's Hatcher accomplished his victory by a similar process of large black support plus a small share of white votes, although Hatcher did not manage to capture nearly as big a share of white support as did Stokes. (In contrast to Stokes who received endorsement from Cleveland's major daily newspapers, Hatcher did not receive similar endorsements. In fact, the local paper discriminated against Hatcher by denying him adequate coverage.)

As Hadden, Masotti, and Thiessen point out, neither Stokes' nor Hatcher's elections depended upon the presence of black majorities. Both men were victorious through a combination of overwhelming black and limited white support. However, in spite of the absence of a black majority, it is necessary to have very large black populations in order to elect a black mayor. Subsequent elections in Newark and Los Angeles have further emphasized this point. Racially polarized Newark elected a black mayor only after the electorate became evenly split between black and white. And Kenneth Gibson's Newark campaign was given a boost among some white voters by the fact that the incumbent administration was on trial in federal court for extorting money from city contractors. (The former mayor was subsequently convicted.) Los Angeles, however, did not elect a black mayor in spite of the black candidate's large plurality in the primary and his opponent's much smaller propertion of the primary vote. In the general election campaign, the incumbent mayor, Samuel Yorty, played upon racial fears to win reelection. The fact that voter turnout in this election was 15 percent higher than in any other previous municipal election demonstrates the interest generated by this contest. In sum, it appears that for blacks to be successful in city-wide elections, they must constitute a large proportion (though not necessarily a majority) of the population, and black candidates must receive overwhelming black support.

Although blacks have been modestly successful in winning political power in some cities, they have been noticeably less successful in attaining power in policy-making positions generally. We have seen in previous selections that many community issues are affected by business and professional interests within the community. And, as Harold M. Baron points out in the fourth selection, blacks have been noticeably unsuccessful in achieving policy-making positions in major urban institutions.

Baron investigated four questions about the role of blacks in Chicago's major institutions: (1) what is the extent of black exclusion from policy-making positions; (2) where blacks are in policy-making positions, what is the nature of the positions; (3) are black policy makers working in the interests of the black community; and (4) what effect would an increase in the number of black policy makers make on black socio-economic status in general?

Answers to these questions were obtained by a census of Chicago's major institutions—governments (city and county) and private establishments (business corporations, major law firms, universities, voluntary organizations, and labor unions)—to find out what proportion of major policy positions were held by blacks. Not surprisingly, the greatest black representation in policy-making positions was found in the governmental sector: blacks hold two and one half times as many important posts in the public sector as they do in the private sector. The black vote is a weapon used to obtain governmental policy posts, although even the power of the black vote is not sufficient to assure black representation in proportions equivalent to the black presence in the general population.

The private sector is another matter. Blacks have no representation in policy-making posts in major law firms or nonfinancial corporations. Their representation in banks, insurance companies, and universities is very small, and much of their representation in banks and insurance firms comes from their positions in primarily black organizations. The greatest concentration of blacks in nongovernmental policy positions is in labor unions and voluntary organizations, especially welfare organizations.

To sum up his findings, Baron postulates a general rule to assess black power: "The actual power vested in Negro policy makers is about one-third as great as the percentage of posts they hold." Baron devalues the power of black policy makers because the policy-making positions held by Chicago's blacks are usually in smaller institutions (such as small banks) or in institutions with little power in the larger society, e.g., welfare organizations.

The inability of urban blacks to achieve power even remotely commensurate with their numbers in the population has contributed to their great frustration and their turn toward violence. Those who see urban ghetto riots as merely looting sprees, the work of "outside agitators," or as aimless expressions of frustration are wrong according to Harlan Hahn ("The Political Objectives of Ghetto Violence"), who presents evidence that many rioters, in fact, have political goals when they engage in riotous behavior.

A large proportion of the rioters or black observers of the riot in Detroit felt that government is unresponsive to the needs of the black community. These people feel that riotous behavior forces government officials to take notice of black political grievances and to take action to right them. Also, according to Hahn, the desire to make governmental institutions more responsive to the black community through mechanisms such as decentralization is much on the minds of rioters and riot sympathizers. In other words, the token representation of blacks in local government is insufficient to satisfy their political demands.

Unlike some European ethnic groups, black Americans have not been successful in attaining political and economic power in urban America. Whereas members of other nationality groups (especially the Irish) attained political offices in fairly large numbers, blacks have taken much longer in attaining political office and they have done so in relatively small numbers in relatively few cities. And, those political achievements which blacks have made have often been only small concessions by white politicians to attract black votes.

It is not surprising, then, that riots have erupted in many black communities across this country. While other nationality groups have been successful in assimilating economically, socially, and politically into American society, black Americans have been kept in ghetto areas at the bottom of the economic, social, and political heap. More fundamental political changes will have to take place before black citizens feel that their grievances have been dealt with fairly. The future will probably see much greater black political gains in cities where they are approaching a majority of the population. However, these gains are slow in coming and blacks' patience appears to be running out.

Negro Politics in the North

JAMES Q. WILSON

Chicago, Detroit, Los Angeles, and New York are important centers of Negro population. Although the proportion of Negroes living in these cities is not as high as elsewhere, in total numbers they are among the very largest.[1] Political activity in these Negro communities is generally high. Three of the four cities have sent a Negro to the United States House of Representatives.[2] In two of the cities, the Negro political leader is a nationally known figure—William L. Dawson in Chicago and Adam Clayton Powell, Jr., in New York. In each city except Los Angeles at least one Negro sits on the City Council, and in Chicago there are six. Each city sends at least one, and usually more, Negroes to the state

Reprinted with permission of The Macmillan Company from *Negro Politics* by James Q. Wilson. © by The Free Press, a Corporation, 1960.

[1] The Negro population of these four cities, during the period 1955–1957 for which the last estimates are available, is approximately as follows:

City	Negro Population	Percent of City Total	Percent Increase, 1950–56
Chicago	631,750	18.0	22.1
Detroit	400,000	22.0	24.1
Los Angeles	254,595	11.3	32.8
New York	948,196	12.2	21.2

Sources: Chicago—Otis Dudley Duncan and Beverly Duncan, *The Negro Population of Chicago* (Chicago: University of Chicago Press, 1957), p. 29. The estimate is for 1955. *Detroit*—average of estimates supplied by the Human Relations Commission and Professor Albert Mayer of Wayne State University. *Los Angeles*—the figures are from the 1956 Special Census of Los Angeles. *New York*—the figures are from the 1956 Special Census of New York City (all five boroughs). The data, in each case, are for the *city* (not the Standard Metropolitan Area) and for *Negroes* (not non-whites). Other sources of estimates are Morton Grodzins, "Metropolitan Segregation," *Scientific American* (1957): 33–41, and R. Norgren et al., *Employing Negroes in American Industry* (New York: Industrial Relations Counsellors, Inc., 1959), p. 161.

[2] William L. Dawson of Chicago, first elected in 1942; Charles Diggs, Jr., of Detroit, first elected in 1954; and Adam Clayton Powell, Jr., of New York, first elected in 1944. Before Dawson, there were two Negro Congressmen from Chicago: Oscar de Priest (1928–34), and Arthur W. Mitchell (1934–42).

legislature. Negro judges sit on the bench in each of the four cities. In every case except Los Angeles, the Negro voters comprise one of the largest single ethnic groups in the central city electorate and a group that is rapidly growing both in absolute size and as a proportion of the total population. This growth, accompanied by the retreat of whites from the periphery of Negro areas, means, among other things, that the size of Negro political representation at all levels of government will continue to grow. In just the four cities under consideration, there are at least six Congressional districts in which substantial numbers of Negroes already live and which are generally expected to elect Negro politicians in the near future.

The growing number of Negroes in northern cities suggests the increased possibility that Negro political power will become a decisive factor in the quest for race goals. Political leadership, based on this large electorate, might presumably be a potent force for change. . . .

The Structure of Negro Politics

The most important single conclusion that emerges from a survey of Negro politics in large northern cities is that, in all cases, the structure and style of Negro politics reflect the politics of the city as a whole. Politics for the Negro, as for other ethnic groups before him, can be viewed as a set of "learned responses" which he acquires from the distinctive political system of the city in which he lives.

Negro politics cannot be understood apart from the city in which it is found. This suggests, happily, that by examining Negro politics on a comparative basis we are at the same time examining American city politics. It also implies that research on this topic must be much broader than the subject itself indicates. The student must cast a wide net; inquiry must begin with the city as a whole in order to understand fully the actions and problems of Negro politicians in that city. This point, obvious by itself, takes on added significance when one considers the nature of the organization and the means by which it induces workers and voters to contribute to it, the pattern of Negro registration and voting, and the relative strengh and unity (or weakness and disunity) of the organization.

The Negro political organization is created and shaped by the poiltical organization of the city. The existence of a Negro machine, as in Chicago, is dependent upon the existence of a white machine. Machine politics requires a centralization of leadership, a sizeable stock of tangible incentives with which to reward contributors, a large group of people in the city who would be attracted by the kinds of rewards a political machine can distribute, and (usually) a ward or district system of selecting party leaders, aldermen, and candidates for public office. The prior existence of a machine, operating under such conditions, means that the entry of Negroes into politics will take place under the forms and rules already established. Where various factors have weakened the city organization and produced a situation of factional rivalry and imperfect solidarity, the Negro political organization will be similarly gripped by internecine warfare and competing leaders. This is the case in Manhattan, where the city organization is weak—i.e., it cannot enforce its rules on its members or maintain an undisputed single leadership. There, the elements of machine politics have been decaying rapidly, and the results are evident in white and Negro areas. In Los Angeles and Detroit, where almost none of the elements of machine control exist, the politics of the city as a whole is characterized by *ad hoc* groupings which come into being in election years to elect good-government, economy-minded leaders whose appeal must be largely based on personality, issues, and newspaper influence. Negroes, where they can enter this kind of political system at all, are forced to do so on its own terms and with the limited resources at hand. No Negro "boss" can spring up where there is not already a white boss. When a strong civil service system, a mobile and prosperous electorate, and a long tradition of "public relations politics" exist as in Los Angeles, Negroes must play the game by the same rules and under the same conditions. In doing so, of course, they are placed at a profound disadvantage.

The most important modification of the statement that Negro politics in northern cities is a reflection of the politics of the cities as a whole is the general time lag in the entry of Negroes into positions of political influence.

Contributing to this lag is the operation of those same factors which have delayed the entry of other, earlier ethnic groups. Big city politics often takes the form of a succession of new arrivals each trying to scale the same ladder of political achievement by pressing those above them for "recognition." Resistance to Negroes is not, in part, different from the general resistance put up by (for example) the Irish political leadership of the big city to the demands for political recognition expressed by Poles, Italians, or Germans. Little is given without a struggle, even when the maintenance needs of the political organization as a whole would seem to require it. The personal interests of those who hold the higher positions inevitably tend to override the organizational interests of the machine which provides them with those positions. In the case of the Negro, however, this resistance is intensified by the frequent operation of personal prejudice and hostility. Negro entry into politics thus far has been less than proportional to their numbers, as expressed in the size of their contribution to the Democratic vote in city elections. Often, as in Chicago's 24th Ward, Los Angeles' 55th and 63rd Assembly Districts, and parts of New York's 13th Assembly District, Negroes can be the largest group in the political unit long before they manage to take control of the leadership of that unit.[3] This is true, again, because Negro voters—unless they are made the objects of really intense, well-led organizational campaigns—will not vote along strictly racial lines in a Negro–white

---

[3] For example, in St. Louis in 1959, six wards returned Negro aldermen but only two of these had Negro ward leaders (wards 18 and 19).

contest, especially when it occurs at the bottom of the ticket in the seemingly unimportant race for ward committeeman or district leader.

In addition to political resistance stiffened by personal hostility and prejudice, another factor works to delay Negro entry into political organizations. Negroes—whose income and educational levels are almost always among the lowest in the city and whose rural background deprives them of sophistication in the ways of the city—are often hard to organize for political ends. Many of them doubt that politics offers any real opportunities. The difficulty in building a Negro organization *from outside the machine* which will then make a bid for recognition and power has been discovered many times in all four cities. This obstacle makes all the more remarkable the achievement of William Dawson of Chicago in rising to power in the 1930s from a powerless base. The aid of Mayor Edward Kelly, valuable as it may have been, was no guarantee of success—if only because of the large number of Negro rivals to Dawson whose factional fights could easily have paralyzed all attempts at coherent organization. In non-machine or weak-machine cities, the active intervention of another strong force which has a vested interest in mobilizing Negroes seems to be necessary to bring them into important polical roles. In Detroit, this has been the function of the CIO. In Los Angeles, where no machine and no intervening organization exists, Negro political organization becomes an immensely difficult task.

The time lag characterizing Negro entry into northern politics has not been uniform in all cities. Negroes held important political offices in Chicago long before they did in New York, and Negroes emerged in New York before they were active in Los Angeles or Detroit. To account for these differences, three factors, in addition to the political organization of the city, appear to be important: (a) the rate of in-migration, (b) the density of the Negro area, and (c) the size of the basic political unit.

In Chicago, Negro entry occurred as early as 1915 when a Negro was elected to the City Council, and later (in 1920) another became a ward committeeman (the real center of political power in the Chicago wards). The powerful city machine was at that time firmly in the hands of the Republicans, and thus the Negro political leaders were at first Republicans. Their entry was partly a reflection of the need of the city organization to insure its strength in the Negro wards by co-opting Negro leaders, and it was partly a product of a bitter struggle by Negroes to gain "recognition" in politics against the opposition of established non-Negro leaders. The machine system in the Negro wards solidified as early as 1920, and by 1928 Negroes were able to elect a member of their own race to Congress.

The relatively early date by which Negroes were able to gain elective office in Chicago, as compared to other northern cities, can be explained by the fact that (a) the concentration of Negroes in one or a few all-Negro areas was, from the first, higher in Chicago and (b) the Chicago political system was based on a large number of relatively small wards usually drawn to conform to the racial, nationality, or religious character of the neighborhood. This demographic concentration in small political units facilitated the entry of Negroes into politics in Chicago, while relatively less concentrated Negro population centers in cities with large districts (or, in some cases, no districts at all) meant that Negro entry was greatly delayed. This was the case in New York, and to an even greater extent in Detroit and Los Angeles.

New York, with even more Negroes than Chicago, and with a political system somewhat comparable, did not have a Negro district leader in Tammany Hall until 1935, and it did not have a second until 1941. In part, this reflected the relatively larger size of New York districts as compared to Chicago wards. This size facilitated a process of gerrymandering that worked to exclude Negroes from important posts. Furthermore, New York districts have been, and still are, divided into halves or even thirds for leadership purposes in order to find compromises between the competing claims of various ethnic groups residing in the district. Thus, a district containing significant numbers of Negroes, Italians, and Jews would be split into three parts, and each part given to a Negro, an Italian, and a Jewish leader. In turn, the single vote which that district had in Tammany Hall would be split into three one-third votes. This often worked to weaken the influence of Negroes even after they had captured a leadership. For this and other reasons which will be taken up later, Negro influence in Tammany was less and increased more slowly than Negro influence in the Cook County Central Committee in Chicago. The first Negro Congressman from New York was not chosen until 1944, after redistricting had created a new Congressional District with a Negro majority. Other things being equal, Negro political strength in city organizations tends to be directly proportional to the size and density of the Negro population, and inversely proportional to the size of the basic political unit.

In Los Angeles, where the growth of the Negro population has been more recent (largely since World War II, rather than World War I as in the case of Chicago and New York), Negro entry into politics has really not occurred at all. The only Negro holding elective office is one member of the State Assembly. No Negroes are on the City Council, and no Negroes are in its Congressional delegation. Los Angeles politics are largely nonpartisan. There are no wards, and no ward leaders. City Councilmen are elected from large heterogeneous districts which must, by law, be reapportioned every four years. Considerable pains have been taken to insure that such redistricting will operate to exclude Negroes from the Council. Civil service is strong in Los Angeles, and there are few material incentives with which to construct a political organization. There is no city-wide organization with a need to attract all segments of the population to support a complete slate of candidates, and hence no group which would have a vested interest in constructing a "balanced ticket" and distributing "recognition" to ethnic, religious, and other easily identifiable groups. Politics is largely the province of white, middle-class, Anglo-Saxon Protestants. Although the sole Negro elective official is formally a Democrat, he has supported Republican Mayor Norris Poulson in both the 1953 and 1957 elections, despite Poulson's stand against public housing. Neither race nor party are clear determinants of political positions in Los Angeles.

One additional factor should be mentioned. The density of Negroes in Los Angeles has been markedly lower than in either Chicago or New York. Los Angeles, for example, has a comparative absence of apartments and tenements in the central city and instead an immense number of small, single-family homes and duplexes. It has, as a result, a Negro population which is spread over a much greater territory than in Chicago. This relative dispersion has many consequences, but one which is important at this juncture is the great ease with which district lines can be drawn to exclude Negroes. A widely spread (but generally contiguous) Negro area can more easily be broken up in such a way that Negroes are in a minority in each district. This would be less feasible in a small but densely-populated area.

Detroit is, in many ways, comparable to Los Angeles. City politics is nonpartisan, and genuinely so. Members of the Common Council are elected at-large from the city as a whole. Each voter has nine votes which he may give to as many as nine different candidates, but no more than one vote per candidate. In the primary, eighteen men are selected from a wide-open field frequently of more than one hundred aspirants. The eighteen compete in a run-off election from which nine emerge. There are no ward leaders, and civil service has put an end to almost all patronage at the city and county level. In such a situation it is not surprising that it was not until 1957 that a Negro was first elected to the Common Council.

The Detroit situation differs from that in Los Angeles because of the existence of a large and powerful labor movement in the former city which has tried to operate as a political organization, endorsing slates of candidates and attempting to organize workers in most of the election precincts. Although this organization, in cooperation with other liberal groups and with the regular Democratic party, has been strikingly successful in electing a Governor and two Senators, as well as a host of other state-wide offices (where the elections are openly *partisan*), it has had much less success in the city itself. It was never able to defeat four-time Mayor Albert E. Cobo, a conservative, nor could it dominate the Common Council.[4]

The CIO United Auto Workers, which was first confronted with Negro laborers in Detroit when they were used as strike-breakers in the 1930s,[5] has since succeeded in incorporating them into the union movement with considerable success. Unlike many craft-oriented unions, the UAW has not segregated the Negroes into separate, all-Negro locals. Rather, Negroes

---

[4] Negro voters were strongly opposed to Mayor Cobo and always voted heavily for his opponent. Many Negro leaders, and some liberal whites, believe that part of Cobo's appeal, especially to middle-class whites who felt threatened by Negro residential expansion, was what they considered to be Cobo's anti-Negro policies in public housing, real estate, and other areas.

[5] See Walter F. White, *A Man Called White* (New York: Viking Press, 1948), pp. 212–19.

are to be found in all the locals in sizeable numbers. Perhaps one-fourth to one-third of the membership of the average local in Detroit is now Negro.[6] In political action, the CIO has concentrated heavily on Negro areas—often with remarkable effect. For example, Negroes are becoming very numerous in the First and Fifteenth Congressional Districts which now return two white Democratic Congressmen, Thaddeus M. Machrowicz and John D. Dingell. Negro Democrats challenged each incumbent in the 1958 primary, but the white leaders—with CIO endorsement —were able to defeat their Negro opponents by substantial margins. Most Negroes voted the CIO ticket rather than on the basis of race. . . .

An interesting variation of the impact of the system of at-large elections on Negro political fortunes is found in Cincinnati. From 1925 until 1957, councilmen were elected at-large under proportional representation. PR modified the effect of the at-large system to the extent that one or two Negroes were usually elected to the city council by receiving as little as 10 percent of the total vote. After PR was abolished in 1957 and a system of at-large elections for nine councilmen was instituted, the leading Negro politician was defeated. An important factor in the campaign against PR was the presumed threat posed by the possibility of Negro political power in the city. Theodore M. Berry, the Negro councilman who had been elected Vice-Mayor in 1955 after running second in a field of twenty-one candidates, was the target of much of this attack. In urging Negroes to vote to retain PR, Berry made explicit reference to the Detroit situation as a warning of what would happen to Negro political representation should PR be rejected.[7] The at-large, nonpartisan election system has similarly helped to exclude Negroes from the Boston Common Council. Negroes held office in Boston for over a century beginning in 1776, but by 1910 they had all been displaced. In the 19th century, Negroes were often elected from predominantly white districts by Yankees who, like the Negroes, were Republicans. After the turn of the century, with the entry of new immigrant groups into political life, particularly as members of the Democratic party, this benevolence ceased. Districts were redrawn to split the Negro vote. In 1949, the district system was abolished altogether, and the nine Council members were elected at large. A Negro running for the Council in 1958 finished fifteenth out of eighteen candidates, although he ran first in the most important Negro ward.[8]

The structure of political competition in these northern areas has implications for the responsiveness of white politicians to Negro goals as well as for the organization of Negro politics itself. The relative success

---

[6] In 1952, Negroes were 19 percent of a random sample of Detroit UAW members. Cf. Arthur Kornhauser, et al., *When Labor Votes* (New York: University Books, 1956), p. 24. At the time, there were about 290,000 UAW members in Detroit or about 30 percent of both the labor force and the eligible voters. *Ibid.*, p. 22.

[7] For a complete account of the impact of the Cincinnati electoral system on Negro politics, see Ralph A. Straetz, *PR Politics in Cincinnati* (New York: New York University Press, 1958), esp. chap. viii.

[8] I am indebted to the researches of Ralph Ottwell, former Niemen Fellow at Harvard, for most of my facts on Boston.

in enacting laws embodying Negro race ends in Michigan and New York, for example, has been due to a large number of factors, including the presence of powerful allies for Negro causes. One factor upon which some speculation seems worthwhile at this point concerns the distribution of Negroes in electoral districts. Although no conclusive evidence can be offered, it is interesting to conjecture about the differences in white politicians' attitudes toward race ends which may be related to a large-district political system (such as New York) as compared to a small-district system (such as Chicago).

Manhattan, which was over 21 percent Negro in 1957, has elected a Negro as borough president. Negro voters in just the four "recognized" Negro districts produced from one-third to one-half of the majorities won by the top of the Democratic ticket between 1954 and 1958.[9] As the strength of Tammany declines, the pressure mounts on city officials, such as the mayor, to move more and more in the direction of meeting the demands of organized minority groups. Mayor Wagner, for example, was a steady supporter of the proposed "open occupancy" ordinance barring discrimination in private housing even though the *Negro* politicians (with one exception) were silent or unenthusiastic. Here we see the Negro benefiting from what may have been the by-product of political and civic action engaged in by entirely different actors and in part for different purposes. White political leaders, it might be hypothesized, meet demands for race ends in such a situation only in part to attract the Negro vote. Their goal is also to attract and hold liberal *white* voters (for example, Jews) who judge a politician in part on the basis of his contribution to the goals of integration and social justice.[10] The Negro may be the unintended beneficiary of such a process. But whatever the audience to which the politician appeals, there is little doubt that in New York—in contrast to Chicago—an appeal must be made. Politics in the former city are more nearly two-party (opponents of the Democratic organization can and do win), and hence greater efforts must be expended to be certain of victory.

Furthermore, New York political units (the districts from which councilmen and borough presidents are elected) are relatively large. Sizable numbers of Negroes live in many of these districts and boroughs.[11]

[9] The four districts are the 11th, 12th, 13th, and 14th Assembly Districts in Harlem. The difference between the Democratic and Republican totals in the four districts is divided by the difference between the Democratic and Republican vote for Manhattan as a whole. The results are: 1954—32.46 percent; 1956—55.57 percent; 1958—49.05 percent.

[10] On Jewish tendencies to vote split tickets, see Lawrence H. Fuchs, *The Political Behavior of American Jews* (Glencoe, Ill.: The Free Press, 1956), pp. 131-49.

[11] The six Manhattan Council districts had, in 1957, an average population of slightly less than 300,000. By comparison, the average size of a Chicago ward (in 1950) was about 72,000 persons. At least four of the six Manhattan Councilmen have sizable Negro areas in their districts, and Negroes are to be found in scattered locations in the other two. There are, in addition, important Negro population centers in the Bronx (134,767), Brooklyn (307,796), Queens (116,193), and Staten Island (8,372). The distribution of Negroes in the various New York City boroughs is of great importance. The Board of

Many white politicians must anticipate the reaction of Negroes to city issues affecting the race. What may be more important, *opponents* of race goals find it harder to gain the support of their political representatives against such measures when the districts these leaders represent are so large and diversified. The larger political unit is a factor which works to deter or delay Negro entry into politics, but it may also be a factor which makes it harder for anti-Negro forces to block race legislation which has strong civic backing. Smaller units in Chicago, on the other hand, facilitate Negro entry into politics but also make it easier for anti-Negro elements in local neighborhoods to mobilize support from their politicians to oppose race measures.

Estimate on which the Borough Presidents sit has substantially greater power than the City Council. It is composed of the Mayor, the Comptroller, the Council President (all elected city-wide) with four votes each and the Borough Presidents from Manhattan, Brooklyn, Queens, the Bronx, and Richmond (with two votes each). Thus, with twelve votes among them, the city-wide officials can dominate the Board and the important decisions it makes, although the necessary unity can be difficult to achieve. The lack of such unity and its consequences are described in Wallace S. Sayre and Herbert Kaufman, *Governing New York City* (New York: Russell Sage Foundation, 1960), chaps. xvii and xviii.

The Making of the Negro Mayors 1967

JEFFREY K. HADDEN, LOUIS H. MASOTTI, and VICTOR THIESSEN

Throughout most of 1967, black power and Vietnam kept this nation in an almost continual state of crisis. The summer months were the longest and hottest in modern U.S. history—many political analysts even felt that the nation was entering its most serious domestic conflict since the Civil War. Over a hundred cities were rocked with violence.

As the summer gave way to autumn, the interest of the nation shifted a little from the summer's riots to the elections on the first Tuesday of November. An unprecedented number of Negroes were running for office, but public attention focused on [two] elections. In Cleveland, Carl

Reprinted from *TRANS-action* 5 (1968): 21–30. Copyright © January/February, 1968 by TRANS-action, Inc. New Brunswick, New Jersey. Reprinted by permission of the publisher.

B. Stokes, a lawyer who in 1962 had become the first Democratic Negro legislator in Ohio, was now seeking to become the first Negro mayor of a large American city. In Gary, Ind., another young Negro lawyer, Richard D. Hatcher, was battling the Republican Party's candidate—as well as his own Democratic Party—to become the first Negro mayor of a "medium-sized" city. . . .

Normally, the nation couldn't care less about who would become the next mayors of Cleveland [and] Gary. But the tenseness of the summer months gave these elections enormous significance. If Stokes and Hatcher lost . . . could Negroes be persuaded to use the power of the ballot box rather than the power of fire bombs?

Fortunately, November 7 proved to be a triumphant day for racial peace. Stokes and Hatcher won squeaker victories, both by margins of only about 1500 votes. . . . Labor leader George Meany was exultant— "American voters have rejected racism as a political issue." Negroes in the two cities were also jubilant. In Gary, the most tense of the cities, Richard Hatcher urged the mostly Negro crowd at his headquarters to "cool it." "I urge that the outcome of this election be unmarred by any incident of any kind. . . . If we spoil this victory with any kind of occurrence here tonight, or anywhere in the city, it will be a hollow victory." The evening *was* cool: Joyous Negroes danced and sang in the streets.

But beyond the exultation of victory remain many hard questions. Now that Cleveland and Gary have Negro mayors, just how much difference will it make in solving the many grave problems that these cities face? Will these victories cool militancy in urban ghettos next summer, or will the momentum of frustration prove too great to put on the brakes? A careful analysis of *how* these candidates won office may help provide the answers.

The focus of this report is on Cleveland because:

As residents of Cleveland, we are more familiar with the campaign and the election.

Cleveland is unique because, in 1965, it had a special census. By matching voting wards with census tracts, we can draw a clearer picture of voting behavior than we could in the other cities, where rapid neighborhood transitions have made 1960 census data quite unreliable in assessing voting patterns. Having examined Cleveland in some detail, we will draw some comparisons with the Gary . . . election, then speculate about their significance and implications.

Cleveland—City in Decline

Cleveland has something less than 2,000,000 residents. Among metropolitan areas in America, it ranks eleventh in size. Like many other American cities, the central city of Cleveland is experiencing an absolute decline in population—residents are fleeing from the decaying core to the surrounding suburbs. The city certainly ranks high both in terms of absolute and proportional decline in the central-city population.

Between 1950 and 1960, the population of the central city declined from 914,808 to 876,050, a loss of almost 39,000. By 1965 the population had sunk to 810,858, an additional loss of 65,000. But these figures are only a partial reflection of the changing composition of the population, since new Negro residents coming into the central city helped offset the white exodus. *Between 1950 and 1960, nearly 142,000 white residents left the central city, and an additional 94,000 left between 1960 and 1965— nearly a quarter of a million in just 15 years.*

During the same period the number of Negro residents of Cleveland rose from 147,847 to 279,352—an increase from 16.1 percent to 34.4 percent of the city's population. There is no evidence that this dramatic population redistribution has changed since the special 1965 census. Some suburbanization of Negroes is beginning on the east and southeast side of the city, but the pace is not nearly so dramatic as for whites. In 1960, approximately 97 percent of the Negroes in the metropolitan area lived in the central city. This percentage has probably declined somewhat since then—16,000 Negro residents have moved to East Cleveland. But the basic pattern of segregation in the metropolitan area remains. The development in East Cleveland is little more than an eastward extension of the ghetto, and the older, decaying residential units the Negroes have moved to are hardly "suburban" in character.

While the population composition of Cleveland is changing rapidly, whites are still a significant majority—about 62 percent. Again like many other central cities, a significant percentage of the white population comprises nationality groups that live in segregated sections, with a strong sense of ethnic identity and a deep fear of Negro encroachment. (In 1964, the bussing of Negro students into Murray Hill, an Italian neighborhood, resulted in rioting.)

In 1960, the census classified 43 percent of the central city's white residents as "foreign stock." In that year, five groups—Germans, Poles, Czechs, Hungarians, and Italians—had populations of 25,000 or greater; at least 20 other nationality groups were large enough to have to be contended with in the political arena. But today these ethnic groups— although unwilling to admit it—have become less than the controlling majority they constituted before 1960.

The Cuyahoga River divides Cleveland, physically as well as socially. When Negroes first began to move into the city, during World War I, they occupied the decaying section to the south and east of the central business district. As their numbers grew, they continued pushing in this direction and now occupy the larger part of the eastside (except for some ethnic strongholds). There are no stable, integrated neighborhoods in the central city—only areas in transition from white to black. To the west, the Cuyahoga River constitutes a barrier to Negro penetration.

Ever since 1941, when Frank Lausche was elected, Cleveland has had a succession of basically honest but unimaginative Democratic mayors. These mayors have kept their hold on City Hall by means of a relatively weak coalition of nationality groups. At no point in this 26-year Lausche dynasty did a mayor gather enough power to seriously confront the long-range needs and problems of the city.

By early 1967, the city had seemingly hit rock bottom. A long procession of reporters began arriving to write about its many problems. The racial unrest of the past several years had, during the summer of 1966, culminated in the worst rioting in Cleveland's history. This unrest was continuing to grow as several militant groups were organizing. Urban renewal was a dismal failure; in January, the Department of Housing and Urban Development even cut off the city's urban-renewal funds, the first such action by the Federal Government. The exodus of whites, along with business, shoved the city to the brink of financial disaster. In February, the Moody Bond Survey reduced the city's credit rating. In May, the Federal Government cut off several million dollars of construction funds—because the construction industry had failed to assure equal job opportunities for minority groups. In short, the city was, and remains, in deep trouble. And while most ethnic groups probably continued to believe that Cleveland was the "Best Location in the Nation," the Negro community—and a growing number of whites—were beginning to feel that Cleveland was the "Mistake on the Lake," and that it was time for a change.

Carl Stokes's campaign for mayor was his second try. In 1965, while serving in the state House of Representatives, he came within 2100 votes of defeating Mayor Ralph S. Locher. Stokes had taken advantage of a city-charter provision that lets a candidate file as an independent, and bypass the partisan primaries. Ralph McAllister, then president of the Cleveland School Board, did the same. For his hard line on *de facto* school segregation, however, McAllister had earned the enmity of the Negro community. The Republican candidate was Ralph Perk, the first Republican elected to a county-wide position (auditor) in many years. A second generation Czech-Bohemian, Perk hoped to win by combining his ethnic appeal with his program for the city (Perk's Plan). He had no opposition for his party's nomination. The fourth candidate was Mayor Locher, who had defeated Mark McElroy, county recorder and perennial candidate for something, in the Democratic primary.

It was in the 1965 Democratic primary that the first signs of a "black bloc" vote emerged. The Negroes, who had previously supported incumbent Democratic mayoral candidates, if not enthusiastically at least consistently, made a concerted effort to dump Locher in favor of McElroy. There were two reasons.

Locher had supported his police chief after the latter had made some tactless remarks about Negroes. Incensed Negro leaders demanded an audience with the mayor, and when he refused, his office was the scene of demonstrations, sit-ins, and arrests. At that point, as one of the local reporters put it, "Ralph Locher became a dirty name in the ghetto."

Stokes, was an independent, and his supporters hoped that the Democratic primary would eliminate the *stronger* candidate, Locher. For then a black bloc would have a good chance of deciding the general election because of an even split in the white vote.

Despite the Negro community's efforts, Locher won the primary and went on to narrowly defeat Stokes. Locher received 37 percent of the vote, Stokes 36 percent, Perk 17 percent, and McAllister 9 percent. Some observers reported that a last-minute whispering campaign in Republican precincts—to the effect that "A vote for Perk is a vote for Stokes"—may have given Locher enough Republican votes to win. The evidence: The popular Perk received only a 17 percent vote in a city where a Republican could be expected something closer to 25 percent. Had Perk gotten anything close to 25 percent, Stokes would have probably been elected two years earlier.

Although he made a strong showing in defeat, Carl Stokes's political future looked bleak. No one expected the Democratic leaders to give Stokes another opportunity to win by means of a split vote. Nor were there other desirable elected offices Stokes could seek. Cleveland has no Negro Congressman—largely because the heavy Negro concentration in the city has been "conveniently" gerrymandered. The only district where Stokes might have had a chance has been represented by Charles Vanik, a popular and liberal white, and as long as Vanik remained in Congress Stokes was locked out. Stokes's state Senate district was predominantly white; and a county or state office seemed politically unrealistic because of his race. So, in 1966, Stokes sought re-election to the state House unopposed.

Between 1965 and 1967, Cleveland went from bad to worse, physically, socially, and financially. With no other immediate possibilities, Stokes began to think about running for mayor again. The big question was whether to risk taking on Locher in the primary—or to file as an independent again.

The Primary Race

In effect, Stokes's decision was made for him. Seth Taft, slated to be the Republican candidate, told Stokes he would withdraw from the election entirely if Stokes filed as an independent in order to gain the advantage of a three-man general election. Taft had concluded that his best strategy was to face a Negro, *alone*, or a faltering incumbent, *alone*, in the general election. But not both. In a three-man race with Locher and Stokes, Taft correctly assumed that he would be the man in the middle with no chance for victory. (Taft would have preferred to run as an independent—to gain Democratic votes—but the county Republican leader threatened to file *another* Republican candidate unless Taft ran as a Republican.)

Meanwhile, Locher committed blunder after blunder—and Democratic party leaders began to question whether he could actually win another election. In the weeks before filing for the primary, Democratic leaders even pressured Locher to accept a Federal judgeship and clear the way for the president of the city council to run. But the Democratic leaders in Cleveland are not noted for their strength or effectiveness, as is evidenced by the fact that none of the Democratic mayors since 1941 were endorsed by the party when they were first elected. When Locher refused to withdraw, the party reluctantly rallied behind him.

Another Democratic candidate was Frank P. Celeste, former mayor of the Republican westside suburb of Lakewood. Celeste established residency in the city, announced his candidacy early, and—despite pressure from the Democratic Party—remained in the primary race.

There was always the possibility that Celeste would withdraw from the primary, which would leave Stokes facing Locher alone. But the threat of Taft's withdrawal from the general election left Stokes with little choice but to face Locher head-on in the primary. A primary race against Locher and a strong Democrat was more appealing than a general election against Locher and a weak Republican.

Now, in 1965 Stokes had received only about 6000 white votes in the city in a 239,000 voter turnout. To win in the primary, he had to enlarge and consolidate the Negro vote—and increase his white support on the westside and in the eastside ethnic wards.

The first part of his strategy was a massive voter-registration drive in the Negro wards—to reinstate the potential Stokes voters dropped from the rolls for failing to vote since the 1964 Presidential election. The Stokes organization—aided by Martin Luther King Jr. and the Southern Christian Leadership Conference, as well as by a grant (in part earmarked for voter registration) from the Ford Foundation to the Cleveland chapter of CORE—did succeed in registering many Negroes. But there was a similar drive mounted by the Democratic Party on behalf of Locher. (Registration figures are not available by race.)

The second part of the Stokes strategy took him across the polluted Cuyahoga River into the white wards that had given him a mere 3 percent of the vote in 1965. He spoke wherever he would be received—to small groups in private homes, in churches, and in public and private halls. While he was not always received enthusiastically, he did not confront many hostile crowds. He faced the race issue squarely and encouraged his audience to judge him on his ability.

Stokes's campaign received a big boost when the *Plain Dealer,* the largest daily in Ohio, endorsed him. Next, the *Cleveland Press* called for a change in City Hall, but declined to endorse either Stokes or Celeste. But since the polls indicated that Celeste was doing very badly, this amounted to an endorsement of Stokes.

More people voted in this primary than in any other in Cleveland's history. When the ballots were counted, Stokes had 52.5 percent of the votes—he had defeated Locher by a plurality of 18,000 votes. Celeste was the man in the middle, getting only 4 percent of the votes, the lowest of any mayoral candidate in recent Cleveland history.

What produced Stokes's clear victory? Table 1 (below) reveals the answer. The decisive factor was the size of the Negro turnout. While Negroes constituted only about 40 percent of the voters, 73.4 percent of them turned out, compared with only 58.4 percent of the whites. Predominantly Negro wards cast 96.2 percent of their votes for Stokes. (Actually

Table 1.

	City Totals			Negro Wards		
	1965 General	1967 Primary	1967 General	1965 General	1967 Primary	1967 General
Registered Voters	337,803	326,003	326,003	103,123	99,885	99,885
Turnout	239,479	210,926	257,157	74,396	73,360	79,591
% Turnout	70.9	64.7	78.9	72.1	73.4	79.7
Stokes Votes	85,716	110,769	129,829	63,550	70,575	75,586
% Stokes Votes	35.8	52.5	50.5	85.4	96.2	95.0
	White Wards			Mixed Wards		
	1965 General	1967 Primary	1967 General	1965 General	1967 Primary	1967 General
Registered Voters	159,419	152,737	152,737	75,261	73,421	73,421
Turnout	111,129	88,525	119,883	53,962	49,105	57,113
% Turnout	69.7	58.0	78.5	71.7	66.9	77.8
Stokes Votes	3,300	13,495	23,158	18,866	26,699	30,872
% Stokes Votes	3.0	15.2	19.3	35.0	54.4	54.1

this figure underrepresents the Negro vote for Stokes, since some of the non-Stokes votes in these wards were cast by whites. Similarly, the 15.4 percent vote for Stokes in the predominantly white wards slightly overestimates the white vote because of the Negro minority.)

Newspaper and magazine reports of the primary election proclaimed that Stokes could not have won without the white vote. Our own estimate —based on matching wards with census tracts, and allowing for only slight shifts in racial composition in some wards since the 1965 special census—is that Stokes received 16,000 white votes. His margin of victory was 18,000. How would the voting have gone if the third man, Celeste, had not been in the race? Many white voters, feeling that Stokes could not win in a two-man race, might not have bothered to vote at all, so perhaps Stokes would have won by an even larger margin. Thus Stokes's inroad into the white vote was not the decisive factor in his primary victory, although it was important.

Stokes emerged from the primary as the odds-on favorite to win—five weeks later—in the general election. And in the first few days of the campaign, it seemed that Stokes had everything going for him.

Stokes was bright, handsome, and articulate. His opponent, Seth Taft, while bright, had never won an election, and his family name, associated with the Taft-Hartley Act, could hardly be an advantage among union members. In addition, he was shy and seemingly uncomfortable in a crowd.

Both the *Plain Dealer* and the *Cleveland Press* endorsed Stokes in the general election.

The wounds of the primary were quickly (if perhaps superficially) healed, and the Democratic candidate was endorsed by both the Democratic Party and Mayor Locher.

Labor—both the A.F.L.-C.I.O. and the Teamsters—also endorsed Stokes.

He had a partisan advantage. Of the 326,003 registered voters, only 34,000 (10 percent) were Republican. The closest any Republican mayoral candidate had come to winning was in 1951, when—in a small turnout—William J. McDermott received 45 percent of the vote.

Stokes had 90,000 or more Negro votes virtually assured, with little possibility that Taft would make more than slight inroads.

Perhaps most important, voting-behavior studies over the years have demonstrated that voters who are confronted by a dilemma react by staying home from the polls. Large numbers of life-long Democrats, faced with voting for a Negro or a Republican by the name of Taft, were likely to stay home.

Had this been a normal election, Democrat Carl Stokes would have won handily. But this was not destined to be a normal election. During the final days of the campaign, Stokes knew he was in a fight for his political life. Those who predicted that the cross-pressures would keep many voters away from the polls forgot that the variable "Negro" had never been involved in an election of this importance.

On Election Day, an estimated 90 percent of those who voted for Locher or Celeste in the Democratic primary shifted to Taft—many pulling a Republican lever for the first time in their life. Was this clearly and unequivocally bigoted backlash? To be sure, bigotry *did* play a major role in the election. But to dismiss the campaign and the election as pure overt bigotry is to miss the significance of what happened in Cleveland and the emerging subtle nature of prejudice in American society.

The Non-Issue of Race

A closer look at the personal characteristics and campaign strategy of Seth Taft, the Republican candidate, reveals the complexity and subtlety of the race issue.

In the final days of the Democratic primary campaign, Taft repeatedly told reporters that he would rather run against Locher and his record than against Carl Stokes. On the evening of the primary, Taft appeared at Stokes's headquarters to congratulate him. As far as he was concerned, Taft said, the campaign issue was, Who could present the most constructive program for change in Cleveland? Further, he said he didn't want people voting for him simply because he was white. A few days later, Taft even presented a strongly-worded statement to his campaign workers:

The Cuyahoga Democratic party has issued a number of vicious statements concerning the candidacy of Carl Stokes, and others have conducted whisper campaigns. We cannot tolerate injection of race into this campaign. . . . Many people will vote for Carl Stokes because he is a Negro. Many people will vote for me because I am white. I regret this fact. I will work hard to convince people they should not vote on a racial basis.

Seth Taft's programs to solve racial tensions may have been paternalistic, not really perceptive of emerging moods of the ghetto. But one thing is clear—he was not a bigot. Every indication is that he remained uncomfortable about being in a race in which his chances to win depended, in large part, upon a backlash vote.

Whether Taft's attempt to silence the race issue was a deliberate strategy or a reflection of deep personal feelings, it probably enhanced his chances of winning. He knew that he had the hard-core bigot vote. His task was to convince those in the middle that they could vote for him and *not* be bigots.

Stokes, on the other hand, had another kind of problem. While he had to draw more white votes, he also had to retain and, if possible, increase the 73 percent Negro turnout that had delivered him 96 percent of the Negro votes in the primary. Stokes's campaign leaders feared a fall-off in the voter turnout from Negro wards—with good reason. The entire primary campaign had pushed the October 3 date so hard that some Negroes could not understand why Carl Stokes was not mayor on October 4. Full-page newspaper ads paid for by CORE had stated, *"If you don't vote Oct. 3rd, forget it. The man who wins will be the next mayor of Cleveland!"* So Stokes felt he had to remobilize the Negro vote.

The moment came during the question-and-answer period of the second of four debates with Taft in the all-white westside. Stokes said:

The personal analysis of Seth Taft—and the analysis of many competent political analysts—is that Seth Taft may win the November 7 election, but for only one reason. That reason is that his skin happens to be white.

The predominantly white crowd booed loudly and angrily for several minutes, and throughout the rest of the evening repeatedly interrupted him. Later, Stokes's campaign manager revealed that his candidate's remark was a calculated risk to arouse Negro interest. Stokes probably succeeded, but he also gave Taft supporters an excuse to bring the race issue into the open. And they could claim that it was *Stokes*, not Taft, who was trying to exploit the race issue.

To be sure, *both* candidates exploited the race issue. But, for the most part, it was done rather subtly. Stokes's campaign posters stated, "Let's do Cleveland Proud"—another way of saying, "Let's show the world that Cleveland is capable of rising above racial bigotry." A full-page ad for Stokes stated in bold print, "Vote for Seth Taft. It Would Be Easy, Wouldn't It?" After the debate, Taft was free to accuse Stokes of using the race issue—itself a subtle way of exploiting the issue. Then there was the letter, signed by the leaders of 22 nationality clubs, that was mailed to 40,000 members in the city. It didn't mention race, but comments such as "protecting our way of life," "safeguard our liberty," and "false charges of police brutality" were blatant in their implications. Taft sidestepped comment on the letter.

No matter how much the candidates may have wanted to keep race out of the picture, race turned out to be the most important issue. Both Taft

The Making of the Negro Mayors

and Stokes could benefit from the issue if they played it right, and both did use it. And although Stokes's remark at the second debate gave white voters an excuse to vote for Taft without feeling that they were bigots, many whites probably would have found another excuse.

Taft as a Strategist

The fact is that Taft, for all his lackluster qualities, emerged as a strong candidate. He was able to turn many of his liabilities into assets.

Table 2. Percent Stokes vote by ward

White Wards	% Negro	1965 General	1967 Primary	1967 General
1	.6	3.2	17.2	20.5
2	.3	1.9	12.8	17.4
3	.9	2.5	13.6	22.1
4	.3	3.0	18.2	20.9
5	.6	1.7	11.8	17.8
6	.8	2.3	15.1	16.7
7	.6	3.4	16.5	23.7
8	3.0	6.1	24.7	29.3
9	.2	1.9	12.4	16.4
14	1.4	1.1	12.7	13.0
15	1.4	1.2	9.2	14.1
22	5.7	8.1	22.5	26.3
26	1.1	2.8	16.3	19.9
32	2.4	2.9	10.0	15.3
33	.3	2.5	17.7	21.4
Average		3.0	15.2	19.3
Negro Wards				
10	91.3	88.7	97.3	96.7
11	91.8	86.3	95.9	96.0
12	82.7	76.9	90.4	90.5
13	75.2	75.8	90.7	88.4
17	99.0	86.6	98.1	97.9
18	89.3	84.0	96.0	95.7
20	91.0	83.0	95.0	92.8
24	92.6	90.6	98.1	98.1
25	90.9	91.3	98.4	98.2
27	85.7	85.2	95.6	94.0
Average		85.4	96.2	95.0
Mixed Wards				
16	56.6	50.7	69.9	70.1
19	25.3	29.2	48.0	39.9
21	61.1	55.2	66.3	68.9
23	20.3	9.8	18.2	23.2
28	28.5	26.5	54.8	57.3
29	24.4	26.8	43.2	42.3
30	51.7	51.5	75.3	71.4
31	21.8	16.9	31.8	39.0
Average		35.0	54.4	54.1

Taft was able to insulate himself against his Republican identity. He successfully dissociated himself from his uncle's position on labor by pointing to his own active role, as a student, against "right to work" laws. At the same time, he hit hard at Stokes's record as an off again–on again Democrat. This strategy neutralized, at least in part, Taft's first political disadvantage—running as a Republican in a Democratic city.

A second liability was that he came from a wealthy family. Taft was an Ivy League intellectual, cast in the role of a "do-gooder." He lived in an exclusive suburb, Pepper Pike, and had bought a modest home in Cleveland only a few weeks before declaring his candidacy. How, it was frequently asked, could such a man understand the problems of the inner-city and of the poor? Almost invariably the answer was: "Did John F. Kennedy, Franklin D. Roosevelt, and Nelson Rockefeller have to be poor in order to understand and respond to the problems of the poor?" Taft's campaign posters were a side profile that bore a striking resemblance to President Kennedy. Whether he was consciously exploiting the Kennedy image is an open question. But there can be little doubt that when Taft mentioned his Republican heritage, he tried to project an image of the new breed of Republican—John Lindsay and Charles Percy. This image didn't come across very well at first, but as he became a seasoned campaigner it became clearer.

Another liability was that Taft had never held an elected office. His opponent tried to exploit this—unsuccessfully. Taft could point to 20 years of active civic service, including the fact that he was one of the authors of the Ohio fair-housing law. Then too, the charge gave Taft an opportunity to point out that Stokes had the worst absentee record of anyone in the state legislature. Stokes never successfully answered this charge until the last of their four debates, when he produced a pre-campaign letter from Taft commending him on his legislative service. But this came moments *after* the TV cameras had gone off the air.

Still another liability emerged during the campaign. Taft's strategy of discussing programs, not personalities, was seemingly getting him nowhere. He presented specific proposals; Stokes, a skilled debater, succeeded in picking them apart. Stokes himself discussed programs only at a general level and contended that he was best-qualified to "cut the red tape" in Washington. His frequent trips to Washington to confer with top Government officials, before and during the campaign, indicated that he had the inside track.

Taft, realizing at this point that his campaign was not gaining much momentum, suddenly switched gears and began attacking Stokes's record (not Stokes personally). Stokes had claimed he would crack-down on slumlords. Taft discovered that Stokes owned a piece of rental property with several code violations—and that it had not been repaired despite an order from the city. He hit hard at Stokes's absenteeism and his record as a "good" Democrat. He put a "bird-dog" on Stokes and, if Stokes told one group one thing and another group something else, the public heard about it.

The upshot was that in the final days of the campaign Taft captured the momentum. Stokes was easily the more flashy debater and projected a superior image; but Taft emerged as the better strategist.

Should Taft Have Withdrawn?

One may ask whether all of this discussion is really relevant, since the final vote was sharply divided along racial lines. In one sense it *is* irrelevant, since it is possible that a weaker candidate than Taft might have run just as well. It is also possible that a white racist might actually have won. Still, this discussion has buttressed two important points.

Taft was not all black, and Stokes was not all white. Taft proved a strong candidate, and—had he been running against Locher instead of Stokes—he might have amassed strong support from Negroes and defeated Locher.

By being a strong candidate, Taft made it much easier for many white Democrats, who might otherwise have been cross-pressured into staying home, to come out and vote for him.

Some people felt that Taft should have withdrawn and let Stokes run uncontested. But many of the same people also decried white liberals who, at recent conferences to form coalitions between black-power advocates and the New Left, let black militants castrate them. It is not traditional in American politics that candidates enter a race to lose. Taft was in to win, and he fought a hard and relatively clean campaign—as high a compliment as can be paid to any candidate.

Yet all of this doesn't change the basic nature of the voting. This is clear from the evidence in Table 2. Stokes won by holding his black bloc, and increasing his white vote from 15 percent in the primary to almost 20 percent in the general. An enormous amount of the white vote was, whether covert or overt, anti-Negro. It is hard to believe that Catholics, ethnic groups, and laborers who never voted for anyone but a Democrat should suddenly decide to evaluate candidates on their qualifications and programs, and—in overwhelming numbers—decide that the Republican candidate was better qualified. The implication is that they were prejudiced. But to assume that such people perceive themselves as bigots is to oversimplify the nature of prejudice. And to call such people bigots is to make their responses even more rigid—as Carl Stokes discovered after his remark in the second debate with Taft.

This, then, is perhaps an important lesson of the Cleveland election: Bigotry cannot be defeated directly, by telling bigots that they are bigoted. For the most part Stokes learned this lesson well, accumulating as many as 30,000 white votes, nearly five times the number he received in 1965. But another slip like the one in the second debate might have cost him the election.

A few words on the voting for Stokes ward by ward, as shown in the table. Wards 9, 14, and 15—which gave Stokes a comparatively low vote—have the highest concentration of ethnic groups in the city. Not only is there the historical element of prejudice in these areas, but there is the ever-present fear among the residents that Negroes will invade their neighborhoods. (This fear is less a factor in ward 9, which is across the river.)

Wards 26 and 32 also gave Stokes a low percentage of votes, and these wards are also the ones most likely to have Negro migration. They are just to the north of East Cleveland, which is currently undergoing heavy transition, and to the east of ward 27, which in the past few years has changed from white to black. In these two wards, then, high ethnic composition and a fear of Negro migration would seem to account for Stokes's 19.9 and 15.3 percentages.

The highest percentage *for* Stokes in predominantly white areas was in wards 8 and 22. Ward 8 has a growing concentration of Puerto Ricans, and—according to newspaper polls—they voted heavily for Stokes. Ward 22 has a very large automobile-assembly plant that employs many Negroes. Now, in 1965 the ward was 5.7 percent Negro—a large increase from 1960. Since 1965, this percentage has probably grown another 2 or 3 percent. Therefore, if one subtracts the Negro vote that Stokes received in this ward, the size of the white vote is about the same as in other wards.

"Imminent Danger" in Gary

The race for mayor in Gary, Ind., was not overtly racist. Still, the racial issue was much less subtle than it was in Cleveland. When Democratic chairman John G. Krupa refused to support Richard D. Hatcher, the Democratic candidate, it was clear that the reason was race. When the Gary newspaper failed to give similar coverage to both candidates and sometimes failed to print news releases from Hatcher headquarters (ostensibly because press deadlines had not been met), it was clear that race was a factor.

Even though race was rarely mentioned openly, the city polarized. While Stokes had the support of the white-owned newspapers and many white campaign workers, many of Hatcher's white supporters preferred to remain in the background—in part, at least, because they feared reprisals from white racists. Hatcher didn't use the black-power slogan, but to the community the election was a contest between black and white. And when the Justice Department supported Hatcher's claim that the election board had illegally removed some 5000 Negro voters from the registration lists and added nonexistent whites, the tension in the city became so great that the Governor, feeling that there was "imminent danger" of violence on election night, called up 4000 National Guardsmen.

Negroes constitute an estimated 55 percent of Gary's 180,000 residents, but white voter registration outnumbers Negroes by 2000 or 3000. Like Stokes, Hatcher—in order to win—had to pull some white votes, or have a significantly higher Negro turnout.

The voter turnout and voting patterns in Cleveland and Gary were very similar. In both cities, almost 80 percent of the registered voters turned out at the polls. In the Glen Park and Miller areas, predominantly white neighborhoods, Joseph B. Radigan—Hatcher's opponent—received more than 90 percent of the votes. In the predominantly Negro areas, Hatcher received an estimated 93 percent of the votes. In all, Hatcher received about 4000 white votes, while losing probably 1000 Negro votes, at most, to Radigan. This relatively small white vote was enough to give him victory. If Stokes's miscalculation in bringing race into the Cleveland campaign gave prejudiced whites an excuse to vote for Taft, the glaring way the Democratic Party in Gary tried to defeat Hatcher probably tipped the scales and gave Hatcher some white votes he wouldn't have received otherwise.

. . . Now let us consider the broader implications these elections will have on the racial crisis in America. To be sure, the immediate implications are quite different from what they would have been if Stokes and Hatcher had lost. . . . If the elections had gone the other way, Summer '68 might well have begun November 8. As Thomas Pettigrew of Harvard put it a few days before the election, "If Stokes and Hatcher lose . . . , then I just wonder how a white man in this country could ever look a Negro in the eye and say, 'Why don't you make it the way we did, through the political system, rather than burning us down?'"

The Meaning of the Elections

But do these victories really alter the basic nature of the racial crisis? There is, true, some reason for hope. But to assume that anything has been fundamentally altered would be disastrous. First of all, it is by no means clear that these elections will pacify militant Negroes—including those in Cleveland and Gary. . . . In Cleveland, most militants remained less than enthusiastic about the possibility of a Stokes victory. Of the militant groups, only CORE worked hard for him. In Gary alone did the candidate have the solid support of militants—probably because Hatcher refused to explicitly rebuke Stokely Carmichael and H. Rap Brown, and because his opponents repeatedly claimed that Hatcher was a black-power advocate.

If the Stokes and Hatcher victories are to represent a turning point in the racial crisis, they must deliver results. Unfortunately, Hatcher faces an unsympathetic Democratic Party and city council. Stokes has gone a long way toward healing the wounds of the bitter primary, but it remains to be seen whether he will receive eager support for his programs. Some councilmen from ethnic wards will almost certainly buck his programs for fear of alienating their constituencies.

Stokes and Hatcher themselves face a difficult and delicate situation.

Their margins of victory were so narrow that they, like Kennedy in 1960, must proceed with great caution.

Enthusiasm and promises of change are not the same as the power to implement change. And the two mayors must share power with whites.

They must demonstrate to Negroes that their presence in City Hall has made a difference. But if their programs seem too preferential toward Negroes, they run the risk of massive white resistance.

This delicate situation was clearly seen in the early days of the Stokes administration. Of his first ten appointments, only two were Negroes. Although relations with the police have been one of the most sensitive issues in the Negro ghetto, Stokes's choice for a new police chief was Michael Blackwell, a 67-year-old "hardliner." This appointment was intended to ease anxieties in the ethnic neighborhoods, but it was not popular in the Negro ghetto. Blackwell, in his first public address after being sworn in, lashed out at the Supreme Court, state laws, and "publicity-seeking clergy and beatniks" for "crippling law enforcement." Cleveland's Negroes are already beginning to wonder whether a Negro in City Hall is going to make any difference.

Some observers believe that Stokes is basically quite conservative, and point to his sponsorship of anti-riot legislation. To be sure, Stokes's position on many issues remains uncertain, but what does seem fairly clear from his early days in office is that his efforts to gain support in white communities is going to lead to disaffection among Negroes. How much and how quickly is a difficult question.

Race relations is only one of many problems that these two new mayors must face. Stokes has inherited all of the problems that brought national attention to Cleveland last spring—poverty, urban renewal, finance, transportation, air and water pollution, and so on. Hatcher faces similar problems in Gary, and must also cope with one of the nation's worst strongholds of organized crime. If they fail, the responsibility will fall heavier on them than had a white man failed. Some whites will generalize the failures to all Negro politicians, and some Negroes will generalize the failures to the "bankruptcy" of the American political system.

Almost certainly, Washington will be a key factor in determining if these two men succeed. The national Democratic Party has a strong interest in making Stokes and Hatcher look good, for it desperately needs to recapture the disaffected Negro voters before the 1968 national election. But how much can the party deliver? The war in Vietnam is draining enormous national resources and Congress is threatening to slash poverty programs. Even if Federal monies were no problem, there is the question whether *any* of Washington's existing programs are directed at the roots of ghetto unrest. Many informed administrators, scientists, and political analysts feel they are not. And the chances for creative Federal programs seem, at this moment, fairly dim.

Another clear implication of these elections is that white resistance to change remains large and widespread. More than 90 percent of the Democrats in Cleveland who voted for a Democrat in the primary switched, in the general election, to the Republican candidate. Now, not many American cities are currently composed of as many as 35 percent Negroes; the possibility of coalitions to elect other Negro candidates appears, except in a handful of cities, remote. Additional Negro mayoral candidates are almost certain to arise, and many will go down to bitter defeat.

Stokes and Hatcher won because black-voter power coalesced with a relatively small minority of liberal whites. It was not a victory of acceptance or even tolerance of Negroes, but a numerical failure of the powers of discrimination, a failure that resulted in large part because of the massive exodus of whites from the central city. The election of Stokes and Hatcher may break down white resistance to voting for a Negro, but this is, at best, problematical. Also problematical is how bigoted whites will react to the election of a Negro mayor. Their organized efforts to resist change may intensify. As we have already indicated, the pace of white exodus from the central city of Cleveland is already alarming. And an acceleration of this pace could push the city into financial bankruptcy.

America Has Bought a Little Time

In short, while the implications of the November 7 elections are ambiguous, it does seem that the victories of Stokes and Hatcher . . . have kept the door open on the growing racial crisis. America has, at best, bought a little time.

On the other hand, we do not find much cause for optimism in those elections—unlike George Meany, and unlike the *New York Times*, which, five days after the election, published a glowing editorial about "the willingness of most voters today to choose men solely on personal quality and impersonal issues." To us, it would seem that the elections have only accelerated the pace of ever-rising expectations among Negroes. And if results don't follow, and rather rapidly, then we believe that the Negro community's frustration with the American political system will almost certainly heighten.

The hard task of demonstrating that Negroes can actually achieve justice and equality in America still lies ahead.

Black Powerlessness in Chicago

HAROLD M. BARON with HARRIET STULMAN, RICHARD ROTHSTEIN, and RENNARD DAVIS

Until recently, the three principal targets of the civil rights movement in the North were discrimination and inferior conditions in (1) housing for Negroes, (2) jobs for Negroes, and (3) the education of Negroes. But after failing to bring about major changes, many Negroes realized that one reason the status quo in housing, jobs, and education continues is that *the black community lacks control over decision-making*. Negroes remain second-class citizens partly because of the discrimination of individual whites, but mainly because of the way whites control the major institutions of our society. And therefore the fourth major goal of Negro organizations and the civil rights movement has become the acquisition of power.

It was because of this concern with power for black people that, more than two years ago, the Chicago Urban League—a social-welfare organization dedicated to changing institutions so as to achieve full racial equality—started to study the decision-making apparatus in Cook County, Ill., and particularly how it affects or ignores Negro citizens. (Cook County takes in the city of Chicago, and two-thirds of the population of the surrounding suburban ring included in the Chicago Standard Metropolitan Statistical area.) Among the questions we posed were:

What is the extent of Negro exclusion from policy-making positions in Chicago?

Where Negroes *are* in policy-making positions, what type of positions are these, and where are Negroes in greatest number and authority?

Do Negroes in policy-making positions represent the interests of the Negro community?

How might an increase in the percentage of Negro policy makers affect socioeconomic conditions for Negroes in general?

What we found was that in 1965 some 20 percent of the people in Cook County were Negro, and 28 percent of the people in Chicago were Negro.

Reprinted from *TRANS-action* 6 (1968): 27–33. Copyright © November, 1968 by TRANS-action, Inc. New Brunswick, New Jersey. Reprinted by permission of the publisher.

Table 1. The exclusion of Negroes from government. Policy-making positions in the Cook County public sector (1965)

	Policy-Making Positions	Positions Held by Negroes	Percent
1. Elected Officials			
U.S. House of Representatives	13	1	8
State Legislature	120	10	8
Cook County—nonjudicial	34	3	9
Chicago—nonjudicial	59	7	12
Cook County—judicial	138	8	6
Total:	364	29	8
2. Appointive Supervisory Boards			
Total:	77	10	13
3. Local Administrative Positions			
City of Chicago	156	2	1
Chicago Board of Education	72	7	9
Metropolitan Sanitary District	7	0	0
Cook County Government	13	1	8
Total:	248	10	4
4. Federal Government			
Civil Service	368	8	2
Presidential Appointments	31	1	3
Total:	399	9	2
Grand Total:	1088	58	5

Yet the representation of Negroes in policy-making positions was minimal. Of the top 10,997 policy-making positions in the major Cook County institutions included in our study, Negroes occupied only 285—or 2.6 percent.

In government (see Table 1), out of a total of 1088 policy-making positions Negroes held just 58. This 5 percent is about one-fourth of the percentage of Negroes in the total county population. Of the 364 elective posts in the survey, however, Negroes occupied 29, or 8 percent, indicating that the franchise has helped give Negroes representation. Yet Negroes had the most positions, percentagewise, on appointed supervisory boards, such as the Board of Education and the Chicago Housing Authority. There they occupied 10 of the 77 policy-making positions, or about 13 percent.

Negroes were better represented on appointed supervisory boards and in elected (nonjudicial) offices than they were in local administrative positions, or in important federal jobs based in Chicago. Thus, Negroes held 12 percent of the nonjudicial elected posts in Chicago's government, but only a little over 1 percent of the appointive policy-making positions in the city administration. The same anomaly appears at the federal level. There is one Negro out of the 13 U.S. Congressmen from Cook County (8 percent), but Negroes held only one out of 31 Presidential appointments (3 percent), and eight of the 368 top federal civil-service posts (2 percent).

Table 2. The exclusion of Negroes from private institutions. Policy-making positions in the Cook County private sector (1965)

	Policy-Making Positions	Positions Held by Negroes	Percent
1. Business Corporations			
Banks	2258	7	*
Insurance	533	35	6
Nonfinancial Corporations	4047	0	0
Total:	6838	42	*
2. Legal Profession			
Total:	757	0	0
3. Universities**			
Total:	380	5	1
4. Voluntary Organizations			
Business & Professional	324	3	1
Welfare & Religious	791	69	9
Total:	1115	72	6
5. Labor Unions			
Internationals	94	15	16
District Councils	211	20	9
Locals	514	73	14
Total:	819	108	13
Grand Total:	9909	227	2
Grand Total for Public & Private Sectors:	10997	285	2

* Below 1 percent.
** Includes the University of Illinois, which is a public body.

Nonetheless, Negroes have—proportionately—two-and-a-half-times as many important posts in the public sector as they have in the private sector. As Table 2 indicates, Negroes are virtually barred from policy-making positions in the large organizations that dominate the private institutions in the Chicago area. Out of a total of 9909 positions, Negroes fill a mere 227. This 2 percent representation is only one-tenth of the proportionate Negro population.

The whitest form of policy making in Chicago is in the control of economic enterprises. Out of 6838 positions identified in business corporations, Negroes held only 42 (six-tenths of 1 percent). Thirty-five of these were in insurance, where Negroes occupy 6 percent of the 533 posts. But all 35 were in two all-Negro insurance firms. The other seven positions were in four smaller banks. In banks in general, Negroes occupied three-tenths of 1 percent of the policy posts. There were no Negro policy-makers at all in manufacturing, communications, transportation, utilities, and trade corporations.

Out of the 372 companies we studied, the Negro-owned insurance companies were the only ones dominated by blacks (see Table 3). And if we had used the same stringent criteria for banks and insurance companies

Black Powerlessness in Chicago

Table 3. The exclusion of Negroes from private establishments. Percentage of Negro policy-makers in the Cook Country private sector by establishment (1965)

	Total Establishments	Percentage of Negro Policy-Makers				
		None	1–5%	6–15%	16–50%	51% +
1. Business Corporations						
Banks	102	98	0	4	0	0
Insurance	30	28	0	0	0	2
Nonfinancial Corporations	240	240	0	0	0	0
2. Legal Professions	54	54	0	0	0	0
3. Universities*	7	5	0	2	0	0
4. Voluntary Organizations						
Business & Professional	5	3	2	0	0	0
Welfare & Religious	14	2	4	7	1	0
5. Labor Unions						
Internationals	4	0	1	1	2	0
District Councils	23	13	0	5	5	0
Locals	33	14	2	8	7	2
Total:	512	457	9	27	15	4

* Includes the University of Illinois, which is a public body.

that we used for nonfinancial institutions, there would have been no black policy makers in the business sector at all.

Now, amazingly enough, Chicago has proportionately more Negro-controlled businesses, larger than neighborhood operations, than any other major city in the North. Therefore, similar surveys in other Northern metropolitan areas would turn up an even smaller percentage of Negro policy makers in the business world.

The legal profession, represented by corporate law firms, had no Negroes at high policy levels. We are convinced that the same situation would be found in other professions, such as advertising and engineering.

The very prestigious universities—the University of Chicago, Northwestern University, Loyola University, DePaul University, Roosevelt University, the Illinois Institute of Technology, and the University of Illinois (the only public university of the seven)—had a negligible 1 percent Negro representation. Most of these universities had few Negro students, faculty members, or administrators. Five of the seven had no Negro policy makers. The University of Illinois had one. Roosevelt University, the sole institution that had a number of Negroes at the top, was the newest, and the one with the *least* public support. When this university was founded, its leaders had made a forthright stand on racial questions and a firm commitment to liberal principles.

We included these major universities in our survey because other institutions—public and private—have been placing increasingly greater value on them. Every year hundreds of millions of dollars in endowment and operating funds are given to the Chicago-area schools. After all, their research activities, and their training of skilled personnel, are considered a key to the region's economic growth. One indication of the tremendous influence these universities have is that they have determined the nature of urban renewal more than any other institutional group in Chicago (aside from the city government). Without a doubt, the universities have real—not nominal—power. And perhaps it is a reflection of this real power that only five out of 380 policy-making positions in these universities are held by Negroes.

The exclusion of Negroes from the private sector carries over to its voluntary organizations: Negroes are found in only 1 percent of the posts there. It is in the voluntary associations that it is easiest to make symbolic concessions to the black community by giving token representation, yet even here Negroes were underrepresented—which highlights the fundamental norms of the entire sector.

The sectors and individual groups in the Chicago area with the highest Negro representation were those with a Negro constituency—elective offices, supervisory boards, labor unions, and religious and welfare organizations. These four groups accounted for 216 of the posts held by Negroes, or 75 percent, although these four groups have only 19 percent of all the policy-making positions we studied. Labor unions had a larger percentage —13 percent—than any other institution in the private sector. In welfare and religious organizations, whose constituents were often largely Negro, Negroes occupied 8 percent of the positions, the same percentage of the elected public offices they held.

Now, either the black constituency elected the Negroes directly (in the case of elective offices and trade unions); or the Negroes were appointed to posts in an operation whose clients were largely Negro (principal of a Negro school, for example); or Negroes were given token representation on bodies that had a broad public purpose (like religious organizations). By "token representation," we mean—following James Q. Wilson—that "he is a man chosen because a Negro is 'needed' in order to legitimate [but not direct] whatever decisions are made by the agency."

Of the three ways a black constituency had of getting itself represented, the most important was the first. The statistics clearly show the importance of the Negro vote. The elected political office and the elected trade-union offices account for only 11 percent of all the policy-making positions in Cook County. Yet almost half of all the Negro policy makers were found in these two areas—137 out of 285.

Nonetheless, even in the major areas where Negro representation was the greatest—labor unions, elective offices, supervisory boards, and religious and welfare organizations—many institutions still excluded Negroes from positions of authority.

There are, of course, few Negroes in the building-trade unions, most of which bar Negroes from membership. Only two out of the 12 building-trade union organizations we studied had even one Negro in a decisive slot. These two Negroes made up a mere one and a half percent of the policy-making positions in the building-trade unions.

The greatest degree of black representation was found in the former CIO industrial unions. Only one-fourth of these units in the survey totally excluded Negroes from leadership. In almost half, the percentage of Negro policy makers was over 15 percent—which is above token levels.

The former AFL unions (not including those in the building trades) had a higher rate of exclusion than those of the CIO. Two-fifths of these AFL unions had no Negroes at all in policy-making posts. But one-third of this group had leaderships that were 15 percent or more Negro. And the only two black-controlled locals large enough to be included in this study were in AFL unions.

In elective offices, the Negro vote certainly does give Negroes some representation—though far below their proportionate number. In public administration, however, where advancement to policy-making offices comes through appointment and influence, Negroes are all but excluded from decisive posts, at both the federal and local levels. Although a very high percentage of all Negro professionals are in public service, they do not reach the top.

The only major governmental operation that had a goodly number of Negroes at the upper level of the bureaucratic hierarchy was the public school system. Nine percent of the top positions were occupied by Negroes. This unique situation is the result of some fairly recent appointments, made as concessions after an intense civil rights campaign directed at the Chicago Board of Education. In this instance, one can consider these civil-rights actions as a proxy for Negro votes. Still, this high-level representation in the Chicago school hierarchy did not seem to reflect any uniform policy of including Negroes in management. At the level of principalship that was not included as a policy-making position in this study, only 3 percent of the positions were occupied by blacks.

The voluntary welfare and religious associations that were sufficiently important to be included in the study usually had at least a few Negro policy-makers. Only two out of 14 bodies had no Negroes in policy positions (see Table 3), while four organizations had token representation—below 5 percent. None had a Negro majority in the key posts. Only the Chicago Urban League (with 43 percent) had Negroes in more than 15 percent of its policy slots. If individual religious denominations had been among the organizations counted in the survey, there would have been some black-dominated groups. As it was, Negro representation in the United Protestant Federation, which *was* included, came largely from the traditionally Negro denominations. It is of interest to note that, in recent years, Protestant groups have provided some of the few instances in which Negroes have been elected to important offices by a constituency that was overwhelmingly white.

Not only were Negroes grossly underrepresented in Chicago's policy-making posts, but even where represented they had less power than white policy makers. The fact is that *the number of posts held by Negroes tended to be inversely related to the power vested in these positions— the more powerful the post, the fewer the black policy makers.*

As we have seen, Negroes were virtually excluded from policy making in the single most powerful institutional sector—the business world. In *all* sectors, they were generally placed in positions in which the authority was delegated from a higher administrator, or divided among a board. Rarely were Negroes in positions of ultimate authority, either as chief executive or as top board officer.

When Negroes ran for a board or for a judicial office on a slate, their number had been limited by the political parties apportioning out the nominations. The percentage of Negroes on such boards or (especially) in judicial offices tended to run lower than the number of Negroes in legislative posts, for which Negroes run individually.

It is also true that no Negro has *ever* been elected to one of the key city-wide or county-wide executive positions such as Mayor, City Clerk, or President of the Cook County Board. These are the positions with the greatest power and patronage.

In welfare agencies, where Negroes have token representation, they are virtually excluded from the key posts of executive director. Only five of the 135 directors of medium and of large welfare agencies were Negro.

Now, it was in the trade-union sector that the highest percentage of Negroes had policy posts—13 percent. We asked several experts on the Chicago trade-union movement to list the number of Negroes among the 100 most powerful trade unionists in the area. Among the 100 people they named, the number of Negroes ranged from two to five. This did not surprise us, for it was compatible with our general knowledge of the number of Negroes with truly powerful posts in other sectors.

A Rule of Thumb on Negro Power

All in all, then, we would suggest the following rule of thumb: *The actual power vested in Negro policy makers is about one-third as great as the percentage of the posts they hold.*

Thus when Negroes elected other Negroes to office, these officers tended to represent small constituencies. For example, the greatest number of Negroes in legislative posts came from relatively small districts that happen to have black majorities. Indeed, according to Cook County tradition, Negroes simply do not hold legislative posts in city, state, or federal government *unless* they represent a district that is mostly black. No district with Negroes in the minority had a Negro representative, even when Negroes constituted the single largest ethnic group. And some districts with a Negro majority had a *white* representative.

Then too, the smaller the district, the more likely it would be homogeneous, and the greater the chances of its having a black majority that could return a Negro to office. In the Chicago area, consequently, Negroes were best represented on the City Council, which is based on 50 relatively small wards, each representing about 70,000 people; Negroes were represented most poorly in the U.S. House of Representatives, for which there are only nine rather large districts in Chicago, each representing about 500,000 people.

Most of the government policy-making posts that Negroes had been appointed to were in operations that had a large Negro clientele, if not a majority—as in the case of the Chicago public schools; or in operations that had largely Negro personnel, as in the case of the post office. On the appointed supervisory boards, in fact, those with as many as two Negro members were the Chicago Board of Education and the Board of Health, both of which serve very large numbers of Negroes.

This limiting of Negro policy makers to Negro constituencies was quite as evident in the private sector. Three of the four banks with Negroes in policy-making posts were in Negro neighborhoods; and two were the smallest of the 102 banks we studied, and the other two were not much larger. The two insurance firms had mainly Negro clients, and were among the smallest of the 30 studied. In the voluntary organizations, the more they served Negroes, the higher the percentage of Negroes on their boards (although representation was by no means proportionate). Thus, the five Negro executive directors of welfare organizations we studied headed all-Negro constituencies: Three directed moderate-sized neighborhood settlements in the ghetto; one directed a virtually all-Negro hospital; and one directed an interracial agency that has traditionally had a Negro executive.

Still another way of limiting the power of Negro policy makers, we discovered, was by "processing" them. Public and private institutions, as indicated, tend to have a token representation of Negroes. And many Negroes in these positions have totally identified with the traditional values and goals of the institution, regardless of what they mean to the mass of Negroes. Some of these Negro policy makers, because of their small numbers and lack of an independent source of power, are neutralized. Others, if they are firm in representing the needs and outlook of the black community, are isolated. The two Negro members of the Chicago Board of Education represented these extremes. Mrs. Wendell Green, a longtime Board member and the elderly widow of a former judge, had been the most diehard supporter of Benjamin Willis, the former Schools Superintendent, through all of his fights against the civil rights movement. The other Negro—Warren Bacon, a business executive—sympathized with the campaign against inferior, segregated housing and, as a result, has been largely isolated on the Board. He was rarely consulted on critical questions. His vote was usually cast with a small minority, and sometimes alone.

The fact is that the norms and traditions of *any* organization or enterprise limit the amount of power held by black policy makers. It is no longer bold to assert that the major institutions and organizations of our society have an operational bias that is racist, even though their *official* policies may be the opposite. The Negro policy maker in one of these institutions (or in a small black-controlled organization dependent upon these institutions, such as the head of a trade-union local) has a certain degree of conflict. If he goes along with the institution, from which he gains power and prestige, he ends up by implementing operations that restrict his minority group. Edward Banfield and James Q. Wilson have neatly pinpointed this dilemma in the political sphere:

Not only are few Negroes elected to office, but those who are elected generally find it necessary to be politicians first and Negroes second. If they are to stay in office, they must soft-pedal the racial issues that are of the most concern to Negroes as Negroes.

This pattern is seen in the failure of William Dawson, Cook County's one Negro Congressman, to obtain many Presidential appointments or top federal civil service posts for the Negroes. Theoretically he is in a more strategic position to influence government operations than any other Chicago-based Congressman, since he has 23 years' seniority and holds the important chairmanship of the Government Operations Committee. Yet in 1965 Negroes held only 2 percent of the top federal jobs in Chicago.

Any examination of the real power of Negroes in Chicago requires an examination of the strongest single organization in the Negro community —the Democratic Party. Wilson's study, *Negro Politics*, points out that the strength and cohesiveness of the Negro Democratic organization is largely dependent upon the strength of the total Cook County Democratic organization. The Negro organization is a "sub-machine" within the larger machine that dominates the city. The Negro sub-machine, however, has basically settled for lesser patronage positions and political favors, rather than using its considerable strength to try to make or change policy. Therefore, this Negro organization avoids controversial questions and seeks to avoid differences with the central organization on such vital issues as urban renewal and the schools.

In short, then, not only are Negroes underrepresented in the major policy-making positions in Cook County, but even where represented their actual power is restricted, or their representatives fail to work for the long-term interests of their constituency. It is therefore safe to estimate that Negroes really hold less than 1 percent of the effective power in the Chicago metropolitan area. Realistically, the power structure of Chicago is hardly less white than that of Mississippi.

From these figures it is clear that, at this time, Negroes in the Chicago area lack the power to make changes in the areas of housing, jobs, and education. The basic subjugation of the black community, however, would not end if there were simply more Negroes in policy-making posts. We have seen the prevalence of tokenism, of whites' choosing Negro leaders who are conservative, of their boxing in Negro leaders who are proved to be liberal, or their giving these leaders less actual power than they give themselves.

Our analysis suggests that the best way to increase both the number *and* the power of Negro policy makers is through unifying the black constituency. Access to policy-making positions could come through both the development of large, black-controlled organizations, and through getting Negroes into white-dominated organizations. If the constituency lacks its own clear set of goals and policies, however, things will surely remain the same. For success depends not just upon formal unity, but upon the nature of the goals set by the black community. In this situation, the overcoming of black powerlessness seems to require the development of a self-conscious community that has the means to determine its own interests, and the cohesiveness to command the loyalty of its representatives. We can safely predict that more and more Negroes will be moved into policy-making positions. The fundamental conflict, therefore, will take place between their cooptation into the established institutions and their accountability to a black constituency.

The Political Objectives of Ghetto Violence

HARLAN HAHN

The riots that erupted in American cities during the nineteen-sixties seem, in several respects, to have caught social scientists relatively unprepared. Despite the traditions of violence or civil disorders that have played a persistent and often determinative role in the development of U.S. politics, the study of riots has not been a significant or distinctive object to scholarly attention. As a result, when policy makers and the public approached the academic community for interpretations of the meaning of urban disorders as well as for solutions to the social problems that they reflected, many political scientists found themselves ill-equipped by either prior theory or research findings for the task. Although there are growing signs that the neglect of urban violence is rapidly being corrected, the social sciences have failed to make the significant progress that many desire in their efforts to contribute to the understanding or solution of America's most pressing social and political problem.

Perhaps a major reason for the lack of information or insights that social scientists, and political scientists in particular, were able to bring to bear on the urban riots has been the preoccupation of many academicians with order and stability. A traditional focus of the study of politics, for example, has concentrated on the processes of orderly change and on the means by which conflict has been kept within legal or constitutional bounds. As a result, political scientists have contributed to what has been

Paper presented at the 1969 Meeting of the American Political Science Association, New York City. Copyright 1969 by the American Political Science Association. Published for the first time in this volume with the permission of the author and the American Political Science Association.

termed "the myth of peaceful progress."[1] If the state is defined in Weberian terms as a legitimate monopoly on physical force or violence, as many social scientists have been prone to do, emphasis naturally has been placed on the methods by which politics is prevented from exploding into violence rather than on the political repercussions and implications of violence.[2] In addition, the perception that riots represented deviant or atypical events has promoted a particular aversion to the subject among political scientists. As one observer has noted, "Political scientists have long ignored the phenomenon of riots, viewing them as aberrant behavior or anomic events which were more the concern of the sociologist than the student of politics."[3] As late as 1966, therefore, Vernon Van Dyke could ask fellow political scientists, "Why do we neglect rioting and revolution?"[4]

Regardless of the sources of this neglect, however, perhaps a major effect of the lack of emphasis on civil disorders has been an inability to provide meaningful guidance or direction for the study of those seemingly new phenomena. For most people, the riots seemed to provoke two salient and interrelated issues: causes and cures. Although the latter problem raised anew many perennial questions concerning programs to improve housing, welfare, education, employment, and other conditions in the ghetto, many political scientists found that they had few distinctive or original insights to contribute to this debate. Since researchers were not theoretically or methodologically prepared to offer specific plans for ameliorating the social tensions that had exploded in violence, attention understandably was directed at the initial problem of attempting to explain the origins of civil disorders. Thus, for political scientists as well as for large segments of the public, the central question of the riots became, why did they happen?

In attempting to grapple with this question, political science—as it has often done—turned to the rich resources of interdisciplinary research for assistance. Much initial research, for example, represented an effort to refute several common theories, promulgated by the public and by political leaders, that the rioters were recent migrants,[5] "riff-raff,"[6] or

---

[1] Jerome H. Skolnick, *The Politics of Protest* (New York: Ballantine Books, 1969), pp. 8–10.

[2] Matthew Stolz, "A Speculation Concerning Politics and Violence," unpublished paper presented at the annual meeting of the Western Political Science Association, Seattle, Washington, March 14–15, 1968.

[3] Peter A. Lupsha, "On Theories of Urban Violence," *Urban Affairs Quarterly*, IV (March 1969), p. 277.

[4] Vernon Van Dyke, "The Optimum Scope of Political Science," in James C. Charlesworth, ed., *A Design for Political Science: Scope, Objectives, and Methods* (Philadelphia: The American Academy of Political and Social Science, 1966), pp. 5–6.

[5] David O. Sears and John B. McConahay, *The Politics of Discontent: Blocked Mechanisms of Grievance Redress and the Psychology of the New Urban Black Man* (Los Angeles: UCLA Institute of Government and Public Affairs, 1967), pp. 5–10.

[6] Robert M. Fogelson and Robert B. Hill, "Who Riots? A Study of Participation in the 1967 Riots," in *Supplemental Studies for the National Advisory Commission on Civil Disorders* (Washington: Government Printing Office, 1968), pp. 221–48.

organized conspirators.[7] As the investigations expanded and intensified, however, both the methods and orientations used to study this subject began to diverge.

The approaches employed by researchers have included such diverse techniques as the examination of ecological characteristics associated with the outbreak of violence,[8] the investigation of the development of a riot,[9] surveys of areas that experienced major disorders,[10] and useful speculation about the sources of civil disturbances.[11] Studies founded on sociological theories of collective behavior often have yielded an inadequate fit and only a limited degree of success.[12] Other researchers, who have based their work on different theoretical concepts and frameworks, have expressed similar complaints.[13]

Perhaps "the most popular explanation" for urban violence, however, has emerged from psychological models of frustration-aggression.[14] The basic principles of the frustration-aggression model often have been elaborated to include the concept of relative deprivation, perceptions of alienation or legitimacy, blocked opportunities, and the intervening capacity of the political system to repress civil disorders.[15] According to this theory, widespread dissatisfaction or felt deprivation coupled with feelings of

[7] *Report of the National Advisory Commission on Civil Disorders* (Washington: Government Printing Office, 1968), p. 89.

[8] Stanley Lieberson and Arnold R. Silverman, "The Precipitants and Underlying Conditions of Race Riots," *American Sociological Review*, XXXI (December, 1965), pp. 887–98; Milton Bloombaum, "The Conditions Underlying Race Riots as Portrayed by Multidimensional Scalogram Analysis: A Reanalysis of Lieberson and Silverman's Data," *American Sociological Review*, XXXIII (February, 1968), pp. 76–91; Bryan T. Downes, "Social and Political Characteristics of Riot Cities: A Comparative Study," *Social Science Quarterly*, XLIX (December, 1968), pp. 504–20; Jules J. Wanderer, "1967 Riots: A Test of the Congruity of Events," *Social Problems*, XXVI (Fall, 1968), pp. 193–98; Jules J. Wanderer, "An Index of Riot Severity and Some Correlates," *American Journal of Sociology*, LXXIV (March, 1969), pp. 500–505.

[9] Ralph W. Conant, "Rioting, Insurrection and Civil Disobedience," *The American Scholar*, XXXVII (Summer, 1968), pp. 420–33; Hans W. Mattick, "The Form and Content of Recent Riots," *Midway*, IX (Summer, 1968), pp. 3–32.

[10] Nathan S. Caplan and Jeffrey M. Paige, "A Study of Ghetto Rioters," *Scientific American*, CXIX (August, 1968), pp. 15–21; Joe R. Feagin and Paul B. Sheatsley, "Ghetto Resident Appraisals of a Riot," *Public Opinion Quarterly*, XXXII (Fall, 1968), pp. 352–62. For an earlier study of this type, see Kenneth B. Clark: "Group Violence: A Preliminary Study of the Attitudinal Pattern of Its Acceptance and Rejection: A Study of the 1943 Harlem Riot," *The Journal of Social Psychology*, XXIX (1944), pp. 319–37.

[11] Robert H. Connery, ed., "Urban Riots: Violence and Social Change," *Proceedings of The Academy of Political Science*, XXIX (1968), pp. 1–190.

[12] James A. Geschwender, "Civil Rights Protest and Riots: A Disappearing Distinction," *Social Science Quarterly*, XLIX (December, 1968), pp. 474–84.

[13] Lupsha, "On Theories of Urban Violence," pp. 273–96; H. L. Hieburg, *Political Violence* (New York: St. Martin's, 1969); Skolnick, *The Politics of Protest*, pp. 329–46.

[14] Leonard Berkowitz, "The Study of Urban Violence: Some Implications of Laboratory Studies of Frustration and Aggression," in Louis H. Masotti and Don R. Bowen, eds., *Riots and Rebellion: Civil Violence in the Urban Community* (Beverly Hills: Sage Publications, 1968), p. 39.

[15] Masotti and Bowen, *Riots and Rebellion*, pp. 35–36, 169–70.

alienation or disaffection from existing political institutions frequently have produced violence as the result of a precipitating incident, if the state is unable to repress the disturbances. While the theoretical orientation of research based on the concepts of frustration and relative deprivation has been directed primarily at the causes of civil disorders, the approach also has contained some significant implications for the prevention or elimination of urban violence. Since riots usually have been inspired by feelings of deprivation or dissatisfaction in nations that do not impose harsh controls on individual aspirations, the solution to the problem of civil disorders often has been regarded as efforts to reduce those frustrations either by improving the social and economic position of deprived populations or by increasing the repressive capabilities of political authorities.

Although relative deprivation and the frustration-aggression hypothesis have offered valid and useful approaches to the study of urban riots, perhaps they have shifted attention away from one of the most significant and interesting aspects of the disorders. In a major respect, the riots represented the process of—as well as a concerted and desperate attempt to induce—social change. As one investigator noted, "The problem with most theoretical conceptualizations of urban violence is that they ignore the essential point that the riots are not just products of frustration and deprivation, they are products of the political system."[16]

Ghetto residents not only were reacting to their own frustrations, but they also seemed to have a definite target. As a report to the National Commission on the Causes and Prevention of Violence concluded, "Implicit in this concept of frustration-aggression is the idea that riots are without purpose or direction."[17] While deprivation and frustration may have formed important sources of urban unrest, the disorders also appeared to reflect goals that have not been implied by those concepts.

An important weakness of the theories of civil disorders based on relative deprivation and the frustration-aggression hypothesis has been their failure to stress the political implications of urban violence. The report to the National Commission on the Causes and Prevention of Violence recommended, "We believe that conventional approaches to the analysis and control of riots have inadequately understood their social and political significance, and need to be revised."[18] Perhaps a sense of relative deprivation has been gradually expanded to include an awareness of political disadvantages; but most discussions of this concept have failed to consider this aspect of ghetto aspirations. As another commentator observed, "One area that has been neglected, although it is often spoken around, is the political side of urban violence."[19] The political component of ghetto disturbances has formed a significant, but frequently ignored, dimension of riots.

[16] Lupsha, "On Theories of Urban Violence," p. 294.
[17] Skolnick, *The Politics of Protest*, p. 340.
[18] *Ibid.*, p. 329.
[19] Lupsha, "On Theories of Urban Violence," pp. 292.

In fact, attacks on political agents or institutions have been the major characteristics that have distinguished civil disorders from other social upheavals.[20] The report to the Violence Commission noted, "The difficulty with most traditional collective behavior theory is that it treats protests and riots as the 'abnormal' behavior of social groups and derives many of its conceptual assumptions from psychological rather than from political premises."[21] Another researcher stated that an important objection to the concept of relative deprivation has been its inability to "suggest mechanisms by which feelings of discontent are directed against institutional targets rather than becoming self-directed."[22] Moreover, the significance of ghetto riots probably has derived from the fact that they were directed at vulnerable political agencies rather than at other social organizations.

Stripped of their political overtones, the riots may have connoted simply an effort to achieve what might be termed as "instant social mobility," or an attempt to short-circuit the frustrations of middle-class strivings by acquiring prized consumer goods through extralegal means. Looting and the burning or destruction of private property have been prominent features of most urban disorders, but few observers have argued that the riots represented nothing more than this activity. The additional elements of civil disturbances, and especially their political goals, have been the principal attributes that have made them both significant and salient objects of social inquiry.

Perhaps civil disturbances, as well as other social phenomena, should be evaluated initially in relation to their objectives. This emphasis on the purposes of ghetto riots not only focuses attention on their cause—that is, what were they trying to achieve?—but it also stresses their impact—or, what did they produce? A definitive answer to the latter question probably would be premature. Neither the effects of the disorders on ghetto residents nor the responses of other segments of the population have become fully evident as yet; but few would argue that the country will remain totally unchanged by the riots—at least it will carry the memory of those outbreaks.

The purpose of the riots, therefore, seemed to provide an important theoretical perspective for the examination of urban unrest. Unlike other forms of violence, however, civil disorders have not reflected a concerted movement to overthrow existing political structures, the deliberate defiance of government policies, or conflict between opposing racial or ethnic groups. The characteristics of riots, including their confinement to ghetto neighborhoods, the lack of immediate targets except local merchants and policemen, as well as the relative absence of direct encounters between white and black combatants, have seemed to distinguish them from many other types of disturbances. Urban disorders apparently have defined the

---

[20] Masotti and Bowen, *Riots and Rebellion*, p. 13.

[21] Skolnick, *The Politics of Protest*, p. 338.

[22] Jay Schulman, "Ghetto-Area Residence, Political Alienation, and Riot Orientation," in Masotti and Bowen, *Riots and Rebellion*, p. 280.

conventional classifications of political violence such as revolutions, civil disobedience, demonstrations, and racial conflict.

As a method of obtaining information about popular grievances and of securing concessions from political authorities, riots or civil disorders have had a long history. During the eighteenth and early nineteenth centuries, some urban areas in England and elsewhere were nearly governed by a type of collective bargaining by riots or violence that continued for many years before these areas were even placed under the surveillance of organized police forces.[23] The riots that exploded in many American cities during the twentieth century have exhibited many similar characteristics of bargaining behavior.[24] In many respects, civil disorders have reflected, to paraphrase von Clausewitz, the conduct of politics by other means, particularly when normal channels for accommodating public complaints have become inadequate for the task.

Racial violence frequently has seemed to signify the failure of regular political processes to resolve critical problems or to satisfy pressing demands. In an analysis of 76 American race riots between 1913 and 1963, Lieberson and Silverman found that the outbreak of rioting was related to "institutional malfunctioning or a racial difficulty which is not met —and perhaps cannot be—by existing social institutions."[25] Subsequent research, employing different methods, also yielded results that were "generally consistent with the theory of institutional breakdown held by Lieberson and Silverman."[26] Perhaps the riots have represented both an attack on structural targets and "an anger directed at the inadequacy of the political system to process demands, and to make allocations in a responsive and responsible manner."[27]

In addition, urban disorders have demonstrated that the occurrence of a major disturbance can produce significant governmental responses, despite debilitating weaknesses in political institutions. An investigation of the nation's four largest cities, for example, found that the size of local anti-poverty grants received from federal sources was directly related to the dispersion of political influence within a city. It also revealed that after the Watts riots of 1965, Los Angeles, which exhibited the most fragmented political structure and which had previously acquired the least OEO funds per poverty-stricken family, suddenly soared to the top of the list in the amount of anti-poverty money obtained.[28] The potential polit-

[23] Eric J. Hobsbawm, *Primitive Rebels* (New York: W. W. Norton, 1963); George Rude, *The Crowd in History* (New York: John Wiley, 1964); Allan Silver, "The Demand for Order in Civil Society: A Review of Some Themes in the History of Urban Crime, Police, and Riot," in David J. Bordua, ed., *The Police* (New York: John Wiley, 1967), pp. 1–24.

[24] Nieburg, *Political Violence*.

[25] Lieberson and Silverman, "The Precipitants and Underlying Conditions of Race Riots," p. 898.

[26] Bloombaum, "The Conditions Underlying Race Riots," p. 90.

[27] Lupsha, "On Theories of Urban Violence," p. 294.

[28] J. David Greenstone and Paul E. Peterson, "Reformers, Machines, and the War on Poverty," in James Q. Wilson, ed., *City Politics and Public Policy* (New York: John Wiley, 1968), pp. 267–92.

ical benefits of riots, therefore, probably have been recognized by ghetto residents as well as by other segments of the public.

One goal of the riots, generally acknowledged by ghetto residents as well as other observers, frequently has been expressed in the concept of protest. In many important respects, the disorders appeared to represent a desperate and extreme method of focusing the attention of the predominantly white public and political leaders on ghetto needs and aspirations. After centuries of denial and neglect, many black Americans demonstrated their dissatisfaction with regular avenues of political expression by adopting one of few forms of protest that could not be easily neglected or ignored. Yet, the riots seemed to represent something more than a mere effort by ghetto residents to arouse the interest of the outside population. In directing their anger at police officers as well as at local businesses, rioters have exhibited their disrespect both for the symbols of the legal order and for the personal and property rights that form the normative bases of political authority. The attacks on important social institutions or rules, manifested by violence, arson, and looting in several major riots, have indicated that the objectives of civil disorders extended beyond the simple display of political discontent. By their statements and behavior, ghetto residents not only were seeking to arouse interest in their needs, but they also seemed to be calling for the establishment of new institutional arrangements to satisfy their grievances. Although protests regarding local grievances have been important elements in most outbreaks of urban violence, the riots also have revealed many characteristics of a form of rebellion or a confrontation with white authorities.

The intensely political nature of riot goals has been particularly evident in the role of law enforcement officers in the start of most urban disorders. To most ghetto residents, the primary tangible representative of external political authority in their community has been the cop on the beat. The presence of policemen in the eruption of civil disorders, therefore, probably has not been accidental. The National Advisory Commission on Civil Disorders noted, for example, "Almost invariably the incident that ignites civil disorders arises from police action."[29] As the principal agents responsible for imposing the legal norms of the outside society upon ghetto neighborhoods, the police have been natural targets of hostility and aggression. The reactions of ghetto residents against existing political control and authority that may have formed an important component of riot goals, therefore, apparently have been underscored by the significance of police behavior in provoking civil disorders.

The outbreak of urban disturbances has seemed to be related to riot purposes. One of the major difficulties with most theoretical considerations of urban violence has been their inability to interpret the role of precipitating events in the development of riots. Research based on frustration-aggression hypotheses and on the concept of relative deprivation, for example, seldom has provided a satisfactory explanation for the fact that most disorders have resulted from contacts with policemen rather

[29] *Report of the National Advisory Commission on Civil Disorders*, p. 206.

than from other types of encounters. The examination of riot behavior from the perspective of their objectives, on the other hand, has indicated a method of joining precipitating incidents with other features of civil disorders by suggesting that the attack on existing political authority and its most accessible or available representatives, the police, has comprised a significant purpose of ghetto disturbances.

Urban violence, therefore, has seemed to contain many of the characteristics of a rebellion. In a fundamental sense, riots have reflected the collapse of normal social mores and a repudiation of external controls. In the chaos of major disturbances, spontaneous congregations of people have created their own rules of conduct in defiance of outside efforts to restrain their behavior. Studies have indicated that relatively well-defined "rules of the game emerge in the course of rioting."[30] Frequently, the newly-formed norms emanating from crowds on the street have protected innocent bystanders or "soul brother" merchants from harm; but perhaps their most significant effect has been to condone destructive acts against policemen and local retailers. By substituting their own moral judgments based on vengeance or other motives for the legal codes prescribed by public officials, the rioters seem to have formed a separate rule-making community and engaged in a kind of political rebellion. The rejection of the regulations enacted by established and supposedly legitimate political institutions, therefore, has necessitated the intervention of the state to protect its authority from competing sources of power. Even in the absence of explicit attempts to overthrow existing government agencies, the riots often have been regarded as a major threat to duly constituted political authority. By raising the specter of renewed violence, moreover, the rioters have sought to ensure that political leaders would not continue to neglect the demands of their neighborhoods.

Civil disorders have constituted a serious attack on existing political institutions as well as on efforts to secure a response from public officials; but they seldom have implied a desire to overthrow or to withdraw from the political order. The riots, therefore, have seemed to reflect a form of confrontation rather than rebellion. The origins of almost all civil disturbances have been associated with a series of grievances; they usually have been accompanied by negotiations between community leaders and white officeholders; and they have sought to demonstrate or dramatize the failure and inability of established structures to satisfy local needs and demands. A major purpose of urban violence, therefore, has been to confront the entire society with the conditions that spawned the disruptions and to secure important modifications of the means by which efforts are made to solve those problems.

The investigation of ghetto riots as a form of violent confrontation provides a means of examining disorders in relation to their goals. By focusing on the political aims of urban disturbances, perhaps the implications of civil disorders can be examined in a broad context that includes their

---

[30] B. Eugene Griessman, "Toward an Understanding of Urban Unrest and Rioting," *Journal of Human Relations*, XVI (Fall, 1968), p. 325.

consequences as well as their origins. As one observer commented, "Perhaps the initial step . . . is to recognize that urban riots, whatever else they are, are political acts, i.e., a primitive form of rebellion, that have a potential for societal transformation as well as social amelioration."[31] This perspective also provides a means of defining the explicit content of riot goals. Most existing theories of civil disorders, as the report to the Violence Commission noted, have been formulated in such broad terms that they "can easily obscure the specificity of political grievances.[32] The principal emphasis of this study, therefore, will be on the aims or objectives of civil disorders.

Ghetto Perceptions of Riot Objectives

Perhaps the primary source for identifying the goals of urban violence has been the people who actually experienced a major riot. While not all of the residents of a ghetto that exploded in violence may have participated in the riots, they at least have been placed in a closer position than other commentators or judges to assess the conditions that spawned the disturbances and to distinguish between purposeless and politically meaningful intentions. The aims of urban riots probably have been reflected most clearly in the perceptions of people who were personally involved or affected by civil disorders.

Data for this study were obtained primarily from a modified quota sample survey of 307 residents of the Twelfth Street area of Detroit, where the nation's worst civil disorders started. The survey was conducted shortly after the riots of 1967. The following sampling procedures were adopted in an effort to secure an adequate cross-section of the neighborhood in the chaotic circumstances that accompanied the disorders: All city blocks in the Twelfth Street neighborhood were stratified on the basis of a composite index of socioeconomic status derived from the median value of dwelling units, the average monthly rent, and the proportion of substandard or dilapidated units according to the 1960 U.S. Census of Housing; blocks were selected randomly within each stratum. Quota assignments in each block were based on the age and race of persons over 21 years of age. Interviewers, who were furnished by the Market Opinion Research Company, and respondents were matched by race.[33] The sample yielded 270 black and 37 white residents. Since sharp racial differences emerged in the survey, however, this investigation has been confined to the attitudes expressed by black respondents.

This study will attempt to explore the association between riot behavior and the political objectives of civil disturbances. Since it has been generally recognized that urban ghettos are not homogeneous or indivisible entities, the perceptions of residents might be expected to reveal

---

[31] Schulman, "Ghetto-Area Residence," p. 282.

[32] Skolnick, *The Politics of Protest*, pp. 337–38.

[33] The author wishes to express his appreciation to the University of Michigan for a special research grant which made this survey possible.

some divisions or disagreements concerning riot goals. By relating beliefs about the purpose of violence to activities during the disorders, however, it may be possible to define what the rioting was intended to accomplish as well as the effects or changes that it actually produced.

One means of determining whether or not the violence contained a significant political purpose is provided by data on the causes of civil disorders. Presumably, if the riots were inspired by meaningful political goals, those aims should be revealed in the perceptions of ghetto residents regarding the grievances that provoked the disturbances. At least the conditions that were identified by local persons as major sources of violence ought to reflect problems or policies that are susceptible to political remedies or solutions. Similarly, of course, perceptions of the intentions of the rioters should disclose a corresponding stress on political aspirations.

In addition, the attitudes of persons located in a riot-torn neighborhood might be expected to display a significant measure of approval or support for the perceived objectives of the disturbances. Perhaps more importantly, if the outbreak and the development of rioting were related to major political demands, people who expressed sympathy with the aims of the rioters may divulge animosity toward existing political institutions as well as an endorsement of violence as a means of securing needed changes. Support for violence among persons who had experienced a major riot also might be translated into growing militancy and a pervasive belief that the disorders might aid in promoting social movements which they favored.

Another significant test of the association between political objectives and riot behavior might be found in ghetto attitudes regarding legal agents of governmental authority as well as by participation in the disorders. It is anticipated that persons who endorsed riot objectives may exhibit greater hostility toward law enforcement officials and higher rates of personal participation than those who disapproved of the violence. Moreover, if the riots represented a purposeful and responsible attempt to achieve political goals, people who had favorable images of riot objectives might be expected to come to the assistance of other persons in different social circumstances.

The influence of riot purposes also might be revealed in ghetto attitudes concerning political actions in the aftermath of the disorders. Perhaps the clearest available expressions of the concrete objectives of the disorders are provided by the political expectations of ghetto residents after the riots. Specifically, residents who supported the goals of the violence may tend to express increased criticism of established public officials and political programs, to eschew traditional methods of gaining political advantages, and, most significantly, to advocate a radical restructuring of existing political institutions as a means of satisfying their demands.

The purpose of this research will be to test those and other propositions or speculation by exploring the connection between assessment of political objectives and aspects of riot behavior or what Tomlinson has termed "riot ideology."[34] Although many attitudes probably have also been influenced by situational factors such as the location of a person on the socioeconomic spectrum, this study will focus primarily on the perceptual links between political aspirations and the characteristics of a riot. In addition, an effort will be made to examine the generality of this theoretical orientation by comparing the findings with the results of similar surveys conducted after civil disturbances in other urban areas.

As has been reported previously,[35] the outcome of the survey in the Twelfth Street area of Detroit revealed greater support for violence and for radical political change than has been found in surveys conducted in communities that have not experienced major disturbances. Most major disorders, however, have been provoked by relatively small numbers of people in limited geographical localities. Any tendency to neglect or ignore the political demands of unique segments of the population that have demonstrated their susceptibility to violence by exploding in a riot has entailed serious risks to the society and the nation.

The Sources and Purpose of Urban Violence

Although the deaths and destructiveness of the Detroit riot of 1967 made it the nation's worst civil disorder, the perceptions of ghetto residents concerning the causes of that riot did not differ significantly from the opinions expressed by black citizens in other localities. The causes that were cited most frequently by persons who lived in the area where the riot started as among "the two or three main reasons for the trouble" were discrimination and deprivation. This interpretation was mentioned by 86 percent of the respondents. Another 24 percent attributed the blame directly to animosity toward the police. Moreover, this finding was confirmed by other studies of areas that have endured riots.[36] As a survey of riot participants in Newark and Detroit concluded, "the continued exclusion of Negroes from American economic and social life is the fundamental cause of riots."[37]

Perhaps the most significant feature of the problems mentioned by ghetto residents as explanations for the riots is that they are all amenable to political amelioration or solution. Since both racial discrimination and

[34] T. M. Tomlinson, "Riot Ideology Among Urban Negroes," in Masotti and Bowen, *Riots and Rebellion*, pp. 417–28.

[35] Harlan Hahn, "Ghetto Sentiments on Violence," *Science and Society* (Spring, 1969), pp. 197–208; Harlan Hahn, "Violence: The View from the Ghetto," *Mental Hygiene*, LIII (October, 1969), pp. 509–12.

[36] Feagin and Sheatsley, "Ghetto Resident Appraisals," p. 354; John F. Kraft, Inc., "The Attitudes of Negroes in Various Cities," in *Federal Role in Urban Affairs*, Hearings before the Subcommittee on Executive Reorganization of the Committee on Government Operations, Part 6, U.S. Senate, 89th Congress, 2nd Session, September 1, 1966, pp. 1387–88; Detroit *Free Press*, August 20, 1967, p. 4–B; T. M. Tomlinson and David O. Sears, *Negro Attitudes Toward the Riots* (Los Angeles: UCLA Institute of Government and Public Affairs, 1967), p. 13.

[37] Caplan and Paige, "A Study of Ghetto Rioters," p. 21.

socioeconomic deprivation, for example, have been sustained and perhaps perpetuated by political decisions, public officials have possessed corresponding means of reducing or eliminating those grievances. In fact, many of the specific complaints that were cited as "causes" of the disorders have been the subject of political consideration and debate for many years. In selecting a way of presenting their views that could not be ignored or dismissed, however, the rioters seemed to be confronting public leaders both with the urgency of their demands and, implicitly, with the need for new methods or mechanisms for resolving their problems. Even though the sources of ghetto discontent have been identified previously, existing political processes were regarded as unable or unwilling to provide satisfactory remedies. By demonstrating their dissatisfaction in a manner that seemed to violate normal rules of political behavior, ghetto residents engaged in actions that conveyed greater meaning than conventional forms of political expression. Moreover, the almost complete unanimity that they displayed in isolating the reasons for the disorders seemed to reinforce and heighten the importance of their attitudes.

Similar evidence from several areas that erupted in civil disorders has indicated that most ghetto dwellers thought that the riots had a definite purpose or objective. In the UCLA survey, for example, 56 percent of the respondents living in Watts and a similar proportion of persons who were arrested in the riot stated that the violence had "a purpose or goal."[38] When the Watts residents were requested to describe the purpose or goal of the riot, 41 percent defined it as an attempt to call attention to the problems faced by black citizens, 33 percent viewed it as an expression of accumulated hostility or rage, and 26 percent regarded it as a means of gaining specific social and economic changes or improvements.[39] Another direct question was posed in the Bedford-Stuyvesant survey, which asked, "What do you think they (the rioters) were trying to do or to show?" The replies indicated that 41 percent of the New York residents felt that they intended to demonstrate their opposition to discrimination and deprivation, a slightly larger proportion identified those motives as the "real cause" of the riots.[40] A relatively large segment of ghetto residents, therefore, believed that the disorders were inspired by goals that contained significant political connotations. In addition, 37 percent of the Twelfth Street residents stated flatly that the riots were "mainly organized," and 57 percent said that the people who started them "had been thinking about it for a long time." "Preliminary analyses of those responses have indicated that organization was intended to mean 'directed activity' and that perceptions of the lack of spontaneity referred to long-standing grievances."[41]

[38] David O. Sears and T. M. Tomlinson, "Riot Ideology in Los Angeles: A Study of Negro Attitudes," *Social Science Quarterly*, XLIX (December, 1968), p. 489.

[39] *Ibid.*, p. 496.

[40] Feagin and Sheatsley, "Ghetto Resident Appraisals," p. 354.

[41] Harlan Hahn, "The Kerner Report and the Political Objectives of Civil Disorders," *Social Science Quarterly*, L (December, 1969), pp. 755–56.

A majority of the inhabitants of the Twelfth Street neighborhood also expressed agreement with the position that the riots represented purposeful activity rather than random or destructive behavior. Fifty-three per cent of the Detroit sample felt that the most important objective of the people who started the riot was "calling attention to their needs," 38 percent thought they were "just taking things and causing trouble," and 8 percent failed to express an opinion on this issue. Although this inquiry may have been useful in identifying persons who presumably were sympathetic to the aims of the riots, it was the only question in the Detroit survey that yielded somewhat less support for recognized political objectives than has been found elsewhere. In Watts, 62 percent of the residents agreed that the riot was "a Negro protest."[42] A survey conducted by Angus Campbell and Howard Schuman in fifteen major U.S. cities also reported that 58 percent of the black respondents saw the riots as "mainly a protest . . . against unfair conditions" rather than as "a way of looting," and an additional 28 percent viewed them at least partially as a protest.[43] In some respects, this slight discrepancy between the findings of the surveys may have been related to different perceptions of the disorders as a means of publicizing local grievances. As Campbell and Schuman noted, "the word 'protest' is a key one."[44] Some evidence has indicated that the people who were directly affected by a major riot may have been influenced by other motives, such as a hope for vengeance and the acquisition of needed economic items, as well as a simple desire to protest ghetto circumstances. In addition, the theft of prized consumer goods and the creation of social disruptions or turmoil may have formed, under some conditions, significant political objectives. Nonetheless, expressions of protest usually have been regarded as a legitimate and necessary initial step to the attainment of broader political goals. As a result, perceptions of riot purposes probably have provided a useful basis for distinguishing persons who regarded the disorders as reflecting rather narrow or self-serving personal ends and those who considered them as representing justifiable collective aspirations with which they sympathized.

Although riot objectives often have been identified by ghetto residents with protests over the failure of public officials to adopt policies that might solve their problems, this attitude has not necessarily implied a general belief that existing political agencies would react favorably to their demands. In fact, people who have had personal experience with a major riot have displayed a striking lack of confidence in governmental institutions and leaders.[45] Ghetto residents may have been seeking to impress white authorities with the pressing need for their demands, but

[42] Sears and Tomlinson, "Riot Ideology in Los Angeles," p. 489.

[43] Angus Campbell and Howard Schuman, "Racial Attitudes in Fifteen American Cities," in *Supplemental Studies for the National Advisory Commission on Civil Disorders* (Washington: Government Printing Office, 1968), p. 47.

[44] *Ibid.*, p. 62.

[45] *Report of the National Advisory Commission on Civil Disorders*, p. 77; David O. Sears, *Political Attitudes of Los Angeles Negroes* (Los Angeles: UCLA Institute of Government and Public Affairs, 1967), p. 20.

their attitudes toward government revealed unmistakable symptoms of political alienation and antagonism.

The political disaffection evident in other riot cities also was found in the Twelfth Street neighborhood of Detroit. Seventy-eight percent of the residents of that area stated that before the riot the government was merely trying "to keep things quiet," while only 18 percent believed that political leaders "really were interested in solving the problems that the Negro faces in this city." This animosity even was directed at fundamental, cherished American institutions such as the legal process and the administration of the law. Ninety-two percent of the respondents did not feel that "most of the laws on the books are fair to all people," and 95 percent did not think that "laws are enforced equally." "People who accept a conventional belief in the impartiality of the law and its enforcement formed a small and nearly imperceptible minority in the ghetto. The prevailing consensus supported the position that injustice pervaded the entire legal system."[46]

Despite the relatively small fraction of persons in the Twelfth Street area who mentioned their loyalty to government and to such basic democratic institutions as the law and law enforcement, those attitudes were related to perceptions of riot objectives. Seventy-five percent of the respondents who believed that government had been trying to solve local problems before the riot started also thought the disorders merely represented a way of "taking things and causing trouble," but 66 percent of those who had been critical of political efforts viewed the disturbances as a means of "calling attention to their needs."[47] Even a majority of the small group of black citizens who retained a faith in the fairness of law[48] and law enforcement[49] ascribed negative connotations to the goals of the rioters, while most of the residents who shared a distrust of legal processes regarded the riots as an attempt to protest their conditions. The view that riot objectives encompassed significant political protest was not confined to persons who expressed confidence in existing political institutions. Since most ghetto residents who perceived protesting as a major goal of the disorders did not actually believe that government would respond to their grievances, the purpose of their actions apparently was not limited to a simple display of dissatisfaction addressed to public officials.

One measure of the extent to which the riots may have reflected a broader political objective than the mere expression of discontent has been provided by perceptions regarding the contribution of the distur-

[46] Harlan Hahn, "Philosophy of Law and Urban Violence," *Soundings*, LII (Spring, 1969), p. 113.

[47] The chi-square value was significant at the .01 level.

[48] While 57 percent of the respondents who felt that the laws were fair stated that the rioters were "just taking things and causing trouble," 61 percent of those who thought laws were unfair viewed the riots as a form of protest.

[49] While 56 percent of the residents who believed that law enforcement was fair expressed a critical view of riot purposes, 58 percent of those who felt law enforcement was unfair considered the riots a form of protest.

bances to other social and political movements such as civil rights progress. Although several studies have revealed a slight increase in the belief that the riots will aid in promoting civil rights, no major survey had discovered a majority that would support this position prior to the Detroit riots of 1967.[50]

The survey conducted in the Twelfth Street neighborhood after the Detroit riots of 1967, on the other hand, revealed that 62 percent of the residents thought that the violence would help "what most civil rights groups are trying to accomplish." Only one-fourth felt it would hurt, and 13 percent were undecided. The percentage of persons who believed that the riots would assist the civil rights movement in this area was nearly twice the proportion uncovered by the other surveys. The perceived benefits of the riots, however, did not emerge from a feeling that political institutions would act to alleviate their needs. While 59 percent of the residents who had confidence in government efforts to solve problems believed that the riots would hurt civil rights progress, 78 percent of those who distrusted political agencies felt that the disorders would aid their cause.[51] In this ghetto, politically disaffected black citizens expressed a belief in the efficacy of riots as a means of securing full equality and freedom; but most of their neighbors who remained loyal to existing political structures felt that the disorders would damage their attempts to gain those rights. The rioting, therefore, seemed to imply something more than an effort to obtain favorable consideration from established leaders.

Participants in civil disorders apparently have sought to achieve important political objectives by engaging in actions that exceeded the limits of normal civic participation. Perhaps the major characteristic distinguishing the riots from conventional methods of protest has been the use of violence. Violence seldom has been employed by groups that did not wish to secure significant readjustments or modifications in existing political systems. The increasingly radical political goals and demands of black Americans have been demonstrated in their attitudes about the use of violence as a means of promoting social change.

In several surveys, support for violence as a means of attaining progress in civil rights has ranged from 12 to 17 percent.[52] On the other hand, nearly one-third of the persons in the Twelfth Street area of Detroit selected violence rather than peaceful protests as the fastest way "for Negroes to get what they want." Although violence was endorsed by only a small segment of the black community, a broadly based commitment

---

[50] Gary T. Marx, *Protest and Prejudice* (New York: Harper and Row, 1967), p. 32; William Brink and Louis Harris, *Black and White* (New York: Simon and Schuster, 1967), pp. 67, 264–65; Campbell and Schuman, "Racial Attitudes in Fifteen American Cities," pp. 48–49; Feagin and Sheatsley, "Ghetto Resident Appraisals," pp. 357–59; Sears and Tomlinson, "Riot Ideology in Los Angeles," p. 490.

[51] The chi-square value was significant at the .01 level.

[52] Joe R. Feagin, "Social Sources of Support for Violence and Nonviolence in a Negro Ghetto," *Social Problems*, XV (Spring, 1968), pp. 432–41; Tomlinson and Sears, *Negro Attitudes Toward the Riots*, pp. 23–24; Campbell and Schuman, "Racial Attitudes in Fifteen American Cities," pp. 51–52.

to this strategy usually has not been required to ignite a major disorder in this neighborhood that had been the scene of the nation's most destructive riot, support for violence apparently was twice as prevalent as in other areas.

Furthermore, the advocacy of violence seemed to be associated with the attainment of important political purposes rather than with simple looting and disruption. While most of the Twelfth Street residents who preferred peaceful protests thought that the rioters were "just taking things and causing trouble," an overwhelming proportion of the persons who favored violence believed that the disorders were a meaningful way of "calling attention to their needs."[53] Other questions have demonstrated, however, that the proponents of violence did not view the riots solely as a form of protest to arouse the interest of the white public and political leaders. When the respondents in the Twelfth Street area were asked if they thought that "people outside this neighborhood" would understand what had happened in the disorders, 59 percent of those who supported nonviolent demonstrations felt that the outside society would understand the rioting. But 56 percent of the people who upheld violence did not believe that outsiders would understand.[54] The principal target of violence-oriented ghetto residents apparently was not the conscience of white society. Black citizens who were prepared to employ violence to advance their cause did not regard the riots as a means of communicating with the rest of the country or as a method of publicizing their needs.

By rejecting the customs and laws that prohibit the use of violence to achieve political aims, rioters have implicitly attempted to repudiate their subjugation to the jurisdiction or constraints of recognized civic authority. The primary means by which the participants in civil disorders have sought to secure this disengagement from normal restrictions on public conduct has been through a direct assault on established social controls. Thus the role of police officers in the outbreak of most civil disturbances has not been coincidental. As the principal agency responsible for imposing social controls on human behavior, the police have become a natural target of ghetto unrest. Moreover, the society usually has depended upon policemen to reassert its authority and control in riot-torn neighborhoods. As a result, ghetto attitudes toward the police probably have had a major impact on the initiation and the objectives of civil disorders.

While several surveys of riot-torn ghettos have disclosed strong criticism of law enforcement practices,[55] the results of the Twelfth Street survey in Detroit indicated that antagonism toward the police may have been more prevalent in that neighborhood than in other areas of the country.

[53] The chi-square value was significant at the .01 level.

[54] When those respondents were asked why outsiders would not understand the riots, they tended to refer to ghetto conditions, police behavior, and other local problems.

[55] Kraft, "The Attitudes of Negroes in Various Cities," pp. 1389, 1408; Detroit *Free Press*, August 20, 1967, p. B-4; Campbell and Schuman, "Racial Attitudes in Fifteen American Cities," pp. 42–43; Walter J. Raine, *The Perception of Police Brutality in South Central Los Angeles* (Los Angeles: UCLA Institute of Government and Public Affairs, 1967).

Eighty-three percent of the respondents did not believe that the Detroit police treated people equally, and 55 percent evaluated the treatment received by local residents before the riot as "not good" or "poor." Perhaps this negative assessment was not based solely on the belief that policemen were guilty of discrimination or inequality in their handling of local citizens. The respondents also endorsed the view that police officers were at least corruptible, if not corrupt. Eighty-nine percent, for example, believed that policemen sometimes "break the rules for their personal gain," and 88 percent attributed the same behavior to city judges. In the past, this criticism may have reflected a general sense of estrangement from political institutions; but the critical role of the police in the enforcement of social restraints also has imbued their sentiments with a special meaning and significance.

Police behavior during the riot apparently reinforced and intensified this prevailing enmity. Perhaps the most striking information elicited by the survey concerned allegations of criminal conduct by police officers. More than 81 percent of the ghetto residents reported that they had heard stories that "some policemen were involved in taking things or burning stores" during the riot. Since police activities during the disorders did little to enhance respect for their functions, the problem of restoring societal authority in riot-torn ghetto neighborhoods perhaps has been greatly exacerbated.

Studies in various cities have discovered a close association between opinions of the police and assessments of riot purposes. The Watts survey, for example, revealed that an index of perceptions of police malpractice was related not only to a measure of favorability toward the riot but also to beliefs about the role of the disorders in promoting civil rights progress.[56] Additionally, a survey conducted in 1966 in Denver, a city which had not experienced a major disturbance, found a significant association between opinions of the police and the approval of violence.[57] The findings were confirmed by the survey in the Twelfth Street neighborhood of Detroit. While 59 percent of the residents who felt that police treatment before the riot had been "very good" or "good" believed that the rioters were "merely taking things and causing trouble," 64 percent of those who gave negative evaluations of police conduct viewed the disorders as a form of protest.[58] Prior attitudes toward the police may have had a marked impact on appraisals of riot goals. The attacks on police officers that have characterized the outbreak of civil disorders, therefore, probably have been linked to the general political purpose of assailing established social institutions and controls.

One of the most significant features of the civil disorders of the 1960s has been the relatively large number of people who were prepared to

[56] Raymond J. Murphy and James M. Watson, *The Structure of Discontent* (Los Angeles: UCLA Institute of Government and Public Affairs, 1967), pp. 46, 48.

[57] David H. Bayley and Harold Mendelsohn, *Minorities and the Police* (New York: The Free Press, 1969), pp. 179–81.

[58] The chi-square value was significant at the .01 level.

defy strong social conventions by engaging in riot activity. Although most major disturbances seemingly were ignited by small groups, they have been joined and supported by many other residents of the neighborhood who shared their attitudes and objectives. The political importance of the disorders, therefore, has been derived in many respects from the proportion of ghetto residents who were willing to repudiate existing social controls and to resist police efforts at restoring those controls by participating in a riot. Although the measurement of riot participation has been a source of considerable controversy, most surveys and other methods have yielded estimates that range from 8 to 15 percent of the neighborhoods in which the disorders occurred.[59]

By a variety of measures, estimates of riot participation based on the survey of the Twelfth Street area of Detroit seemed to be somewhat higher than have been reported by prior research. One question revealed that during the riot 61 percent of the residents "got out to see what was happening." Many of these persons probably were passive bystanders, counter-rioters, or others who did not engage in illegal behavior; but nearly all of them contributed to the size of the crowds on the street and to the general impressions of riot activity formed by outside observers. In addition, the respondents were asked to estimate the percentage of the neighborhood that was directly involved in the disorders. Despite the fact that one-fourth of the residents declined to offer a conjecture, 58 percent projected that participation encompassed more than one in ten persons and nearly one-third reported it was 25 percent or higher. Furthermore, an indirect measure based on the participation ascribed to various groups in the community such as whites, black homeowners, unemployed black youths, and militant supporters of black power by persons who were themselves included in that group resulted in an estimate of 36 percent. All of the measures based on the Twelfth Street survey, therefore, reflected more extensive participation in the Detroit riots of 1967 than the 11 percent figure based on arrest data and other studies.[60]

Perhaps some of the most interesting responses in the survey, however, were provoked by a hypothetical question that attempted to tap the reflexes of the community toward a situation that involved "a policeman beating up someone from the neighborhood." Since most civil disorders have been ignited by an incident inspired by police action, the replies may have provided a relatively clear indication of the proportion of ghetto dwellers who would react to a precipitating event with conduct that might lead to the outbreak of a major disturbance. In response to the

---

[59] Fogelson and Hill, "Who Riots?," p. 231; Feagin and Sheatsley, "Ghetto Resident Appraisals," p. 357; Kraft, "The Attitudes of Negroes in Various Cities," p. 1386; Caplan and Paige, "A Study of Ghetto Rioters," p. 16; Brink and Harris, *Black and White*, pp. 67, 266–67; Campbell and Schuman, "Racial Attitudes in Fifteen American Cities," p. 51–53; Ben W. Gilbert, et al., *Ten Blocks from the White House* (New York: Frederick A. Praeger, 1968), pp. 224–25; David O. Sears and John B. McConahay, *Riot Participation* (Los Angeles: UCLA Institute of Government and Public Affairs, 1967), p. 6.

[60] Fogelson and Hill, "Who Riots?," p. 231; Caplan and Paige, "A Study of Ghetto Rioters," p. 16.

situation, 15 percent were uncertain about their probable conduct, but just 3 percent said they would ignore it. Only 44 percent stated that they would follow the formally approved procedure of filing a complaint. The remaining replies—"going to other people for help," mentioned by 27 percent; and "waiting around to see what happens," referred to by 10 percent—seemed to imply behavior that usually has been associated with the start of civil disorders. The potential for actions that might contribute to the eruption of another disturbance in the Twelfth Street area, therefore, seemed to be relatively high.

Despite the problems associated with identifying riot activity, the participants in civil disturbances have formed an especially critical segment of the ghetto population. One measure of the extent to which riots may have reflected important political goals, for example, has been provided by determining whether or not the persons who supported those goals actually participated in the disorders. The results of the Twelfth Street survey revealed that personal contact or exposure to the Detroit riot was related to the perception of the disorders as reflecting major political objectives. While 88 percent of those who viewed the riots as a type of protest said they had gone out in the neighborhood "to see what was happening," 61 percent of the people who felt that rioters were "just taking things and causing trouble" reported that they had not left their homes during the disorders.[61] Personal or direct involvement also was associated with a distrust of political institutions. Two-thirds of the residents who felt that the government was "merely trying to keep things quiet" got out in the disorders, but an identical proportion of those who believed that politicians really were attempting to solve local problems had not gone out during the riots.[62] Similarly, three-fourths of the respondents who endorsed violence as the fastest means of securing progress reported that they had been on the street, but 53 percent of those who advocate "peaceful protests" had remained inside their homes.[63] Moreover, a desire for revenge seemed to be related to personal experience with the riots. Although 65 percent of the people who had been outside during the disorders believed that stores were burned "because the owners deserved it," 52 percent of those who stayed inside attributed the burning to other reasons.[64]

In addition, the estimates of riot participation offered by residents of the Twelfth Street ghetto were associated with the objectives of the disorders. While 70 percent of those who thought the rioters were simply looting and causing trouble guessed that participation included one-tenth or less of the neighborhood, 52 percent of the residents who saw the riot as a form of protest estimated participation at one-fourth or more.[65] Furthermore, 65 percent of the residents who favored progress by "peace-

---

[61] The chi-square value was significant at the .01 level.
[62] The chi-square value was significant at the .01 level.
[63] The chi-square value was significant at the .01 level.
[64] The chi-square value was significant at the .01 level.
[65] The chi-square value was significant at the .01 level.

Table 1. Ghetto perceptions of riot objectives and reactions to police brutality

	Reactions to Police Brutality (Percent)			
Evaluations of police treatment before the riot:	Ignore it	Call the police	Wait around	Go to others for help
Very good or good	6% (5)	62% (53)	11% (10)	21% (18)
Not good or poor	3 (4)	42 (52)	12 (15)	43 (53)
Fastest means of securing progess:				
Peaceful protests	4% (5)	72% (91)	10% (13)	14% (18)
Causing trouble	5 (4)	32 (24)	15 (11)	47 (35)
Purpose of rioters:				
Taking things and causing trouble	4% (3)	72% (64)	10% (9)	14% (13)
Calling attention to needs	4 (5)	38 (47)	11 (14)	47 (58)

ful protests" placed participation at one-tenth or less; but 57 percent of those who approved of violence estimated it at one-quarter or more.[66] Interestingly enough, expanded estimates of participation also were associated with the view that the looting represented a clear and necessary purpose. While participation was projected at one-fourth or more of the area by 59 percent of the people who said that looters mainly stole goods "they needed but could not afford," 61 percent of those who felt that one-tenth or fewer were involved thought that the looters took "anything they could get their hands on."[67]

Perhaps the clearest test of the political goals of the rioters, however, was provided by the responses of ghetto residents to a hypothetical precipitating incident. The associations between reactions to this event and several measures of riot objectives are presented in Table 1. As the principal representatives of public authority in ghetto communities, police officers often have been both the primary targets of civil violence and a major source of the estrangement and hostility that has exploded in riots. As Table 1 demonstrates, prior perceptions of police behavior were closely related to probable reactions to an encounter with the police that might trigger serious disorders. While most of the residents who had positive images of police treatment before the riot would respond to the police beating by notifying the department, a majority of those who had unfavorable views of police conduct would respond in a potentially provocative manner by waiting around or securing other help. Similarly, 72 percent of the respondents who supported "peaceful protest" and who criticized the aims of the rioters, respectively, said that they would react by follow-

---

[66] The chi-square value was significant at the .01 level.
[67] The chi-square value was significant at the .05 level.

Table 2. Ghetto perceptions of motives for arson and reactions to automobile accident

	Reactions to Automobile Accident (Percent)			
Perceptions of motives for arson:	Ignore it	Wait around	Call police	Go to others for help
Storeowners deserved it	47% (35)	64% (39)	58% (54)	80% (8)
Other reasons	53 (40)	36 (22)	42 (40)	20 (2)

ing the official approved procedure of contacting or filing a complaint with the police. But most of the residents who adopted more militant or radical positions reported that they would respond to this hypothetical case of police brutality by remaining at the scene or seeking help from others. Probable reactions to an inflammatory precipitating incident, therefore, also seemed to be associated with perceptions of riot purposes.

As a desperate and powerful attempt to exert political influence, the riots seemed to attract the support—and the participation—of persons who shared their objectives. The issue of whether or not the disorders represented a *responsible* effort to secure basic alterations in existing social and political institutions, however, has remained a controversial question. In fact, some evidence has suggested that riot participants have displayed less social responsibility than persons who were not embroiled in the disorders. The Detroit Urban League survey, for example, found that persons who would report their neighbors to bill collectors were twice as likely to be self-reported rioters than those who would not give them information.[68] Persons who admitted that they were active in the riots seemed to feel less concern about the plight of their neighbors than those who had not been involved.

In many respects, civil disturbances have exhibited few signs of social responsibility. By engaging in violence, rioters have violated acceptable limits of political protest and they have provoked needless death and destruction. Moreover, urban disorders have been sustained by other relatively unsavory intentions such as attacks on the police, theft and looting, as well as a desire for vengeance. To examine the social concerns of Twelfth Street residents, support for the latter motive of revenge against ghetto storeowners was related to possible reactions to a hypothetical incident involving an automobile accident. As Table 2 indicates, most of the respondents who said that they would respond by calling the police, going to others for help, or remaining at the scene of the accident also believed that stores were burned during the riots because "the owners deserved it." On the other hand, a majority of those who would simply ignore the accident, without waiting or attempting to offer assistance, cited other reasons as the cause of the burning. Perceptions of vengeance in the disorders, therefore, did not necessarily imply socially irresponsible

[68] Detroit *Free Press*, August 20, 1967, p. B–1.

conduct in other circumstances. While additional research is needed to clarify the association between attitudes toward the disorders and a sense of personal or moral obligation, preliminary evidence has not demonstrated that the approval of riot behavior was related to a lack of concern about the problems of other people.

Although the riots may have represented an extreme—and, to many, an unacceptable—method of promoting desired social changes, the information gathered from ghetto residents has demonstrated that the disturbances were directed at significant political objectives. The unrest that ignited the disorders seemed to have its origin in political grievances. Moreover, a large proportion of the residents of neighborhoods that had erupted in violence acknowledged that the disturbances encompassed political goals. Perhaps most significantly, however, perceptions that riots reflected politically purposeful rather than meaningless or self-serving activity were related to the distrust of government, a belief that the incidents will aid the struggle for civil rights, support for violence, hostility toward major agencies of social control such as the police, and participation in the disorders. Urban civil disorders, therefore, have seemed to contain many of the goals and characteristics of a radical political movement. Perhaps the clearest expressions of the meaning and implications of riot objectives, however, were found in the political sentiments voiced by ghetto residents after the disorders had subsided.

The Political Effects of Ghetto Violence

The riots that have exploded in many American cities have not only been spawned by distrust or dissatisfaction regarding governmental institutions, but they also have had a major impact on the political attitudes of ghetto populations. In several surveys, for example, the residents of riot-torn neighborhoods have offered negative assessments of incumbent political leaders.[69] In Detroit, 36 percent of the people in the Twelfth Street neighborhood regarded Mayor Cavanaugh's action during the riot as "not good" or "poor," and 23 percent viewed his behavior as "very good." On the other hand, 43 percent judged the way that Michigan Governor George Romney handled the disorders as "not good" or "poor," and only 13 percent said it was "very good." The respondents also were asked about a movement initiated by local conservatives before the riot to recall Mayor Cavanaugh from office because of his alleged failure to take a tough stand on the "law-and-order" issue. Surprisingly, perhaps, 22 percent stated that they would vote to have the mayor "recalled and removed from office."

Although a sizeable number of Twelfth Street residents shared the aims of those who were attempting to oust Mayor Cavanaugh, they overwhelm-

---

[69] Feagin and Sheatsley, "Ghetto Resident Appraisals," p. 356; Sears, *Political Attitudes of Los Angeles Negroes*, p. 8; Campbell and Schuman, "Racial Attitudes in Fifteen American Cities," p. 41.

ingly rejected the motives behind that movement. Seventy-nine percent of the black respondents who sought to secure civil rights through "peaceful protests," for example, wanted Cavanaugh to remain in office; but the residents who favored violence were evenly divided by the recall issue.[70] The principal opponents of the mayor in this neighborhood were not voters who wanted him to impose harsh or repressive measures to end crime and disorders. On the contrary, some of his major critics were persons who espoused the use of violence and who apparently entertained the almost radical or revolutionary hope that the leader who replaced him might be more sympathetic to their interests and objectives. The disorders, therefore, seemed to encourage a desire to turn incumbent and even supposedly liberal public officials out of office.

In addition, people who regarded the riot as an effort to advance political goals have not appeared to be strongly disposed to work through regular political channels such as the major parties to achieve social changes. The Twelfth Street survey found that 69 percent of the respondents regarded themselves as Democrats, only 3 percent considered themselves to be Republicans, and about one-fourth reported that they were independents. In contrast to the usual image of independent voters as apolitical or disinterested citizens, however, the survey revealed that the independents were somewhat more likely to regard the riots as a form of protest[71] and to believe that the disorders had aided the civil rights movement[72] than those who identified with the major political parties. Moreover, while 68 percent of the residents who classified themselves as either Republicans or Democrats advocated "peaceful protests," as the fastest means of securing civil rights progress, the independents were almost evenly divided between support for violent and nonviolent strategies.[73] Similarly, 84 percent of the independents considered vengeance to be the principal motive for the burning of stores during the riot; but only half of those who identified with a political party agreed, and the other half ascribed the burning to other causes.[74] Furthermore, more independents than party identifiers admitted that they had been involved in the disorders.[75] For many black citizens who were not affiliated with either the Democratic or the Republican party, the riots may have represented a rapid and feasible means of securing desired political objectives. The failure of those persons to participate in normal political activities, however, did not necessarily imply that they had abandoned all political goals and interests; in fact, their attitudes toward the disorders seemed to offer further evidence of the political significance of the riots and of their dissatisfaction with existing governmental processes.

Another indication of the political discontent that prevailed among the

---

[70] The chi-square value was significant at the .01 level.
[71] The chi-square value, however, was not statistically significant.
[72] The chi-square value, however, was not statistically significant.
[73] The chi-square value was significant at the .05 level.
[74] The chi-square value was significant at the .01 level.
[75] The chi-square value was significant at the .05 level.

residents of the Twelfth Street neighborhood was found in their opinions of established approaches to ghetto problems such as the federal antipoverty program. When the respondents were asked about the way the program was being handled in Detroit, 41 percent replied that they disapproved of it, only 36 percent approved, and 23 percent were undecided. Criticism of the antipoverty program in this area was considerably greater than in other parts of the country.[76]

In rejecting this program, the residents of the Twelfth Street area seemed to be calling for the creation of new policies and new structural arrangements for solving their problems. Opposition to the current program, for example, was concentrated among persons who favored somewhat radical or revolutionary political goals. While 55 percent of the residents who supported "peaceful protests" to achieve civil rights progress agreed with the antipoverty program, 76 percent of those who endorsed violence disapproved of it.[77] The advocacy of violence as a means of gaining political objectives, therefore, was not associated with a simple desire to augment or enlarge existing social and economic policies such as the antipoverty program. The residents of a ghetto that had experienced a major riot did not merely wish to gain increased support for established programs to alleviate their needs but they also may have sought basic changes in the political process that had designed and enacted those programs.

The purposes of the disorders may have not been confined to a simple protest concerning the lack of public support for existing policies to improve ghetto conditions. In the Twelfth Street survey, only 27 percent of the respondents felt that the riots "could have been avoided," but 57 percent thought that they "had to happen sooner or later." A large proportion of ghetto residents appeared to accept the almost fatalistic belief that political leaders could not have prevented the outbreak of civil disorders. When the respondents were asked why the riots had to happen or how they could have been avoided, most of them cited basic social problems such as the lack of equal rights, job discrimination, or police practices. Yet, most of the people who felt that the disorders included a political purpose or reflected a type of protest did not believe that the trouble was avoidable. While 63 percent of those who viewed the rioters as merely "taking things and causing trouble" said that the riots could have been prevented, 67 percent of the respondents who considered the disorders as an attempt to "call attention to their needs" thought they were inevitable or unavoidable.[78] The implications of this association seemed to be relatively direct. Since most of the residents who felt that the riots could have been avoided regarded them as purposeless theft or destruction, firm or repressive measures to stop the outbreak of rioting

---

[76] Sears, *Political Attitudes of Los Angeles Negroes*, pp. 11–12; Brink and Harris, *Black and White*, pp. 242–43; Campbell and Schuman, "Racial Attitudes in Fifteen American Cities," pp. 41–42.

[77] The chi-square value was significant at the .01 level.

[78] The chi-square value was significant at the .01 level.

might have been supported by some segments of the neighborhood. However, the opinion that the violence could have been averted and that it represented a form of protest, which seemed to imply a belief that existing policies were simply inadequate or insufficient to stem the outbreak of disorders, was held by only a small proportion of the respondents. The majority of the people who perceived the riots as an attempt to call attention to their needs, coupled with the feeling that they were inevitable, seemed to lack faith in the ability or capacity of present leaders and programs to satisfy their demands. For many respondents, the disorders were not merely an expression of protest designed to promote the expansion of existing projects.

One manifestation of the relatively radical political goals that existed among the residents of the Twelfth Street neighborhood was evident in their sentiments about black separatism. Several surveys conducted elsewhere have found that the supporters of black nationalism or racial separation have included only a miniscule percentage of the black population in the country.[79]

In response to a question about whether black people should "integrate with whites or try to get along without whites," by contrast, support for black separatism in the Twelfth Street ghetto jumped to 22 percent. Furthermore, separatists were more than twice as likely as integrationists to express a distrust of government,[80] to say that the riots had not harmed the civil rights movement,[81] to advocate violence as the fastest means of achieving progress,[82] to admit that they got outdoors during the disorders,[83] to claim that the owners deserved the burning of their stores,[84] to reject the antipoverty program,[85] and to argue that outsiders would not understand the rioting.[86] The approval of black separatism in the Twelfth Street area, which was nearly double than that found in any comparable surveys, was related to the endorsement of riot objectives and apparently reflected a relatively widespread intention to disassociate themselves from white values and standards. By rejecting the ends of integration, many black residents of this area may have been seeking to withdraw from the social or political supervision of the white public and

---

[79] Marx, *Protest and Prejudice*, p. 108; Brink and Harris, *Black and White*, pp. 262–63; Campbell and Schuman, "Racial Attitudes in Fifteen American Cities," p. 16; Joel D. Aberbach and Jack L. Walker, "The Meanings of Black Power: A Comparison of White and Black Interpretations of a Political Slogan," unpublished paper presented at the annual meeting of the American Political Science Association, Washington, D.C., 1968; "Report from Black America," *Newsweek*, June 30, 1969, p. 20; see, however, Harlan Hahn, "Black Separatists: Attitudes and Objectives in a Northern Ghetto," *Journal of Black Studies*, I (September, 1970), pp. 35–53.

[80] The chi-square value was significant at the .01 level.
[81] The chi-square value was significant at the .01 level.
[82] The chi-square value was significant at the .01 level.
[83] The chi-square value was significant at the .01 level.
[84] The chi-square value was significant at the .01 level.
[85] The chi-square value was significant at the .01 level.
[86] The chi-square value was significant at the .01 level.

political leaders. This sentiment, therefore, constituted a direct threat to the political authority of the outside society.

Other evidence of this desire for a dis-annexation from white customs and institutions was present in the political attitudes expressed by residents of the Twelfth Street neighborhood. Even among those persons who retained their faith in integration and who did not favor black separation, there was considerable sentiment favoring increased public participation in government decisions, a stronger sense of community, and greater independence from predominantly white political agencies. The political goals of the disorders seemed to include the hope that existing political processes and arrangements might be restructured to provide for improved means of satisfying the needs of this neighborhood.

Perhaps the clearest statement of the political objectives of many ghetto residents was contained in their responses to a series of questions about their attitudes toward government after the riots had subsided. The feeling that local people would enjoy increased opportunities for political participation after the disorders, for example, was supported by 73 percent of the residents who thought that they would have "more to say about what should be done in this neighborhood." Twenty percent felt that they would have about the same amount of influence, and only 2 percent predicted that they would have less to say about decisions affecting projects in their area. The remaining 5 percent were uncertain. In addition, the riots seemed to instill a belief that the Twelfth Street neighborhood would not continue to be neglected or ignored by political leaders. While 61 percent of the residents believed that the needs of the neighborhood would receive "more attention" from city officials, 31 percent guessed that they would get about the same amount of attention as before the disturbances, and only 3 percent said they would obtain less attention. Again, 5 percent were undecided about this issue. Finally, in reply to a direct question about whether the people in the neighborhood would have "more power, less power, or about the same amount of power than they did before the trouble started," 46 percent of the respondents stated flatly that they would have more power, 34 percent estimated that they would have about the same amount of power, only 3 percent anticipated less power, and 17 percent were unable to make a prediction. The attitudes of Twelfth Street residents toward major issues affecting their relationships to government after the disorders, including neighborhood participation, recognition, and power, therefore, seemed to constitute the clearest available statement of the political objectives of the riots.

Although the responses to all three questions seemed to imply a hope that the neighborhood would become an increasingly autonomous or self-governing unit, the residents expressed greater optimism about the prospects for increased public participation in local decisions than they did about the possibility of receiving more attention from city officials; and they displayed somewhat more faith in both the growth of opportunities for political participation and the probable concern of local officeholders than they did in their own power. In part, this relative lack of confidence in city officials as well as the potential influence of the neighborhood may have reflected a basic distrust of established political processes and structures. Perhaps some residents did not feel that the riot would end governmental neglect of their neighborhood or that it would give them increased power, even though they foresaw expanded openings for political participation, simply because they did not believe that political institutions were really interested in solving their problems. Even more striking than the slight differences in their responses to the three questions, however, was the prevailing hope for major structural changes to improve the relationship between neighborhood citizens and government. Only a small proportion of the residents felt that existing political arrangements would remain essentially unchanged after the disturbances, and even fewer thought that they would grow worse. For many persons, experience with a major riot apparently evoked strong expectations that the political objectives of civil disorders would be fulfilled.

The political objectives of the civil disorders in Detroit seemed to be basically similar to the concepts of "neighborhood corporations" or "community control"[87] of education, law enforcement, and other municipal services that have been widely discussed as a possible solution to the alienation and hostility that has accompanied the growth of ghetto problems. Other research has shown that black citizens have displayed the greatest interest in neighborhood problems, but whites have expressed the most interest in national problems and the least interest in neighborhood issues.[88] While elaborate political mechanisms have been created to process complaints and to solve the national or city-wide problems that trouble white voters, no comparable organizations have been established at the neighborhood level. Although urban black residents have been compelled by traditional patterns of segregation and discrimination to live exclusively in designated areas, municipal policies and services usually have been extended on the assumptions that local problems can be resolved on a community-wide basis and that all sections of a city have similar needs and requirements. Relatively little attention has been devoted to the distinctive political grievances and demands of minority groups in most urban areas. In local politics, black citizens have been forced to compete with the wishes of the more numerous and more influential white population. Despite the deep racial cleavages that permeate most major cities, local governments have failed to establish means of accommodating the special interests and aspirations of the residents of black neighborhoods.

In general, support for the political aspirations of the riots was strongly related to the belief that the neighborhood would enjoy increased influence and authority afterwards. While 59 percent of the residents who perceived the disorders as a form of protest expected the neighborhood to

---

[87] See, for example, Aaron Wildavsky, "The Empty-head Blues: Black Rebellion and White Reaction," *The Public Interest* (Spring, 1968), pp. 3–16; Maurice R. Berube and Marilyn Gittell, eds., *Confrontation at Ocean Hill-Brownsville* (New York: Frederick A. Praeger, 1969).

[88] Harlan Hahn, *Race Relations and Community Structure* (forthcoming).

have more power, for example, 52 percent of those who thought the rioters were merely "taking things and causing trouble" predicted it would have the same or less power.[89] Similarly, 63 percent of the respondents who felt that the rioting would help the civil rights movement anticipated more power, but 56 percent who viewed the disorders as harmful to civil rights foresaw the same or less power for the neighborhood.[90] The approval of violence as a means of securing civil rights progress also seemed to promote the conviction that the neighborhood would gain increased power. Sixty-eight percent of the people who supported violence estimated that they would have more power, but 52 percent of those who favored "peaceful protests" believed that the area would possess similar or declining power after the disorders.[91] Furthermore, 64 percent of the respondents who felt that police behavior before the riot had been "not good" or "poor" sought enhanced neighborhood power; but 55 percent of those with favorable perceptions of prior police conduct thought that their neighbors would have relatively stable or decreasing influence after the disturbances.[92] Expressions of animosity toward the major agents of social control as well as support for the riots and their goals, therefore, were associated with the growth of political aspirations and expectations for the neighborhood in the aftermath of the disorders.

Although the riots may have reflected an effort by politically discontented or deprived segments of the population to secure expanded local influence and authority, their activities provided relatively little direct evidence about how they intended to achieve their purpose. Since there was no discernible attempt to perpetuate the informal organization of neighborhood people that developed on the streets during the disturbances, the rioters apparently did not expect to establish permanent independence from external supervision or control. Many of the ghetto residents sought some major modifications in the existing political system, but they did not plan to create new political structures through the destruction or overthrowing of governmental institutions. Even though a large proportion of people in the Twelfth Street area did not believe that the government was interested in solving their problems, they seemed to think that they could attain their objectives without a full-scale rebellion or revolution.

The belief that the riots had at least partially fulfilled their political goals also was implied by the attitudes of Twelfth Street residents toward government after the disorders. Whereas only 23 percent of the people in the area had expressed confidence in the willingness of government to solve local problems before the riots, this proportion grew to 38 percent in the aftermath of the disturbances. As might have been expected, political sentiments after the disorders depended to some extent on prior perceptions of the government. Ninety-five percent of the respondents who

---

[89] The chi-square value, however, was not significant.
[90] The chi-square value was significant at the .05 level.
[91] The chi-square value was significant at the .05 level.
[92] The chi-square value was significant at the .01 level.

felt that public officials would merely try to "keep things quiet" afterwards, for example, had not substantially altered their political attitudes as a result of the riots. In addition, 54 percent of the people who expected political agencies to "solve problems" after the disorders had expressed their faith in government previously. Yet 46 percent of those who believed that government would attempt to solve problems afterwards had modified their earlier sentiment of political skepticism.[93] While the riots had not changed a large number of minds about government intentions, a small but significant segment of the population did express growing trust in the ability of government leaders to solve critical problems after the disturbances were over.

Moreover, this increasing faith in government emerged primarily from persons who regarded the riots as a form of protest rather than as purposeless theft and destruction. Among the respondents who felt that the disorders represented an attempt to "call attention to their needs," 81 percent of those who believed government would attempt to solve local problems after the riots previously had been convinced that politicians were simply trying to keep things quiet; but, among the people who viewed the disturbances primarily as looting and violence, only 29 percent of those who thought that government would solve problems afterwards had been converted from a position of political distrust. Persons who felt that the riots reflected a political purpose, therefore, experienced the most dramatic growth of confidence in government after the disorders.[94]

Summary and Discussion

This increasing faith in political institutions has imposed heavy burdens and responsibilities on public officials. Although many ghetto residents have harbored a basic distrust of existing political structures, they have not sought to overturn or destroy those structures. By recognizing restraints that have prevented riots from exploding into rebellions or insurrections, the participants in civil disorders have implicitly displayed at least some confidence in the ability of the political system to produce desired changes. They apparently have not abandoned their hopes that established political arrangements can be restructured to satisfy their grievances and demands.

The aspirations for increased local participation and influence, by threatening to deprive other political agencies of their existing prerogatives, has presented public leaders with a serious challenge. Moreover, the prospect of adding what might amount to "another layer of federalism" to the existing political system has not been greeted by widespread enthusiasm. Although the outcome of this controversy may severely tax the capacity of the political process to ameliorate major conflicts, its

---

[93] The chi-square value was significant, however, at the .01 level.
[94] Harlan Hahn, "The Aftermath of a Riot," *Discourse*, XII (Autumn, 1969), pp. 549–53.

development has not been unlike the struggle of other ethnic groups for greater power and autonomy, which often has entailed prolonged violence. Most of those skirmishes were resolved either by harsh repression, such as American Indians experienced, or by the needs of a rapidly expanding economy which permitted the social and political integration of entire groups including European immigrants into the existing structure of society.[95] Several characteristics affecting the struggle of black Americans including their visibility, their historical experience, as well as contemporary trends such as the altered demands of a technological economy and growing political centralization, have greatly exacerbated the difficulty of their quest for equal rights. To avoid the emergence of a massive revolutionary movement in America, therefore, public officeholders have been forced to confront the possibility of granting to black citizens the increased local independence and self-regulation that were historically denied to other minorities as a result of propitious intervening economic and political forces.

The demands by ghetto residents for decentralization or for increasing control of their own neighborhoods have raised some crucial and vexing questions regarding forms of government that might contribute to the reduction of racial tensions. One study of racial disturbances and features of municipal government such as electoral districts and the size of city councils, for example, concluded that "the more direct the relation between voter and government, the less likely are riots to occur."[96] A subsequent investigation, however, found that cities displaying attributes of relatively centralized political influence such as council-manager governments, nonpartisan elections, and small councils were less likely to experience racial violence than communities that lacked those characteristics.[97] Perhaps a relatively close relationship between voters and their elected representatives has provided government officials within improved information about community grievances; or perhaps a less dispersed political process has permitted the concentration of resources and decision-making authority that might be necessary for expeditious action on those complaints to prevent violence. Regardless of the role that either consolidated or fragmented political structures have played in the outbreak of riots, however, relatively centralized local governments have seemed to be most responsive to the needs of black citizens after the disorders. An examination of the twenty cities studied in depth by the Kerner Commission, for example, revealed that the actions taken by communities in the aftermath of riots formed a cumulative scale that was related to the dispersion of influence in city government. Even though the Commission failed to notice this distribution or its association with structural characteristics, cities that launched a large number of programs to alleviate ghetto conditions after the disorders were more likely to have at-large elections, a

---

[95] Skolnick, *The Politics of Protest*, pp. 17–21.

[96] Lieberson and Silverman, "The Precipitants and Underlying Conditions of Race Riots," p. 896.

[97] Downes, "Social and Political Characteristics of Riot Cities," pp. 516–18.

strong mayor-council system, a longer term of office for the mayor, and more citizen complaints annually than localities that were less responsive to riots.[98] Apparently, the centralization of authority in some cities has enabled them to mobilize and to initiate policy changes promptly in an effort to avert further disruptions in public order. The potential for this type of civic reaction, however, has seemed to be somewhat inconsistent with the objectives of increased participation and decentralization in the policy-making process.

This study of the attitudes of persons who had experienced a major riot has not meant to infer that all residents of the neighborhood believed that the disorders reflected political goals. Many people may have participated in the riots for other reasons. Many also did not feel that the disorders implied political objectives, nor did they approve of those aspirations. Yet, an important segment of the neighborhood that had direct contact with a destructive riot expressed strong convictions that it contained a political purpose. Moreover, the belief that the disorders exemplified political goals was associated with various aspects of riot behavior and ideology including estrangement from existing political institutions, orientations concerning violence, hostility toward the social control imposed by the police, participation in the disorders, antipathy regarding other means of securing political access or power, and a hope for increased local autonomy. This perception of riot objectives might not have been found in other areas of the country or even in other black ghettos. One of the basic points of this study, however, has been that the Twelfth Street neighborhood may have represented a unique portion of the society; but it has not been any less important for that reason. Most riots have been precipitated by relatively small groups of people in somewhat unusual sectors of urban areas, but any plans to avert future violence that overlook or ignore the aspirations of those special pockets of the society may be doomed to failure. For a critical segment of the population, the disorders seemed to represent a purposeful attempt to achieve significant political goals rather than a blind effort to strike out at the external society as a primary source of frustration or an emotional reaction to the vast gap that has separated white and black Americans.

By seeking to examine the objectives of civil disorders, this study has revealed that the riots were directed at a political purpose that might not have been identified by an investigation based on commonly accepted approaches such as relative deprivation or the frustration-aggression hypothesis. Simultaneously, it has opened up numerous opportunities for further research. A need has emerged for additional explorations of the concept of community control of black neighborhoods and the political structures that ghetto residents want to establish to achieve enhanced local participation, recognition, and authority. The perceived objectives of the disorders embodied in increased local independence and decentralization also have raised some important questions about the characteristics

---

[98] Harlan Hahn, "Civic Responses to Riots: A Reappraisal of Kerner Commission Data," *Public Opinion Quarterly*, XXXIV (Spring, 1970), pp. 101–7.

of the persons who supported those goals. Have prior experiences with the political process induced them to view violence as a final resort to secure desired changes, for example, or have they been relatively insulated from previous political activity? Have they developed any specific plans to overcome anticipated resistance to their demands for autonomy? An emphasis on the distinctively political aspects of civil disorders might enable social scientists to gain a clearer image of what the rioters were attempting to accomplish than research based on usual theoretical concepts has been able to provide.

Perhaps a basic reason for the weaknesses or inadequacies of completed research on urban unrest has been related to contrasting perceptions of the political system. Most white Americans, including political scientists and other members of the academic community, have not lost their faith in the democratic process and in its ability to adjust to new demands, to accommodate divergent interests, and to resolve divisive conflict. Their assumptions have prompted them to interpret the riots within a framework that has ranged from criminal behavior to a display of protest or discontent. On the other hand, a large proportion of the residents of black ghettos have either lost their trust in existing political institutions, or they have retained only a marginal hope that those structures may yield basic changes after they have been attacked by violence. As a result, their objectives have embodied a desire to radically restructure the political process for solving their own problems. The demand by ghetto residents for increased autonomy probably has confronted government officials with one of the most fundamental political issues that this nation has been forced to resolve, and it has also compelled the white public and its leaders to face the possibility that the political aspirations represented by civil disorders may emerge again as sweeping rebellions or insurrections.

7

Recent Developments in Urban Politics

Professionalization and
Bureaucratization,
Urban Renewal,
and Metropolitan Government

Industrialization in America transformed this society from an agrarian society to an overwhelmingly industrialized and urbanized one. America's cities grew both in size and number and spread out over their traditional political boundaries into vast urbanized areas which encompassed both cities and suburbs. These vast changes in the shape of urban areas have brought profound problems with which cities must now contend—increasing layers of government, urban renewal, and regional considerations. These are the problems discussed in this section.

Our earliest cities performed very few functions, perhaps the maintenance of a police force and a fire brigade (which was often volunteer) but often little else. Modern methods of sanitation were unknown and not subject to city control. Problems of mass transit did not exist and vast highway networks were not needed. Building and zoning codes were not developed and city planning was almost unheard of. In sum, during America's early history, city functions were minimal.

However, as more and more people were attracted to cities by new industries hungry for a large labor force, the cities rapidly had to assume new functions. Problems of sanitation required the construction of sewer systems, disposal facilities, and garbage collection. People had to be housed. Vast numbers of daily commuters required new modes of transportation—often mass transportation regulated by franchises under city control. Electric power systems had to be built and expanded—systems sometimes owned or regulated by municipalities. A growing number of economic functions in cities also created the need for zoning regulations and safety codes administered by city agencies. And the list could go on.

In addition to the problems raised by expanding populations and economic activity, the expansion of cities led to the development of suburbs. Populations soon spilled over central city boundaries into the outlying areas. Many people wanted to escape from urban congestion to a more rural-like suburban atmosphere, although they often continued to work in the central city. Compounding city problems presented by their own residents are the problems presented to central cities by the large number of suburban commuters: people who utilize city services but who do not pay taxes to support those services. (Of course, some cities which now have income taxes levy it against suburbanites who earn their living in the city.) In addition to their use of city services, large numbers of suburban commuters exacerbate problems of mass transportation and highway congestion.

To meet the problems caused by growing populations, cities have had to develop mechanisms to coordinate and control diverse urban activities. Like other segments of society faced with large-scale administrative problems, cities have bureaucratized and professionalized municipal departments and staffs. It is this phenomenon which is the topic of the first selection.

Instead of using historical data to investigate the phenomenon of bureaucratization and professionalization of municipal government, Robert Alford uses comparative data. He assumes that as cities increase in size they encounter certain common problems at each size level. Therefore, he predicts, and his data support him, that the level of bureaucratization will increase as city size increases.

In fact, other historical evidence indicates that as cities increase in size they assume larger numbers of functions which they handle with bureaucratic control. The democratization of city governments by increasing the number of elective offices, such as occurred during the Jacksonian era, had to be reversed as cities took on more functions. City governments were too fragmented because large numbers of semi-autonomous elected officials decentralized power. One (albeit informal) mechanism to centralize city government was the political machine with a "boss" as the central leader. However, machines became unacceptable to the urban electorate and machines have been replaced by more formal mechanisms of centralization and control.

In addition to the relationship between city size and bureaucratization, Alford also demonstrates that elements of bureaucratization are related to each other. For example, the presence of a full-time personnel officer is related to the form of government, the proportion of city employees covered by civil service, and full-time employees per capita. One might make the inference that bureaucratization is a systemic phenomenon. That is, once a city begins to bureaucratize and professionalize its governmental structure and processes, it does so throughout the governmental arena rather than in just one isolated area or department. This systematization of bureaucratic government is due to the increasing complexity of city functions and because relations between city departments and services themselves are becoming more complex. Therefore, interagency coordination itself necessitates a bureaucratic structure.

Urban growth not only necessitates the bureaucratization of municipal government but also necessitates urban renewal. As theories of city growth such as Ernest Burgess' concentric zone theory, Richard Hurd's axial growth theory, or Homer Hoyt's sector theory demonstrate, cities grow outwardly with new businesses and housing added at the periphery. A consequence of new building in this area is that older structures located near the city center are often neglected and allowed to decay. The development of flexible transportation such as the automobile and the truck has accelerated this decentralization process. Each year more and more homes and businesses (retail, wholesale, manufacturing, services, etc.) are built in outlying areas. The decay of centrally located businesses and residences necessitates the implementation of urban renewal programs. Because private investors are reluctant to invest in the central city, government urban renewal money is used to stimulate the redevelopment of central city areas.

The next selection by Michael Aiken and Robert Alford discusses community social structure associated with the presence of urban renewal programs. They find that conditions of need—e.g., the existence of dilapidated housing, etc.—are associated with such programs. However, they also find that need alone is probably not a sufficient explanation. Certain social structural features must be present in the community for the successful adoption and implementation of these programs.

Aiken and Alford discuss five theories of community innovation—(1) political culture, (2) centralization of formal political structures, (3) concentration or diffusion of community power, (4) community differentiation and continuity, and (5) community integration—and find all of them lacking in terms of the support their data give to these theories. In place of these theories, they offer an alternative hypothesis to explain why some communities innovate in areas not requiring a vote of the people.

They suggest that "the more differentiated the organizational structure of a city, the more innovative it will be." Their data show that the number of manufacturing establishments with 100 or more employees, the number of independent banks with assets of fifty million dollars or more, and the percentage of plant workers unionized among all industries in the community are associated with the presence or absence of urban renewal programs, the speed of introduction of the innovation into the community, and the program output (per capita expenditures).

According to Aiken and Alford, organizational differentiation is indicative of the "nature and state of interorganizational networks" in cities. As communities age and mature, associations within them are able to develop interorganizational networks—patterns of interaction between organizational units and their leaders. In communities with relatively stable populations, these networks become settled and are not disrupted by the continual influx of newcomers.

The organizations in a community are "centers of power." These power centers are linked to each other by mechanisms Aiken and Alford call "interfaces" which consist not only of current linkages in the community, but also of historical "accumulations of knowledge and experience among various centers of power." Communities with the greatest number of power centers and which possess comprehensive interfaces, according to Aiken and Alford, are the communities most likely to innovate because a minimum coalition can probably be formed. The authors caution, however, that this model may only be adequate for community decisions in which the major participants are organizations. In decisions where individuals are mobilized, e.g., fluoridation referendums, changes in city charters, etc., this model may be either insufficient or inappropriate.

One innovation which often requires a vote of the people is annexation or metropolitan reorganization measures (i.e., the formation of metropolitan governments). The need to correct regional problems and to insure sufficient tax bases and financing of city government has centered attention on the need for urban reorganization into metropolitan governments. However, the advocates of metropolitan government have made little headway—only a few of these governments exist in the United States. Because of the lack of success in achieving metropolitan government, the next selection focuses on the stumbling blocks to this form of governmental reorganization.

The article by Robert Wood ("The Political Economy of the Future") focuses on the structural roadblocks to metropolitan reorganization. He lists three stresses in the New York metropolitan area. (These stresses are equally applicable to other large metropolitan regions.) First, given the population movements and economic change since World War II, there is the ability of present governmental units to remain financially solvent.

Second, there is the ability of the system to continue to improve service levels commensurate with public demand and with improvements since World War II. And, third, there is the question as to how serious are the sporadic displays of public dissatisfaction with the way the New York region is going.

Wood says that unless the above three problems or stresses are insoluble, the status quo will prevail in the New York region. Are, in fact, the above three problems insoluble? No, says Wood. With respect to impending municipal bankruptcy, the reorganization proponents argue that expenditures will increase faster than revenues, especially since property taxes tend to lag behind economic growth. There is, according to the forecasters of municipal economic disaster, a "peril point" beyond which taxes cannot go without bringing down the system. However, Wood points out that when expenditure and revenue trends are compared, both did not grow very much, relative to the gross national product or other measures of the national or regional economy. In other words, there has been no large-scale diversion of income or capital to local expenditures. Although there are a few cities (e.g., New York and some New Jersey cities) facing increasing economic stringency (slowly growing or declining tax bases), these cities are a minority. The relative positions of the "haves" and "have-nots" has remained stable.

In addition, the starvation thesis (that is, local municipalities are underspending relative to their needs) is not supported, according to Wood. Improvements in public spending (average per capita operating expenditures in constant dollars) have been registered in the period 1945 to 1955. The quality of municipal services is at least holding steady and schools have been improved.

Finally, there are political payoffs in the going system. No deterioration in services or expenditures has occurred. What has occurred is a body of opinion which wants to divert more of society's revenues to the public sector and to obtain more positive regional policies. Such a radical change (especially for regional development) would involve regional governmental reorganization. However, there are political, legal, and constitutional roadblocks to metropolitan government. Politicians have a vested interest in the status quo and there is no public groundswell for change. Public apathy towards the matter seems to prevail. Unless public opinion can be mobilized, there will be no metropolitan governmental reorganization.

Since Wood wrote his analysis, two significant developments have taken place: (1) the growing influence of black voters in urban areas and the election of some black mayors; and (2) a heightening of the urban financial crisis.

Several critics of metropolitan reorganization point out that metropolitan government would mean the death of black political power at a time when such power is making itself felt. The migration of blacks to the central cities and the subsequent flight of whites to the suburbs has produced a number of cities with large black populations—large enough to represent a potent political force. Metropolitan government—government over the central city and surrounding suburbs—would dilute black power by producing a large white majority in the new political unit. Blacks and others sympathetic to the black cause will undoubtedly resist efforts at metropolitan reorganization as will many suburbanites who fled to the suburbs to escape the city and its problems.

Second, the urban financial crisis has reached such a magnitude in late 1970 and early 1971 that some cities have been forced to lay off municipal workers. This financial crisis, while most seriously affecting our largest cities, is also affecting suburbs and state governments as well. City and state revenues have not been able to keep pace with expenditures. For the cities, then, metropolitan reorganization might no longer be an answer to financial woes (although metropolitan government would undoubtedly provide efficiencies in municipal operation). Currently, there is agitation for federal revenue sharing with local governments, since federal income tax receipts tend to rise as fast as personal and corporate income and because the federal government can engae in deficit spending. Perhaps metropolitan government will fade into the background (although it has never been well received) as new sources of revenue from the federal government become available.

The growth of cities, then, has produced complex problems of administration and the distribution of resources. The selections in this section have illustrated some reasons for the response or lack of response to some of these problems. Problems of administration have been met by the bureaucratization and professionalization of municipal government. The peripheral expansion of cities has produced decaying inner areas which have been subject to urban renewal programs. And the growth of metropolitan areas has produced problems of governmental coordination, distribution of services, and financing which have not been adequately dealt with. Perhaps federal revenue sharing (if it is enacted) will represent at least a partial answer to the most pressing financial needs of urban America. There is little prospect for wholesale governmental reorganization on the metropolitan level.

The Bureaucratization of Urban Government

ROBERT R. ALFORD

Increasing bureaucratization of urban government is well-known. The growth of urban areas has continually posed new problems for the local governments within those areas, problems which have been met by expanding staffs, establishing new departments, and hiring professional specialists to handle the technical tasks involved in traffic engineering, city planning, budgeting and sheer administrative control. Even in the absence of urban growth, expectations by voters of better and more services have led to expansion of personnel and increased organizational complexity.

These secular pressures upon local government have not been the same in all communities, nor have the responses of local leaders and officials been the same to similar pressures. It is our thesis that variations in bureaucratization between cities are not completely explained by the objective problems posed by growth and the technicalities of administration. The value placed upon bureaucracy and professionalism has varied from one community to another.

We first discuss the interrelated character of bureaucracy and professionalism in order to treat them as aspects of a single continuum or process of development in middle-sized American cities. Then we present various indicators, together with a discussion of problems of measurement and data. The association of the indicators shows that we can regard bureaucratization as a general tendency of American local political systems, not just as a property of particular governmental institutions. Bureaucratization, it is concluded, is associated with city size, but size alone does not account for the variations found between American cities.

Published for the first time in this volume, this paper was written in 1967 and has not been revised to take account of later literature. Some of the themes which it presents are dealt with in more detail in the author's book, *Bureaucracy and Participation* (Chicago: Rand McNally, 1969), which concerns itself with four Wisconsin cities.

The Growth of City Functions, Staffs, and Expenditures

The increase of governmental functions with the growth of a city is illustrated by the history of Milwaukee, Wisconsin, which was chartered in 1846 and reached a population of 50,000 by 1880 and over 600,000 by 1950. In its first year, ordinances were passed authorizing legislation, enforcement of ordinances, conduct of elections, registration of chattel mortgages, plotting of land, operation of public buildings, house numbering, licensing of occupations and trades, recording and publication of council proceedings, etc. (The author names a total of 48.)[1] Established in subsequent years were: care of dependent children (1849), dog pound (1856), maintenance of a general hospital (1857), bathing beaches (1878), parks (1889), conservatory (1899), maintenance of a tuberculosis hospital (1907), symphony concerts (1910), tuberculosis preventorium (1911), golf courses (1914), park nursery (1915), refectories (1923), aviary (1930), open air swimming pool (1932). Only a few minor activities were discontinued: voting machines (1902), special assessments for collection of ashes and rubbish (1907), hospital library service and tourist camp (1922), special assessments for tree borders (1925), publication of land value maps (1930). Taken over by the county were: registration of chattel mortgages, outdoor relief, hospitalization of the sick poor, and the almshouse. Taken over by the state was the examination of school teachers, a duty first performed by the city. Some functions changed in form and control, of course, although not in substance.

Milwaukee is undoubtedly typical in the scope of functions performed by the "average" city government, if not in the exact dates at which they were established, and this list gives some idea of the expansion of city activities since the mid-eighteenth century.

Growth of the population within a city does not mean simply a regular increase of the scope of urban government. A city does not simply add one fireman for every 10,000 additional population, one more library employee, one more policeman. Instead, there is a steep increase as cities grow in the complexity, specialization and sheer number of functions performed. There is a corresponding need for both professionals and organizational techniques for controlling personnel recruitment, allocation and performance, as well as the necessary financing.

Table 1 shows that there is a direct and linear correlation of the proportion of full-time employees per capita with city size. Not only does the absolute size of the staff employed by the city increase as the city grows, but also the relative size, indicating indirectly the expansion of city government functions and services as cities grow. We would expect analogous

---

[1] Bayard Still, *Milwaukee: The History of a City* (Madison: The State Historical Society of Wisconsin, 1948), Appendix, Table 8, pp. 584–90. Still summarizes the city ordinances authorizing various governmental activities from 1846 to 1940. He also includes those activities which, by 1947, had been assumed by the county, the state, private contract, or had been discontinued.

Table 1. Per capita full-time city employees and per capita general expenditures, by city size. All cities over 25,000 population in 1960

			Size Range (000's)			
25–50	50–100	100–150	150–250	250–500	500 or more	Total

Per cent with more than nine employees per capita

43%	51%	55%	63%	67%	90%	50%
(356)	(180)	(49)	(30)	(30)	(21)	(666)

Per cent with more than $67 per capita general expenditure

47%	59%	67%	90%	80%	95%	57%
(360)	(180)	(49)	(30)	(30)	(21)	(670)

Data are for 1960. Data on employees were not available for 10 cities between 25 and 50,000 population in the 1962 City and County Data Book. Data for expenditures were not available for 6 cities. The cutting points were chosen because the data were dichotomized, as the totals indicate. The same patterns appear regardless of the cutting points, but no meaning attaches to the absolute figures.

geometric increases in city budgets, and this is also the case. (Revenues increase similarly.)

Although our interest is in the *process* of bureaucratization, as well as its causes and consequences, we have little data directly bearing upon historical change. We must, therefore, infer historical processes of change from differences in bureaucratization between cities differing in size. We assume that there will be pressures upon city governments to adopt certain kinds of decision-making processes when they reach a certain size. The indirect evidence for this is only the actual correlation of city size both with *conditions* of bureaucratization (increasing size of staff and amount of money spent) and with *measures* of bureaucratization itself. It seems unlikely that those cities which, in 1960, had a chief personnel officer or a civil service system always had one, regardless of their size. The variations in bureaucratization among cities of approximately equal sizes we attribute to variations in the local social structure and the dominance of particular political subcultures which define local government and political processes in different ways.

Just what do we mean by bureaucratization? We turn to this question.

The Meaning of Bureaucracy and Professionalism

Bureaucracy is related to and yet not identical with professionalism, centralization, specialization, and hierarchy. In American cities it is possible to regard several of these aspects of decision-making organization as part of a central trend toward bureaucratization, but their analytical independence requires brief discussion.

Bureaucratization means the elaboration of differentiated organizational units in a hierarchy, with appointed officials at the head. Professionalization (in an organization) means the appointment of technically trained experts to positions with a relatively high degree of autonomy and judgment held by the incumbent, with only ultimate judgment of performance by the organizational heads, not immediate day-by-day supervision. These two aspects of the increasing elaboration and complexity of the structure and functioning of an organization are associated if there are many specialized and immediate tasks to be performed which require both considerable training, technical skill, and a large staff. Bureaucratization exists without professionalization where there is a large staff performing relatively unskilled jobs (as in a large office of clerks, an assembly line, or an army). Professionalization exists without bureaucratization where there is a relatively small staff performing highly specialized tasks, such as a medical clinic (not a hospital), a university department, or a crew of building tradesmen.

Tensions between the two principles of organization develop when the two basic conditions leading to one or the other (size of staff leading to bureaucratization and specialized tasks leading to the hiring of professionals) are in conflict. Bureaucratic officials attempt to preserve the hierarchical principle by breaking the ties of their technical specialists to outside professional organizations, or by asserting the superiority of organizational claims over professional ones. As the size of the organization increases, so do these pressures. Conversely, technical specialists attempt to preserve the principle of autonomy as the technical requirements of the job increase by asserting the prior claims of the professional organization to define responsibility and standards.

To restate the central point, the key meaning of bureaucratization is specialization and structural differentiation: the performance of tasks by separate persons or organizational units consciously assigned those tasks and supervised in their performance by superiors. The essential meaning of professionalization is training, competence, and membership in a body of collegial equals who set standards of performance. A critical index of bureaucratization would be the number, elaboration and specificity of the rules governing the activities of individuals in an organization: who does what, when, and how. A critical index of professionalization would be the number of persons in the organization with specialized training which is the basis for their position in the organization and which justifies their membership in an external organization setting the requirements for performance of their task and governing the admission of persons to the position labeled by the professional title.

City governments, by and large, follow a middle path as they grow. They neither have such a large staff nor such imperatively coordinated tasks as to require strict hierarchical control, nor do they have such specialized and highly technical tasks as to require the hiring of a predominantly professional staff. Although there is some conflict between the administration and its staff over the relative autonomy of work, particularly among planners, traffic engineers, and other specialists, generally we can regard a middle-sized city government as following the path of increasing bureaucratization and professionalization simultaneously. We feel justified in treating the several indicators as measures of a single abstract continuum which we shall call "bureaucratization."

Although bureaucratization is frequently associated with centralization of decision-making authority, this is not necessarily the case. As functions become specialized, one part of the local government may become "centralized" in the sense that a set of officials are made responsible for a given set of decisions, but the total system may become more decentralized. Conversely, a mayor or city manager who consolidates power in his own hands is presiding over a centralized but not necessarily bureaucratized system. The sources of direction of separate agencies might be many: the mayor, the city council, the city manager, the school board. In a system with little executive centralization, sources of policy can be many and varied.

Also, in an urban area with many local governments, each of them might be highly bureaucratized, but the "metropolitan government" as a whole would be highly fragmented. Thus, such simple structural indices of bureaucratization as the number of decision-making units within a political system are not adequate in and of themselves. If the number of decision-making units were the criterion, then the more local government units within a metropolitan region, the more bureaucratized the regional government would be, and this seems to be a case we would want to exclude.

Sheer differentiation of decision locations is not an index of bureaucratization per se. Probably the establishing of, and the number of, *specialized* decision-making units within a single coordinated system is a key characteristic. Specialization (traffic, streets, health, welfare departments) is an important element in bureaucratization, not merely the proliferation of decision units with possibly overlapping jurisdictions.

The implications of this point, however, are that some degree of centralization and coordination is necessary to avoid overlapping and thus to achieve a true division of labor or functions. Probably an evaluation of the actual functioning of agencies would be necessary to assess these qualitative features of bureaucracies: the extent of coordination, control of function, and evaluation of performance.

The Process of Bureaucratization

The process of bureaucratization of urban government has not been systematically studied by any of the several subfields which might logically have dealt with the problem: community power, organizational theory, public administration, and "community" studies in sociology, although all of these perspectives are useful in a broader approach.

Studies of community power can locate the relative influence of administrators. Studies of bureaucratic organizations can locate the internal incentives for innovation and expansion. Studies of community life can locate the impact, upon neighborhood and other primary groups, of various bureaucratic decisions. But, the incomplete and open nature of a local community means that another analytical approach to the process of bureaucratization is necessary.

We hold that while there are indeed two "principles" of social organization which may conveniently be summarized as "bureaucratic" and "community," these two tendencies of social life should be thought of somewhat differently than is usual. Rather than postulating either a steady drift toward the bureaucratization of all social life, or a segmentation of society into separate spheres governed by fundamentally different principles of human relationships, rather than isolating a single organization out for internal analysis regardless of its environment, we believe that, particularly for studies of urban government, the two principles may usefully be seen as sets of solutions to problems which present persistent dilemmas for action. Precisely because there is great variation in the level of bureaucratization between cities, even those of similar size and objective situation, it seems clear that there is tension between the two principles of organization. The structural and cultural sources of the political processes leading to particular patterns in different types of cities are our chief concern. In this paper we deal only with the structural correlates of bureaucratization.

Problems of Measurement and Data

A number of indicators of bureaucratization are available, and we will discuss each of them briefly. Since we assume that professionalization is empirically closely related to bureaucratization among American cities, we will consider how each indicator measures both characteristics. The six indicators to be used are: form of government (manager vs. mayor-council), the level of development of a civil service system, the existence of a chief personnel officer, the number of planning department employees and planning expenditures, and the existence of a capital budget. Unfortunately, all of these are indirect measures of bureaucratization and professionalization, since we do not know from these data just how elaborate is the system of rules governing the behavior of employees, controlling the hierarchy of authority, and allocating resources within the organization. Nor do we know how many fully professionalized employees the city has, nor the nature of their training, autonomy, and orientation toward an external professional organization.

FORM OF GOVERNMENT

The city-manager form is a direct index of bureaucratization since the installation of a manager means that an official with hiring and firing powers has been appointed. Centralization of an organizational hierarchy has increased. The city-manager form is also a direct index of professionalization, since the manager usually now has specialized training, is probably a member of the International City Managers' Association, and is probably conscious of standards of performance besides those set by the local council.

Civil Service

The existence of a civil service system is an indirect indication of bureaucratization, since a stable system of hiring, promotion, and firing is likely to coexist with an established set of positions with defined jurisdictions and place in an organizational hierarchy.

Chief Personnel Officer

The existence of a chief personnel officer is a direct indication of bureaucratization, since a personnel officer is more likely to be necessary where there is a large staff and many specialized positions. It is also an indirect indication of professionalization, since such an officer himself represents an additional specialized function.

Planning Department Employees

The more planning department employees, the more likely the city is to devote resources to long-range consideration of the coordination of various city services and the impact upon the welfare of the city. Thus, this is a direct indication of professionalization, because such a task requires specialized knowledge.

Planning Expenditures

This is a parallel indicator to the number of planning department employees, indicating professionalization.

Capital Budget

The existence of a capital budget (and its length) is a direct indication of professionalization, like planning, because it requires a consideration of the growth of staff, the functions to be served in the future and how they are to be financed, and, therefore, specialized knowledge and probably a staff to plan the budget.

The mere existence of one of these indicators of bureaucratization of local government does not mean that any particular institution functions in a way which would normally be viewed as efficient and rational. The civil service may be shot through with favoritism, the capital budget ignored, the planning department recommendations spurned, the chief personnel officer the nephew of the mayor, the manager a home-town boy without any college education. We assume that this is not often the case.

It seems clear that precisely because a set of situational factors—the concerns of local leadership at any given time to push for a given decision vs. another one, if nothing else—that any given indicator of bureaucratization may or may not be present in a given city at a given time, regardless of whatever might be the "real" level of commitment to a professionalized and bureaucratized local government. Such modifications as a change of a capital budget from five to seven years, or the hiring of a few more planning employees because a large federal grant came through obviously may change the position of any particular city on a particular indicator. What we assume is that the pattern revealed by the several indicators is a systematic difference and not a random one.

It may well be true that each of these characteristics could be regarded as indicating an important subtype of local bureaucracy. That is, the presence or absence of a civil service system per se may well be an important indication of the qualitative character of a local bureaucracy. Or, possessing the city-manager form may well carry with it certain consequences quite independent of any of the other characteristics with which we are dealing. Again, this is a complication which is important but which we must neglect within our present scope.

There is no doubt some bias in the missing data; cities which are probably less bureaucratized were less likely to respond to the mailed questionnaire from the International City Managers' Association. Smaller cities and mayor-council cities were less likely to have reported the data. Probably, since these characteristics are themselves associated with bureaucratization (as will be seen), those cities which did send back their questionnaires are more highly bureaucratized than those which did not. This does not solve the problem of the characteristics of those who did not respond at all, but in any case the direction of bias is probably to inflate the estimate of bureaucratization for those cities which did respond, and to reduce the differences between them and other cities.

It will be noted that the years for which data were gathered differ for several of the variables. Data on the capital budget, for example, apply to 1964, while data on civil service coverage apply to 1962. (The Municipal Yearbook did not supply capital budget data in 1963 or 1964.) We assume that this bias has the effect of reducing any associations we find, since a later time of measurement will find more and more cities, regardless of their other characteristics, adopting a capital budget, since it becomes the "modern, progressive" way of running a city.

Unfortunately, we do not have quantitative data showing precisely the changes in the degree of bureaucratization in American cities, but only differences between cities at one point in time. This makes it impossible to differentiate between the effects of city size per se and changes in the level of expectation of bureaucratization regardless of city size. That is, we would expect that cities of the same size would be more bureaucratized in 1960 than they were in 1930 because of technical changes and differences in the level of expectation of performance of services.

The only characteristic that we do have data on concerns the form of government, and here the trend is clear that more and more cities, except for the very largest cities, have adopted the manager form. We would assume that the same has been the case for other aspects of bureaucratization: civil service, personnel officers, capital budgets, and planning development.[2]

The historically-relative character of indicators of a given complex structural phenomenon is quite clear in the case of the level of bureaucratization and professionalization of local governments. Over 90 percent of all local governments by 1962 had a planning board, for example, so that this characteristic no longer distinguishes one government from another in the way that it might have twenty years ago. We know very little about the sheer time order in which local governments adopt innovations let alone the conditions which lead to adoption. What we assume is that we have located a series of indicators which, in the 1960s and in the United States, measure the level of attainment of bureaucratization and professionalization. In England at the same time probably quite a different set of indicators for the same phenomenon would have to be chosen, but, if our theory about the conditions underlying bureaucratization is correct, the causes should be the same, even if the specific evidence of the consequences is different.

Bureaucratization in American Cities

In order to justify talking about the bureaucratization of the local government *as a whole*, we must show that (1) there are intercorrelations between the various indicators, so that we can justifiably talk about a movement in a general direction: larger staffs, numbers of employees in planning, the number of departments, the numbers of functions serviced, the complexity and time span of budgeting, etc. We are only justified in ranking total systems and inquiring about the *general* causes and consequences of more or less bureaucratized systems if such is the case.

Table 1 showed that employees and expenditures both increase with city size. These characteristic consequences of growth may be regarded as intervening variables which create direct pressures for bureaucratization, although the number of employees per capita has no independent influence upon bureaucratization. (Data will not be presented in table form to document this assertion, but there is no association between full-time employees per capita and any of the indicators of bureaucratization when city size is controlled, among cities between 25 and 250,000 population.) Either full-time employees per capita or city size itself could be used as a control for the objective external pressures toward bureaucratization. At this point, when we are dealing with all cities over 25,000 population in the United States, we shall use full-time employees per capita as a crude control for one objective condition of bureaucratization.

[2] See Daniel N. Gordon, "The Social Bases of Municipal Government," unpublished Ph.D. thesis, Department of Sociology, University of Wisconsin, 1967, for data on changes in form of government since 1933 and correlations with various social characteristics.

Table 2. Percent of cities with a full-time personnel officer (1962), by form of government (1958), full-time city employees per capita (1960) and proportion of employees under civil service (1962), all cities

Cities with a full-time personnel officer (Percent)	(N)	Form	Full-time Employees	Civil Service
			All Three "High"	
62	(76)	Manager	High	High
			Two "High"	
59	(68)	Mayor-council	High	High
51	(95)	Manager	Low	High
28	(50)	Manager	High	Low
36	(22)	Mayor-council	Low	High
35	(20)	Mayor-council	High	Low
25	(48)	Manager	Low	Low
			All Three "Low"	
15	(26)	Mayor-council	Low	Low
44	(405)	Total		

Effect parameters: civil service + 26, employees + 14, manager form + 5. See James S. Coleman, *Introduction to Mathematical Sociology* (New York: The Free Press, 1964), Chap. 6, for a discussion of effect parameters. Commission cities are excluded from this table. "High" full-time employees means nine or more city employees per capita population in October, 1960. "High" civil service means that all or most employees were covered by a civil service system in 1962, as reported in the 1963 *Municipal Yearbook* (Table VIII). Data on the personnel officer were obtained from the same source. Data for all variables were only available on 405 cities out of the 676 over 25,000 population. Of the 492 cities for which personnel data were available, 43 per cent had a full-time personnel officer.

The association of three conditions and indicators of bureaucratization with a fourth is shown in Table 2: form of government, the full-time employees of the city per capita, the scope of civil service coverage of city employees, and the presence of a full-time personnel officer. The effect parameters (average percentage differences) are all positive, indicating that all three factors are associated with the presence of a full-time personnel officer, but they differ in strength. Cities with all or most of their employees under civil service are more likely than cities without developed civil service coverage to have a full-time personnel officer, regardless of the size of their staffs or their governmental form. But, with one exception, cities with bigger staffs and professional managers are somewhat more likely to have a full-time personnel officer. Thus, 62 percent of the cities with a manager had more than nine city employees per capita and a developed civil service system and also had a full-time personnel officer compared to only 15 percent of the mayor-council cities with relatively smaller staffs per capita and lower civil service coverage.

One critical decision—which might be the hiring of a city manager—may imply a series of subsequent decisions in the same "direction": increasing the bureaucratization of city government. A city which fol-

Table 3. Percent of cities with more than four planning department employees (1964), by form of government (1958), full-time employees per capita (1960), full-time personnel officer (1962), and civil service coverage (1962), all cities

Cities with more than four planning employees (Percent)	(N)	Form of Government	Full-time Employees	Civil Service Coverage	Full-time Personnel Officer
			All Four "High"		
79	(43)	Manager	High	High	Yes
			Three "High"		
85	(46)	Manager	Low	High	Yes
77	(13)	Manager	High	Low	Yes
71	(28)	Mayor-council	High	High	Yes
			Two "High"		
43	(35)	Manager	Low	High	No
43	(28)	Manager	High	Low	No
38	(21)	Mayor-council	High	Low	No
			Three "Low"		
18	(27)	Manager	Low	Low	No
9	(11)	Mayor-council	Low	High	No
			All Four "Low"		
33	(12)	Mayor-council	Low	Low	No
56	(307)	Total			

See Table 2 for the measures of "High" and "Low." Only those categories of cities are included for which data were available on all five characteristics, and only those categories are given for which there were data on at least 10 cities, except for the total, which includes all cities. Missing data have biassed this table, since 73% of the 462 cities for which planning employment figures were available had more than four full-time employees, however, it is assumed that the relationships would not be reduced. Effect parameters were computed for those cells with more than 10 cities, and the results were as follows, with the number of comparisons possible in parentheses: effect of personnel officer + 31 (5), full-time employees + 13 (5), manager form of government + 7 (4), civil service coverage + 6 (5).

lowed a different initial path might institute a quite different set of organizational incentives, leading to continuous expansion and growth in a gradual series of stages, without the discontinuation of the other process. We have no evidence, unfortunately, on the stages at which cities acquire various professional specialties, nor the speed with which one innovation follows another as a city grows, but there is no reason to assume a slow and continuous pattern of change.

Table 3 shows the relationship of various combinations of five indicators of bureaucratization. All of the characteristics are positively related to the number of planning department employees. The more conditions for increased bureaucratization that are present (with minor exceptions), the more likely a city is to have more than four planning department employees. The fact that a full-time personnel officer is most closely associated with a larger planning staff has no easy explanation, but the general point can be made again that we may be dealing with a process

Table 4. Size of community and bureaucratization of local government, 676 cities

Index of Bureaucratization	Size of Community (000's)				
	25-50	50-100	100-250	250 and over	Total
Percent with a city manager	47 (366)	46 (180)	47 (79)	32 (50)	45 (675)
Percent with more than nine full-time city employees per capita	44 (356)	51 (180)	58 (79)	76 (51)	50 (666)
Percent with all or most employees under civil service	51 (307)	65 (147)	67 (70)	96 (45)	60 (569)
Percent with chief personnel officer	18 (252)	52 (136)	89 (61)	93 (43)	43 (492)
Percent with more than four full-time planning employees	26 (227)	61 (132)	100 (56)	100 (42)	52 (462)
Percent with more than $27,000 spent on planning	29 (252)	65 (137)	87 (53)	100 (44)	52 (494)
Percent with a capital budget	47 (193)	59 (141)	77 (60)	83 (46)	57 (540)

which is not smooth and continuous, but jerky and discontinuous. Once a certain level of size of staff and professional organization is reached, certain additional "decisions," such as the addition of certain types of professional specialists, are almost universal.

Because the sheer size of the city is so closely related to the pressures for bureaucratization of local government, we must deal with the problem of the effect of size in order to consider the possibility that the patterns we find are not simply a result of the fact that cities differ in size.

Size is closely correlated with level of bureaucratization as is shown in Table 4. We have already shown that the number of city employees per capita increases with city size, showing that there is probably a geometrical increase of the complexity of governmental functions as city size increases. Correspondingly, the larger the city, the more likely its employees are to be under civil service, to have a chief personnel officer, a larger planning department and expenditures (*and* expenditures per capita). Large cities are less likely to have city managers however, indicating that they are less likely to have professionalized certain functions.

The implication is that when we examine the association of various aspects of bureaucratization and professionalization within a certain size category of city, we have controlled for the major *structural* factors affecting the *general* level of bureaucratization; the number of city employees and the necessity for a minimum degree of organizational control of their activities (civil service, personnel officer, etc.). We have also controlled for at least one aspect of political culture: the general and "normal" level of the quality and quantity of services expected in the United States to be performed by a local government in the 1950s and 1960s. As Wood, Williams and others have shown, the "bundle" of services to be performed and the general level of expenditures for them are highly correlated with the size of the community.[3]

Conclusions

What are the implications of these findings about the systematic variations between U.S. cities in the level of bureaucratization of local government? Given these patterns, what consequences do they have for the functioning of decision making, the processes by which influence is gained and power exercised in the cities? The implications and consequences follow from our initial definition of the meaning of bureaucratization. The detailed studies of decision-making processes which would be necessary to prove these hypotheses are beyond our scope.

Cities with highly bureaucratized and professionalized local governments are probably more likely than cities which are less bureaucratized: (1) to have removed many decisions from the public arena for debate and popular influence to the hands of technicians; (2) to have formalized the channels for the raising of issues and demands from "outside" the government such as hearings and public meetings; (3) to have formalized the channels "within" the government for negotiations between departments over budgets, jurisdictions, and authority.

Note that we are avoiding any implication that one level of bureaucratization is more "democratic" than another. There is no a priori reason to assume that the formalized method of operation of a bureaucratized system is less (or more) open to organized influence which follows proper channels than is the informal mode of operation of a less bureaucratized system.

The level of bureaucratization is related to the exercise of power in the community in the sense that frequently the fruits of victory in a controversy are the institutionalization of a new function which then becomes a permanent part of the repertory of city services. Once a certain policy has been established, political "decisions" in the usual sense are no longer necessary and routine actions implement the policy. (Clearly the conditions under which policies are reopened for renewed debate are important to analyze, but we know that once established, few services are abolished.) Thus, the level of bureaucratization and the consequent scope of institutionalized and routine "decisions" is relevant when attempting to assess the distribution of political power at a given time. Many factors which might affect the outcome of political struggle over an issue may not be operating because the relevant actors, groups, and interests

---

[3] Population size alone accounted for 83 percent of the variation in the public expenditures of 64 middle-sized municipalities in New Jersey. Robert Wood, *1400 Governments* (New York: Anchor Books, 1964), pp. 39–40. The same finding is reported in a study of 238 local governments in Pennsylvania by William Oliver, Harold Herman, Charles S. Liebman, and Thomas R. Dye, *Suburban Differences and Metropolitan Policies* (Philadelphia: University of Pennsylvania Press, 1965), p. 92.

have removed themselves from the political arena after a previous victory.

Since both the absolute and relative size and complexity of the bureaucracy increases as cities grow, we may expect that its continuing growth will be initiated more and more from internal forces. That is, officials themselves, particularly as they become more professionalized, will attempt to expand the scope of services they perform and therefore the number of personnel they employ. This, in and of itself, may partly account for the increasing proportion of employees per capita as cities grow. While cities are small, the spur for the initial establishing of a department or service comes from "outside" the local government itself, from a citizen's group recommending that a park department be formed and the like. At a certain stage of growth the political system may become fregmented, with segments of the bureaucracy responding to particular outside constituencies, and the local legislature serving only to moderate or mediate conflicts which cannot be settled at any lower level. In this sense, those "laws" which can be passed without severe jurisdictional conflict will be "passed" at lower levels by administrative units. The factors which lead to jurisdictional conflict and therefore the shifting of a dispute to a higher level are beyond our scope here.

The effects of increasing size, whether of the community or of a bureaucratic organization itself, are not automatic. Conceptions of the proper functioning of the organization, or of the proper level and quality of services to be provided to the community, affect the behavior of decision makers: public leaders and organizational officials. These intervening processes are not easy to trace, but they clearly must exist and help to account for the close correlation between city size and the size of city staffs, between complexity of function and size of organization.

These conceptions or norms, which they are insofar as they constrain the behavior of leaders, probably vary in strength and scope from community to community. Persons with different party loyalties and political persuasions will hold different notions about the proper ends and means of local government activity.

The perspective of a *process* of bureaucratization which we have adopted here requires a final word on the relationship of local government to the dichotomy of "community" and "bureaucracy" in much sociological literature. A city cannot be defined as simply a community or a bureaucracy; the nature of many elements of its social organization combine elements of both, and in addition, as we have shown, communities are undergoing bureaucratization. Local governments fit neither the usual ideal-types of community (family, friendship group, neighborhood) nor bureaucracy (army, factory). Instead, the local government of a city exhibits contradictory principles at work. Its size is not so great that administrative decisions are necessarily invisible to interested and affected external constituencies. The urgency of its tasks is not so great as to create a great pressure to insulate its personnel from outside pressures in order to get the job done. Thus, the local government is under no tremendous constraints to become a full-fledged classic bureaucracy.

Conversely, there are important, and yet not dominant, elements of "community" in local government. Because, in small and middle-sized cities at least, particularly those with many aldermen, ward elections, and well-defined neighborhoods, whether their identification is based on ethnic, class, religious or racial grounds, there is a tendency to define the local government in personal and particularistic terms. Even in large cities, the "machine" was an attempt to respond in particularistic terms to needs and demands. The "machine" was seen as anachronistic or inappropriate precisely because it existed in large cities where informal mechanisms of help, cutting through the machinery of bureaucracy, were regarded as illegitimate, at least by groups holding certain political perspectives. In smaller communities the pressures for bureaucratization are not so great, and there can be greater bending of the "rules," if rules analogous to bureaucratic ones even exist.

Local government is thus subject to conflicting views of its very nature which stem from fundamental principles of social organization. Is it an instrument for the achievement of consensus, a repository for the common values of the community which define its tasks and its role? Or is it a task-oriented organization designed to achieve a set of technically definable tasks as efficiently and as cheaply as possible? The very fact that these questions can be raised and that no easy answer can be given, except "both," indicates that the structure and functioning of local government is ambiguous. We may therefore expect considerable conflict over its scope and role.

The contradictory principles of community and bureaucracy may now be redefined with special reference to the problem of local government. What we are dealing with are two sets of norms: one enjoining leaders, officials, and voters to behave *as if* the government were a "community," and another set enjoing them to behave *as if* it were a "bureaucracy." Conflicts in a community over local issues and decisions frequently take the form of struggles to *define the situation* as one appropriate for one set of norms over another. The victorious strategy will partly determine the outcome. *If* government is based on the principles of community, it should be informal, respond quickly to particularistic demands and needs, and be closely integrated with neighborhood, religious, ethnic, and other group demands for representation. *If* government is based on the principles of bureaucracy, it should be formalized, insulate itself from particularistic demands, and base itself upon criteria of rationality and efficiency which may be inconsistent with demands of particular ethnic or neighborhood groups.

By formulating the problem in this way, we avoid the need for defining exactly what a local government "is," nor do we have to decide in what spheres it "should" respond to particularistic appeals, in which it must remain aloof and unresponsive. Forces of change in the larger society—the growth of cities, technological and economic change, the centralization of many political functions—have an impact on this struggle, conditioning the arguments of leaders and the interests of groups, removing certain options from the debate, casting weight on one side or another. The level of bureaucratization is an important structural constraint upon the actions of leaders and voters, although the level itself is due in part to those actions.

Community Structure and Innovation: The Case of Urban Renewal*

MICHAEL AIKEN and ROBERT R. ALFORD

The search for determinants of public policy innovation in American cities has received little attention from social scientists. The controversy over "community power structure" focused almost entirely upon case studies of "who governs" in particular cities and barely at all upon the policy consequences of different configurations of power in the local community.[1] However, a number of comparative studies have appeared recently focusing upon such policy outputs as urban renewal, fluoridation, and desegregation. The data used in these studies, often rather crudely, indicate the concepts they allegedly represent. Such slippage between available data and theoretical constructs has resulted in the proliferation of diffuse explanations of public policy innovations and identical or even contradictory empirical indicators.

In this paper we shall review a number of theories of community policy innovation, examine some empirical findings about innovation

Reprinted from the *American Sociological Review* 35 (1970): 650–65. Copyright 1970 by the American Sociological Association. Reprinted by permission of the publisher.

* This research was supported in part by funds granted to the Institute for Research on Poverty at the University of Wisconsin by the Office of Economic Opportunity pursuant to the provisions of the Economic Opportunity Act of 1964. The conclusions are the sole responsibility of the authors. We are indebted to Terry N. Clark, Robert L. Crain, and Paul E. Mott for their detailed and helpful comments. We are grateful to the Institute for its research and administrative support, and to Elizabeth Balcer, Janet Jensen, and Ann Wallace for their competent and vital research assistance.

[1] Herbert Jacob and Michael Lipsky, "Outputs, Structure and Power: An Assessment of the Changes in the Study of State and Local Politics," *Journal of Politics* 30 (1968): 510–38; Robert R. Alford with the collaboration of Harry M. Scoble, *Bureaucracy and Participation: Political Cultures in Four Wisconsin Cities* (Chicago: Rand McNally, 1969); Michael Aiken, "The Distribution of Community Power: Structural Bases and Social Consequences," in *The Structure of Community Power: An Anthology*, Michael Aiken and Paul E. Mott, eds. (New York: Random House, 1970).

in urban renewal, and conclude by suggesting an alternative theory which conceives of the community as an interorganizational system. Parallel papers to this one analyze innovation in public housing and in poverty programs.[2]

The Nature of Community Innovation

Little attention has been given to innovation in communities, although they are continually introducing new ideas, activities, processes, and services. In the comparative perspective utilized here, we are interested not only in knowing those structures and processes in communities that are associated with the *adoption* of an innovation, but also with the *speed* of the innovation and the *level of output* or performance of the innovative activity. In particular, we are interested in identifying the underlying structural properties and community processes that explain why some communities moved quickly to enter the urban renewal program while others were either slow to innovate or have never participated at all in this federal program. At least five theories of innovation which are relevant to this question can be found in the recent social science literature. Nowhere have these various explanations of community innovation been brought together. In part this lack of theoretical integration is due to the diverse concepts used; what we consider to be innovation has also been called community decision making, community decision outcomes, and policy outputs.

Some Theories of Community Innovation

The five general hypotheses of community innovation are as follows:

(1) *Political Culture:* Cities with majorities holding "public-regarding" values are more innovative with respect to policies benefiting the community as a whole than cities dominated by groups with "private-regarding" values.[3]

(2) *Centralization of Formal Political Structure:* Cities with centralized administrative arrangements and a strong mayor, that is, cities with city manager or partisan mayor-council governmental structures, are more innovative.[4]

[2] Michael Aiken and Robert R. Alford, "Community Structure and Innovations: The Case of Public Housing," *American Political Science Review* 64 (1970), 843–64, and "Community Structure and the War on Poverty: Theoretical and Methodological Considerations," in *Studies in Political Ecology*, Mattei Dogan, ed. (Paris, 1970).

[3] Raymond E. Wolfinger and John Osgood Field, "Political Ethos and the Structure of City Government," *American Political Science Review* 60 (1966): 306–26; James Q. Wilson, "Innovation in Organization: Notes Toward a Theory," in *Approaches to Organizational Design*, James D. Thompson, ed. (Pittsburgh: University of Pittsburgh Press, 1966), pp. 193–218.

[4] Robert L. Crain, Elihu Katz, and Donald B. Rosenthal, *The Politics of Community Conflict: The Fluoridation Decision* (Indianapolis: Bobbs-Merrill, 1969); J. David Greenstone and Paul E. Peterson, "Reformers, Machines, and the War on Poverty," in *City Politics and Public Policy*, James Q. Wilson, ed. (New York: John Wiley, 1968), pp. 267–92.

(3) *Concentration or Diffusion of Community Power:* There are two aspects to this argument: concentration of systemic power[5] and diffusion of power through mass citizen participation.[6] In both cases the hypothesis is the same: the greater the concentration of power, the greater the degree of innovation.

(4) *Community Differentiation and Continuity:* Older and larger cities are more bureaucratic and consequently less receptive to policy innovations than younger and smaller cities.[7]

(5) *Community Integration:* Cities in which community integration breaks down or is extremely low have a lower probability of innovation or other collective actions. Consequently innovation should be highest in integrated communities.[8]

We have presented these five explanations separately because it is possible to conceive of them as five independent factors. However, one or more of these factors may be either spurious or intervening variables for the operation of another more fundamental factor, such as the sheer need for a program. Also, as we shall see, the indicators of the theoretical variables have been quite diverse, overlapping, and are sometimes used for quite different concepts. This diversity in the use of the same empirical indicators is partly a result of the great "distance" of the easily available quantitative indicators from the theoretical variables of greatest concern to most scholars.

Most of the data we use are no better, but we have the advantage of bringing together most of the various indicators used in the previous literature, as well as adding several measures which have the merit of being considerably closer to the theoretical variables to which they refer, although they have defects of their own.

Data and Methods

Urban renewal programs have been the most frequently studied aspect of public policy making in American cities in recent years. In the scholarly literature, the aspects studied have been diverse, including whether or not a program had reached a planning or execution stage in a given city, urban renewal expenditures, and the number of years a city took to enter the program. The problems which have led to its study include community power structure, the political ethos of the city, and the capa-

---

[5] Amos H. Hawley, "Community Power Structure and Urban Renewal Success," *American Journal of Sociology* 68 (1963): 422–31.

[6] Robert L. Crain and Donald B. Rosenthal, "Community Status as a Dimension of Local Decision-making," *American Sociological Review* 32 (1967): 970–84.

[7] Thomas R. Dye, "Urban School Segregation: A Comparative Analysis," *Urban Affairs Quarterly* 4 (1968): 141–65.

[8] James S. Coleman, *Community Conflict* (New York: Free Press, 1957); Maurice Pinard, "Structural Attachments and Political Support in Urban Politics: A Case of a Fluoridation Referendum," *American Journal of Sociology* 68 (1963): 513–26.

city of shrewd political leaders to generate support. (There seems to be little doubt that the main effect of the program has been to reduce the stock of low-cost housing, since the original legislation explicitly forbade local governments to use income from the sale of land to build new low-rent housing, and relatively few cities have built public housing with other funds, whether federal or nonfederal.)

The findings of this study are based on the universe of 582 American cities in 1960 with the following characteristics: (1) incorporated urban places of size 25,000 population or more, (2) location in states that had state enabling legislation prior to 1958 permitting cities to enter the urban renewal program, and (3) cities in existence in 1950. Of the 676 incorporated urban places of size 25,000 population or more in 1960, 74 are omitted because they were located in 11 states which did not get enabling legislation until 1958 or later (Idaho, Montana, New Mexico, Utah, and Wyoming), or which had highly restrictive enabling legislation, reversals of decision, or no enabling legislation at all as of June 30, 1966, or had a combination of these (Florida, Louisiana, Maryland, Mississippi, Oklahoma, and South Carolina). Another 20 cities that did not exist in 1950 are also omitted.

Since the cities that are included in this study constitute the population of all eligible cities of 25,000 or more, one may question the appropriateness of using statistical tests of significance. The use of statistical tests of significance when the data do not meet the assumptions of those tests (as in the case here) has been a continual problem for sociologists.[9] Even though we have exhausted all the units in the universe, there is still the possibility that the observations were produced by errors of measurement. In addition, because we have no other criteria, we utilize significance tests to distinguish between negligible and appreciable correlations, although we recognize that this test, strictly speaking, is not one of statistical significance, nor does it provide assurance of substantive significance.[10]

The various measures of community structure were taken from the *Municipal Year Books* of 1963 and 1964, the 1950 Census of Housing, and the 1960 Census of Population. Information about the innovation measure, i.e., participation in the urban renewal program, was taken from the *Urban Renewal Directory: June 30, 1966,* Department of Housing and Urban Development, U.S. Government, Washington, D.C., 1966.

We shall ignore in this paper changes in federal urban renewal legislation from 1949 on, although such changes may alter the incentives of different cities to obtain such resources. The original 1949 act required that 55%, or more, of the project area be residential either before or after renewal in order to qualify for federal assistance. This requirement was gradually eased by subsequent legislation. Undoubtedly the incentives of

---

[9] David Gold, "Statistical Tests and Substantive Significance," *American Sociologist* 4 (1969): 42–46; Denton E. Morrison and Ramon E. Henzel, "Significance Tests Reconsidered," *American Sociologist* 4 (1969): 131–39; Robert F. Winch and Donald T. Campbell, "Proof? No. Evidence? Yes. The Significance of Tests of Significance," *American Sociologist* 4 (1969): 140–43.

[10] Gold, "Statistical Tests and Substantive Significance."

local industrialists, real estate investors, and local groups of residents to initiate, support, or oppose urban renewal were altered by these changes, and therefore the probabilities of a given program being carried through, but we do not have the data to investigate this possibility.[11]

We measure the presence or absence of innovation by whether or not a community has ever participated in the urban renewal program. Of the 582 cities in the analysis here, 372 (or 64%) had innovated an urban renewal program, although 32 of these later dropped out of the program. Among the remaining 340 cities, 187 had completed at least one urban renewal program as of June 30, 1966; 130 others had reached the execution stage of the program; and the other 23 were still in planning. There were 210 communities that had never innovated an urban renewal program.

The speed of community innovation is measured by the number of years after 1949 before the city entered the urban renewal program. This is similar to a measure developed by Straits in his critique of Hawley's work,[12] although Straits used 1951 to calculate the speed with which a community entered the urban renewal program. The distribution of this variable was slightly skewed toward the lower end of the distribution, but skewness was not of sufficient magnitude to warrant a transformation of this variable.[13]

Since some cities were located in states that did not enact enabling legislation until after 1949, another measure of speed in innovation was constructed: the number of years it took the city to enter the program after state enabling legislation was enacted.

The level of output measure is the number of urban renewal dollars reserved per capita as of June 30, 1966. This measure is similar to those used by Wolfinger and Field and Clark, although not strictly comparable.[14] The measure used here was computed by determining the total number of dollars reserved for all urban renewal projects as of June 30, 1966, and then standardizing this figure by the population size, thus yielding a dollar amount reserved per capita for all urban renewal projects. This distribution was highly skewed toward the upper end of the scale so that a natural logarithm transformation of this variable (which was approximately normally distributed) was used in the computation of correlation coefficients.

The relationships among these measures of innovation are quite high, as shown in Table 1, although not so high as to make them equivalent measures. Nor are they logically the same.

[11] Francis T. Ventre, "Local Initiatives in Urban Industrial Development," *Urban Affairs Quarterly* 2 (1966): 53–67.

[12] Hawley, "Community Power Structure."

[13] Bruce C. Straits, "Community Adoption and Implementation of Urban Renewal," *American Journal of Sociology* 71 (1965): 77–82.

[14] Wolfinger and Field, "Political Ethos," and Terry N. Clark, "Community Structure, Decision-making, Budget Expenditures, and Urban Renewal in 51 American Communities," *American Sociological Review* 33 (1968): 576–93.

Table 1. Relationships among indicators of community innovation

	Presence of Innovation	Speed of Innovation		Level of Output
	Presence of Urban Renewal Program	Number of Years After 1949 Before Entering the Urban Renewal Program	Number of Years It Took After State Enabling Legislation Was Present	Number of Dollars Reserved Per Capita (Natural Log)
Presence of participation in the urban renewal program		—.69***	—.62***	.86***
Number of years after 1949 before the community entered the urban renewal program			.88***	—.80***
Number of years it took after state enabling legislation was present				—.71***
Number of urban renewal dollars reserved per capita (natural logarithm)				

*** $p < .001$.

Note: The number of cases is 582 except for the proportion of registrants voting, which was 370. The presence of urban renewal programs of one or another form of political structure was treated as a "dummy" (binary) variable for purposes of correlations and regressions in subsequent analysis. The natural logarithm of four highly skewed variables was used for correlation analysis, in order to produce an approximately normal distribution.

Findings

A preliminary test of the several different theories of community innovation is found in Table 2. We have classified each indicator under only one theoretical concept, although it may have been used to measure more than one concept.

First, *political culture*. There is some question about the authorship of this theory. Wilson has written that he and Banfield[15] never developed the theory that Wolfinger and Field attributed to them.[16] In spite of the question of exactly whose theory this is, we still include it here as an alternative theory of community innovation. According to this theory, a low proportion of foreign born in the city's population, a small proportion of Catholics, and a high proportion of the population that is middle class have been regarded as indicators of a likelihood that a community is composed of a majority of individuals and groups holding "public-regarding" values. The consequence should be a high level of performance on policies which do not directly benefit the persons voting. While

---

[15] James Q. Wilson and Edward C. Banfield, Communication to the Editor, *American Political Science Review* 60 (1966): 998–99.
[16] Wolfinger and Field, "Political Ethos."

it can be argued that urban renewal directly benefits downtown businessmen rather than the poor, at least one study has tentatively accepted the appropriateness of measuring the consequence of public-regarding values by urban renewal outputs.[17]

In addition, we have added the percent voting for the Democratic candidate for president in 1964 as an additional indicator of the presence of a population holding private-regarding values. Cities that are heavily Democratic (as measured by the Democratic vote in 1964) are likely to be highly ethnic ($r = .32$), have many Catholics (as measured by the proportion of school children in private schools, $r = .23$), and have many working-class persons ($r = .22$). This is surely a more direct political measure than any of these demographic characteristics. Thus, if the political culture theory works, we should find that Democratic communities are less likely to have urban renewal.

Table 2 shows that of the 16 relationships between the four indicators of political culture and four indicators of community innovativeness, only one is in the expected direction. Most of the relationships between percent in private schools, median family income, and percent voting Democratic in 1964 are in the opposite of the predicted direction. In the case of percent of foreign stock, one of the indicators of speed of innovation is significant and in the predicted direction, but the others have no relationship with this measure of political culture. The political culture theory is thus (with one exception) not supported by any of the indicators and is contradicted by an additional one—percent voting Democratic in 1964.

Second, *centralization of formal political structure*. This argument has two aspects, one based on centralization of formal power, the second related to the political culture argument. In the first place, the thesis in the literature is that the more centralized the formal political structure, the more innovative it should be and the more capable it is of policy outputs.[18] There is some disagreement on what the indicators of centralization should be, since the usual conception of "reform" government is that its structural devices—the city-manager form, nonpartisan elections, at-large elections, small city councils—were intended to centralize power in the hands of a small executive and a professional manager at the same time that potential power in the hands of citizen groups was fragmented and dispersed by removing the instruments of the political party and the ward organization. On the other hand, some have argued that strong political parties were the most effective device for centralizing power. But in either case there was agreement that administrative or political centralization should lead to a greater capability for innovation and greater policy outputs, regardless of the institutional form which centralization took.

The second aspect of political structure is related to the political culture argument, because it has been argued that reform political insti-

---

[17] Wolfinger and Field, "Political Ethos."
[18] Crain et al., *Politics of Community Conflict*.

Table 2. Relationships between indicators of innovation, speed, and outputs and various measures of community structure and culture

Theoretical Categories and Empirical Indicators	Presence of Innovation — Presence of Urban Renewal Program	Speed of Innovation — Number of Years After 1949 Before Entering the Urban Renewal Program	Speed of Innovation — Number of Years It Took After State Enabling Legislation Was Present	Level of Output — Number of Dollars Reserved Per Capita (Natural Log)
Political Culture				
Percent of native population of foreign or mixed parentage[a]	−.01	−.04	.10*	.02
Percent of elementary school children in private schools[a]	.06	−.08*	.05	.08*
Median family income[a]	−.33***	.26***	.37***	−.29***
Percent voting Democratic, 1964[b]	.09*	−.13***	−.10*	.08*
Political Structure				
Presence of a city-manager form of government[c]	−.16***	.14***	.05	−.14***
Presence of nonpartisan elections[c]	−.14***	.14***	.04	−.18***
Percent of city council elected at large[c]	−.04	−.04	−.10*	−.02
Number of members of the city council[c]	.16***	−.13***	−.04	.14***
Centralization of Community Power				
MPO ratio[a]	−.30***	.29***	.21***	−.32***
Citizen Participation				
Percent of adult population with four years of high school education[a]	−.38***	.36***	.32***	−.38***
Percent of registrants voting[d]	.18***	−.20***	−.10*	.18***
Community Differentiation and Continuity				
Age of the city (census year city reached 10,000 population)[a]	−.48***	.54***	.46***	−.48***
Size of the city (natural logarithm)	.33***	−.49***	−.49***	.33***
Community Integration				
Percent unemployed[a]	.23***	−.25***	−.24***	.25***
Percent migrant[a]	−.23***	.25***	.12***	−.24***
Poverty				
Percent of housing dilapidated, 1950[a]	.20***	−.14***	−.28***	.13***
Percent of families with less than $3,000 income per year, 1959[a]	.26***	−.22***	−.34***	.21***
Percent adult with less than five years education (natural logarithm)	.36***	−.36***	−.40***	.34***
Percent 14–17 year olds in school[a]	−.33***	.29***	.35***	−.30***
Percent of population that is nonwhite (natural logarithm)	.37***	−.44***	−.46***	.39***

Table 2. *Notes*

* $p < .05$.
** $p < .01$.
*** $p < .001$.

Sources of the data are as follow:

a U.S. Census of Population, 1960.

b *County and City Data Book*, 1967. The county Democratic vote in 1960 was coded as follows: 60% or more Republican, 55–59% Republican, 50–54% Republican, 50–52% Democratic, 53–58% Democratic, 59% or more Democratic, to create six nearly equal groups. The two cities for which data were not available (Washington, D. C., and New York) were assigned to the mean category.

c *The Municipal Year Book*, 1963 (International City Managers' Association, 1963). Four or five cities with missing data on one or more of the measures of political structure were assigned to the mean category. The categories for the number of members of the city council were collapsed as follows: 3–4, 5, 6, 7, 8, 9, 10–19, 20–29, 30–50.

d Data are from a survey taken by Eugene C. Lee, Director, Institute of Governmental Studies, University of California at Berkeley. For further details and analysis of the voting data, see Robert R. Alford and Eugene C. Lee, "Voting Turnout in American Cities," *American Political Science Review* 62 (1968): 796–813.

tutions were part of the array of policies favored by groups with public-regarding values, and presumably the instruments of such values should produce consequences similar to that of sheer demographic composition.

In most respects, the predictions of innovation which would be made by either the administrative centralization or political cultural interpretation of the indicators of political structure would be the same. The prediction is ambiguous only in the case of the form of election. If nonpartisan elections are regarded as decentralized, then, according to this line of reasoning, they should be associated with less innovation. But if they are regarded as instruments of groups with public-regarding values, then nonpartisan elections should be associated with more innovation.

Table 2 shows that the relationships of urban renewal innovation and output with political structure contradict the centralization of formal political structure hypothesis completely. Manager, nonpartisan, at-large, small council cities are with one exception either *less* likely to innovate, or there is no relationship. The relationship between at-large elections and the modified speed of innovation measure is in the predicted direction, but this is the only one. The centralization argument is also contradicted, unless one wishes to accept the argument that partisan elections lead to administrative centralization, and therefore greater innovation. The data support the latter proposition.

Third, *concentration or diffusion of community power*. We refer here to two related explanations of community structure and consequences for the distribution of power: the ecological or systemic theory which sees power as a property of dominant institutions, and a mass participation theory which argues that those structural features which reduce mass participation will, as a consequence, concentrate power. We cannot test with our data a third, an "elite-participation" hypothesis, which argues that the smaller the number of elite participants and the more homogeneous their interests, the more centralized the power structure and the greater the policy outputs.[19] While these theories differ in the feature of community organization which they single out as the critical measure or cause of concentration of power, they share the general assumption that the fewer the actors, whether mass or elite, and the more those actors represent dominant institutions, the more concentrated the power. The further inference that concentrated power leads to greater innovation is not always explicitly stated, but we believe that it is a justified extension of the theories.

In his study of urban renewal, Hawley argued that communities with a greater concentration of power will have a high probability of success in any collective action affecting the welfare of the whole.[20] Hawley used participation in urban renewal programs as his measure of a successful collective action, and he used the MPO ratio (the proportion of the employed civilian labor force that are managers, proprietors, or officials) as his measure of the degree of concentration of community power. He reasoned that system power is exercised through managerial functions, and that those functions can be more readily coordinated if there are few positions performing those functions relative to the number of all other positions.

The data in Table 2 support Hawley's empirical prediction: cities with high MPO ratios are less likely to innovate in all respects that we have measured than cities with low MPO ratios.

Other data drawn from case studies raise questions about the meaning of the MPO ratio, however. Aiken classified 31 case studies of community power on a four-point scale of concentration of power ranging from "monolithic" to "pyramidal" to "pluralistic" to "dispersed power" arrangements, using qualitative judgments of the number of groups involved in major issues in the community as the measure of degree of dispersion of power.[21] The results show a tendency for less centralized communities to have higher levels of innovation and outputs, and for cities having high MPO ratios to have higher concentrations of power than cities with low MPO ratios. Another study of 51 cities found that the greater the decentralization of community power as measured by the number of persons involved in decision making in four issues (urban renewal, air pollution, poverty programs, and the selection of the mayor), the greater the number of urban renewal dollars per capita secured from the federal government.[22]

Thus, cities with high MPO ratios are found to have little urban renewal, as Hawley predicted, but few active power centers, which finding appears to be inconsistent with his thesis. But since centralization for Hawley referred to the distribution of systemic power while the meaning of centralization here refers to elite participation, this does not mean that Hawley's thesis is necessarily wrong. Systemic power may be highly

---

[19] Clark, "Community Structure, Decision-making."
[20] Hawley, "Community Power Structure."
[21] Aiken, "Distribution of Community Power."
[22] Clark, "Community Structure, Decision-making."

dispersed, yet few actors or power centers may be active. Still, such an inconsistency does raise interesting questions about the meaning of centralization and about an adequate explanation for this inconsistency.

The second aspect of the concentration of power theory refers to citizen participation. Crain and Rosenthal argued that the higher the level of education in a community, the higher the political participation, which in turn leads to higher conflict, then stalemate, and consequently less innovation in urban renewal.[23] Their hypothesis links a high level of educational attainment with a low degree of community innovation and output, and posits an intervening process of heightened political participation and consequent community conflict and blockage. The relationship between the percent of adults with a high school education and the four measures of innovation supports this hypothesis (Table 2).

While the empirical relationships between these variables are clear, the meaning of this educational variable and the intervening process may be questioned. Does a high level of educational attainment in a community reflect the presence of many well-educated, relatively affluent persons? Or does it reflect merely the absence of a poor population and less urban decay? Do cities with many well-educated persons have greater citizen participation and consequently more stalemate and inaction, or do they simply have less of an apparent need for urban renewal? Among cities over 25,000 population, the correlations between median education and the upper extremes—percent of adults who have completed college and percent of families with incomes of $10,000 or more per year—are .62 and .63 respectively. But cities with high median education also have fewer adults with less than five years of education ($r = -.77$), fewer families with incomes of less than $3,000 per year ($r = -.53$), less housing built before 1929 ($r = -.48$), and less dilapidated housing ($r = -.39$). The interpretation of educational level clearly depends on which end of the stratification scale one wants to emphasize, the degree of poverty, low educational attainment and poor housing stock, or the degree to which an articulate middle class is present.

In the analysis of 31 case studies of community power it was found that there were fewer power centers active in cities with high educational levels than in those with low educational levels, although the relationship was not a strong one.[24] Similarly, Clark found a positive relationship between the median educational level of a city and the degree of centralization (i.e., fewer elites participating in the four decision areas examined).[25] If centralization refers to the degree of elite participation, middle-class cities appear to be more centralized than working-class cities. Even if this is true, it is still possible that citizen participation is greater in highly educated cities, thus accounting for less innovation in urban renewal. They, like we, lack direct data on the key intervening variable of participation. Unfortunately, adequate data on political par-

[23] Crain and Rosenthal, "Community Status."
[24] Aiken, "Distribution of Community Power."
[25] Clark, "Community Structure, Decision-making."

ticipation do not exist for a large sample of cities. If voting turnout can be regarded as a crude indicator, a recent study has shown that better-educated cities have lower voting turnout than less well educated cities.[26] We find among the 381 cities in our study for which data on voting turnout are available that *higher* voting turnout is associated with greater innovation, although the relationship is not a strong one (see Table 2).

Our empirical relationships between level of education and innovation in urban renewal are quite consistent with the findings of Crain and Rosenthal, although empirical indicators vary slightly. Middle-class cities have less urban renewal, but they also apparently have *less* elite participation. If centralization means elite participation, then we find that there is less urban renewal in centralized cities. If centralization means citizen participation (as measured by educational levels) or dispersed systemic power (as measured by the MPO ratio), then we find that there is less urban renewal in decentralized systems. We do not mean to suggest that the well-reasoned theories of Hawley and Crain and Rosenthal are incorrect; we don't have the evidence to demonstrate that. But we do wish to point out the various usages of the term centralization in the literature on comparative community decision making and to call attention to an inconsistency in conclusions about the relationship between centralization of power and innovation. Clearly, greater conceptual refinement and additional research using more direct measures of mass participation and distribution of systemic power will be necessary to unravel the meaning of an inconsistency such as this.

Fourth, *community differentiation and continuity*. As noted at the outset, the few articles that have used the variables of age and size of cities have disagreed about their interpretation, arguing on the one hand that older and larger cities would be more rigid, more set in their ways, more complex and, therefore, more incapable of action, and, on the other hand, that such cities should be more adaptable, more experienced, more flexible.[27]

The data of Table 2 show that older and larger cities are in fact more likely than younger and smaller cities to have innovation in urban renewal. The correlation coefficients of these two characteristics with the various innovation measures are the largest of any in Table 2. Whether or not age and size are merely a reflection of a high level of structural degradation of the housing and building stock, and hence only a reflection of need for urban redevelopment, is a question which will be addressed later.

Fifth, *community integration*. The argument here is that more highly integrated communities, i.e., those with highly developed networks of communication and contact among social groups, should suffer less from paralyzing conflict in the case of a new issue requiring decision, because, on the one hand, channels of communication to work out

[26] Alford and Lee, "Voting Turnout."

[27] Dye, "Urban School Segregation," and Lawrence B. Mohr, "Determinants of Innovation in Organization," *American Political Science Review* 63 (1969): 111–26.

compromises exist and, on the other hand, isolated factions standing fast on their own positions would not be present.[28] The indicators used for community integration are quite diverse, and include several already mentioned under other headings, but two additional variables—the unemployment level in the community and the amount of migration— are also included in this argument. Pinard's thesis is that high unemployment levels will produce disintegration of community life by reducing attachments to community institutions resulting in high conflict levels and low innovation capabilities. High levels of city growth and in-migration reduce integration because they disrupt long-standing networks of communication and interchange between the organizations comprising the community. He also argues that racial and ethnic diversity and large city size indicate low community integration and that high political participation indicates the bringing into the political system of those least attached to the community, therefore those most likely to oppose innovation.

Table 2 shows that in the case of urban renewal these theoretical expectations, with one exception, are not supported. As already seen, highly ethnic and large cities are *more* likely to innovate, as are cities with high voting turnout. And cities with high unemployment are more likely to have urban renewal, contradicting the hypothesis. Cities with high levels of in-migration have less urban renewal, in accordance with the hypothesis.

Few of the hypothesized relationships drawn from the literature are borne out completely; in the case of those that were supported, we have noted some inconsistencies in the meaning of the concept of centralization. Our main empirical findings are that older and larger cities and those with low levels of education and income, high unemployment, fewer managers and officials, and low levels of in-migration and growth are more innovative.

The first question which these results raise is whether or not a community's innovation in urban renewal is simply a function of the poor quality of the housing stock, the deterioration of the central business district, and the generally lower levels of economic growth in older cities. To answer this question, we have included some additional measures of poverty and housing conditions in Table 2. Cities with more dilapidated housing in 1950, more poor families, fewer well-educated families, and more nonwhites were far more likely to have entered the urban renewal program, entered it faster, and have higher levels of participation in the program.

Given the strong and consistent relationships between city size and these need measures and innovation in urban renewal, we may pose the question whether or not many of the previously discussed relationships, regardless of the concepts they were alleged to represent, are not simply functions of a high degree of community need for urban renewal. To answer this question, we computed a series of partial correlations between

---

[28] Pinard, "Structural Attachments and Political Support."

Table 3. Partial correlations between community characteristics and speed of innovation (after enabling legislation) and level of output, controlling for size of community and percent of housing dilapidated in 1950

	Speed of Innovation (After Enabling Legislation)	Log N Urban Renewal Dollars Per Capita
Political Culture		
Percent of native population of foreign or mixed parentage	−.04	.09
Percent of elementary school children in private schools	−.02	.11**
Median family income	.23***	−.24**
Percent in the county voting Democratic, 1964	−.03	.02
Political Structure		
Presence of a city-manager form of government	.01	−.12**
Presence of nonpartisan elections	.04	−.18***
Percent of city council elected at large	−.10*	−.03
Number of members of the city council	.09*	.06
Concentration and Diffusion of Community power		
MPO ratio	.14***	−.28**
Percent of adult population with four years' high school education	.21***	−.34***
Community Continuity		
Age of city (year city reached 10,000 population [log n])	.26***	−.38***
Community Integration		
Percent unemployed	−.14**	.21***
Percent migrant	.08*	−.21***
Poverty and Need		
Percent of families with less than $3,000 income per year	−.19***	.18***
Percent of adults with less than five years' education (log n)	−.24***	.28***
Percent 14–17 year olds in school	.17***	−.22***
Percent population that is nonwhite (log n)	−.25***	.29***

* $p < .05$.
** $p < .01$.
*** $p < .001$.

two measures of innovation and most of the variables in Table 2, controlling for city size and level of dilapidated housing. As shown in Table 3, the relationships between the variables that were strongly related to the innovation measures in Table 2 are still relatively strong when city size and the amount of dilapidated housing are partialed out.

Stepwise, regression analyses which introduced the five "need" measures were first performed, and showed that approximately 18% of the variance was accounted for by those measures. Additional variables, each accounting for at least 1% of the variance, were age of city, city size, percent migrant, percent foreign stock, and median family income (listed in order of selection).

A few words are necessary on the relationships between both the inde-

Table 4. Means of indicators of innovation in urban renewal within region

Region[a]	Number of Cities	Presence of Urban Renewal Program	Number of Years After 1949 Before Community Entered Urban Renewal Program	Number of Years It Took After State Enabling Legislation Was Present	Number of Dollars Reserved Per Capita (Natural Log)
Northeast	164	82%	9.1	8.9	7.25
South	191	62	11.5	8.0	5.18
Midwest	219	48	13.5	12.7	3.86
Far West	102	36	13.9	13.0	3.10
All Cities	676	58	11.9	10.6	4.97

[a] The states included in each region are as follows:

Northeast: Maine, New Hampshire, Vermont, Massachusetts, Connecticut, Rhode Island, New York, New Jersey, Pennsylvania, Maryland, Delaware, and District of Columbia.

South: Texas, Oklahoma, Kansas, Missouri, Arkansas, Louisiana, Alabama, Mississippi, Florida, Georgia, North Carolina, South Carolina, Virginia, West Virginia, Kentucky, and Tennessee.

Midwest: Ohio, Indiana, Illinois, Michigan, Wisconsin, Minesota, Iowa, North Dakota, South Dakota, Nebraska, Montana, Idaho, Colorado, Utah, Wyoming, Arizona, and New Mexico.

Far West: California, Oregon, Washington, Nevada, Alaska, and Hawaii.

pendent and dependent variables and the regional location of a city. Cities in the Northeast are most likely to have urban renewal, followed in order by cities in the South, the Midwest, and the Far West, as shown in Table 4. Similarly, Northeastern cities were faster in applying for and more successful in obtaining money for urban renewal. But these cities are also likely to be older, poorer, and have higher levels of ethnicity and out-migration. The question can be raised whether all of these relationships are accounted for by regional location of a city.

Although we cannot present the data in detail, the major findings hold up when they are examined within the four regions. Age and size of city are closely related to all four measures of innovation in all four regions, as are education, income, MPO ratio, and nonwhite composition, with only a few exceptions. Almost all of the original relationships that were low remain low in all four regions, except for a few cells for which we have only ad hoc explanations. Political structure, Democratic vote, and voting turnout are significantly associated with innovation only in the Far West, for example. Our general conclusion, however, is that the findings previously discussed are, with some exceptions, also true even within regions in spite of strong regional variations in innovation rates.[29]

We have also examined the correlation coefficients between the various independent variables and the speed and output measures among the 372 cities that had ever entered the urban renewal program. This is a very conservative procedure since it excludes cities that never innovated in urban renewal. We would expect the correlations between the various independent variables and the speed and output measures of innovation to be attenuated. While the size of the correlations among this subset of 372 cities that have ever innovated is indeed reduced, the major findings

---

[29] Aiken and Alford, "Community Structure and Innovation."

remain intact. Age, size, nonwhite composition, low income and low education are still related in the same direction to the speed and output measures. Evidently the same factors that contribute to innovation in the first place also affect the speed with which innovating cities enter the urban renewal program and their level of outputs in the program.

But even if we know which are the best predictors or that our results are not simply a function of the size and level of need, regional variations, or results produced by including noninnovating cities in our study, we still do not know why and how some communities enter the urban renewal program and others do not. The mind is not set at rest by such findings. In the first place the relationships are not strong. In the second place the condition of housing or the age of a city does not tell us anything about the intervening processes which enabled some cities to displace their blacks for new businesses or expensive appartments while others did not use urban renewal in this way.

Structural Differentiation and Community Innovation

Let us start negatively by reviewing the rejected explanations. Global properties of the political ethos of majorities and integration seemed to fare most poorly. While the zero-order predictions of Hawley and Crain and Rosenthal were as predicted, we have shown that even these relationships can be removed by partialing procedures. That is, hypotheses referring to properties of the city as a whole rather than properties of groups or organizations making up that city seemed (1) to use concepts most distant from the available data and (2) to be supported most weakly by the data. If anything, the data point in the opposite direction. Cities that appear to be heterogeneous, differentiated, and fragmented—as indicated by ethnicity, a large working class, nonwhite composition, size, and the qualitative data on centralization (elite participation) in the works of Clark and Aiken—are most likely to have innovated in urban renewal.[30] The same studies show that the more groups and actors participating in current decisions, the higher is the level of innovation and outputs.

Additional and more directly relevant data support the proposition that the more differentiated the organizational structure of a city, the more innovative it will be. A more direct measure of organizational complexity than simply city size would be a count of the number of organizations of various types which play some role in community life. We have data on three such types of organizations—manufacturing firms, banks, and trade unions—although only for a subsample of cities in each case. Unfortunately, we lack data on other more crucial types of organizations such as political parties, voluntary associations or the local government.

Not only the sheer number of organizations may be important, but also the number having sufficient resources to affect critically the course of community innovation. For this reason we have chosen the number of

[30] Clark, "Community Structure, Decision-making," and Aiken, "Distribution of Community Power."

Table 5. Differentiation of economic structure and innovation in urban renewal in American cities[a]

	Manufacturing — Number of Establishments of Size 100 or More	Banking — Number of Independent Banks with Assets of Fifty Million Dollars or More	Unionization — Percent of Plant Workers Unionized, among All Industries — North	Unionization — South
Innovation				
Presence of urban renewal	.27***	.33***	.22*	.33**
Speed of Innovation				
Number of years after 1949 it took the city to enter the urban renewal program	−.42***	−.46***	−.15	−.48***
Number of years it took after state enabling legislation was present	−.33***	−.37***	−.03	−.03
Outputs				
Log N urban renewal dollars reserved per capita	.32***	.36***	.24**	.40**
	N = (217)	(217)	(77)	(35)

[a] Source: Manufacturing and banking data are available for the 217 nonsuburban cities in the size range 25,000 to 250,000 population which had 20% or more of their labor force in manufacturing in 1960. The unionization of munufacturing establishments is avaliable for 84 metropolitan areas, which provide an estimate of unionization in 112 cities within them. See Michael Aiken, "Economic Concentration and Community Innovation," unpublished manuscript, 1969, for details on the construction of the measures. The banking data were taken from *Polk's Bank Directory* (Nashville: R. L. Polk and Co., March, 1966). The data on unions are drawn from Bulletin No. 1465–86, Bureau of Labor Statistics, U.S. Department of Labor, Washington, D.C., October, 1966, titled *Wages and Related Benefits: Part I, 84 Metoropolitan Areas, 1965–66*. The measure is the approximate percent of all plant workers employed in establishments in which a union contract covered a majority of workers during the period July, 1964 to June, 1966. We have assigned the degree of unionization in the SMSA to the urban place as the best estimate we have of the unionization of the city itself.

* $p < .05$.
** $p < .01$.
*** $p < .001$.

manufacturing establishments with 100 or more employees and the number of independent banks with assets of at least fifty million dollars as our measures of organizational complexity and differentiation. Unfortunately, the unionization data cannot be treated in exactly the same way. But because larger firms are more likely to be unionized and because the data include all establishments in which a majority of the plant workers are unionized, we believe that this measure is an appropriate indicator of the organizational complexity of a community.

These data relating structural differentiation and community innovation are presented in Table 5. Because the level and character of unionization can be presumed to be different in the North and the South, the data for that variable are presented by region. The results are consistent with our expectations. The more manufacturing establishments, the more independent banks, and the more unionized plants that a city has, the more innovative it is.

These measures of structural differentiation can be regarded as ways of spelling out more precisely what it means to be a large city as far as capacity to innovate is concerned. Large cities have a greater diversity of social organizations, and they also have greater innovation.

An Alternative Explanation

Because we find none of the previously discussed theories completely satisfactory, we here propose one approach that seems to be more consistent with the previous findings. Our alternative explanation of the findings can be only a suggestion since we do not have the empirical data to test directly our ideas. Therefore, we shall only suggest here some of the concepts that appear to us at this time to be most relevant in explaining innovation in such decision-areas as urban renewal, public housing, and the war on poverty.

Our tentative alternative explanation is that such innovations are a product of the nature and state of interorganizational networks in communities.[31] Such networks are properties of community systems that have developed historically through the interaction of organizational units and their leaders. If the population of a community is relatively stable, these interorganizational networks are not likely to be disrupted by the continuous influx of new citizens and organizations, and thus greater potential exists for increasing their capacity for coordination over time.

The degree of historical continuity in a community structure—especially as it affects interorganizational networks—may aslo influence innovation. Presumably older cities have had a longer time for existing organizations to work out patterns of interactions, alliances, factions, or coalitions. In such communities the state of knowledge in the community system about the orientations, needs, and probable reactions to varying proposals for community action is likely to be quite high, thus increasing the probability of developing a sufficiently high level of coordination in order to implement successfully a community innovation.

The degree of structural differentiation and complexity of a community may also influence innovation for two reasons. First, larger cities are likely to have more organizations devoted to specific kinds of decision-areas—i.e., more likely to have a redevelopment agency, a housing agency, a community action agency, a city development agency for Model Cities, welfare councils, and other community decision organizations. Such organizations are likely to have larger, more specialized, and more professional staffs to provide the technical, administrative, and political knowledge required to innovate successfully, not only within their organizations, but also in the activation of interorganizational relationships and estab-

---

[31] Herman Turk, "Interorganizational Networks in Urban Society: Initial Perspective and Comparative Research," *American Sociological Review* 35 (1970): 1–19.

lishment of critical coalitions.[32] Secondly, it is precisely in the larger, more structurally differentiated communities that coalitions that can implement an innovation will be easiest to establish. If we assume that only a limited number of organizational units need to be mobilized to bring about a successful innovation, then it follows that in large, highly differentiated communities a lower proportion of the available organizations will participate in such decisions, and that there will be wider latitude in selecting organizations for these critical coalitions. In other words, the "issue arena" involved in the innovation will require the participation of only a few of the organizations that exist in the community system. In one sense, this proposition is simply a spelling out of what is meant by "structural differentiation" or "functional specialization." The more highly differentiated or specialized a community system, the higher the proportion of decisions that are likely to be made by subsystems and the less likely the entire system will be activated on most issues.

The extent to which the interorganizational field is "turbulent" may also influence innovation.[33] Where many people are moving out of the city, the existing historically developed network of organizational relationships may be relatively undisturbed, except insofar as out-migration indicates an economic or perhaps political crisis which existing institutions cannot handle. Conversely, where many people are moving in, bringing with them different ideas about the appropriate functions of local government, and perhaps creating demands for new services, newly established organizations may be severely limited since they are less likely to be in an organizational network which can aid in achieving an adequate level of coordination for a proposed community innovation.

We thus suggest that three properties—structural differentiation, the accumulation of experience and information, and the stability and extensiveness of interorganizational networks—may contribute to the capacity of a community to innovate. Let us turn to more concrete concepts and hypotheses that might be consistent with this particular approach.

Community systems can be conceived of as interorganizational fields in which the basic interaction units are *centers of power*. A center of power can be defined as an organization which possesses a high degree of autonomy, resources, and cohesion. The linking mechanisms among centers of power in a community system we call *interfaces*.[34] Interfaces are not only the current set of interorganizational relationships in the community, but more importantly include the historical accumulation of knowledge and experience among various centers of power. An *issue arena* is the organization set of centers of power which must be activated on a given issue in order to effectuate a decision.[35]

[32] Mohr, "Determinants of Innovation."

[33] Shirley Terreberry, "The Evolution of Organizational Environments," *Administrative Science Quarterly* 12 (1968): 590–613.

[34] Paul E. Mott, "Configurations of Power," in *The Structure of Community Power: An Anthology*, Michael Aiken and Paul E. Mott, eds. (New York: Random House, 1970).

[35] William Evan, "The Organization-set: Toward a Theory of Interorganizational Relations," in *Approaches to Organizational Design*, James D. Thompson, ed. (Pittsburgh: University of Pittsburgh Press, 1966), pp. 173–91.

We hypothesize that the greater the number of centers of power in a community and the more pervasive and encompassing the interfaces, the higher the probability of innovation in a given issue arena. In other words, the more choice among acting units in the system—centers of power—and the greater the state of information about organizational actors, the higher the probability that a minimum coalition can be formed. For many issues this will mean the creation of an organization whose specific task is the implementation of the decision to innovate. Warren refers to these as "community decision organizations," and he cites community action agencies, housing authorities, welfare councils, health departments as examples.[36] The community decision organization is a special type of center of power whose mission is to supervise the planning, coordination, and delivery of the innovated activity. The professional staffs of such organizations are likely to generate further innovations.

The structural conditions in the community that lead to the introduction of an innovation in a given activity—organizational differentiation and historical continuity—may not be the factors that are most conducive to high levels of performance by community decision organizations. Once the innovation has been introduced, the community decision organization may seek to develop relatively tightly controlled relationships with cooperating organizations in their issue arena and thus gain legitimacy for an exclusive mandate from other community decision organizations. If so, communities with high levels of performance in various community action activities may well be those in which relatively autonomous issue arenas have emerged. It may be that the structures of relationships within such subsystems are indeed "centralized" in the sense of a given organization having strong control over units within that issue arena. If this is true, it would suggest that Hawley's thesis may be appropriate if a community subsystem is taken as the unit of analysis.

It is possible, however, that this model is only applicable to decisions for which the major actors are organizations. To the extent that private citizens are mobilized on a given decision—such as in the case of fluoridation—this model may not be appropriate, or at least it may be incomplete.

What we have suggested is a two-stage process in which the overall state of a community system may be most important for understanding the community's propensity for innovation across a wide spectrum of issues, but that the appropriate analytic unit for understanding specific innovations, as well as performance in such innovations, is a subsystem of a community in which the central actor is the community decision organization. Our data do not permit us to test the validity of assertions such as these; that would require a completely different type of comparative study. But this particular approach appears to us to be as consistent with the data presented in this paper as any of the theories we have examined, if not more so.

---

[36] Roland L. Warren, "Interaction of Community Decision Organizations: Some Basic Concepts and Needed Research," *Social Service Review* 41 (1967): 261–70; and "The Interorganizational Field as a Focus for Investigation," *Administrative Science Quarterly* 12 (1967): 396–419.

The Political Economy of the Future

ROBERT C. WOOD

The Systems within the Sector

... The most significant fact about the governments of the New York Region circa 1960 is not the size of the public budgets, the number of dollars allocated or about to be allocated to one program or another, or the trends in these budgets and allocations. The most significant fact is that two different types of political systems rule the public sector today—the local governments and the Regional enterprises.

The inference to be drawn from this finding is that these systems, by the attitudes of the participants, the nature of the political processes, and the rules of the political game, strengthen the economic trends in being. They leave most of the important decisions for Regional development to the private marketplace. They work in ways which by and large encourage firms and households to continue "doing what comes naturally."

To be sure, the two systems arrive at their positions of negative influence by quite separate routes. That system . . . subsumed under the title of "local government"—the units of general jurisdiction and their satellites, the small special-purpose districts—is ineffective in the aggregate principally because its parts tend to cancel one another out. The system of quasi-governmental agencies, the Authorities and public corporations with programs which leap over municipal boundary lines, buttresses the marketplace more as a matter of conscious design. In this instance considerations of institutional survival often tend toward programs which accelerate trends already underway. But the net effect remains the same: public policy rarely seems to be the initiating force in the pattern of population settlement or economic growth.

There is nothing mysterious, of course, about why this vacuum in public policy occurs. For all their frantic bustlings with economic devel-

Reprinted by permission of the publishers from Robert C. Wood, *1400 Governments* (Cambridge, Mass.: Harvard University Press), Copyright, 1961, by the Regional Plan Association, Inc.

opment programs, land-use controls, and building regulations, each local government, even that of New York City, commands only a small portion of the Region's territory. As each strives to preserve its own local identity, doctrines of municipal mercantilism become natural lines of action. Indeed they are close to being the only politically palatable policies so long as both a desire for high quality urban services *and* continued independence make up a common municipal credo. Yet, from the point of view of the Region, no common policy emerges from the welter of elaborately and individually concocted strategies of manipulation and maneuver. Instead, there is only a number of options from which businessmen and households can choose.

In a different way, but just as understandably, the present development of agencies with more or less Regional responsibilities makes public direction of economic growth difficult. In the oligopolistic sphere of the transportation giants, the half-way house of water politics, and in the complex realm of intergovernmental housing activities, the program most likely to succeed is the one that supports—not contradicts—the marketplace. Success seems to smile on the transport agencies that favor the auto, the housing project that reclaims a potentially profitable downtown site, the water resources program which responds to a present need rather than anticipating—and helping shape—the future pattern of development. Though these agencies are concerned with questions of over-all Regional policy with a vengeance, typically they ride with, rather than oppose, the main currents in the private sector.

It is these characteristics of the political systems that allow us to discount the programs and policies of local governments so heavily. So long as the individual strategies of individual municipalities are condemned to frustration because of the sheer number of their neighbors, so long as prudence dictates that Regional institutions abet the economic forces already at work, public programs and public policies are of little consequence. Costs of urban government may continue to rise, but they will not substantially influence the preference patterns of families and locational choices of entrepreneurs. The most stringent policies of land-use control or the most ardent wooing of industries will not in the end determine the broad pattern of settlement. While these systems continue, the economist is safe in basing his projections on a consideration of the economic factors involved in Regional growth.

Checklist for a Revolution

But will be political systems continue to function in 1970 or 1980 or 1985 as they have today? Is it plausible to expect that . . . changes in living and working patterns . . . will take place while political styles remain unaffected? Already, in Dade County, Florida, one metropolitan area in the United States has effected a comprehensive structural reorganization and there are more modest but nonetheless significant reforms in other metropolitan centers. Already, one distinguished scholar of urban affairs speaks of "a vast and growing dissatisfaction with life in and around the great cities" and suggests that popular action is impending.[1] Within the New York Region itself in recent years, new governmental agencies have been established, new procedures for intergovernmental collaboration have developed, and new proposals for more fundamental rearrangements have been put forward. With such apparent signals of impending change flying, is it conceivable that twenty-five years will pass without the emergence of a new ideology and structure of public bodies, equipped with new capacities and motivations to intervene in the affairs of the private sector? In short, is not the gravest danger in sketching the Region of the future that of underestimating—or even ignoring—the prospects of revolution?

This sort of proposition is a difficult one to tackle—but it is not an impossible one. It is difficult because the question is not how much government but what kind of government, and in this instance the projection of trends "as they are" may confuse rather than clarify the issue. But the proposition remains manageable, for there is nothing inherently unpredictable about the process of radical change. We are not called upon to contemplate a disorderly or violent future for the New York Region; we are not involved in the business of forecasting municipal socialism or conjuring up visions of irate citizens marching on City Hall. We are asked instead to consider whether certain major stresses and strains in the public sector will require transformations in political habits and major new governmental arrangements—not marginal changes but changes of the character not seen since the boroughs of New York City formed a more perfect union or the Port of New York Authority was established.

Conceived in these terms, the inquiry becomes both a familiar and a limited one. It is familiar because we are covering ground for the New York Region which has been carefully examined elsewhere before in the 100-odd studies of the conditions requiring governmental reorganization in metropolitan areas which have been authorized since World War II. So the situation in New York has strong parallels to Miami and Toronto where reorganizations were put into effect and to St. Louis and Cleveland where they were rejected.

The inquiry is limited, because three specific stresses are involved in the New York situation. We are concerned first with the capacity of the present systems to remain financially solvent given the pattern of population movement and economic change. . . . Second, we need to make a judgment about the ability of the systems to improve service levels, at least at a rate approximating that since World War II, against the background of new public demands and new expectations of government. Finally, we have to evaluate the sporadic displays of public dissatisfaction over the ways the Region is developing and judge how serious is the inclination for widespread public intervention.

If we can establish a plausible case that the present systems can handle these problems, then our prognosis will be against a local revolution. For

[1] Luther Gulick, *Metro: Changing Problems and Lines of Attack* (Washington, 1957).

our presumption is that the governments in the New York Region will continue doing business as usual unless there is compelling evidence that a breakdown is at hand. Ideological satisfaction, historical lethargy, and the calculus of politics are on the side of the status quo. Prudent politicians, committed to the present system as "going concerns" and uneasy at the uncertainties of change, will, we expect, make minimal—not maximum—adjustments.

The Burning Issues:
(1) The Case for Municipal Bankruptcy

By all odds, the most widely publicized basis for expecting dramatic changes in the structure of the Region's governments and the reallocation of duties and responsibility is the one built upon the so-called "gaslight government" thesis. The bare bones of this position are that the revenue base of local government is hopelessly antiquated, narrow, inefficient, and inadequate. Local revenues—so the argument runs—are far less sensitive to changes in income or production than are federal or state taxes. Particularly the property tax fails to expand its yield proportionately with other revenues, and yet the structure of local government is such that other tax sources are even less politically or administratively feasible. As a consequence, the Region's governments are rapidly approaching the point where they cannot provide even the additional services required by population growth or the extension of urban settlement. With such a rigid tax base they face fiscal disaster—unless there occurs a major overhaul, at least in the revenue system and more likely in the formal structure of government.

In one sense, this argument is only a Regional variation of a national analysis: a conviction that the Region's plight is symptomatic of nationwide conditions. Otto Eckstein, for example, projecting net cash expenditures of all state and local governments in the United States to 1968 on the bases of "past policy decisions and the interplay of political and economic forces," arrives at a "medium projection" in current dollars of $53.7 billion, in comparison with the 1958 total of $36.2 billion. On the assumption that present revenue rates and sources will remain unchanged, he forecasts a state and local deficit of $3.4 billion by 1968—a ten-year increase of $1.7 billion. Eckstein believes that, if conditions of inflation intensify, the situation will become even worse, for "property tax assessments notoriously lag behind value changes; gasoline and other specific taxes also lag; only income and general sales taxes may have a better than proportionate response." Even without inflation, an average increase in tax rates of 8 percent would be required between 1958 and 1963 to erase the deficit.[2]

But, if local governments everywhere are headed for deficit spending,

---

[2] Otto Eckstein, *Trends in Public Expenditures in the Next Decade*, Supplementary Paper of the Committee for Economic Development (New York, 1959).

their prospects for borrowing the money they need also seem dim. Paralleling Eckstein's estimates of total expenditures and revenue for the future, Harry L. Severson has projected new construction costs, program by program, for the next decade. He arrives at a capital outlay total for state and local governments in 1968 of $25.2 billion, and estimates the new state and local bond offerings of that year at $16.3.[3] Both of those figures are more than double the 1958 levels. But even as the rate or volume of borrowing increases, the position of these governments in the security market grows worse. Fiscal experts attribute this partly to the depressant effect that expanded offerings would have on the market. Another reason is that the tax-exemption proviso of local bonds is no longer the drawing card it once was. "The natural size of the market has been narrowing while the demand for funds has been broadening. State and local governments have had to bargain away most of the advantages of tax exemptions to investors. Prospects for an increased interest rate, greater difficulty in securing investors in the marketing of general obligation bonds seem to compound the financial troubles of the local unit. The lone investor with the large income who was forced to state and local purchases in order to reserve some of his earnings from the National Treasury no longer is sufficient to handle the volume of offerings now current. The relative bargaining position of borrower and lender has consequently shifted and major reforms seem necessary if this source of finance is to prove adequate to the demands ahead."[4]

At the level of the New York Metropolitan Region, this national analysis is, by the testimony of many observers, doubled in spades. Not since the twenties, for example, has New York City been able to receive a clean bill of financial health from any of the numerous state or municipal investigating commissions. Typically, the City is usually characterized as operating in a financial strait jacket, with a tax base that cannot meet even the requirements of normal growth. So, the Temporary Commission on the Fiscal Affairs of the State Government concluded in 1955 that, by 1961, the City would require $511 million more than in the 1954–55 budget and that only about one-half of the increase could be received from the existing tax levies.[5] (As it turned out, the predictions came true three years before the 1961 target date.) Continuing the tradition, the Commission on Governmental Operations of the City of New York, established in 1959, observed that between 1949 and 1958 the City's total operating costs increased by almost 82 percent while the property tax base estimated at market value expanded by only 56 percent and the

---

[3] Harry L. Severson, "The Rising Volume of Municipal Bonds," *The Daily Bond Buyer* (June 10, 1958). This article provides a summary of his analysis. Severson has prepared an extensive review and series of projections for private circulation.

[4] Roland I. Robinson, "Postwar Market for State and Local Government Securities," manuscript for National Bureau of Economic Research, dated April, 1957.

[5] Temporary Commission on the Fiscal Affairs of State Government, *Report*, Vol. II (Albany, 1955), p. 644.

residents' personal income after income tax withholdings rose by only 23 percent.[6]

The City's capital outlay program is similarly in tight circumstances. In 1958 the Planning Commission set the capital requirements for the City at $300 million annually for a "barely minimum capital program." An adequate program over the next ten years, in the Commission's judgment, would call for a yearly expenditure of $380 million and even this would only "permit reasonable progress in meeting our real needs without frills. It makes no allowance for increased costs and it would not permit any major additional transit expenses." In contrast the actual capital expenditure had not exceeded $200 million in any postwar year to 1958 and is not budgeted to go much higher in the years immediately ahead.[7]

The largest city in the Region is not the only one that appears, on the surface, to have reached the limits of its revenue yields. Surveying in 1959 the postwar experience of the Region's suburban government, Merrill Folsom reports a growing concern over the present level of taxation among officials and residents; cries of "strangulation" as "the real estate tax burden is being shifted from the urban industrial areas to the new homes of commuters"; and statements that "taxes are becoming overwhelming." Within affluent Westchester County, where real estate levies increased from $61.5 to $136.7 million between 1948 and 1958, Folsom calculated that at current levels, an average property owner's lifetime taxes on real estate will be $7,710.[8]

Less impressionistically, Samuel F. Thomas supplements Folsom's finding, focusing on the extraordinary growth in school expenditures in Nassau County. Between 1945 and 1954, Thomas reports, school operating expenditures rose over 300 percent and total school expenditures went up 657 percent. In the one year between 1953–54 and 1954–55 the school operating expenditures rose by one third, leaving Thomas to suggest "that the tax burden on the real estate owner in Nassau County is greater and is increasing at a faster pace than the tax burden on the property owner in New York City."[9]

Perhaps the bluntest warning of tax insufficiency in New York has come from New York State's Commissioner of Education, James E. Allen, Jr. Anticipating necessary educational outlays in New York in 1965 at double their 1958 level, Allen estimates that—even having made "liberal allowances for the growth of real property valuation" in the meantime—

---

[6] Commission on Governmental Operations of the City of New York, *Interim Report* (Feb. 1, 1960), p. 80.

[7] City of New York, Planning Commission, *Capital Budget Message* (New York, 1957), p. 5.

[8] Merrill Folsom, "Taxes in the Suburbs Heading Up As Demand for Services Keeps Increasing," *New York Times* (Oct. 1, 1959), p. 7.

[9] Samuel F. Thomas, *New York City: Its Expenditure and Revenue Patterns* (mimeographed, 1958), pp. 58–59.

local property tax rates would have to increase by about 40 percent to finance new school budgets. In his judgment "the real estate tax will not suffice for meeting the educational burdens of the years immediately ahead."[10]

The same cries of tax crises echo with special intensity in New Jersey. With a much heavier dependence on the property tax, the Garden State has doubled the amount so levied between 1948 and 1958. The New Jersey Commission on State Tax Policy in its 1958 report concludes, "The policy of no new taxes has succeeded only in part. Its success has been limited largely to the legislative halls. Its effect may well have been to commit New Jersey to the support of its governmental services primarily from the property tax to the point of no return."[11]

Paper Tigers in Public Finance

But what precisely is "the point of no return" in estimating the capacity of a tax system? One is not disposed to ignore steadily rising tax rates nor prophecies of disasters when issued by responsible observers. Nonetheless, the minor and often underemphasized premise of the municipal bankruptcy argument is that there is somewhere an economic or political peril point beyond which taxes cannot go without the system collapsing. Specifically there is the notion that Eckstein's 8 percent increase in effective taxes (that is, tax levels expressed as a percentage of tax base, either income or market property value) is very hard to come by in the world of practical affairs.

Yet, actually, the facts do not bear out this contention. Once expenditure and revenue trends are laid along trends in economic growth, more than a little sunshine breaks through the gloom. On a national basis in 1958, after a decade of dramatic growth in absolute terms, total expenditures of local governments amounted to 5.8 percent of the gross national product—about the same as in 1927. State and local capital expenditures in the same period closely paralleled earlier experience; they totaled 2.4 percent of the gross national product in 1955 as contrasted to 2.1 percent in 1927.[12]

Nor do the years ahead appear to place substantially more drastic burdens on the economy. Eckstein's projections of expenditures assume that state and local expenditures will move in the 1958–1968 period from 8.3 percent of the gross national product to 8.6 percent—certainly not an extraordinary rise.[13] Making similar forecasts, Dick Netzer arrives at a

---

[10] James E. Allen, Jr., Address to the Columbia University Conference on Problems of Large School Districts (mimeographed, March 17, 1959).

[11] State of New Jersey, Commission on State Tax Policy, *Ninth Report* (Trenton, 1958), p. XIX.

[12] Jesse Burkhead, "Metropolitan Area Budget Structures and Their Significance for Expenditures," a paper delivered at the 52nd Annual Conference of the National Tax Association, Houston, Texas, Oct. 28, 1959.

[13] Eckstein, *Trends in Public Expenditures*, p. 9.

1970 "moderate" projection in the range of between 8.4 and 8.9 percent of the gross national product.[14] His "substantial" projection—the highest range of expenditures which he believes possible—is between 10 and 10.6 percent. Other analyses project a 1970 state–local ratio of expenditures to gross national product at approximately 10 percent.[15]

When we move to the most accurate indicators of "available" revenues —real property valuations and tax rates expressed as a percentage of market value—the desperate straits of local fiscal capacity seem even less desperate. Despite the persuasive logical arguments to the contrary, nationwide the property tax has proven far from sluggish in recent years. Netzer estimates that between 1946 and 1957 the percentage change in the property tax base for all state and local governments was about 151 percent, an increase just about equal to that of the gross national product. During the same period, the increase in the average effective tax rate —as a proportion of value—has been about 5 percent, and between 1946 and 1952 the effective tax rates across the country appear actually to have declined.[16]

Once again, the evidence which can be assembled on a Regional basis supports a conclusion that the experience of the New York Metropolitan Region parallels that of the nation. As a proportion of personal income, total local government *expenditures* rose between 1945 and 1955 from 5.9 percent to 9 percent for the total Region, from 5.7 percent to 10.3 percent for New York City, from 7.0 to 9.3 percent for other New York governments and from 5.9 percent to 6.4 percent for New Jersey units. No dramatic signs of upheaval in local *revenue* burdens appeared. As Table 1 indicates, total property tax levies show no sharply rising trend relative to personal income outside New York City. Further, our investigations in New York State indicate that total local property taxes as a percentage of market value declined between 1950 and 1955 an average of 30 percent for the governments in the counties outside New York City. A further indication of the "water" remaining in the existing tax structure is the fact that in 1951 the average ratio of the assessed valuation to market value for the New Jersey counties of the Region was 33.1 percent and in 1957 was 28.7 percent.[17] Throughout a decade of substantial population changes and pent-up demands for public services spilling over from the war years, New Jersey has maintained its policy of "no new taxes" because it extracted over one-half billion dollars in additional revenue from the taxes it already had.

It is true that local school taxes on real property rose considerably, in absolute terms, an average of 121 percent between 1950 and 1955.[18] But

[14] Dick Netzer, "The Outlook for Fiscal Needs and Resources of State and Local Governments," *Proceedings of the American Economic Association* (1958): 317–27.
[15] Burkhead, "Metropolitan Area Budget Structures."
[16] Netzer, "Outlook for Fiscal Needs and Resources."
[17] State of New Jersey, *Ninth Report*, p. 3.
[18] These figures are from a series constructed by the New York Metropolitan Region Study from reports by the Comptroller of the State of New York and by the New Jersey Department of the Treasury.

Table 1. Total property tax revenue of local governments compared with personal income[a] of population, New York metropolitan region[b]

	Personal income (millions)	Local property taxes (millions)	Property taxes as percentage of income
Region			
1945	$20,287	$ 619	3.05
1950	27,876	998	3.58
1955	35,766	1,495	4.17
New York City			
1945	13,124	300	2.28
1950	16,247	541	3.32
1955	18,663	763	4.08
Other New York counties			
1945	2,412	112	4.64
1950	4,328	161	3.71
1955	6,814	305	4.47
New Jersey counties			
1945	4,751	207	4.35
1950	7,301	296	4.05
1955	10,289	427	4.15

[a] Personal income figures for 1945 and 1950 were interpolated from New York Metropolitan Region Study estimates for 1939, 1947, and 1955.

[b] Excluding Fairfield County, Connecticut, for which figures are not available.

when these school taxes are shown as a percentage of personal income and of market value of property (where these figures were available), the increase is not so sharp. Here the New York experience again approximated that of the nation: local school taxes doubled, but in the relatively low range of from 1.5 to 3.0 percent of personal income.

In summary, these figures suggest that however intense the spending pressures in the Region's public sector generated by urbanization and growth since World War II may appear for the Region as a whole, they have certainly not brought about a massive diversion of income or capital to public purposes. More important, in an economic sense (except possibly for a long-term shift in consumer expenditures away from housing expenditures and a consequent slowing down in the accumulation of taxable property values) the resilience of public revenue does not seem as low as is often supposed. For the "gaps" between projected expenditures and projected revenues, more often than not in the postwar period, have been filled by an increase in revenue rather than a reduction in expenditures, demonstrating an elasticity in taxes not suspected when the trends of expenditures and revenues are extrapolated independently of one another. In the end, the case for municipal bankruptcy rests on the incapacity of the political process to divert funds to public policy—not on "an objective economic constraint to taxes . . . or a measurable limit on the fraction of economic activity that a community may wish to channel through the public sector."[19]

[19] Burkhead, "Metropolitan Area Budget Structures."

But this supposed political incapacity has not shown itself in the New York Metropolitan Region. In New York City, beginning with the complete reorganization of grants-in-aid under the Moore Plan in 1946, continuing in the state's uniform reassessment of local property values, and extending to Governor Rockefeller's proposal to equip the local school districts with general powers of taxation, again and again the size of the revenue structure has been expanded.[20] Less dramatically, New Jersey has moved in the same direction: first, by a grant-in-aid breakthrough so far as education is concerned; second, by the business earnings tax in 1958; third, by the court rulings on assessments which in effect have doubled the taxing capacity of all local jurisdictions. When these state actions are coupled with the adoption of local sales and nuisance taxes at the county and municipal level, and with much heavier rates of borrowing, it is clear that over-all the political process has displayed few signs of incapacity to adjust. Simultaneously, it has indicated little disposition to undergo comprehensive or fundamental structural or financial reform.

It is quite true that this picture of the Regional public sector as a whole does not fit equally well all parts of the Region. On a relative basis, not only New York City but the older municipalities in the inlying New Jersey counties have experienced conditions of increasing stringency. In the six years between 1951 and 1957, Jersey City, Newark, Elizabeth, Paterson, Bayonne, and Hoboken have all faced increased tax rates against a background of tax bases which were either rising much more slowly or actually declining. These six registered changes of between 2.2 percent and 45.9 percent in the local property tax rate per thousand dollars in full market value. In the case of Hoboken and Bayonne, where the increases were 45.9 percent and 12.2 percent respectively, these changes were accompanied by absolute losses in both assessed and market value. Clearly, these cities have not found the last few years easy going.

Yet these municipalities still seem more the exception than the rule—there is little evidence that the division between the "haves" and the "have-nots" in other parts of the Region grows worse. On the contrary, what little evidence can be assembled hints at an opposite process underway. When New York towns were compared in the estimated per capita full market value of taxable property for the years 1945, 1950, and 1955, no trend toward greater disparities among the governments' revenue base was detectable. Although there is an increasing spread in the values of these series (as indicated in the increase in the standard deviation from $1180 in 1945 to $2350 in 1955), the degree of dispersion relative to their average level remains roughly the same.[21]

Very probably even the absolute increase in the ranges of these values reflects more the Regionwide growth in property holdings and the impact of inflation than any tendency toward an increasing "clustering" of values. One can reason from this pattern that, though differences in residential

---

[20] On the latest New York consideration of a major tax reform see *New York Times* accounts of Governor Rockefeller's 1960 proposals, Jan. 8, 1960.

[21] Note 18, above.

values among localities continue to grow, the process of commercial and industrial diffusion works in the opposite direction. New shopping centers and new industrial plants leaven the sprawl of comparatively low-value residential settlement in Bergen, Rockland, and Suffolk Counties to offer tax relief to beleaguered officials.

Clearly we are on tenuous ground either in forecasting that the older cities will muddle through or that the respective positions of the "haves" and "have-nots" will stay about the same. For one thing, a ten-year time is too short to determine reliably what is happening to the spread in municipal tax bases. For another, . . . municipalities *try* very hard to acquire that kind of residential and industrial government which returns more in taxes than it costs in public services, and intent becomes entangled with effect. Undoubtedly once a government scores an initial success in this strategy a snowballing tendency may get underway—for it is easier for "them that has" not only to "get" but to get more. Still there are few signs, as we have seen, that these intentions are generally matched by deeds. To the contrary, a gradual bunching of effective tax rates is underway, a leveling out in the per capita differences in respective tax bases. As another volume in this Study has pointed out: "The scope for variation in the tax levels of different areas contained within a single state is narrowing. More and more of the total tax bill is coming to be represented by state and federal taxes, correspondingly less of it by local taxes . . . on top of this, the leveling of population densities in the Region of the future may well add to the general equalization of local tax rates."[22]

The Burning Issues: (2) The Demand for Services

If one can feel sanguine about the future supply of public monies in the Region, what other pressures might drive the governments to radical reform? Paradoxically enough, the very fact that public budgets *can* be balanced is often taken as a distress signal. The second major indictment of the present systems is that expenditures are set now and in the future at far too low a level. Malnutrition, not galloping consumption, according to this argument, is the fatal ailment of the public sector.

This is by no means a new argument in the United States, but it is an especially fashionable one right now. Its main thrust is that the American economy suffers from underspending so far as social investment and services are concerned; that national prosperity depends on channeling more resources to the support of government. Or, in one of the more pungent phrases of its advocates, the present mechanisms for allocating resources between the public and private sectors pay too much attention to "private wants" and not enough to "public needs."[23]

---

[22] Edgar M. Hoover and Raymond Vernon, *Anatomy of a Metropolis* (Garden City, New York: Doubleday Anchor Books, 1962), p. 55.

[23] Francis Bator, *The Question of Government Spending: Public Needs vs. Private Wants* (New York, 1960).

One can catch a sense of what the New Spenders regard as appropriate expenditure levels by reviewing the "needs" established by professional specialists in the main public programs. Writing in 1955, and concerned with projecting government expenditures to 1960, Willie Kilpatrick and Robert Drury attributed past changes in expenditures to such relatively impersonal and typical forces as prices, population growth, age distribution, income, and urbanization. Looking to the future, however, they distinguished between demands and needs and provided two 1960 estimates: the "probable" and the "needed," according to the lights of experts in the public programs involved. Wherever a "direct measure of need" was available, the authors employed it, usually maintaining the same ratio between probable and needed expenditures for 1960 as existed in 1950. In their calculations, total state and local expenditures in 1960, using 1950 prices, would "probably" total $37 billion, whereas $42 billion would be actually "needed." Thus, a series of "deficiencies"—the gaps between the probable and the needed—appeared: $1 billion for schools, $165 million for highways, $455 million for welfare and corrections, and so on, adding up to a grand total of over $5 billion.[24]

The same sort of balance, this time for public investment rather than annual spending, was struck in 1957 by the Special Assistant to the President for Public Works Planning. His office estimated a backlog of $204 billion worth of public facilities required by 1965, including $92 billion for highways, $42 billion for education, $22 billion for hospitals, and $25 billion for water and sewage. In effect, the Special Assistant called for construction spending at the rate of $20 billion at a time when the annual rate was 42 percent of that amount.[25]

Yet, just as with the bankruptcy argument, the starvation thesis fails to come to grips with the reality of the problems of the public sector. Estimates of needs can put dollar signs on the expectations of experts concerned about the quality of public service today—but they cannot turn the preferences of the experts into the preferences of the public. Even if they could, the popular preferences would not be immediately registered on the governments involved. At best, what the estimates give us are standards by which to evaluate services. They never free us from the problems of determining whether any given set of standards actually expresses preferences—or whether any set of standards is likely to be realized. Thus, one can readily admit that the impersonal forces of population growth, industrialization, density, and so forth push up the demand for public services, without arriving at the conclusion that failure to meet certain defined standards courts political disaster. One can concede that while schools are crowded there will be articulated demands for additional classrooms—and that while streams are polluted, there will be

---

[24] See Kilpatrick and Drury in J. Frederick Dewhurst and associates, *America's Needs and Resources* (New York: Twentieth Century Fund, 1955), chap. 18.

[25] U.S. Government, Special Assistant to the President for Public Works Planning, *Planning and Public Works* (Washington, 1957). See also Department of Commerce, *Survey of Construction Plans of State and Local Government* (April 4, 1955).

judicial decisions requiring the installation of more disposal systems—and still not accept the proposition that these voices and decisions will inexorably prevail. No greater mistake can be made than to suppose that the apparently objective and impersonal chronicling of "requirements" is anything more than presumptive evidence that some individuals are unhappy about the present state of affairs.

What is most relevant in estimating the relation of service levels to political stability is not their deviation from utopia but an understanding of the drift of present affairs in terms of the temper of the Region's residents. What we need to know are not the opinions of agitators as much as the general record of recent accomplishments. By and large, are public services showing some signs of improving quality that can be determined in any reasonably objective way? Are the most "pressing needs" being fulfilled first? Are the politically active and influential elements in the Region's constituencies mollified by the recent trend of events?

On all these counts, on the basis of the evidence which is available, the record of the Region suggests that the systems are more likely to survive than go under. So far as the over-all trends are concerned, it seems clear that improvements in the quality of public services are being registered. Between 1945 and 1955, the average per capita operating expenditure for the Region in constant 1954 dollars rose from $160.71 to $211.90, an increase of 35.1 percent.[26]

Undoubtedly some of this increase may have been due to the growing complications of providing a roughly constant level of services under more difficult circumstances—extra police assignments in the slums of older cities, for instance, or more fire engines for a new suburban development. Some could also be set down to increased factor costs—changes in real wages and fringe benefits without any improvement in the services involved. But even if we take these aspects into account for the Region as a whole, there has been, in fact, an increase in services—in more policemen per 1000 population in New York City, more hospital beds in Newark, more teachers per thousand pupils in the New York suburbs, more teachers with an A.B. degree in the New Jersey suburbs. Fire rating improved in Long Island towns; the average age of the subway cars declined; school property value per pupil across the Region almost doubled. Even in those older cities with stable or declining populations, significant changes in major services seem to have occurred. Between 1947 and 1957, the number of firemen in Yonkers, Elizabeth, Newark, and New York City increased 19, 20, 18, and 65 percent respectively. The number of policemen rose 32, 27, 17, and 46 percent. In short, if as experts in municipal finance have long contended, the citizen gets what he pays for—if service standards are principally a function of money—quality has improved for almost every service in every part of the Region. On a per person,

---

[26] Note 18, above.

constant dollar basis, more money has been put to public purposes at a faster rate than in any other ten-year period in the Region's history.[27]

If the Region's over-all performance shows up favorably, what about the record for the services which loom most important in the public eye? As far as the largest public program—education—is concerned, absolutely and proportionately more money has gone into this activity than any other. Between 1955–56 and 1959–60 the average school operating expenditure per pupil in New York State has risen from $378 to $491; and during the 1959–60 school year the foundation "minimum" program amount of $356 was exceeded in 95 percent of major school districts. Indeed, if one were disposed to accept the referenda on school bond issues as a true expression of the public will, the decision would be inescapable in New York that school progress has been too rapid. For the 1958–59 school year, 38 percent of all bond issues put to a vote failed to carry.[28]

If the quality of municipal services seems at least to be holding steady, and schools improving rapidly, prospects are just as good for improvements in another sensitive area, transportation. At any rate, facilities for the movement of automobile and air traffic are being constructed at a rate and on standards of service which have never been undertaken before. No one could accuse the Port of New York Authority, for example, of lack of imagination and enterprise in its planning and building of the new Idlewild Airport. The designs of the new bridges and expressways similarly display continuing pursuit of engineering excellence. The gross annual operating expenditures of the Port Authority between 1945 and 1955 increased 170 percent—compared to an increase by the City of New York of about 80 percent, and an average increase of 120 percent in nonschool operating expenditures outside New York City. Only the suburban school districts have registered a greater percentage rise on the average, topping the 200 percent mark in their expenditure increases during the same period.[29]

Of course, . . . both the school districts and the transportation authorities operate in very special circumstances. The districts have developed sophisticated and financially remunerative relations with state authorities, resulting in large and growing grants-in-aid programs. The transportation agencies are supported by user charges which feed on larger and larger volumes of traffic or substantial federal grants. In both instances, public officials responsible for the programs are able to considerable degree to define "needs" according to their own standards and then proceed to satisfy them. Given these capabilities, it is not surprising that

---

[27] For an evaluation of New York City performance specifically, see Commission on Governmental Operations of the City of New York, *Interim Report* (Feb. 1, 1960).

[28] See mimeographed statement by Arthur Levitt, comptroller, State of New York, "Financial Circumstances of School Districts and Implications for State Aid Policy," (Dec. 13, 1959).

[29] Note 18, above.

these programs function on a self-starter basis and their records of improving standards of service are the best in the Region.

As in the case of the revenue question, then, the problem of public expenditures in the Region turns out at rock bottom to be one of political attitudes and behavior. Just as any allocation of resources between the public and the private sectors from 1 to 100 percent is theoretically possible, so, given public desires which are intense enough, almost any "need" can be fulfilled. In Lyle Fitch's words, "Fiscal stress in the modern American community is often more psychological than economic."[30] All that our expenditure calculations can yield is the knowledge that, in ways more or less related to the type of government involved, public spending has been increasing, and that one is justified again, with some qualifications, in inferring that quality has been upgraded in public programs. Whether the quality is good "enough" and the responsiveness rapid "enough" are issues which no expenditure series or professional criteria of excellence can answer.

Political Payoffs in the Going Systems

We have been seeking evidence that a substantial change in the nature of public ideology and organization impends in the New York Region—one which will alter the trends which economic analysis has identified. The burden of the foregoing two sections has been that the indices customarily employed to gauge the effectiveness of the present system are not really relevant to the issue. The Region's governments theoretically can never go bankrupt, and they can never achieve the utopian standards that program specialists advocate.

But even if we took the indices seriously, the recent history of the Region would give us little cause for alarm. No "cruel burden" present or impending seems to rest upon the taxpayer, even if the most pessimistic estimates of new levies are accepted. No abnormally low service standards prevail, at least when considered in historical perspective. What has occurred—when one considers criticism of school conditions in New York City or renewal programs in New Jersey—is a sizable redefinition of what we consider "adequate" today, at least in experts' eyes. What obviously exists is a body of opinion which wants more funds allocated to the public sector and more positive public policies toward the use of natural resources in the Region, the planning of the transportation network, and the rebuilding of the Region's centrally located cities. The question is whether or not that body of opinion will be politically effective enough in the next twenty-five years to accomplish its objectives.

We should be as specific as possible here about what the revolution would constitute now that it seems clear it will not come with Hegelian naturalness. It would involve, first off, a much more rapid diversion of

---

[30] Lyle Fitch, "Metropolitan Financial Problems," *The Annals of the American Academy of Political and Social Science* 314 (1957): 73.

resources to the public sector: at a rate which, say, diverted at least one-half of all productivity gains to government rather than private spending. More important, however, it would involve the establishment of a governmental structure which possessed the jurisdiction and the authority to make decisions about alternative forms of Regional development, more or less consciously and more or less comprehensively. More specifically, there would be some type of Regional organization empowered to set aside land for recreational purposes on the basis of a Regional plan and not on the sporadic acquisitions of states, localities, and independent authorities or bequests by private citizens. There would be some type of Regional organization empowered to subsidize commuter transportation, if this were in accord with a general plan. And, to be fully satisfactory to the body of opinion which Jesse Burkhead has termed the "view with alarm" school of metropolitan affairs, the organization should probably be responsible to a Regional electorate and draw revenue from a common revenue pool.

To sketch the skeleton of a government sufficient to redirect the pattern of economic development in the Region—even in the minimum terms above—is to indicate at once the rocky road to reform. For, if the dissidents are to be effective, they must attract a sizable number of politically influential supporters; they must gain the acquiescence of the majority of the Region's residents; and, finally, they must overcome formidable legal, constitutional, and political obstacles, to make the groundswell of opinion legally applicable. These are difficult tasks. Slow evolution over the next twenty-five years, not decisive action to alter the main lines of development, seems the course of least resistance.

Perhaps the most formidable obstacle to changing either the structure or the philosophy of the Region's governments would be the assembling of a coalition of effective political figures. . . . It is hard even to conceive how such a coalition might come about. At the outset, three governors, the mayor of New York City, and the chief office-holders of the 17 counties surrounding the City would have to be persuaded that their present performance in their offices was unsatisfactory; that their failure was due to severe structural deficiencies in the present organization; and that only the creation of new arrangements would solve the problems they face.

That these officials know they have problems is already clear. Since 1956, the Metropolitan Regional Council has included in its 30-man body the top elected officials of all the counties and major cities of the Region as well as a number of smaller municipalities.[31] As an informed,

[31] Newspaper comment on the Metropolitan Regional Council has been substantial in the last few years, and the organization publishes a periodic *Bulletin* respecting its activities. Maxwell Lehman, deputy administrator for the City of New York, whose office functions as Secretariat to the Council, and William Cassella of the National Municipal League, who has observed the Council's activities since its inception, have furnished valuable information and observations. A summary evaluation of the Council was made by the Special Committee on Metropolitan Governmental Affairs of the Regional Plan Association in its report published in the *New York Times* (Jan. 9, 1959), p. 16. See also Regional Plan Association, *The Handling of Metropolitan Problems in Selected Regions* (mimeographed, April, 1958).

consultative association, the Council has been able both to develop common policies with respect to some matters of law enforcement and traffic control and to initiate major investigations into Regional problems. It has been hailed therefore as having a "great potential for becoming an official regional leadership institution."[32]

The potential exists—but so far the evolution of the Council into an agency with the capacity to set goals, analyze resources, and recommend development policies has been slow. It remains a confederation, requiring unanimous consent from all its members before taking any important step. For two years, one of its committees held hearings to determine if it should acquire legal status. But the upshot of this self-analysis remains inconclusive, for while the Council has ultimately decided that its role should be legitimized, a strong minority is reported as reluctant to see the organization gain official recognition. Some outside groups have suggested that the Council take on operating responsibilities. Among these groups were the Citizens' Union, the Metropolitan Committee on Planning, and the Association of Real Estate Syndicators. But the more noteworthy of the Council's supporters—the Regional Plan Association of New York, the Citizens Budget Committee, and the State Citizen Council—have carefully refrained from suggesting that it acquire independent financial resources or assume major operating responsibilities.

Meantime, there are few signs that the usual pattern of political behavior is undergoing a metamorphosis. Officials continue to cling to their favorite slogan "cooperation" as the panacea for the very real conflicts of interests which exist. The conflicts themselves, however, show few signs of diminishing. A new state study committee has been created to criticize the City's administration and to cast doubt about the capacity of the largest government organization in the Region to conduct its own affairs. Recent mayors of the City and the recent comptrollers of the state have continued in the tradition of their predecessors to dispute openly the program needs of the City government. The city and the Port Authority continue to announce and activate separate programs for port development. The New Jersey municipalities and the Port Authority continue to disagree on their respective responsibilities with respect to a metropolitan district plan for pooling transit revenues. As between the states themselves, problems over the taxation of New Jersey residents by New York, of air pollution control, and the strain of persistent crises in mass transportation have led to predictions of "an era of hostile rivalry such as has not existed since Colonial days." Said Walter Jones, New Jersey state senator and Republican party leader in Bergen County, "The very purposes of the bi-state compact establishing the Port of New York Authority are in grave danger. A desire for vengeance is in the air."[33] Given there performances, one is disinclined to believe that major surrenders of existing prerogatives are close at hand.

---

[32] *New York Herald Tribune* (Aug. 24, 1959), p. 24.
[33] *New York Times* (May 1, 1960).

In the less formal circles of political activity, much the same characteristics of divisiveness are on display. The business community, in various garbs, has been represented as concerned with economic development across the Region. So far, however, this concern has evidenced itself principally with respect to maintaining or increasing land values in Manhattan and Newark and to urging the limited development of the Metropolitan Regional Council. The renewal projects which the private interests have sparked directly are located in areas where the forces of regeneration already exist (as with the Downtown–Lower Manhattan Association) or where matters of special institutional concern are apparent (Morningside adjacent to Columbia University or the Bloomingdale Neighborhood Conservation Project). So far as other Regional problems are concerned, the failure of private concerns to provide financial support for the Metropolitan Rapid Transit Commission emphasized the difficulties which even vitally concerned interests have in mobilizing themselves to attack this issue. As for general development plans, even private associations dedicated to progress in government and planning find it difficult to agree. Thus, the Regional Plan Association and the City Club of New York criticize each other's analyses and reports, almost before they are published.

Other elements of diversity and insularity also underscore the difficulty of coordinate action among the political activities. Within the City, the predominant majority party has more than its usual number of factions —its leadership undergoing serious attack from members claiming that racial favoritism intrudes on party councils and from those concerned with issues of party integrity and policy. The governors of the three states meet cautiously but inconclusively on transportation and other matters; to date they prefer to work separately on the resolution of the problems. And suburban party figures show little enthusiasm for closer collaboration with their neighbors if new election districts are involved. Indeed, in many matters, suburban governments go their separate ways, impervious to entreaties of party or state loyalties.

So, in November 1959, Democratic Hudson County, fearing local revenue losses, opposed Democratic Governor Meyner in his proposal to divert turnpike funds to mass transit purposes.[34] So, in January 1960, the Republican New York legislators were reported "cool" to a Republican governor's proposal to give school districts local taxing power, the first reason being their feeling that "school board members in many areas do not exhibit enough independence as taxpayers representatives, tending rather to be 'yes men' for school superintendents."[35] Except for study committees, a thesis that the existing leadership in the Region stands poised for reform and reorganization, restrained only by lack of public understanding, hardly seems plausible. It is easy to see how incumbents might suffer in a major reshuffle; it is hard to see who would get ahead.

If the Region's leadership shows little inclinaton to take giant strides,

[34] *New York Times* (Nov. 3, 1959), p. 1.
[35] *New York Times* (Jan. 8, 1960), p. 1.

it is not likely to be pushed by the Region's electorate. No massive mumblings demanding reform seem at hand. As far as one can detect, there are no insurgent elements in either party demanding "metropolitan government"; no civic associations in Long Island, Rockland, or Monmouth seeking union now with New York City. To be sure, a formal proposal for a change in governmental structure was made in 1959, coming on the heels of Governor Rockefeller's tax proposals, but it was scarcely a move toward unity. On the contrary, at that time the cry went out—and rapidly waned—for New York City to secede from the state and establish itself as a separate commonwealth.[36] Elsewhere attitudes toward metropolitan reform appear to have paralleled those expressed in Bergen County in 1958 when a survey asking what should be done about metropolitan problems of transportation, planning, and resource development disclosed that most voters felt they were "somebody else's headache."[37] Apathy, not anxiety, seems to be the prevalent popular mood. Political change when public problems become pressing seems quite possible. But the anticipation of problems by the localities and the development of policies and structures to meet them is another matter.

It is possible, of course, that the stimulus for reform may come from political institutions at higher echelons in the American federal system. Over a period of years, the state governments may take to heart the injunction of one study commission after another that their programs and policies are inextricably intertwined with those of the local governments in the Region. They may also accept the commissions' recommendations that the activities of the Regional enterprises authorized by state law need to be more effectively coordinated and rationalized. Alternatively the federal government might be persuaded to apply its not inconsiderable influence in the shaping of the pattern of development within the Region. If Washington adopted standards in its home loan and guaranty programs which considered the impact of new housing developments on the suburban community concerned, as well as the effect upon the homeowners and the lender, the character of residential settlement might be quite different. If the Congress were to provide federal aid for mass transportation as well as for highways, the location of both homes and factories would be further affected. If renewal and development programs, and assistance in the fields of water resources and open space, were conducted according to metropolitan rather than municipal plans, the federal influence could be felt in still a more comprehensive way. In each instance, these developments might take place without so direct and obvious a challenge to the going political systems that exist within the Region itself.

The prospects seem even more substantial that informal nongovernmental concern with the course of Regional economic development will sharply increase. There are strong traditions in the Region for private concern with metropolitan planning; for educational and philanthropic

[36] *New York Times* (Jan. 17, 1959), p. 1.
[37] *Bergen Evening Record* (Dec. 3, 1958), p. 1.

activities designed to offer alternative courses of action which are professionally prepared; and for the sounding of alarms at what appear to be untoward governmental proposals. These traditions may now trigger off a rapid evolution of quasi-public, quasi-private programs which reflect many interests but which require no formal grants of authority. These programs could move to strengthen the prospects of coordinated guidance of urban growth.

As for the probability of actions within the formal systems themselves, however, the odds seem smaller. Certainly the evidence we have just cited concerning the disinclination of the professional political leaders to move rapidly and the unconcern of the electorate should come as no surprise. For the expectations of the reformers do violence to what we know about the objectives and mode of operation of the Region's political systems. In actuality, what the reformers suggest should take place is the establishment of institutions which will "ensure the Region's optimum development" and "maximize the usefulness of the Region's human and material resources." The goal they see as both desirable and possible for the Region's government is a major and continuing concern with the shape of the Region's development.

Yet the plain fact is, of course, that few inhabitants of the Region, or of the nation for that matter, have ever looked to their local governments to "optimize" or "maximize" anything. On the contrary, people have regarded these units as necessary but not especially admirable service units to provide programs which did not seem supportable through private enterprise. It has never been in the Region's tradition to charge local government with the responsibility for physical and economic development. The price mechanism and the marketplace are our chosen instruments for those purposes.

We seem, now, somehow concerned at the end-products issuing from the instruments on which we have relied. And, somewhat wistfully and somewhat vaguely, we think that possibly a system of human relationships neither designed nor oriented toward that purpose can be restructured to do better. We wish this restructured system, possibly, to reconsider the transportation or land-use or water-use or recreational activities that the marketplace has encouraged. We wish it to come to grips with problems in blight, obsolescence, and poverty which the marketplace has not solved. And we would prefer it to do so quickly.

Yet, to these new purposes, we endow the system with no special urgency. On the contrary, we devise ways and means—though grants-in-aid, minimal boundary changes, new sources of revenue, and new contractual relationships—for the old set of institutions and working arrangements to survive, to improve their services, and to adjust bit by bit to changing circumstances. We make sure that in extreme crises some palliative action is taken. Wherever we can, we pattern the agency organization after the very mechanism we have found defective—and then express concern when these agencies act like their ancestors. If, in any given part of the Region, public service levels fall too low, or conditions of blight and obsolescence become too severe for our taste, many of us simply move out farther into the suburbs. This is in the great American pioneering tradition of abandoning settlements we have despoiled.

It is possible, of course, that even under these circumstances of ambivalence, drastic changes will occur. Leadership may forswear present power and prerogative; the public may adopt a new consciousness toward their neighbors and embrace an ideology of metropolitan citizenship. Both may seek not the tolerable environment, but the best conditions of Regional growth—a New Yorker's interpretation of the *arete* of the Greek city-state.

In a discipline as uncertain and rudimentary in its techniques of prediction as political science, we do not dismiss these possibilities out of hand. We simply record that we know of no other time when a revolution took place when the existing system was solidly established and its citizens, as they understood the goals of their domestic society, content.